SARMATIA

Dniester R.

Don R.

[...]ga R.

CASPIAN SEA

BLACK SEA

BYZANTINE EMPIRE

Constantinople

ASIA

TURKEY

Boghazkoy

PERSIAN EMPIRE

IRAN

PHRYGIA

HITTITE EMPIRE

ASSYRIA

Nineveh

[...]oy

Pergamum

MINOR

KINGDOM OF
MITANNI

LYDIA

Sardis

ANATOLIA

MESOPOTAMIA

Tigris R.

IONIA

Ephesus

Perge

Tarsus

Miletus

Euphrates R.

RHODES

Babylon

BABYLONIA

SUMER

Byblos

PHOENICIA

SYRIA

CYPRUS

Tyre

Ur

CHALDEA

SEA

PHILISTIA

CANAAN

ISRAEL

Jericho

PALESTINE

Jerusalem

PERSIAN
GULF

Alexandria

Memphis

EGYPT

ARABIA

RED SEA

Ptolemais

Theb[...]

Syene

FREEDOM IN THE ANCIENT WORLD

Books by Herbert J. Muller

FREEDOM IN THE ANCIENT WORLD

ISSUES OF FREEDOM

THE LOOM OF HISTORY

THE SPIRIT OF TRAGEDY

THE USES OF THE PAST

THOMAS WOLFE

SCIENCE AND CRITICISM

MODERN FICTION

FREEDOM IN THE

Secker & Warburg London

HERBERT J. MULLER

ANCIENT WORLD

To the memory of my father

CONTENTS

A*

ILLUSTRATIONS

The following are grouped in a separate section after page 172.

Prehistoric art: bison from Lascaux
Ziggurat at Ur
Early Sumerian sculpture
Sumerian royal jewelry from Ur
Victory tablet of King Narmer: Old Kingdom, Egypt
"Village Mayor": Old Kingdom
The Great Sphinx
Throne of Tutankhamon, from his tomb at Thebes
The Last Judgment before Osiris
Statue of Ramses II at Luxor
Code of Hammurabi, the "god-fearing" prince
Business records from Babylon
Ruins of Babylon
Throne room in the Palace of Minos, Knossos
Assyrian King (Ashurnasirpal) on a lion hunt
Obelisk of Shalmanisu III, with picture of captive Israelite king, John
Late Hittite sculpture
The stables of King Solomon at Megiddo (reconstructed)
King Solomon's temple (cross section of a reconstructed model)
The Moses of Michelangelo
The spoils of Jerusalem, from the Arch of Titus in Rome
Archaic Greek sculpture: "Apollo type" from the seventh century, B.C.
Attic vase of the sixth century: Ajax and Achilles throwing dice
Attic cup: Dionysus in a boat
Acropolis of Athens
Athena mourning (fifth century)

xi

PREFACE

The subject of this work is freedom in the broadest sense of the word. I am adhering to the relatively neutral, objective definition stated in my *Issues of Freedom*: "the condition of being able to choose and to carry out purposes." This involves the primary dictionary meaning, the absence of external constraints, or the common idea of freedom *from* coercion. It also includes the idea of practicable purposes, an actual ability with available means, or effective freedom *to* do what one wishes. With this ability it assumes a power of conscious choice between known alternatives, or freedom *of* mind and spirit, as the distinctive freedom that man is capable of, beyond the ability of other animals to carry out their instinctive purposes. Add a positive desire to make choices, and my definition corresponds to that of Christian Bay in *The Structure of Freedom*: "A person is free to the extent that he has the capacity, the opportunity, and the incentive to give expression to what is in him and to develop his potentialities."

So defined, freedom means concretely freedoms of various kinds. I am ruling out, however, the various concepts of "true freedom" that philosophers have been fond of: the notion that a person is "really" free only when he is avoiding "license," acting virtuously, doing his duty to the state, being perfectly rational, serving God, or being his "true self." These concepts all come down to the idea that freedom consists in doing what is right and good—by the standards of the writer. Thinkers are notoriously unable to agree on these standards, or on the nature of the alleged "true self." From this point of view I mean by freedom a state in which a person may decide for himself what is right and good, what to do with his freedom, what kind of self to become. While the question of freedom *for* what is always pertinent, indeed inescapable, it may be discussed more profitably if we hold to a neutral definition and distinguish the problem of the nature of freedom from the problem of its proper uses or ends. We should all know by now that free men are not necessarily virtuous or wise.

It follows that freedom is more than a political matter. Men brought up in a consciously free society generally assume, with good reason, that rights or civil liberties guaranteed by law are its essential condition. (I am making no distinction between *freedom* and *liberty*, which in common usage are interchangeable.) Nevertheless, I assume that a historian must consider freedom in relation not only to government but to mores, technology, commerce, art, religion—the culture as a whole. Its history begins with the appearance of man's distinctive powers of mind, a meddling with the natural environment that gave him increasing power, or more effective freedom. This culminated in the rise of civilization, the creation of an elaborate world of man's own. Civilization made political power a major problem ever after, but it also widened the range of man's choices, gave freer rein to his creative powers, made possible a fuller realization of his potentialities. Eventually it produced the higher religions, philosophy, and science, which cannot possibly be ignored in a history of freedom.

My subject is therefore a very large, deep, complex one; and my effort to cover it may seem more pretentious because I have also plunged into the philosophy of freedom, tried to meet head on the issues it raises about the nature of man and his relations to the cosmos. But here I plead a degree of modesty. While I have naturally sought to be cool and impartial, and first of all to record objectively the actual historical developments, I do not pretend that this study is pure unvarnished truth, free from any preconception or bias. Not only am I deeply committed to the ideal of freedom, but the very effort at objectivity calls for an immediate admission that no historian ever is or can be wholly objective when dealing with such vital issues.

"The one great Bible which cannot lie," wrote Froude, "is the history of the human race." Still, we have to interpret this Bible too, and historians have read into it as diverse meanings as Christians have found in their Scriptures. For they cannot take a God's-eye view of this history, or record it from nobody's point of view. Apart from the more obvious forms of bias—temperamental, class, national, religious—their interpretation of it is inevitably influenced by the climate of opinion in their age. It is always based on assumptions about the human race, what is natural or normal for man, what is important or good for him; and these assumptions are always debatable. Thus the effort at impartiality itself premises a belief in the values of truth, the love of truth, the intellectual freedom and honesty essential to the pursuit of truth—values that may now seem self-evident, but that have not been universally recognized, even by the highest authorities. The authors of the historical books of the Bible hardly tried to be objective or impartial. The truths self-evident to them should remind us of the most insidious form of bias: the silent or unconscious assumptions, all that "goes without saying," and therefore without thinking. I have accordingly endeavored to lay all my basic assumptions on the table. If I sometimes like to think that I am writing on behalf of Man, immediately I am writing as a twentieth-century American. I have entitled this work *a* history of freedom, not *the* history.

Yet such admissions by no means imply that history is a *merely* personal or provincial interpretation. Simple respect for the stubborn facts counts for a good deal, the more because of modern methods of sifting and checking the historical evidence. The effort at objectivity counts for no less. This is reinforced by the publicity of the scientific method, which invites constant criticism by other members of the professional community; scholars can always be trusted to supplement, discount, and correct one another's efforts, and so to expose their common fallibility. And the very awareness of cultural bias—of the limits of objectivity—is a distinct gain in objectivity. The archaeological, historical, sociological, and anthropological research over the last hundred years has not only built up an immense body of positive, reliable knowledge about human history, but has given us a much longer, wider perspective on the one great Bible. It has made possible a more sympathetic understanding of the many diverse cultures, and a more detached view of our own. It has enabled me to undertake such a work as this, which could not have been written two centuries ago, or even conceived in any civilization but our own.

Hence I can maintain that I am not betraying cultural conceit when I concentrate, as I do, on the history of the Western world—on Greece and Rome in this volume, and on our own civilization in the volumes to come. It would be pleasant to believe with Lord Acton that the growth of freedom has been the central theme of man's entire history, and represents God's plan for man; but the record suggests nothing so uniform or universal. The West has unquestionably made the major contributions to the theory and conscious practice of freedom. To be sure, the early civilizations of the East wrote an all-important chapter by embarking on the astonishing adventure of civilization. The later civilizations cultivated values that may be deemed higher or holier than freedom, in particular a peace of mind that many free men now yearn for. But none of the great Eastern societies were basically free societies, dedicated to any proposition of liberty and equality, or of government of and by the people. Their characteristic ideals—from patience, obedience, and resignation to nonattachment and renunciation—bred a natural indifference to the ideal of freedom. Today the non-Western world is astir with Western ideas and ideals; and the drama is so fascinating and momentous precisely because hundreds of millions of men are beginning to realize capacities, demand opportunities, and cherish aspirations hitherto largely confined to a small minority of the human race.

My main concern is the living tradition of freedom: what has entered the broad stream leading to the consciousness of modern man, and lately to the almost universal acceptance in theory of the once-revolutionary principle of "human rights," or the rights of man. This point of view also calls for an initial apology, as it not only suggests the insufferable conceit of modernity but involves what may be called the unpardonable sin for a historian. While I have of course tried to understand the mentality of ancient peoples, I have not sought primarily to present them as they saw themselves, or to record their history for its own sake, and I have slighted or virtually ignored many peoples who left memorials of intrinsic interest and dignity. In effect I have dwelt rather on their contributions to *us*, and their shortcomings by *our* standards. Nevertheless, my concern is essentially pious. It makes possible a charitable judgment of ancient peoples, in an awareness of their limited material and intellectual resources, limited consciousness or power of choice. It calls for a recognition of many contributions, as to technology, that have commonly been neglected. It leads to a clearer, fuller realization of our immense indebtedness to innumerable peoples, in the steady accumulation of arts and skills, the broadening stream of ideas and ideals. It points to the strongest argument for the usually conceited assumption of Westerners that their history is the main stream of human history; for they have drawn most heavily and consciously on the achievements of other societies, past and present, and in spreading all over the world began the writing of world history, laid the foundations for the United Nations.

In any case, I have not attempted a play-by-play, country-by-country, century-by-century history of freedom, but instead have concentrated on what seem to me the major developments. Here my only apology is for a deal of unavoidable self-plagiarism. In *The Loom of History* I dwelt on the historic drama of East and West, in which—as I read it—

freedom has been a major issue. I also dwelt on this issue in *The Uses of the Past,* and to some extent in *The Spirit of Tragedy.* In my present work I have substantially repeated some passages from these earlier works, as well as from *Issues of Freedom,* when I felt (both happily and unhappily) that I had nothing better to say. But in the main I have attempted a fresh treatment of such materials, in keeping—I must hope—with a clearer, more comprehensive view of my subject, and a sharper focus on it.

Lastly, I can acknowledge nothing like the full extent of my obligation to friends, students, colleagues, and historians. But I wish at least to end on a note of gratitude, in particular to Cass Canfield, for his warm encouragement from the outset of this project; to Professors Joel Feinberg, Richard McKeon, and Welsey B. Carroll for critical readings of sections of my manuscript; and to the many scholars not cited in my text upon whose works I have drawn, directly and indirectly, over the years.

Herbert J. Muller

FREEDOM IN THE ANCIENT WORLD

| Chapter One | *THE BEGINNINGS* |

1. *The Evolution of Man*

Some half a million or so years ago, an apelike creature that had long before dropped from the trees to the ground, and developed the habit of standing on its hind legs, was well on its way to becoming a man, the "highest" form of animal life. The chief means to its rise in the world was a growth in brain power. Although many links in this process are still missing, and unlikely to be found, all scientific students of man now regard human evolution as an established fact. Most religious students also have come to accept the idea that it was in such a way that God created man, as well as all other forms of life. "There is grandeur in this view of life," Darwin concluded in *The Origin of Species,* noting reverently that "from so simple a beginning endless forms most beautiful and most wonderful have been, and are being evolved."

There is also considerable mystery in this view of life. The direction of evolution has in general been from simple to more complex forms of life, with increasingly elaborate, specialized means of adaptation to the environment; but the development has not been a clear, uniform progress, toward any apparent goal. In the animal world it has entailed a ceaseless, bloody struggle for survival, in which death has been the universal fate of individuals and extinction the common fate of species. If man assumes that he is the main point of the whole evolutionary process, he must wonder why the Creator chose such a painfully slow, tortuous, wasteful way of achieving his purpose. To the biologist it looks like a mindless process, in which natural selection has worked on random, mostly useless variations to achieve only temporary successes. A wonderful adaptation to the environment has led many a

1

species to extinction, as the environment changed. Innumerable complex forms of life have become extinct while the simple amoeba survived; other forms, such as parasites, succeeded by becoming simpler. If survival is the goal, or the test of fitness, one of nature's most brilliant successes is the oyster: it has endured in essentially its present form for two hundred million years or more. By the standard of dominance of environment, insects may look like the lords of creation.

Man might wonder, too, at some of the most beautiful products of natural selection. A number of species have developed sexual display characteristics, such as the trains of peacocks and the antlers of deer, that serve to attract females but otherwise appear to handicap the animal in its struggle for survival; and with all due respect to females, most species manage to woo them without such fancy equipment, and the oyster has got along without any at all. This development may be one of nature's extravagances. And so might man himself—the parvenu of the monkey family. It has been suggested that the human brain is a kind of tumor, a monstrous overgrowth that has enabled him to indulge in biologically preposterous behavior, and that will eventually destroy him. Certainly he is now capable of self-destruction, as no other species is. Pleased to consider himself the highest form of life, he may now be conscious of the profoundly ambiguous consequences of his distinctive power of choice. It has meant the constant possibility of foolish or even fatal choices, because of which no other animal is so stupid as a human fool.

Hence he might take comfort in the knowledge that he is still kin to other animals. Many of them exhibit the rudiments of intelligence in their capacity to learn, as well as some sort of awareness of their environment. Many others enjoy a rudimentary social life, in schools, flocks, and herds. In this respect lowly insects most nearly anticipated man, developing marvelously efficient societies, with some astonishing approximations of human customs. One ant, for example, keeps smaller ants as slaves to do all the domestic work while it confines itself to the business of war; another ant domesticates a beetle that exudes a sticky stuff it dotes on.[1] Their small size, however, has barred insects from the

---

[1] Their relationship is another mystery of natural selection, for it is harmful to both the host and the guest. The self-indulgent ants take better care of the beetle larvae than they do of their own, many of which are eaten by the little beetles; the ant colony may die out from having too many guests. The beetles in turn suffer because the ants cover all the larvae with earth, to enable them to spin cocoons, and then expose the cocoons to the sunlight, which is fatal to the beetles. The beetle colony survives only because its well-fed hosts overlook some of its cocoons.

development of brain power that has marked the whole primate order, from the tree shrew to the ape. Man is naturally most akin to his simian ancestors.

Monkeys and apes are distinguished by a high degree of curiosity, a kind of pleasure in the world about them. They are also exceptionally sociable, showing an active interest in their fellows, even a sympathy for those in distress, that goes far beyond the mere cohesiveness of flocks and herds or the mechanical relations of insects. But most obviously they are distinguished by their intelligence, in which man's closest rival is his evolutionary cousin, the ape. Koehler's experiments with chimpanzees demonstrated conclusively that they not only can solve problems but do so by no mechanical trial-and-error methods; they suddenly size up the situation, get the solution by an apparent insight or flash of intuition. Likewise they enjoy learning tricks, such as riding cycles, and seem to enjoy them most when the trick is most difficult. They can actually beat man at his own game. When the Kelloggs brought up a baby chimpanzee with their own baby, under conditions as nearly alike as possible, they observed that the ape was somewhat better at solving novel problems, as well as quicker in developing motor skills. He would also become self-sufficient much sooner than the human youngster, whose prolonged helplessness might remind us of the trials of our remote ancestors. As parents they had reason to envy their ape-cousins.

Meanwhile, however, the Kellogg baby was learning to talk. The bright chimpanzee never tried to talk. He had the better of it only in the first year or so of growth, while the human youngster would profit from his prolonged helplessness by continuing to learn. The ape would never pass on the benefits of his education to his own youngsters; they would end up essentially the same as their ancestors of a million years ago. The quick intelligence of the ape sets off the strictly unique power of the human brain—a natural outcome of one line of development that is not clearly the goal of the whole evolutionary process, nor a guarantee of man's lordship of creation, but that is in any case the source of his unique freedom and the key to his unique history.

For 450,000 years, Carl Becker observed, the Dawn Men lived like "anachronistic disciples of Walter Pater," burning with a hard gem-like flame. They kept chipping flints, quite unaware that they were contributing to the progress of the human race, aware only that they were chipping flints. Actually, of course, we can never know just what went on in their heads. Nevertheless, we can be sure that they were not living simply for the moment: unlike the apes, they were making tools. In so doing they were taking thought of the morrow, thinking of things that were not, acting on premeditated instead of merely instinctive purposes—choosing as well as carrying out their purposes. They were already monkeying systematically with the world around them. For this purpose the meddlers had another great biological advantage in the possession of hands. Other animals developed highly specialized instruments, such as claws and beaks, by which they became exquisitely adapted to their environment; the less specialized hand—inferior for walking, climbing, tearing, fighting—enabled man to do many different things, adapt himself to different environments, and become a specialist in ways of his own choosing. By the collaboration of brain and hand he became a Maker.

In other words, the Dawn Men were acquiring power. Eventually men would realize the dangers of power, make it an ugly word; yet the race would always cherish it, cling to every gain in it, for plain enough reasons. In view of its evil reputation we must first emphasize the obvious, that without power there can be no freedom and that there is no good in impotence per se. Technology, ignored by historians until recent times, provided the indispensable material basis for all other freedoms. It also represented an indispensable intellectual means, as a work of reason, and for a long time the only source of reliable knowledge about the natural world. The clearest progress of the race has been made in and through technology. The Dawn Men made a considerable advance, for they were experts in stoneworking well before a hundred thousand years ago.

This was a very slow advance, to be sure. For countless generations men were divided into two main groups: the core-people, who fashioned their tools by chipping down to a central core, and the flake-people, who fashioned them by striking off and working up large flakes; and each group continued in its own way, without benefit from the experience of the other. Archaeologists have been struck by the uniformity in patterns, and in the sequence of forms, of tools found all over Europe and Asia. The uniformity emphasizes the extreme conservatism of a creature who is by no means so inventive and adventurous by nature as he sometimes likes to think. It suggests that he very early became subject to cultural tradition, since individuals left to themselves might be expected to introduce more variety even in simple implements. Nevertheless, some individuals did manage to break in with ideas of their own. Ingenuity eventually produced such implements as stone axes, which require great technical skill as well as patience—as modern men learned when they tried to duplicate these crude-looking tools. And however gradual and unplanned this process, it was not an automatic one: invention is the work of inventors. There were unsung geniuses among the Dawn Men.

These men were also embryo artists: their artifacts became more pleasing to the eye, more polished than utility required. It is not too clear how or why an aesthetic sense evolved by natural selection, or what biological use it had in the early struggle for survival. If it was associated with the sexual display characteristics that some species developed, mammals were unable to appreciate some beauties until they reached the primate stage, for excepting monkeys and apes, all seem to be color-blind; none have hide or fur splashed with the blues, greens, and pure reds that nature has lavished on so many of its other creatures. With the primates, at any rate, such possibilities reappeared, and an aesthetic sense somehow became part of man's biological equipment. As he evolved and began to realize his mental potentialities, its uses became more apparent, for purposes other than sexual display. It reinforced his natural curiosity, or impulse to explore and comprehend the world about him (an impulse too seldom included in the "basic drives" listed in the textbooks on psychology). It stimulated his creativity and inventiveness. In time it would become a major means to the creation of a world of his own.

Most important by far, however, was the early development of language. Other animals can communicate after a fashion by signs and noises, and bees have even developed the rudiments of symbols in their dance-language, by which the foraging bee can inform the hive of the direction, distance, and precise location of the honey hoard it has found; but man is the only wordmaker. By language he climbed to a different plane of existence, put an immeasurable gulf between him and the apes. Again we can never know how or when the Dawn Men made this supreme contribution to the race. The bowwow, dingdong, poohpooh, and other theories of the origin of language are necessarily conjectural, and merely point to the natural conditions that made it possible. Perhaps it began to develop as soon as men began to make tools, since they transmitted the new skills to their children. Its elaboration must have been very slow and largely unconscious, much as a child learns to talk without being aware of the complex system of grammar he is employing. No genius could have devised this whole system, for to do so would have required a power of conceptual thought that is conceivable only after language has become highly developed. What is important is that language made possible conceptual thought, the realization of genius.

Immediately it made possible a pooling of experience, and a more developed social life. Language emphasizes an elementary but often neglected truth, that man is by nature a social animal. The traditional emphasis on his natural depravity, the habits of a highly competitive society, and (since Darwin) the common talk of the struggle for survival have obscured the plain fact that man rose in the world primarily by co-operating, not struggling with his fellows. While there is evidence of homicide and cannibalism among the Dawn Men, there is no evidence of the anarchic individualism, the war of "every man against every man," that Hobbes pictured as the state of nature—"and the life of man, solitary, poor, nasty, brutish, and short." His early life might have been poor and short enough, but as far back as we can see him it was never solitary or simply brutish.

Language was likewise the primary means to the growth of culture —all the behavior and belief that man is taught during his long childhood. It was the beginning of an evolution no longer biological, not transmitted in the genes. The efficient organization of insect societies is wholly regulated by instinct and built-in structure, which in ant and termite colonies includes such strange biological castes as doorkeepers with pluglike heads. Human society is never so stable and orderly as insect societies because its order is not genetically inherited or regulated by instinct, every individual having to learn his job and his role; but for the same reason culture is much more flexible, making possible a wide range and variety of adaptation to environment, and a growth in power over it. Cultural evolution became much more rapid than biological evolution, effecting radical changes in man's mode of life while his bodily structure was undergoing only slight change. The most important product of Man the Maker is man himself.

Here we must pause; for with culture appear the profound ambiguities of man's history, the basic paradoxes that will mark every major advance in freedom. Unlike power, *culture* is not an ugly word; as a creation of the human mind, it comes down to a "spiritual" affair. Yet it has never meant a simple emancipation of mind or spirit. Immediately it also imprisoned man in a world of his own making, often ill-made for intelligent purposes. It engrained habits and beliefs that generally tended to discourage enterprise and impede further growth.

Finally it culminated in civilization: a remarkable demonstration of man's powers, and expansion of his range of purpose, by which he created more elaborate, rigid forms of bondage. Grown self-conscious, he would have increasing misgivings about all his works, and begin to envy the apparent freedom of wild animals. He would regard culture as an artificial creation.

But simply because in a sense it is indeed artificial, as man-made, we should first note that cultural evolution was not essentially an unnatural, discontinuous, superpsychic process. It was a natural fulfillment of the potentialities of brain power developed by biological evolution, or immediately of the thought required to make and use tools. It included mores required by the social life that is as natural to man, and necessary for his survival. Its growth was facilitated by the wide range of variations in the most highly individualized of animals, and also by a seeming biological handicap, the prolonged care required by the human offspring. It was always affected by the natural environment in which it perforce took place. The man-made "spiritual" world is always a reflection, however distorted, of the material world.

The early stages of this development are best known through Neanderthal man, whose remains have been excavated in many sites in Europe, Asia, and Africa. He appeared on the scene perhaps a hundred thousand years ago. A short creature, not wholly erect, with little forehead and less chin, he was still apelike in appearance and not a lineal ancestor of modern man, or Homo sapiens; yet he was definitely a man, with some reason to think that he was the apex of development. Entering Europe toward the onset of the last ice age, he was able to stick it out, thus anticipating the many later peoples who rose in the world by first rising to the challenge of adversity, not by exploiting relative ease and plenty. He belonged to the late flake-people, who had finally been stimulated by association with the core-folk. He was a skilled workman, able to make specialized tools and weapons, and also a skilled hunter. Evidently he had some sort of social organization, for he killed mammoths and rhinoceroses, a feat that lone hunters would hardly be capable of. He used fire to keep himself warm, though apparently not to cook; probably he did not know how to make a fire, as no traces of it have been found in some of his caves. (Even in modern times some primitive peoples have used fire without knowing how to make it.) That Neanderthal man did not get very far during his many millennia on earth, and gave way to other races, testified to the importance of cultural evolution; for he had a brain capacity as large as that of modern man. He was only beginning to learn how to use his head.

Yet he was already doing some thinking, about first and last things. The most suggestive, haunting remains of Neanderthal man are his graves. He buried his dead ceremonially, in formal postures suggesting tenderness, and with them he buried their weapons and some joints of meat. It would seem that he had some notion of a life after death. In religious terms, he had a soul.

Or did he? What were his thoughts and feelings? He could never know that death, which is not clearly inherent in the properties of protoplasm, was a product of evolution and a necessity for further evolution. We may doubt, too, that he had come to the shattering realization—unknown to the apes—that all men must die; for in primitive myth death is commonly treated as an accident, not a natural necessity or law of life. It is little more likely that he was comforted by dreams of a happy hunting ground, which are rare among primitives. Like many later peoples with similar burial customs, he probably had only vague ideas about a shadowy afterlife, with some fears of ghosts. But we cannot know how painful a thing death was for him, or whether he buried his dead in fear or in hope, to appease or to gladden their spirit. Just possibly Neanderthal man might have been expressing simple piety toward his dead, as many of us do who have no belief in immortality. (Archaeologists excavating our graves a thousand years hence might conclude that we expected to enter the hereafter all dressed up in our best clothes.) At any rate, this chinless, browless creature was human enough to express some sort of sentiment. He was dealing in some fashion with the problem of death, anticipating the resolute refusal of almost all men to accept the evidence of their senses and believe that death is the end. Whatever his thoughts were, something like his death cult was to persist ever after.

Toward the end of the last ice age, the Neanderthalers were superseded in Europe by Homo sapiens, best known in the handsome variety called Cro-Magnon man. Less rugged, he stood erect and looked essentially like modern man. He and his fellows developed a far superior culture, or rather variety of cultures, which gave them more to do and think about. They were skilled fishers as well as hunters. They had more efficient tools, including tools to make tools, and with stone they worked bone, horn, and ivory. They started man on his long career as a mechanic by devising the first known engines—spear throwers and bows. They knew how to make fire, which they used not only to heat

and light their caves but to cook their food. By now man had learned
to control one of the great natural forces: a Promethean feat commemorated by the fire worship in nearly all ancient and primitive
religions. The graves of these men also suggest a plainer defiance of
death: they sprinkled their pallid dead with red ocher, perhaps to
restore the complexion of life, and buried with them their personal
ornaments. But the most striking evidence of their more advanced
mentality and complex culture is the work of men who must have
been at least part-time specialists—the artists who executed the superb
animal drawings in their caves. They had achieved an astonishing
mastery of realistic portrayal, unexcelled to this day. Some worked in
polychromes, which signified a remarkable technological feat as well.
There was nothing "primitive" about these drawings—except their
intent.

The motives of these prehistoric masters were not primarily aesthetic.
Their drawings do not adorn the entrance of the caves, where they
lived, but are found far back in dark recesses, usually at the end of a
tortuous passage; their artistry is more astonishing because they had
to work in a cramped position, in the dim light provided by some sort
of crude lamp or torch. The drawings served some magical purpose:
perhaps to give man power over the animals, perhaps to enable him to
participate in their splendor, perhaps to placate their spirits. They may
have been the beginning of totemism. Another suggestion of incipient
religion is the fertility idols found in the same dark recesses: hideous
female figurines with huge breasts and vulva, these were progenitors
of the oldest known deity, the Mother Goddess.

We have come upon another great power in man's life—magic, or
religion. At this stage we cannot clearly distinguish the two; but lacking
any evidence as yet of a lofty spirituality, we might start from the premises suggested by Gordon Childe, considering magic "a way of making
people believe they are going to get what they want" and religion "a
system for persuading them that they ought to want what they get."
The cave drawings look more like magic. No doubt the belief went
far back, magical lore growing with practical success in toolmaking.
(Childe proposed a likely formula of Neanderthal man: "To make a
D-scraper, collect a flint nodule (1) at full moon, (2) after fasting all
day, (3) address him politely with 'words of power,' (4) . . . strike him
thus with a hammerstone, (5) smeared with the blood of a sacrificed
mouse.") There is more doubt, however, about the effects of magic
on man's freedom. It may well have involved some oppressive fear of

the unknown, or of the unseen powers men thought they knew; Santayana observed that man is always afraid of a universe that leaves him alone. By the same token magic is a means of overcoming such fears, renewing confidence. The illusion of power it gave might have been strengthened by rituals that also strengthened the solidarity of the group and heightened its effectiveness. Hence Freud saw in primitive ritual a belief in "the omnipotence of thought," not the recognition of man's limitations that it seemed to Malinowski. A layman would think that it might signify both, given the common ambivalence of man's attitudes in such matters, and that the dominant feeling—of power or of anxiety—would depend upon the culture and its fortunes. As for the prehistoric cave men, their animal drawings give a strong impression of confidence, a feeling of mastery.

Yet these artists went to a great deal of trouble, to achieve a purely illusory power. Whatever freedom it gave them was subjective rather than objective, a matter of *feeling* free, not *being* free—an important distinction that we must keep in mind when we come to the "spiritual freedom" offered by religion. It amounted to a false security, and tended to distract them from seeking more intelligent, effective means of mastering their world. Significantly, they were much poorer at portraying the human figure, as they did in some hunting scenes. Their female figurines have no faces or features—no humanity; they have only an impersonal, monstrously exaggerated sex. It is therefore symbolically appropriate that these artists worked in darkness. Unconsciously they worked for posterity, and illustrated a paradox that was to become more pronounced with the approach of civilization. In the quest of supernatural power man was displaying natural gifts and powers greater than he knew, obscuring his actual progress. As he learned more, he would multiply error and become more enslaved by superstition.

Further generalizations about man at the Cro-Magnon stage must be hedged by cautions against popular simplicities. The human scene was now diverse and confused. A number of different peoples with different cultures occupied south-central Europe and north Africa, and the cultures distinguished by archaeologists do not coincide with the races distinguished by anatomists. (Among the latter were the Negroid Grimaldians.) In the Near East there is evidence that incoming Homo sapiens mixed with Neanderthal man, to produce a breed more rugged than his own; in China Mongoloid and Melanesian types might occupy the same cave. Unwittingly, prehistoric man had the wit to interbreed and so to broaden his genetic base, produce a wide variety of types, and facilitate adaptation to new or changing environments as he spread over the world. Unfortunately, many civilized men would fail to appreciate this contribution to the success of the human race, and would also forget the basic unity of mankind. The human race today is literally one race, in which all men are variants of a single species of a single genus.

It was once believed that the three main races of popular classification—the white, the yellow, and the black—descended from different subhuman ancestors. Authorities now find no grounds for this belief, emphasizing rather that very little is known about the origin and development of Homo sapiens, or of the three races, which specialists have broken down into thirty or more races. Some of the racial differences, as in stature, body build, and color, appear to have resulted from natural selection; others were most likely promoted by cultural preferences, different tastes in what constituted handsomeness in males and beauty in females. But the most pronounced differences, such as the color of skin and the shape of head, bulk small in the common human inheritance. Whatever biological importance they may have had in the early struggle for survival, they have no apparent connection with man's basic capacities for making, speaking, and thinking. No race is pure, no one clearly defined race took and maintained the lead in the growth of human freedom. The key to this growth is not race but culture; and in the long view, culture was the work of mankind as a whole.

Cultural evolution was likewise oversimplified by early theorists. They commonly assumed development in a straight line, through uniform stages, always from simple to more complex in the manner of biological evolution (although this too was not actually so uniform). We may indeed roughly distinguish some main stages in cultural evolution—the Stone Age and the Bronze Age, for instance—and describe the development in general as from lower to higher levels of culture. Nevertheless, the diversity of culture that is so conspicuous in primitive societies today was already apparent in Cro-Magnon times. Custom and belief need not have been uniformly simpler than in later times; primitive languages today are often more complex than civilized languages. The development that followed was not the uniformly linear development outlined in early theories, as from magic to monotheism or from promiscuity to monogamy. (There is no evidence of a promiscuous stage, incidentally, but good reason to believe that the life of early man was too hard to permit such luxuries.) In short, prehistoric men were somewhat freer in their behavior than orderly thinkers might like to have them. They were not so rigidly governed by any determinate historical law of development.

Again, biological evolution led thinkers to assume that at given stages of their development men in different parts of the world independently made the same basic discoveries and inventions, arrived at the same basic customs and beliefs, in keeping with their common needs and common powers of intelligence. This may well have been true of some discoveries, especially the simpler ones. It is difficult, however, to imagine men all over the world independently thinking up so complex a mechanism as the bow and arrow. Like almost all the more advanced inventions, the bow is not in fact found everywhere, it is still unknown to some primitive peoples, and it is not strictly a "need." Hence most students of prehistoric man are now agreed that cultural evolution was due primarily to diffusion, a slow spread of new skills and practices. There is evidence of trade in very early times, such as Mediterranean seashells found in caves well in the interior, and with such goods men might well exchange ideas. As we approach historic times, almost every excavation yields more evidence of the travels of artifacts and ideas.[2]

Such diffusion belies other common assumptions. Necessity may not be the mother of invention, since the inventions were not literal necessities; men had got along without them for many thousands of years, as some needy peoples still do. Freedom may be called the mother of invention—and therefore of necessity, as the inventions became necessities to men acquainted with them. The diffusion then obliges us to repeat that man is not by nature a restless spirit or a born inventor. He was not quick, either, to adopt superior tools and techniques; the travel of new artifacts was usually very slow, and no doubt was resisted by the prehistoric wise men or priests. But his engrained conservatism also emphasizes again the importance of the rare pioneers—the creative individuals who hit upon new ideas, the troublemakers who succeeded in defying tradition. It bids us pause with Collingwood to honor the incredible genius who tied the first knot, unaware that the lives of millions of men thereafter would often depend upon the strength of knots. Another agreeable implication of cultural diffusion is a measure of civility, which for Collingwood was summed up by the

---

[2] We can follow, for example, the stages by which the Greek custom of offering meat sacrifices to the gods worked its way to the wild men of Borneo, where it survived, while it was superseded by later practices at other stations en route.

spirit of Chaucer's Clerk: "And gladly would he learn, and gladly teach." We may suspect that prehistoric men did not learn very gladly, and taught less so—at least in their dealings with outsiders; the tribe may have jealously guarded their magic lore. Still, they did teach all they knew to their young, and their intercourse with other tribes was sociable enough to permit the eventual transmission of all the basic discoveries and inventions. Unwittingly they were creating deeper bonds among men, in a common indebtedness to the pioneers in a common adventure.

There were few troublemakers among them, however—too few. Man's conservatism can get him into deeper trouble. We may now risk some final speculation about Cro-Magnon man and his contemporaries, in the knowledge that their cultures died out and their glorious art left not a trace on their successors.

It is doubtful that man at this stage had yet become a problem to himself. He was good at hunting, for which his biological development fitted him; his animal drawings suggest that he felt at home in his world. But he must have paid some price for his wider range of interest and activity. Because he could take more thought of the morrow he could worry about it, and he could always depend upon nature to provide sufficient occasion for worry and grief. At least it seems clear that he eventually paid a price for his magical power. It recalls us to the artificial aspect of culture, by which man makes the natural world intelligible but to a considerable extent invariably misrepresents it. Culture misrepresents as well its own work, invoking supernatural sanctions for its traditions, creating a false past. Language itself, so indispensable to the growth of thought, has always worked to confuse thought, leading men to mistake words for things, names for powers. The power that Cro-Magnon man presumably got by incantation, in a language that will never be known, failed him over a long, hard pull.

The apparent reason for his failure was a change in the environment to which he had so successfully adapted himself. Toward 10,000 B.C. the Ice Age came to an end. As the glaciers retreated, the grasslands gave way to forests, and the mammoth, the rhinoceros, and the reindeer disappeared. The cave men had kept drawing these animals magnificently, but evidently they were unable to readapt themselves to the new life of the forest. They failed to develop such new tools as the stone ax, which helped later peoples to cope with the forest.

Unlike some of the animals on which he fed, Homo sapiens remained adaptable, and did not become extinct. While the reindeer went north and the mammoth went under, he learned to live in the new climate. The immediate successors of Cro-Magnon man and his contemporaries also learned to domesticate dogs as hunting partners or companions. Otherwise, however, they made no significant advances and left no such brilliant memorials as the cave drawings. They may even have forgotten that they had souls, for they seem not to have buried their dead ceremoniously. The next great step would come when man discovered a humbler possibility in the natural environment. His power over the mighty mammoth was negligible compared to the power he acquired through the seed, the discovery of agriculture.

2. *The Neolithic Revolution*

The so-called neolithic revolution that transformed man from a food hunter or food gatherer into a food producer, and from a cave dweller into a villager, got under way some eight or ten thousand years ago. It was a slow, quiet affair, scarcely a revolution in the modern sense of the word. Its authors were no rebels but apparently poor peoples who had become more dependent on wild vegetables as game grew scarce, and were suffering from the desiccation that was making deserts of large areas of the world. Many peoples remained food hunters and food gatherers, as some have been in recent times; others continued to concentrate on hunting, leaving their womenfolk to do a little planting on the side, as American Indians did; and some continued to live in caves. Those who devoted themselves to agriculture surely took a long time to master the art. Yet the discovery of agriculture did revolutionize man's whole way of life. It led to far more rapid change than he had ever known before, inaugurating one of the greatest creative periods in his history. His cultural advance made possible a far more rapid spread, all over the world; one of the rarer mammals became one of the most numerous. Culture now clearly dominated his life and directed his evolution. In the village he laid the foundations of society as we know it, and worked out a pattern of life that was to remain the basic pattern for most men to this day. Outside the advanced industrial countries, most people are still busy at the tasks invented by neolithic men.

Unfortunately for the fame of these pioneers, they did not go in for making the kind of precious objects that attract the directors of museums and the wealthy sponsors of archaeological expeditions; so until recently very few of their villages were excavated. Little is known about the early stages of their discoveries. But somehow they learned to grow such basic crops as wheat and barley, legumes, and oil seeds, and also learned to domesticate animals. Although authorities are still debating the precise origins of these plants and animals, they generally agree that the major development occurred in the Near East, in or about Mesopotamia. Archaeologists have now traced the main course of the remarkable doings of neolithic men at a number of sites —Sialk in Iran, Tepe Gawra in Assyria, Ras Shamra in Syria, Jericho in Palestine. From this region the new mode of life, and the arts and skills that went with it, spread westward to Asia Minor and Europe, eastward to India and China. A possibly independent development in southeastern Asia was based on the cultivation of rice, the most profitable of crops.

At least we have learned enough to appreciate our immense indebtedness to these anonymous neolithic "barbarians." They discovered all the major food plants in use today, by trial and error that must often have made them sick. They domesticated all the major animals that man still employs, and in the process learned how to breed them. They set about developing the whole complex of inventions called for by the new mode of life—sickles for harvesting, baskets for collecting and transporting, pottery for cooking and storing. They went on to make most of the basic inventions, such as the plow, the loom, the brick, the wheel, the sail. By about 4000 B.C. they were ushering in a new age by learning to work metals, discovering in fire the key to man's conquest of nature.

Now, we cannot be certain of the mentality of the neolithic villagers, since they were not yet able to record their thought and feeling in writing. We must also be wary in speaking of *the* village, and we must not assume a uniform, static mentality; the greatly expanded range of activity was reflected in a considerable variety of cultures. Nevertheless, the basic pattern of neolithic culture was fairly uniform. We know that the village everywhere meant a more developed social order, a more elaborate economy, and more routine work, and we can get some specific idea of its common life from its dwellings and its artifacts. Aided by inference from our knowledge of primitive peoples living under comparable conditions in recent times, we can speculate with some confidence about its basic institutions and modes of thought. At any rate, we must speculate about a way of life very different from our own, yet much closer to us than the life of the cave men, by no means simply alien; for we are still subject to attitudes and habits of thought that neolithic men engrained in "human nature."

As the new way of life most plainly limited the freedom of the individual, we may begin by wondering: Did neolithic men feel confined in the village? Did they think wistfully of the good old days when men had been free to roam? Possibly so, to judge by the traces of nostalgia in later myth and legend. Dim memories of a painful change may be preserved in the myth of the expulsion from the Garden of Eden, which biblical chronology places in this period. Some peoples did keep roaming, migrating out of need or restlessness. The new mode of life was resisted in some regions where game was plentiful; hunting is more exciting than growing things, fresh meat more palatable than porridge. The revolutionary advance—the greatest progress that man had yet made—in fact meant immediately a less adventurous life, and more sweat and toil if not tears.

Still, most men evidently led a settled life out of preference, and grew thoroughly accustomed to it. They stuck to agriculture wherever it became known; they clung to the village, which remained the center of neolithic culture.[3] And if they had any memories of the choice made by their ancestors, they had reason to applaud it. Living close to the soil, with their livestock, they could scarcely have felt that the village was an artificial world; yet they could enjoy the advantages of a settled world of their own. They had a higher standard of living than the food gatherers, materially and culturally. They may well have enjoyed most of the pleasures of an ordered social life—games and sports, dancing, joking, feasting, visiting, courting, gift-giving—that are found in every known historic culture. It is certain that they soon came to know the pleasures of beer, to free the spirit. (Possibly their food-gathering ancestors had made this discovery, for it has been suggested that the discovery of agriculture was inspired by the desire for beer, not bread.) In general, they were freer to make and do things for themselves. The possible satisfactions of such freedom were most apparent in their pottery. As they learned that they could fashion a lump of clay into whatever shape they pleased, they began turning out much more

---

[3] Although archaeologists are unlikely to stumble on isolated dwellings, it seems still more unlikely that there were such dwellings, for even today the isolated farmhouse is rare outside the new or the more advanced industrial countries, such as America. Over most of the world peasants continue to live in villages surrounded by their fields, as they have all through history.

elaborate shapes than utility required, and also began decorating their pots with abstract designs: designs that may have had a symbolical significance, and soon became formal conventions, but initially suggest that men were finding enjoyment in creating designs all their own, not merely copying nature. They began developing the characteristic styles in art and thought that would most clearly distinguish the great societies to come.

Such freedom contributed to the variety of neolithic cultures. While the plainest reason for the variety was the physical environment —differences in climate, rainfall, soil, natural resources—the environment set the conditions, not the ends of cultural development. It might determine, for example, whether houses were made of wood, stone, or mud-brick; their styles were a matter of social preference, perhaps even personal whim. Neolithic men living in similar environments were perverse enough to display different tastes, which a determinist may describe as not yet explained, but to others look like a kind of freedom in choice. The range in choice was widened by trade; for if the neolithic village was basically or potentially self-sufficient, it chose not to remain so. The earliest villages have yielded materials (such as obsidian) the nearest source of which was hundreds of miles away; and trade grew ever brisker as neolithic culture developed.

So the profit motive entered history, to enrich and complicate the life of man. At this stage, however, it was no serious complication. Though property arrangements in the village are uncertain, they almost certainly caused little trouble by modern standards. The grave furnishings show that the villagers had some personal possessions, as people do in all known societies, but they could hardly have had a clear concept of private property in the basic means of production, for this everywhere appears late in history. Most likely they had communal land for grazing, the normal practice of modern barbarians, and families held plots by some kind of communal allotment. In any case, holdings seem to have been more or less uniform in the early villages; there are no marked differences in dwellings or grave furnishings. Conspicuous inequalities in wealth and class distinctions were a later development. It is safe to conclude that economic interests, individual greed, or the "acquisitive instinct"—the ruling motives of man, according to many modern thinkers—played a minor role, or at least were as definitely subordinated to social relationships and noneconomic ends as they are in most primitive societies. The old Adam had yet to discover these original forms of sin, which threaten the freedom of the many.

The social organization of the village is likewise uncertain, but there is little or no question about some of its elements. That there was a definite organization is indicated by the regular arrangement of dwellings. The basic unit was always the family—not the individual; the family is one of the universals of human culture. Its universality might seem strange, in view of the sexual proclivities of man, were it not for one plain social need: children have to be reared and educated. (If some peoples possibly did attempt some substitute for the family, they disappeared without leaving a trace.) It was not necessarily a patriarchal family, nor was the mother necessarily the head of it if descent was traced through her, but authority would naturally be lodged with some elder or elders, as it is everywhere in all kinds of families. So too with the larger kin-group, the tribe that made up the village. The early village was a homogeneous group, held together by common understanding rather than formal government, and certainly not ruled by a king; but even so authority would be exercised by elders or natural leaders. The primary reason was not natural depravity or lust for power (there are no jails or police in primitive societies) but the need for leadership in co-operative action. The prehistoric cave men must have had leaders of sorts when they hunted mammoths in packs, and the neolithic villagers had more need of leadership in their more highly organized life, as in the building of fences to protect their livestock, later of ramparts to keep out human foes. Since authority, like power, has acquired an evil name through obvious abuses, we need to keep in mind its naturalness and necessity. We may assume that in the neolithic village leaders did not ruthlessly or even consciously impose their will on the group, just as there is ordinarily no brutal, tyrannical abuse of authority in primitive societies.

Perhaps as illuminating for sophisticates was the status of woman, who then as now made up half the human race (a fact slighted in almost all histories). While nothing whatever is known of early sexual behavior, and there is every reason to believe that it varied widely, the behavior of primitives would lead us to believe that woman suffered from the universal fear of menstruation, had to put up with some repulsive taboos. She was never an object of romantic adoration or idealization, and rarely if ever honored for virginity in her prime. Yet she had more reason to rejoice than she could have realized. Apart from the power that she may have exercised in matrilinear societies, or the sexual freedom she may have enjoyed in her youth, she had an essentially more honorable status than she would have in later civilizations. She profited from the universal worship of fertility among prehistoric men. Unless physically abnormal, she always had a husband, she was never either a prostitute or a frustrated old maid. She was also protected from contempt and from neurosis by a natural division of labor that made her of further value to the community. Students of prehistory assume that, as in almost all known agricultural societies, men took care of the flocks and the plowing, women did the cooking, weaving, and homemaking; they generally credit woman with the invention of pottery and the loom.[4] On all counts she retained a high status until well into the history of civilization, when slaves took over some of her functions, and the rise of philosophy and the higher religions deprived her of some of her natural dignity, making her a distraction or a threat to the spiritual concerns of men.

Meanwhile woman had the help of religion. The fertility idols found in the prehistoric caves reappear in great numbers in the early villages. To the cave men they must have assured human fertility and perhaps had some Freudian significance, the cave symbolizing the womb, but to the villagers they assured as well the fertility of the soil, the success of the crops. The Mother Goddess was emerging—the great mother of all life, who would become known as Inanna, Astarte, Cybele, Isis, Demeter, and Diana of the Ephesians, among many other goddesses, and who as the Virgin Mary would restore the feminine element excluded from the Christian Godhead. In the early neolithic village she apparently had it all her own way, for there is no sign of a male deity until civilization approaches. Like some primitives in recent times, the villagers may not have known of the relation between father and child, though stock breeding should have taught them the necessity of the male principle in procreation. By the time they became aware of this necessity, at any rate, tradition had enshrined the Great Mother.

Here we are still in the realm of magic, but approaching religion; and this awesome subject calls for a preliminary note of caution. The theory of evolution has generated a vast deal of speculation about the

---

[4] These may now seem like simple inventions, befitting the ordinary practicality of women, but they required a great deal of ingenuity. In *Man Makes Himself,* Gordon Childe takes more than a page to note some of the things that had to be learned about clay and the process of firing and coloring it before a decent pot could be turned out (pp. 77-78). It is also quite possible that women discovered agriculture too.

origin of religion, which has been located variously in magic, animism, totemism, ancestor worship, and the Oedipus complex. We can never be certain, of course, how it began, but the main reason for caution is the intellectual passion for reducing the many to One—the inveterate tendency to look for *the* origin. It is never clear why there must have been a single root for the whole complex of beliefs associated with historical religions, beyond some very general awareness that there are powers greater than man, and that he had better try to get them on his side. The obsession with the One is the more dangerous here because of the common genetic fallacy, the assumption that the origin of something is the key to its essence. Those who trace religion to the Oedipus complex or to magic born of fear are likely to conclude that its essence is still guilt or anxiety; those who discover that Zeus began life in Crete as a snake may forget that he became something utterly different. Speculation on how any institution began may always be illuminating; but our major concern should be how it developed, what it became, where it ends.

The Mother Goddess almost certainly began as a local, not a universal deity, and took on her many different manifestations as culture spread and grew more diverse. In the village she was not yet the Mother of the Gods, inasmuch as there were no other gods.[5] The villagers may have used any or all of the common religious ways of dealing with their patron, such as prayer, flattery, bribery, and ritual etiquette. They unquestionably helped out with magic; everywhere they made amulets. They had some inclination to totemism as well; such totemic bonds as cave men may have felt were strengthened by the domestication of animals, for the Mother Goddess came to wear cow's horns, alike in Asia and Africa. Animal worship was widespread in the early civilizations.

In all this we may sense an enviable feeling of harmony between man, nature, and deity. We may become aware of advantages that the neolithic barbarian had over us. For all his ignorance, he knew his little world much better than the modern city dweller can ever hope to know his. He knew his tools, his job, his purposes, his fellows, his place in the community, his service of the god—he knew all the basic conditions of his life, the reasons for the happenings in his world, and what he must do about these happenings. He had no problem of ad-

---

[5] The neolithic village seems to refute Father Schmidt's theory that monotheism was the original religion of mankind, unless it be assumed that the villagers mistook God for a woman, or that long before them man had suffered another Fall.

justment, or of personal liberty. Granted a few troublesome or mal-adjusted individuals, such as we find even in primitive societies, we may safely assume that the homogeneous neolithic village was united in a common understanding of roles and duties, a common acceptance of custom and tradition. It was essentially a moral order, but with little or no moral problem; right and wrong were clear and fixed. Religion was truly "catholic"; there were no protestants, no claims of conscience against the accepted beliefs. There were no deep splits between body and soul, nature and culture, reason and passion, theory and practice. Religion, art, and business were one. Add that there was no money or gold—no root for evil—and the neolithic village might seem to approximate Rousseau's dream of the ideal primitive state, before the corruptions of civilization.

This was strictly a dream, however. It is still a haunting dream, as men long for the simple, closed, tribal community, the social womb of the race; so there is need of emphasizing that even apart from substantial evidence that neolithic life was far from idyllic, every one of its apparent advantages must be qualified. The village was no doubt very well integrated, its members were very well adjusted—magic words for the social scientist; but the close bonds of community were bonds in the less agreeable sense of shackles on its members, who could not ask what kind of life they were adjusted to. The village approached the perfect order and stability that would become the ideal of political philosophers; but such approximation of the beehive meant a dearth of variety and new possibility, the want of any provision for change and growth. The whole order was based on unquestioned certainties, which religious teachers have sought mightily to restore; but the certainties precluded real freedom of mind or spirit. Likewise the absence of moral problems signified an absence of moral judgment, or of real moral sense, typified by the taboo and punishment without regard for intent. In particular, it signified a lack of personal responsibility and personal initiative.

Except again for the rare troublemakers, there was no problem of individual liberty because there were no self-conscious individuals. The village did not deliberately suppress the individual—he had simply not emerged yet. The villager who knew his world so thoroughly knew everything but his *self*. He was not idealistically surrendering himself to the community, because he had not yet found himself. Hence he could not even have a full, vivid consciousness of community, for to realize oneness it is necessary to realize difference.

B*

And such consciousness of community as he did have took the form of another universal of human culture—the incivility of tribalism. Loyalty to the group meant suspicion of the stranger, hostility to the outsider—a constant source of conflict with other groups.

Now, we still know this tribalism of the neolithic village, as we also know its conservatism, its blind adherence to custom; and it gives us pause. Unreasoned though it was, the loyalty was as natural and necessary as it had been when men lived in the cave. Today men must still live as members of a limited, if much larger group; only a very few can live either as solitaries or as citizens of the world. Tribalism is still a necessity, loyalty still a virtue. But we hardly need to emphasize this, given a tradition so old, universal, and deeply engrained. Our need is to transcend the narrow group interest that has always been a menace to the freedom of other groups, and that today menaces the survival of the human race. We may forget that the selfishness and aggressiveness commonly attributed to the unsocial nature of man, or to original sin, have been most conspicuous in the behavior of societies, and have been intensified by the loyalty of the individual to his tribe or his nation, his readiness even to die for the group.

Similarly the neolithic village affords a perspective on the ideal of personal liberty that we have set up. The complete subordination of the individual was also quite natural at this stage, and a necessity for survival; natural selection would weed out whatever undisciplined, lawless groups there may have been. Today we still have to reconcile our ideal with the necessities of social order. If we declare that the individual is an end in himself, we cannot allow him to be a law unto himself; the collective interest must still prevail over private interests. Knowing the dangers of individual selfishness and greed, we perhaps need to emphasize most of all the social obligations of the individual, the duties he owes in return for his precious rights. Only again we may forget the powerful pressures to conformity and uniformity, backed by a universal tradition many thousands of years old. Apparently most men want first of all to be well adjusted, and have little more disposition than the neolithic villager to ponder the question what kind of life they want to be adjusted to.

So we may reconsider, finally, the unquestioned certainties that gave the village its stable order, perhaps a deep feeling of security— but not freedom. The essential conditions of freedom are uncertainty, instability, a measure of insecurity, a measure of disunity and disorder.

The price may come high. But the neolithic villager also paid a price for his literally enchanted life.

While he knew his little world inside out, much of what he knew was illusion. The increasing numbers of idols and amulets found in the later villages reveal that as men acquired more actual power over nature, they acquired a stronger conviction of the efficacy and the necessity of magic. Their devotion to it is understandable, even though magic is not clearly easier or less time consuming than rational effort. Usually it works—the crops do grow, the patient gets well; and always its successes are more memorable than its failures. Still, it often did fail the villagers. They were necessarily much more concerned about the weather than cave men had been, and the weather in the region of Mesopotamia is always uncertain, often cruel. Tempest, flood, or drought might destroy their crops and their herds—and then strengthen instead of weaken their belief in the necessity of magic. Primitive societies having a hard time of it seem least disposed to risk any departure from the traditional sanctities.

Again we may wonder how the villagers felt about their magic—whether they were chiefly relieved or oppressed by their belief in it. A possible clue is suggested by Huizinga in *Homo Ludens*. In all known cultures men play; and play, he argues, is at the root of all the great archetypal activities of human culture. It is a voluntary, disinterested activity, done in "free time," for "fun"; it is always different from "real" or ordinary life, involving some sense of "only pretending" or "make-believe"; yet it is typically performed with intense seriousness, earning its universal significance by expressing rhythm, creating order, resolving tension and uncertainty, and so "enchanting" us—freeing the spirit. In this broad sense play enters into not only sport but ritual, myth, poetry, art, drama, war, law, even philosophy; and all the world's a stage. In perceiving these significant connections, however, one may lose sight (as Huizinga tends to) of the strictly playful element, the fun. Thus we may assume that the neolithic villagers played in some fashion, and we must hope that they had some fun, enjoyed in some sort their ritual make-believe. But then we must ask: Was their magic a *conscious* make-believe? There is little suggestion of playfulness or fun in their artifacts. All we know of primitive magic makes it doubtful that their ritual practice was a free, spontaneous activity, much less a disinterested one. If it necessarily involved some hocuspocus different from ordinary life, they were likely to have played it in

dead earnest, as an absolute necessity of "real" life. It may have done much to smother delight in the natural world, which in children seems natural. At least it had a compulsive air that makes the literally enchanted world of the villager not very enchanting to those who know better.

The Mother Goddess was not simply bountiful and benevolent, and certainly not the loving, sorrowing Mother who would comfort civilized men. Whether or not one agrees with followers of Jung that the Mother reigned over the primordial Unconscious, and was hostile to conscious personality, there were good reasons for the "Hero" to overcome and kill her, as he did in many later myths. While she had a gentle aspect, symbolized by her cow horns, she also had a ferocious aspect, symbolized by the lions who presently accompanied her, and by her frequent demand for the sacrifice of the first-born children. She destroyed and devoured as well as nourished, brought death as well as life; she long continued to show a preference for living in caves, entrances to the dark underworld. And if we cannot know just how the villagers felt toward her, it appears that whatever sense of power they got from her was not a sense of freedom, or simply a source of joy. Their fertility idols are generally crude objects, aesthetically much inferior to the animal drawings of the cave men, and to their own pottery; they give little suggestion of having been fashioned with loving care or in simple piety. Rather they anticipate the many grotesque or ugly gods that were to be made by man, in a subhuman or inhuman image. Altogether, neolithic religion does not look like a mode of spiritual freedom. The advance "from the idol to the ideal" was still a long way off.

In this light we may better understand and appreciate the worldly advances that the neolithic barbarians nevertheless continued to make, perhaps with the help of inspiration from the Mother, but finally at her expense. Magic did not entirely govern their thought and practice. It merely confused them, clouded their awareness of their own creative achievements, and so complicated the problems resulting from their creativity. The most momentous of these achievements was their discovery of how to work metals, by which they unconsciously prepared for the next revolutionary advance in human life—the rise of civilization.

At first merely hammering copper, to get an edge little if any better than that of their stone tools, they eventually learned to smelt copper in furnaces and to cast it in shapes difficult or impossible with stone. They proceeded to reduce other metals, such as lead, silver, and gold, and to develop alloys, in particular the alloy of copper and tin that gave its name to the Early Bronze Age.[6] The direct consequence of their discoveries was better tools, less likely to break, but if broken easy to resmelt and recast, whereas a broken stone ax is gone for good. Much more important were the unforeseen consequences. Metallurgy not only provided more wealth and power in itself but stimulated all other productive activities, transformed the economy, and shook up the whole life of the village.

As the most abstruse and exacting art yet mastered by man, it gave birth immediately to specialized industry. Metal tools could not be made in the home, in spare time, but required skilled craftsmen. To whatever specialists the village had already developed—chiefly such types as the medicine man—were now added miners and smiths. In order to supply the growing market these had to be relieved of the job of growing their own food. Quite likely some smiths took to the road, carrying ingots and making tools to order, but in any case itinerant traders peddled their wares. Trade was now a vital matter, involving material necessities as well as shells, amber, and other magical accessories. The village was no longer self-sufficient; it rarely had copper mines in its vicinity, and might be hundreds of miles from the nearest sources of supply. To purchase the new weapons and tools, it had to produce more food, clothing, or other goods than it needed itself. It became more used to the sight of the stranger, got news of a much wider world. A spirit of adventure was in the air. Explorers for new sources of metal must have set out in something like the spirit of modern gold seekers, while the itinerant merchants were themselves bold adventurers, leaving home and village to make their fortune.

Metallurgy might also be considered the·beginning of physical science, except that the empirical knowledge of the early smiths must surely have been mixed up with magic and more or less secret lore. The villagers doubtless looked upon them with awe, as magicians who could "turn stones into metal." In time their craft suffered from such attitudes. They were looked down upon by priests and scribes, specialists in a higher kind of magic; the smith occupied a lowly status in the Near East. His status rose in the later Western world only when his craft was divested of mystery and magic; here hosts of smiths became solid citizens, and a poet celebrated even the blacksmith as a mighty

---

[6] It should be remembered that this conventional label marks a phase in culture, not a chronological period. The Bronze Age in Europe came many centuries after that in the Near East.

man. But even here writers have echoed the sentiments of some early poets and thinkers, who deplored the evil that came into man's life with metal. At least it intensified his aggressive tendencies; so it brings us back to the invariable complications of human progress in freedom. All major creativity has been attended by destructiveness.

Although the early villagers seem everywhere to have been peaceful types, the neolithic revolution itself had destructive potentialities. If man was no longer merely preying on nature, killing for his livelihood, he was exploiting nature more aggressively and beginning to disrupt the natural economy. In domesticating animals he made helpless parasites of them, defying natural selection, while also providing opportunities for other parasitic creatures less amenable to his purposes. He was transforming the landscape in unpleasing ways by exhausting or eroding the soil, starting to make dust bowls. And as he prospered he began struggling more violently for survival against his own kind. The spread of neolithic culture stimulated cupidity and conflict as well as creativity; the fences around early villages gave way to ramparts. The abrupt changes in culture that sometimes appear in the layers of settlements found in Near Eastern mounds suggest that invaders conquered the previous inhabitants. The newcomers may not have exterminated them, but put them to work and then learned something from them; in the long run the mixture resulting from such conquests would prove a major means to the development and enrichment of culture. The process was none the less hard on the villager, the embryonic slave.

Conflict became more extensive with the search for metals and the improvement of metal weapons. To this period we may date the beginning of the institution of war. There must have been some fighting among the cave men, but they had neither the means nor the incentive for systematic warfare; such "savagery," which was still unknown to some primitive peoples in recent times, came late in history, and came into its own only with civilization. One of its early consequences was the rise of the chieftain—the war leader, the potential king. The authority he exercised was still essentially natural, and not simple tyranny for his followers; men are more disposed to welcome than to resent leadership, especially in war. An anthropologist writes that every society gives its leaders prerogatives and dignities because public service is not self-rewarding. One may suspect, however, that the rewards soon became obvious enough, and leaders tempted to seize prerogatives. At least neolithic society developed sufficiently to be approaching the political problem. And with it the class problem: the grave furnishings found in later villages show that some groups in the community were distinctly wealthier than others. We may presume that economic motives had grown stronger, habits of conspicuous consumption more formal.

But those who profited most from the increasing wealth were the gods, or their agents. The village shrines began growing into temples. Temples cannot take care of themselves—nor gods either, for that matter: they require ministers. The earliest specialist in the village was probably the medicine man, the embryo healer, intellectual, oracle, and priest. Now he became a full-fledged priest. As the specialist in propitiating the gods, and through them magically controlling nature, he would naturally come to control men too. Priesthood, wrote Carleton Coon, is "the most efficient and least expensive agency for law enforcement" in a homogeneous community. It was evidently efficient, but it would become pretty expensive. Whatever "spiritual freedom" it gave the community was purchased at some expense of social, economic, and political freedom.

In every respect the changing world was becoming more and more a man's world. Men did the mining, smelting, and casting, the trading and exploring. They were probably responsible for all the later inventions, and certainly monopolized the exploitation of them. After the invention of the potter's wheel, for example, women might still make pots in the home, but wheel-made pots were turned out by male specialists. High priests as well as war-leaders were men—"of course," one might add today; though it is by no means clear why God must have only male ministers, or even why he must be *He*. (One story has it that She is black.) Hosts of male deities were now showing up, to take over functions unsuited to the Mother Goddess, or perhaps beyond her capacity. When a supreme deity began to emerge from the crowd, he was everywhere a male.

If women resented their confinement to the home, they might have been comforted by the thought that the Mother Goddess not only remained popular but sired the most important of the new deities. This was a young male god, generally credited with the introduction of agriculture, who was somehow both her lover and her son. In helping her to assure good crops, he became the ritual symbol of the cycle of life, death, and new life again: a dying god who was annually resurrected. As such, he was not a supreme god; but he was a more authentic immortal, due to outlive all the supreme gods of early civilization and to remain the major spiritual legacy of neolithic man. From the

physical survival of the community he went on to assure the spiritual
survival of the individual, who like him might be resurrected. By his
promise of new life, and then of life everlasting, he became an ideal
symbol of spiritual freedom. But there was nothing of play or make-
believe about him. The ritual dramas commemorating his annual
death and resurrection had an ambiguous aspect: sublime in the self-
surrender of his worshipers, and rather pitiful in their monotonous
persistence, the implication of poverty of imagination and spirit. Men
would believe that they could attain their heart's desire through him,
and attain nothing without him.

3. The Rise of Civilization

Much as we owe to neolithic men, and as we may cherish inklings of
their humanity, we cannot be greatly stirred or warmed by their doings.
The diversities in culture that excite specialists—the different styles in
tool and pot—seem superficial. They do not alter the essential sameness of life in the village everywhere, and the monotony over many
centuries. Even apart from our scanty knowledge of it, prehistory may
strike us chiefly as an absence of real history. We are separated from
neolithic men by still more than some thousands of years in time. The
rise of civilization meant a difference not merely in scale but radically
in kind from the life of the village.

Like the neolithic revolution, the so-called urban revolution that led
to civilization was not a sudden, dramatic affair. Trade and industry became more and more extensive; villages grew into towns of some size.
It is impossible to say at just what point in this gradual process culture
became complex and elaborate enough to be dignified as civilization.
But again these changes literally revolutionized the life of man. They
were much more rapid and stirring than changes in the neolithic age.
They look more purposeful, and certainly involved more active intelligence and planned effort. They raise the curtain on history as we
know it and feel it because they included the invention of writing—
by general consent the clearest index to the emergence of civilization.
(One exception was the Incas of Peru, who without writing managed
to become great builders and administrators.) Another index is the
rise of the city, which ever after would remain the main center of all
the distinctive activities of civilization. In the city, too, man unmistak-

ably became a problem to himself; he created the social, moral, and political problems that we are still wrestling with. But for this reason too we must first try to understand and do justice to an extraordinary pioneering achievement.

The authors of this achievement professed the belief that it was the work of the gods. In Mesopotamia the city belonged to a god, whose priests managed his estate; writing was invented in order to keep the god's accounts. To us civilization looks like man's own free doing, directed by practical motives. The immediate means to its rise was a technological feat, the organization of a large-scale drainage and irrigation system; the first recognizable civilizations all grew up in river valleys with such systems—the Tigris-Euphrates in Mesopotamia, the Nile in Egypt, and the Indus in India. The earliest of these civilizations, the Sumerian in Mesopotamia, happily left the most complete archaeological record. We do not know where these Sumerians came from, and we cannot know why they proved so much more original than other contemporary peoples, but we can follow the course of their progress from the time they entered Mesopotamia in the fourth millennium B.C.

Although they spoke a language unrelated to any other known language, the Sumerians brought with them a Copper Age culture much like that found in settlements in Syria, Assyria, and Iran. No doubt they migrated out of need, the continued desiccation in the Near East, for they settled in the Tigris-Euphrates Delta, valleys rich in alluvial soil and teeming with fish and game, but all in jungle-swamps at the mercy of floods. Like the gods in their creation myths, they set about the task of bringing order out of watery chaos—draining the swamps, creating the land on which they built their villages. To control the waters they developed the system of canals that modern Iraq is trying to emulate.[7] As they began building more substantially they had to import all their timber, stone, and metals. All along they had to contend against the menace of floods, such as the great flood of Sumerian legend that inspired the legend of Noah, and that at Ur left eight solid feet of sediment. Their own arduous labors left fifty feet or more of debris of successive settlements at various sites. But by 3000 B.C. their villages had become full-fledged cities—Ur, Erech, Eridu, Lagash, and

---

[7] Their homeland is today largely a desert, crisscrossed by small dirt mounds that mark the routes of the ancient canals. The rivers have changed their course and have also filled up the gulf on which such cities as Ur were once located; the desert mound of Ur is now many miles inland.

a dozen others. In each the village shrine, a few feet square, had grown into a ziggurat—an artificial terraced mountain of brick, crowned by a temple, which might be 200 by 100 feet.

Monumental architecture, another sign of civilization, points to all its essential conditions. It is a product of material wealth, the surplus of a society no longer busy at mere subsistence, now free to cultivate the "higher" values. It is likewise a product of co-operative effort, literally a public work, requiring a high degree of social organization. It requires as well a considerable technical skill, involving an empirical knowledge of mathematics and mechanics. In its form, and in the art that adorns it, it reveals a mastery of materials for aesthetic purposes, and imaginative freedom to create new shapes out of brick, stone, and metal. It expresses the distinctive style of the society, enhancing its solidarity, heightening its pride in its achievement, symbolizing its conquest of the environment, or the transformation of nature into culture. For even though it is usually dedicated to the gods, it exhibits a superb confidence in man's own powers. Let us turn aside to contemplate the incredible daring of Khufu-onekh, the architect of the Great Pyramid of Gizeh: only three generations after Egyptians started building in stone, he planned a structure that would take almost two and a half million blocks, each weighing two and a half tons.

Although no one feat of the Sumerians was as bold as this, their total achievement was even more breath-taking. They worked up all the knowledge, the new skills, and the complex new institutions needed to keep a civilization going. To manage their great drainage system and their far-flung trade, they established large-scale government, creating a formal state with formal laws, and systematized large-scale business by standard weights and measures, a standard medium of exchange, the institution of credit, and devices for timekeeping. (We owe them our 24-hour day.) They developed writing, the art of the pen that is indeed mightier than the sword, as the most potent means to the civilization that the sword may destroy but can never create. With writing they introduced formal education, evolved mathematics, and created literature, in forms ranging from the proverb to the epic. They produced the originals of famous works long attributed to later peoples, such as Hammurabi's law code and the Babylonian Epic of Gilgamesh. They stimulated far more creativity than can ever be known as the influence of their civilization radiated in all directions, at length reaching Europe and China.

This whole development now looks so natural and logical, as one step led to another, that historians are wont to describe it as inevitable. Once man had learned to work metals, they say, civilization was bound to come. Nevertheless it was a literally extraordinary development, by no means automatic. Civilization did not flower by itself in a favored land; the Sumerians made their land a rich one by their own works. Call in Toynbee's principle of challenge-and-response, and the fact remains that other peoples failed to respond to similar challenges; many have stayed primitive to this day. Once the process was under way, the impetus and the rhythm generated opportunities such as could not be realized by the potentially most gifted individuals in primitive cultures; but at every stage the situation was open to different possibilities, and the main point remains that Sumerian genius brilliantly exploited its opportunities. Many other peoples who indirectly profited from the Sumerian achievement, or caught something of its impetus, failed to go on and take all the natural, logical steps. European peoples would take more than two thousand years to catch up with the Sumerians, who by then had disappeared from history.

A student of freedom should not be distressed by the implication that we cannot wholly explain the rise of civilization, any more than we can the work of genius. We could explain it only if history were completely governed by determinate laws, or by the will of a God whose designs were completely known. As it is, a historian must recognize the deep, impersonal processes of social change, with consequences always unintended and unforeseen by men, just as no group of early Sumerians sat down and planned a civilization; but he is not obliged to conclude that unplanned developments are wholly involuntary, automatic, or predetermined. Instead of ultimate causes, he may be content to specify the essential conditions and factors of civilization, the frame of necessities within which man's power of choice operates. Assuming sufficient natural resources (such as are not available to Eskimos or Bedouins), it requires an adequate technology to provide an economic surplus. More basically, it requires creative thought, first to design and build up the technology, then to employ the surplus in the cultivation of aesthetic, intellectual, spiritual interests. On both counts it requires a great deal of co-operation and organization, in particular a division of labor. The temple records of Sumer disclose that the city god had a staff of "divine" servants—a butler, a coachman, a musician, a gamekeeper, a sheriff, etc. He had a much larger staff of human servants, including brewers, bakers, smiths, clerks, and female spinners and weavers. There can be no civilization without many such specialists, to provide both its material and its spiritual goods.

Hence the Sumerian city was no longer a homogeneous community. Although many or perhaps most of its people still worked in the surrounding fields, many were artisans of various kinds. Over them were administrators, served by scribes; under them were slaves; around them were professional merchants, including visitors or settlers from other cities. The records of the city indicate that it was comprised of different linguistic and cultural stocks. The land of Sumer as a whole was similarly diversified. It had a basically uniform culture, it recognized common gods, its people identified themselves as the "black-headed" people; but it was made up of a congeries of city-states, each under its own god, behind its own walls.

Now, as we are all too familiar with the problems of civilized life, we may be disposed to overlook the positive goods it brought to man, goods we now take for granted. Immediately it brought material abundance, reflected in an immense increase in population. Man was no longer at the mercy of the annual flood, the scorching wind, the periodic drought; by trade and by the surplus stored in his granaries he could tide over the lean years. He had achieved a measure of supremacy over nature. If he was still close to it, likely to work in the fields, the landscape about him was his own creation too; he had made these well-watered gardens and fields, just as his ancestors had created the very land on which his city stood. He could enjoy the imported goods that made up for the deficiencies of nature in his own region. In Sumer he was very conscious of the pleasures of abundance.

The inevitable constraints imposed by the more complex life of civilization may likewise obscure the positive gains in freedom. Life in the city was much more varied, colorful, and stimulating than life in the village. It provided much more scope for creative ability, much more opportunity for self-realization. The young in particular might enjoy such opportunities; whereas education in the village trained the child to do and to be just like his father, education in Sumer might train him to do something different or to become something better. "Better" might not mean more contented—freedom has never been a guarantee of contentment. As Whitehead said, civilization comes down to a program for discontent. But its justification comes down to the only possible reasons why it is better to be a man than an oyster, an intelligent man than a moron, an educated man than an illiterate, a free man than a slave. It lies in the expansion, refinement, and enrichment of man's distinctive consciousness, the realization of his distinctive capacities for knowing, feeling, striving, and creating.

In the city the restrictions on him were also means of realizing more real freedom in thought and practice. With specialization of labor a man was tied down to his job, no longer self-sufficient; but at the same time he was relieved of the necessity of growing his own food and taking care of all his material needs. He might realize his creative potentialities more fully by sticking to one vocation, while sharing in the more abundant material and spiritual goods that obviously accrued to the community as a whole. (Today he may enjoy as well the sentimental illusion of self-sufficiency by hunting his own game, building his own cabin, or like Thoreau going "back to nature"—in order to become a sophisticated writer, and forget that no great artist has ever been self-sufficient.) If for the same reason man became dependent upon the city, bound to it, he was no more bound than the villager had been, and he evidently stayed in it by conscious preference. The always crowded, restless, noisy, wicked city would in time be deplored by many writers, denounced by many more preachers; and it would always remain the mecca of bright, ambitious young men from the countryside. It stimulated intelligence, perhaps even increased brain power; there is some evidence that native intelligence declines in a stable environment. The interdependence of civilized life by no means prohibits independence of spirit, but requires more of it.

Above all, the notorious wickedness of the city was a sign of more moral and intellectual freedom—and not merely for dissolute spirits. The homogeneous village had no serious moral problems because it bred an unthinking acceptance; morality was pure custom, bound by taboo. The heterogeneous city created moral problems by creating moral consciousness. Men began thinking about the relation of man to man, not merely of man to nature or the gods. Right conduct became a matter of conscious choice, personal responsibility. The Sumerians formulated a moral code, setting up such ideals as truthfulness, righteousness, justice, compassion, and mercy. They began trying to hold up even their gods to these high standards, as villagers could hardly dream of doing—the gods of nature are plainly as amoral as the weather, having no concern whatever for justice. Sumerian kings repeatedly boasted of how they had protected the poor from the rich, restored justice, and abolished iniquity.

Their boasts, however, give away the sad truth. Justice was never restored for long, iniquity never abolished at all. We must now consider the problems that came with civilization—problems due not so much to the sinful nature of man as to the nature of the city. "Friendship lasts a day" ran a Sumerian proverb; "kinship endures forever."[8] The heterogeneous city was no longer held together by the bonds of kinship. Even the family was unstable. "For his pleasure: marriage," ran another proverb; "on his thinking it over: divorce." Hence the Sumerians could no longer depend on the informal controls of custom or common understanding that had sufficed to maintain order in the village. They had to supplement custom by political controls, a system of laws, backed by both force and moral persuasion. In this sense the city created the problem of evil. Here, not in Eden, occurred the Fall.

More specifically, the rise of civilization forced the social question that is still with us. By their great drainage and irrigation system the Sumerians were able to produce an increasing surplus of material wealth. The question is: Who was to possess and enjoy this wealth? The answer in Sumer was to be the invariable one: Chiefly a privileged few. The god who in theory owned it all in fact required the services of priestly bailiffs, and before long these were doing more than their share in assisting him to enjoy it, at the expense of the many menials beneath them. Class divisions grew more pronounced in the divine household, as in the city at large. The skilled artisans of Sumer, whose work in metals and gems has hardly ever been surpassed, became a proletariat, unable to afford their own products. "The valet always wears dirty clothes" noted the Sumerian scribe. Other proverbs dwelt on the troubles of the poor:

> The poor man is better dead than alive;
> If he has bread, he has no salt,
> If he has salt, he has no bread.

The poor have not always been with us. As a class, they came with civilization. There was also the new type of the slave: victors in war had discovered that it was even more profitable to domesticate human captives than other types of animals. And outside its walls the city created still another type of man—the peasant. The villager had been preliterate, on a cultural par with his fellows; the peasant was illiterate, aware of the writing he did not know, aware of his dependence on the powers of the city, and liable to exploitation by them. Altogether, the urban revolution produced the anomaly that would become more glaring with the Industrial Revolution. As the collective wealth increased,

---

[8] This and subsequent translations from the Sumerian are by Samuel Noah Kramer, in *From the Tablets of Sumer.*

many men were worse off, and many more felt worse off, than the neolithic villager had been.

Similarly the great irrigation system posed a political problem: Who would control the organization it required, exercise the power it gave? The answer was the same—a privileged few. As the temple estate grew into a city, the priesthood needed more secular help, especially in time of war. Sumerian legend retained memories of some sort of democratic assembly in the early cities, but it emphasized that after the Flood "kingship descended from heaven." The gods had sent kings to maintain order and to assure the proper service of them upon which the city's welfare depended. This was not a pure heavenly boon, judging by the Sumerian myth of a Golden Age before the Flood: an Eden of peace and plenty in which there was no snake, scorpion, hyena, lion, wild dog, wolf—"There was no fear, no terror. Man had no rival." At any rate, the divinely appointed king ruled as an absolute monarch, and might be a terror. With him descended a plague of locusts—the tax collectors. Again civilization meant an anomaly: as the collective achieved much more effective freedom, many individuals enjoyed less freedom than prehistoric villagers had.

In Sumer these problems were aggravated by a profounder paradox. All along, we have seen, man had come to depend more and more on supernatural means of power as he extended his own power over nature. Now, with the most triumphant demonstration of his creative powers, he became convinced of his utter dependence upon the gods, his utter powerlessness without them. The monumental architecture of the Sumerians exemplifies this crowning paradox. The ziggurat, which inspired the Hebrew myth of the Tower of Babel, was by no means the symbol of human presumption that Jehovah mistook it for—it was a symbol of abject subservience. Sumerian myth taught that man had been created simply to be the slave of the gods; he did all the dirty work, that they might rest and freely enjoy. They got the credit for all the highest achievements of the Sumerians. They also got the prime benefits, since the works of the city were dedicated to the promotion of their welfare, not man's welfare.

Such servility is still understandable. If men had made a world really their own in the walled city, life in it was never actually secure, as its very walls indicated. Other cities might attack it, natural disaster might still strike. Sometimes the floodwaters got out of control; then its inhabitants were more helpless than the prehistoric villagers, who could pick up their simple belongings and move on to new pastures. Always they had to deal with the problems created by the more rapid change in their society, and before long they knew that it might be change for the worse; they began experiencing the cycle of rise and fall that would ever after recur in civilized societies, as it does not in primitive ones. Meanwhile the individual in particular could no longer know his world so well as the villager had known it, nor have an illusion of mastery. He was more dependent on a social system that was growing more complex, on powers that were growing more remote and impersonal. He had a more vivid sense of the temporal, the perishable, the mortal —of a gulf between man and deity, if not an opposition between culture and nature. The Sumerians paid the price of their livelier, fuller consciousness. Reflection leads man to an awareness of strictly insoluble problems, mysteries that remain unfathomable even after religion has provided a solution; for faith itself—and still more the felt *need* of faith, the insistence of the godly that man *must* have faith—testifies to a painful mystery.

As it was material success that the Sumerians chiefly sought from their gods, they could remain aggressively devoted to the pursuit of wealth, pleasure, and worldly prestige. Their religion was doubtless a positive inspiration, given all the great works executed in its name. Looking back from our vantage point, we can always see that men have acted on mistaken beliefs; so we must guard against the illogical but common conclusion that the beliefs counted for nothing, and that the "real" cause of their doings must have been something different (usually more discreditable). But considered either as illusion or as a positive power, the religion of the Sumerians gives a melancholy cast to their achievement. If on the face of their record it did not crush their spirit, it remained a constant source of anxiety. It brought little apparent spiritual freedom or peace of mind.

While believing that everything depended upon the gods, the Sumerians felt that the gods could never really be depended upon. They might insist that the gods were just, but in their hearts they knew differently. Their myths told how the gods could be violent in wrath, could be irresponsible (especially when they had had too much beer), could be simply heedless. In effect the Sumerians acknowledged that the divine will was inscrutable. The gods might send floods or droughts, or even let their own city be destroyed by enemies, for reasons that their unhappy worshipers could never fathom. Nor did it always help that every man had a personal god whom he might plead to, or bribe to get favors from the higher gods. (The favorite seal of the Sumerians represents this good angel introducing a worshiper to a god.) At best these were favors, not rights to be earned by righteousness; and the personal god too might fall down on his job. In general, the Sumerians had come to conceive of a cosmic order that was comparable to the order they had established in their own state, and that therefore was not a secure, clearly rational, consistently lawful order. The gods themselves were insecure, limited in power, in a cosmos that had not been created by an Almighty, but had arisen out of chaos by heavenly violence.

At this stage the whole development may be summed up by a document in which appears the first recorded use of the word "freedom." In the twenty-fourth century B.C. King Urukagina of Lagash, the first social reformer known to history, issued decrees revealing that the Sumerians were still conscious of lost liberties: he "established the freedom" of his citizen-subjects by restoring their ancient rights. In the name of Ningirsu, the god of Lagash, he rid the city of the ubiquitous tax collectors; he put a stop to the practices of the high priest, who was treating the god's property as his own and the god's servants as his personal slaves; he made a special covenant with Ningirsu to protect widows and orphans from "men of power." But the god evidently did not approve of his deeds. He allowed King Urukagina and his city of Lagash to be overwhelmed by the king of another city, after a reign of less than ten years. The scribe who gratefully recorded the reforms of Urukagina did not complain of the ingratitude of Ningirsu; he took for granted the arbitrary ways of the god. He brings us back to the basic mentality of the Sumerians, who accomplished so much in spite of the inscrutable gods, but always in the name of the gods. In his new man-made world, man was not yet really conscious of himself as a maker. Neither did he become so in any other of the civilizations of the ancient East.

| # THE EARLY CIVILIZATIONS

1. The Basic Mentality

As we cherish the human spirit, and seek to refresh and to fortify it, we must keep returning to the manifold diversity of its creations, the evidence of its spontaneity and its freedom. Such diversity grew much more marked in the early civilizations. True, men followed a similar course as they developed their irrigation systems, and with these the basic institutions required by civilization. The peoples in the Nile and Indus valleys were indebted to the pioneering Sumerians; thus the Egyptians seem to have got from them the cylinder seal, the use of brick for monumental architecture, and the idea of writing, while there is no evidence of Egyptian influence on Sumer. Nevertheless, the Egyptians went on to build an essentially original civilization, with a characteristic style of their own. If in so doing they were influenced by a different environment, a land of perpetual sunshine, their response to this environment was no more predetermined or predictable than the brilliant Sumerian response; they created their unique style, just as Khufu-onekh planned the incredible Great Pyramid that still awes us. Likewise the people in the Indus Valley pursued an independent course. Over a spread of some 800 miles they evolved a remarkably homogeneous, static culture that lived on in some of the distinctive forms and motifs of the later Hindu civilization in India. Within the conditions imposed by the environment, and with the aid of commerce, men were elaborating their culture to suit their own tastes and purposes.

Yet their purposes were cramped by similar obsessions. As we cherish the human spirit, we must also dwell on the severe limits of its freedom in the early civilizations. To a student of culture, in particular of the

arts, the most interesting thing about these civilizations is their differences in style. To a student of freedom, more significant is an essential
sameness in the mentality underlying these differences. Their culture
was based squarely on religion, of an unedifying kind. The key to
their religion, and to their basic mentality, is myth.

As usual, this is no simple matter. Scholars are still seeking the key
to myth itself, and locking as many doors as they open in their disposition to find a single explanation, which may then look suspiciously
like a scientific myth. (Among the weirder examples is Freud's notion
of the murder of the primeval father that generated all religion and
art.) Speculation about the origin, content, and purpose of myth has
grown more earnest and more confused with the awareness that it is
still very much alive in our own thought. It is indeed a universal expression of the human spirit, and now dear to devotees of "mystic" or
"timeless" truths; but for this reason we had better pause to qualify
some popular ideas about its universal meanings.

Followers of Jung, for instance, have made a fruitful search for the
archetypal patterns that he conceives as located in the "racial unconscious," somehow embedded in the structure of the brain. They have
found ancient images, such as the primordial Mother, the Divine
Child, and the mysterious Hero, that are deeply embedded in our
heritage and that haunt our poetry and our dreams. But none turns out
to be actually universal. The Mother Goddess disappeared in the early
civilizations of America, to be replaced by such ferocious goddesses as
the Eagle-Woman of the Aztecs. Neither do we find everywhere the
image of the dying, resurrected god. We might expect him to be a
universal symbol, in view of the universal cycle of life and death; but
early America did not know him, the Far East failed to make much
of him, and Israel and Islam would have nothing to do with him.

The most apparent clue to the universality of myth is not its
specific content but its purpose, the needs it has served. These too
appear variable. The early seekers of origins saw the "real" meaning
of myth in an effort to explain the mystery of the universe and the facts
of man's life, implying that prehistoric man was an embryonic
metaphysician. Durkheim interpreted it as a kind of allegorical in-
doctrination, serving to adapt the individual to the group. Today most
specialists regard it as an outgrowth of ritual—the magical thing said
corresponding to the magical thing done. But at least there is now
pretty general agreement on some broad generalizations. Early myth
was not purely or freely imaginative, and was not designed to satisfy

curiosity, to symbolize universal truth, or consciously to idealize high aspiration. Its essential functions were tribal and sacramental: to maintain the traditional ways of the tribe and its traditional dealings with the supernatural, to guarantee the efficacy of the ritual, or in general to confirm "togetherness," within the group and with its deities, and so to assure the communal welfare. Its content might be vague and various, as we find considerable diversity of myth over large areas in which ritual was basically uniform; but like ritual it commanded absolute belief. As a conscious "make-believe" or a merely symbolical tale it would not have served its very practical purposes or had the necessary efficacy.

The genetic fallacy, however, is still likely to obscure the implications of the growing diversity of myth, in contrast with the stability of ritual. By the time myths were recorded they seem clearly to have taken on new meanings. Some, notably the creation myths, do look very much like efforts to explain the cosmos, or to help men endure it. Others were plainly efforts to rationalize rituals the original meaning of which had long since been forgotten—for instance, the Greek myth that explained why, in offering sacrifices to the gods, men feasted on the choicest portions of the animal while the gods got the leftovers. Still others suggest what we might expect, that fancy began embroidering the traditional myths out of mere delight in story, escape from boredom, or possibly just for the hell of it, as men do in folk and fairy tale. In humanity, we should be pleased to see some free imagination and playfulness in the Sumerian myths about how the gods cut up when they had had too much beer.

Still, we cannot be sure. We are dealing with a mentality that is in some fundamental respects strange to us, and that has therefore been given widely different interpretations. Lévy-Bruhl described primitive mentality as "prelogical": a scheme of thought that was consistent, granted its premise of a kind of mystic continuum between man and nature, but that lacked any comprehension of causal connections or idea of logical contradiction. Although he later qualified his theory, students of early civilization have taken over the idea of a mystic continuum. Man in Egypt and Mesopotamia, wrote Henri Frankfort, simply did not know an inanimate world; for him nature was not It but a living Thou. While showing some capacity for logical thought, he did not regard such thought as autonomous or necessary, and he made no distinction between subjective and objective, appearance and reality, symbol and the thing it stood for. If so, the difficulty remains that his thought was not consistently mythopoeic. All the empirical knowledge he had acquired, as in agriculture, metallurgy, and medicine, suggests that in practice he did make some distinctions. Clearly he did not depend on magic ritual alone to assure the communal welfare. His proverbs express a very practical wisdom, usually without reference to the Thou, in effect recognizing a separate human realm.[1] His frequent anxiety intimates that whatever feeling he had of the unity of man and nature was far from a feeling of perfect community or real identity. Ritual itself implies a possible awareness that he was in some sense a stranger in the world, who unlike other animals—animals he might imitate in dances—had to take pains to keep on good terms with the Thou. In his anxiety, at any rate, he was led to reflect about the mysterious ways of his gods, seek not merely to divine but to comprehend their will. He was at least engaged in the quest of an intelligible world.

It was often a painful quest, especially in Mesopotamia. Frankfort wrote that just as man at this stage made no sharp distinction between appearance and reality, so he made no sharp separation between the living and the dead; but elsewhere he noted that the Sumerians and the peoples who succeeded them did make a sharp enough one. Their mentality was in this respect basically different from that of the Egyptians. In their smiling land the Egyptians looked forward to an afterlife that was a continuation of the best of this life—all this and heaven too. The Mesopotamian peoples enjoyed no such prospect. While their grave furnishings imply the common belief in some kind of spiritual survival, the furnishings include no clearly religious symbols or figurines, and their myths, hymns, and proverbs express no hope of heavenly bliss; the world of the dead was at best a dreary one, like the Hades of the later Greeks. Some kings apparently dreamed of a royal hereafter, befitting agents of the gods, but all ordinary mortals had to make the best of an always uncertain life on earth. Even the great hero Gilgamesh had failed miserably when he rebelled against death and spent his last years in a quest of immortality. Hence the problem of evil on earth was more acute. The author of "Ludlul Bel Nemeqi," a poem on the Job theme, made a reasoned effort to understand the gods, only to conclude that there is no understanding them:

---

[1] For one thing, he everywhere prohibited incest, which his gods were wont to indulge in freely. The most apparent reason for the universal taboo on incest, which goes far back into prehistoric times, was not knowledge of the biological dangers of inbreeding, but the need of preventing sexual conflict within the family.

What to one's heart seems bad is good before one's god.
Who may comprehend the mind of the gods in heaven's depth?
The thoughts of a god are like deep waters, who could fathom
them?[2]

This was not, however, the conclusion of the poem. Its author evaded
the whole problem of the sufferings of the righteous by an illogical
happy ending, restoring the health and wealth of his hero, asserting
in effect that god-fearing righteousness is always rewarded. He brings
us back to the common limitations of the mentality of both Egyptians
and Mesopotamians, as formed and symbolized by myth. Granted the
necessary qualifications—the diversities in their views, the rational
elements in their thought, the rudiments of philosophy and science—
their thought remained basically nonrational. Magic remained its
premise, myth its conclusion. If not prelogical, it was at least precritical
and prescientific; these men never reached any clear, consistent distinction between fact and myth, natural and supernatural. They had as
little sense of logical inconsistency as of empirical improbability. Their
thought about the cosmos was free in that it was undisciplined, un-
fettered by logic or empirical test; but by the same token it was at the
mercy of irrational hopes and fears.

Its limitations are plainest in their devotion to magic. Because magic
is generally more matter-of-fact and everyday than mythology, and
always serves a more definite purpose, Malinowski described it as rudimentary science: it developed systematic techniques to control nature,
thereby implying a belief in the lawfulness of nature. Yet in the
ancient East it remained at the opposite pole from science. It was never
a disinterested pursuit of truth, it employed nothing like scientific
methods, it had no means of formulating questions and verifying answers, and it involved no comprehension of scientific laws. Neither the
Egyptians nor the Mesopotamians recorded a coherent theory of magic.
The rudiments of science are to be found rather in their considerable
empirical knowledge, but this only emphasizes their failure ever to
separate such knowledge clearly from their magic. They had no word
for "nature" in our sense, nor did they ever attain to a steady conception
of natural causes, ever see through the fallacy of *post hoc, propter hoc*.
If they presumably had in mind some criterion of truth, we can only
guess what it was. In practice it seems to have been just this *post hoc*
fallacy.

---

[2] Translation by Mrs. Henri Frankfort.

Together, magic and myth obviously served real needs. "Needs" have acquired an aura of sanctity since anthropologists discovered, rather belatedly, that the most fantastic primitive customs serve them. Hence men may forget the obvious questions—not only what these needs are, and whether they are really necessary, but how well they are served. Nobody, I take it, would argue that magic does as well as science for practical purposes. But it seems necessary to emphasize the basic irrationality of ancient mythopoeic thought, now that we have become aware of the possible value of myth and have discounted the early scientific view of it as a mere aberration of thought, or "disease of language."

Romantic poets and critics began to revere it as poetry, or "imaginative truth." Myth may express the deep affinities between the life of nature and the life of man reflected in the animism of everyday language—threatening clouds and raging seas, murmuring forests and smiling landscapes, Father Time and Mother Earth. It may symbolize further truths about his own life, as in the myth of Adam and Eve and the birth of sin, the burden of consciousness. Accordingly, the classical definition has it that myth states what never happened, but is forever true. Literary men who are now pleased to find in it their version of the highest or holiest truth may draw on the authority of Jung: he insists that we must revere the archetypes as essential correctives of the extravagances of the conscious mind, which always tends to separate and isolate. Others, who are content to dignify myth as a symbolical expression of mystery, or of hard realities that can be coped with only symbolically, may cite Malinowski, who declares that we should regard it as not pre- but post-scientific, a necessary means of validating our cultural beliefs. Still others may add that religion, philosophy, and science alike are all founded on what amounts to a mythology, as imaginative schemes of thought, versions of the supreme metaphor Reality. The most sober students of our society emphasize that in any case myth has indelibly stamped our religion, the silent assumptions of our thought, the legends and the symbols of our national life. Skeptics tell us that all ideology is mythology.

Yet all this talk is highly self-conscious. When writers celebrate the myth they begin to deprive it of its original vital function, for they celebrate a conscious fiction, a merely symbolical truth. They date it more positively when they spell out its "timeless" truth, which then satisfies the needs chiefly of some contemporary sophisticates, or gives them the illusion of having recaptured a lost innocence.[3] Above all, they tend to forget the distinction between fact and fable that they began with. Aware of the limits of reason and the dangers of a narrow rationalism, we might agree that myths are necessary to symbolize and vitalize the strictly undemonstrable beliefs that men must live by, and that hold a society together; but we still can and must make the basic distinction between fact and fable. Mythology is not identical with poetry, religion, philosophy, or ideology as we know them. Taken symbolically, the myth can be rich in imaginative value. Taken literally, it can be an intellectual nuisance, or simple superstition.

In the ancient East men took their basic myths literally, with entire seriousness. They never spoke or thought of *myths*—they had no such word in their lexicon. They never considered them mere poetry, which with us always involves a degree of conscious make-believe, and never interpreted them as allegory, which implies a conscious symbolism. Lacking any clear distinction between real and ideal, they could not consciously use them to express lofty ideals or "mystic" truths. They could imaginatively embroider, elaborate, multiply them, but they had no rational means of translating, discounting, or criticizing them. We need not "explode" the myth unless it is taken literally, or until it becomes as dangerous as Hitler's racial mythology. They were simply unable to explode it: they took fable for fact, and were stuck with it. They were ignorant of their ignorance.

For such reasons we can never really share all their thought and feeling about the cosmos and the gods, even if we could be sure of the meanings of their key words. With the best of will, it is hard to do them full justice. The most sympathetic students of the early civilizations, such as Henri Frankfort, are therefore likely to combat our cultural conceit by insisting that their values are incommensurate with our own. Yet a student of freedom cannot let it go at this. We have learned a great deal about these peoples, and at least know them much better than they could ever have known us. Given the advantage of our greater knowledge, our wider outlook, and our capacity for a degree of both

---

[3] I should confess that a literary critic once pointed out that I obviously lack the faintest idea of what "imaginative truth" is. In the interest of "more accurate thought," he proceeded to define it: "Imaginative truth is simply that type of truth which, as long as we can contemplate it, overwhelms us." I believe I have been bowled over often enough by imaginative literature; but since men have been overwhelmed by innumerable visions, from voodoo to the dream of a world dominated by the Aryan race, I still consider this experience a doubtful criterion of truth, and think it accurate to say that the imaginative may be purely imaginary. A historian, at any rate, should presumably try to keep his head.

sympathetic and objective understanding, it is not only our privilege but our intellectual duty to judge their values. We have the right to declare flatly that their ruling beliefs were rooted in ignorance and a basic irrationality. In humanity we should add that their irrationality was not a moral fault, and by no means an unpardonable perversity. For the sake of humanity we must declare it for what it was—the more emphatically because it is still with us.

In this history I again take for my text the parable of the Grand Inquisitor in Dostoyevsky's *The Brothers Karamazov:* the Spanish Inquisitor who recognized the true Christ, come back to earth, but nevertheless sentenced him to death again. Christ, he said, was offering men freedom of choice and conscience—and for the great masses of men such freedom is an intolerable burden. What they need first of all is bread, and then "miracle, mystery, and authority." What they seek is not God but the miraculous. Although there is some question about the good will of the Grand Inquisitor, this need not concern us. The critical question is: Is he right? About man in the ancient East there is no question—he was.

The early civilizations were all based on "miracle, mystery, and authority." What men sought from divinity was not holiness but divination, magical power, to assure good crops, health, virility, success in war—the worldly goods that ordinary men still pray for. The difference was that men then really depended on the gods to produce these goods, and in return had to serve them and their priests. Although they might complain when the gods seemed careless or heedless, they scarcely dreamed of spiritual freedom. Unquestioning obedience to authority was likewise the ruling principle of their political life. Their government was absolute monarchy, divinely ordained; the monarch was the agent of the gods when not himself a god. And this was to remain the basic form of government in almost all the great societies, under all the world's religions, until recent centuries.

Men in the Western world, beginning with the ancient Greeks, have tried to order their society on a more rational basis; but their history still gives reason to fear that the Grand Inquisitor might be right. We must therefore seek a clear understanding of the sacred monarchy. In particular we must face up to the fact that on this basis Egypt endured for almost three thousand years. By ordinary practical standards of success, what "works," it was the most successful state in history. Free Americans, in their noisy infant nation, cannot afford to forget Egypt.

2. *The Basic Pattern of the Sacred Monarchy*

The essential similarity of the political structures of Egypt and Mesopotamia may seem more surprising because their peoples arrived at their common destination by quite different routes. In Sumer, as we have seen, civilization arose in independent city-states, which initially had popular assemblies. After "kingship descended from heaven," the cities were sometimes welded into temporary kingdoms by war, and about 2350 B.C. Sargon of Agade (or Akkad) succeeded in dominating the whole land, going on to conquer most of western Asia, and create the first great empire in history; yet Sumer never became a real nation.[4] Sargon's empire collapsed within a century, as did a subsequent one under the Third Dynasty of Ur; thereafter Mesopotamia was ruled by a succession of different peoples—Elamites, Amorites, Kassites, Assyrians, Chaldeans—who overthrew one another when they were not overthrown by foreign invaders. In Egypt, on the other hand, history began with the unification of the land under a king (or series of kings) known as Menes, who ruled a predominantly rural domain from a capital at Memphis; and thereafter the Egyptians were always a nation. Their history falls into three major phases, the Old, Middle, and New Kingdoms, punctuated by a period of anarchy and a period of domination under foreign invaders, the Hyksos; but throughout they retained their identity, their gods, and their basic institutions. Each kingdom was presided over by Pharaoh, their divine king.

The basic attitudes of the peoples differed correspondingly. The insecure, anxious Sumerians devoted their writing, learning, and art primarily to the service of the gods; in a land dominated by the ziggurat, the king himself was only an agent of the gods. The Egyptians, living in a united, isolated, relatively secure land, blessed by perpetual sunshine and the punctual beneficence of the overflowing Nile—unique among great rivers in that it never brought raging floods—had more apparent confidence in man's powers, and at first glance seem less obsessed by religion. Royal themes predominated in the art of Egypt,

---

[4] At this stage exact dates—as of Sargon and his successors—are uncertain. Recent historians generally favor the "short" chronology, which brings Mesopotamian dynasties several centuries closer to us, and early Egyptian dynasties still closer, than the older textbooks indicate; but it is still approximate. For my present purposes, however, exact dates are unnecessary. I insert occasional dates (following the short chronology) chiefly as an aid to the reader in keeping his bearings.

whose early monumental architecture was not the temple but the pyramid, the royal tomb, built grandly in permanent stone. It had no flood myth to dispel the idea of the permanence of its works.

Yet its culture was not actually more humanistic or naturalistic. To the end the Egyptians were united in the belief that their welfare depended wholly upon Pharaoh—and Pharaoh was himself a god, no mere deputy. In the Old Kingdom his subjects owed their very souls to him; he conferred upon his officials the boon of immortality. In theory he owned the whole land and had entire management of its affairs. In fact, as the Great Pyramid testifies, the Egyptians worked even harder to serve their divine monarch than the Sumerians did to serve their gods, and they had less freedom in going about their own business; no pharaoh ever "established the freedom" of his subjects as King Urukagina did. The homogeneous, isolated land of Egypt may be said to have worked out the "ideal" form of the sacred monarchy, which all other societies in the East merely approximated.

The ideal was pure absolutism, under a sacred autocrat. Pharaoh was literally the state, wielding all executive, legislative, and judicial power. His exercise of this power was naturally limited by custom and simple prudence, but there were no constitutional checks on it, no lawful means of resisting his decrees. To us his divine status looks somewhat confused, as do the hosts of gods worshiped in Egypt; although admittedly born of a mortal woman, he was the son of the sun-god Re, he was also Horus, and when dead he became Osiris. To the Egyptian all was clear, or at least as clear as the supreme realities of miracle and mystery can be. Like all supreme gods, Pharaoh was both gracious and terrible—in their own words, "that beneficent god, the fear of whom is throughout the countries." When he appeared in public, his people fell on their faces before him. He alone worshiped the other great gods on behalf of his people. He knew everything: "there is no subject which he has not comprehended." He and he alone did everything; in war he defeated the enemy singlehanded (sometimes even before news of his victory reached him). He had to have absolute power because everything depended on him.

In spite of his supernatural abilities, Pharoah understandably needed some human assistance in taking care of the details of administration. As he appointed high priests to perform the ceremonies of worship, so he appointed officials to manage the irrigation system, collect taxes, store grain, administer justice. He ruled through a bureaucracy, a hierarchy headed by a vizier and trained in the palace school. The bureaucracy managed the whole basic economy, including foreign trade; it brought in the copper from Sinai, the gold from Nubia, the cedar from Lebanon, luxury goods from elsewhere in Asia. As might be expected, the high officials acquired considerable wealth and power, more especially since many had royal blood; Pharaoh had a number of wives and concubines. (As a god, he was also privileged to commit incest and sometimes married his daughter—presumably to keep the royal or divine blood pure.) But this ruling class was not an independent class with constitutional powers and privileges. High officials were appointed by Pharaoh, responsible to him alone, and always subject to arbitrary dismissal; they had no legal rights to office.

In theory, accordingly, Egypt was a totalitarian state, and in fact a managerial state of a high order of organization, with a planned economy—a striking anticipation of modern collectivism. Its social structure was not rigid, permitting commoners to rise in the world, but they were always subject to conscription for work on the dikes or in the building of palace, pyramid, and temple. (Herodotus reported the tradition that the Great Pyramid required the labor of 100,000 men for twenty years.) Likewise the early artisans worked chiefly in palaces and temples, as there was little other market for their wares; few were independent or acquired any means to speak of. In general, what freedoms were permitted were a matter of custom and convenience, not political principle. Commoners had no political rights, no voice in the government. There was no idea that government existed primarily to serve their interests; they existed to serve Pharaoh. There were no public affairs because there was no means of debating the public interest, no clear idea of any such thing apart from the interest of Pharaoh. If Pharaoh was ideally a good shepherd, the people were always his sheep.

Since he was divine, and ruled in a land of regular flood and sunshine, the Egyptians naturally conceived their society as static and permanent. Their pyramids, their massive temples in stone, the unblinking stare of their statues in immobile attitudes, the annals of their dynasties reaching far back into antiquity—all express their ideal of immutability. There could be no new things under a sun that in effect was Pharaoh himself. Naturally, too, some changes did take place in spite of the Egyptians, even apart from the periods of disorder between the kingdoms. In the later kingdoms a middle class emerged, enjoying a measure of economic freedom; high officials revealed an increasing mobility by boasting more often of how they had risen from lowly origins; nobles entered the hereafter on their own, without need of the grace of Pharaoh, as in time even commoners did; the priesthood grew in size, wealth, and power. Yet there was never a fundamental change in the political structure of Egypt, or a serious effort at any such change. Pharaoh retained his absolute authority. However feeble he might be in practice, no independent power within the society was strong enough to oppose him on principle. If his harem, his ministers, and his high priests might intrigue or conspire against him, no party set up a public standard of opposition. Throughout the long centuries of Egypt's history there was never a popular rebellion to unseat Pharaoh.

As mere mortals, the kings of Sumer could hardly boast of such eminence. Even the great Sargon was known to have been a poor boy, and Urukagina did not conceal the fact that he had assassinated the priest-king before him. When divinity hedged the later kings in Mesopotamia they became vainglorious enough, but they still fell short of the supernatural powers of Pharaoh. The greatest kings were prey to anxiety, in the knowledge that their success depended upon conformity to the will of their gods, and that the most meticulous attention to omens might yet fail to divine his will. (With more than two thousand years of royal experience in divination behind him, Ashurbanipal, the Great King of Assyria, left a piteous inscription lamenting the strange evils that had befallen him, the holiest of kings, in his old age.) Similarly the rulers of Mesopotamia permitted more latitude to private enterprise. Sumerian kings left foreign trade largely to merchants, and though their successors extended bureaucratic controls, keeping the economy under strict regulation, they did not try to supplant the merchants with their own officials. A middle class of enterprising business-men flourished all along in the land of the two rivers.

Yet absolute monarchy was the rule here too, and in time it came closer to the Egyptian ideal. The king was at least appointed by the gods, if in ways that are not very clear. With imperial success he began entertaining a more exalted idea of his role. After Sargon became "King of the Universe," his grandson proclaimed himself "the divine Naramsin, the mighty, god of Agade." Although his empire fell to semi-barbarians, who wiped out Agade, his style did not go out of fashion; later kings were commonly honored, or honored themselves, by some sort of deification. In any case, the state was an extension of the despotic cosmic order. "The command of the palace, like the command of Anu, cannot be altered," we read in the royal annals. "The king's word is right; his utterance, like that of a god, cannot be changed." There was no legitimate way of opposing him if his inalterable word chanced to be wrong, his subjects having no more voice in their government than in the weather. The succession of peoples and empires in unsettled Mesopotamia introduced the popular Oriental theme of regeneration, as founders of new dynasties were pleased to announce themselves as heaven-sent saviors or restorers; but the new dynasties never changed the basic pattern of the absolute monarchy. The primary virtue of their subjects remained unquestioning obedience; in theory all were the slaves of the king. The correct posture in the royal presence was the typical Oriental symbol of total submission—prostration.

Now, to a Western eye this sacred monarchy looks like simple despotism. "Oriental despotism" is indeed the name given it by Karl Wittfogel, who has made the closest, most exhaustive study of it to date. As he emphasizes, however, it remained the commonest, longest-lived form of state in history; so we must take the more pains to understand it. Actually it was not a simple tyranny. Neither was it simply a brutal exploitation of the masses in the interests of selfishness, greed, lust for power, or any cynical motives; we must reckon with the significant fact that the "despots" managed without a police force (the police is a typical Western institution) and did not use their armies to hold down the masses. Nothing in the tradition of either the Sumerians or the Egyptians indicates that the kings rose to power by sheer violence. Some violence there must have been; but all we know of early history suggests that kingship was generally a natural, an unforced, and on the whole a welcome development.

Ideally, a society would advance to civilization with all its members abreast, in step. Neolithic society had been more or less egalitarian, as primitive societies typically are, and out of its inchoate democracy there might here and there have emerged something like the democratic Iroquois confederacy in prehistoric America, based on implicit if unformulated principles of liberty, equality, and fraternity. Thus the early Sumerians, with their popular assemblies, conceivably might have advanced in unison. Yet in all history no known people has risen to civilization in this manner. Peoples have invariably risen under the leadership of a few; a ruling class provided the necessary direction, maintained the necessary order, developed the necessary arts and learning—and enjoyed the wealth. Indeed, it could hardly be otherwise. In Egypt and Mesopotamia the building and maintenance of the vast drainage and irrigation systems clearly required a strong central authority; and it is difficult to imagine town meetings achieving such a feat—especially in Egypt, where villages were strung along the Nile for hundreds of miles.

There can be little doubt that the earliest kings exercised the natural authority of the chieftains who began to appear in neolithic society: an authority based primarily on natural ability, not on economic power or naked force. They still led their followers in person, were still bound by tribal custom. If their authority might sometimes be resented (as men are prone to resentment of the father, the god, or any symbol of authority), it was generally welcomed, and gratefully rewarded after successful ventures. The real problem arose with success on a large scale—the growth in numbers of the group, and in size of its dominions. We may assume that the problem first appeared in all its magnitude with Menes, the great pharaoh who unified the land of Egypt. Whether a farsighted statesman or a simple warrior, an unselfish patriot or a power-hungry adventurer, the king was now of necessity remote from most of his subjects, apart from the community, and of course above it. The scope of his job, if not of his self-importance, further removed him from ordinary occupations, and so augmented his majesty. Now, too, his great authority had to be institutionalized and legitimatized. The natural way of transmitting it was to keep it in the family; though by this or any other formal procedure it might pass to a man without pre-eminent ability, or natural claim to authority. The natural way of legitimatizing his sovereign powers was to declare that he got them from the gods.

This need not have been a conscious solution to the problem, proposed by either a wise statesman or a cynical despot. Much more probably it was unpremeditated. Given the basic mentality of men at this stage, in fact, it might be called a foregone conclusion. One specific preparation for it, and explanation of it, was the annual ritual drama of the dying, resurrected god, which in various forms had long been enacted all over the Near East. No routine ceremonial, as are most rituals today, this was literally a matter of life and death—the survival of the community depended on it. We know that in later times it still excited intense emotion: anguish over the suffering and death of the god, ecstasy over his triumphant resurrection, both perhaps intensified rather than tempered by the knowledge that neither the death nor the resurrection was permanent—next year he would have to go through it again. And the king early took the place of the god in this annual drama, becoming a kind of ritual scapegoat. Quite likely he was at first actually killed, until men learned the need of being thriftier with leaders. Thereafter he played a formal but symbolically no less important role in the annual drama, traces of which remained in the coronation ceremonies of kings in the Western world.

The common veneration of European kings and of the "crown"— the circle that in antiquity more clearly symbolized continuity and completeness—recalls the ideal aspect of kingship. This was unquestionably still more real to early peoples. The Egyptians rejoiced in the belief that their society had been completely ordered and would be permanently maintained by Pharaoh, a divine being who was yet visibly, daily, miraculously on the job. "It was an ideal," wrote Henri Frankfort, "which ought to thrill a Western historian by its novelty, for it falls entirely outside the experience of Greek or Roman or Modern Man. . . . It represents a harmony between man and the divine which is beyond our boldest dreams." The anxious Sumerians could only dream of such harmony; but they too believed that kingship was a gift of the gods, an indispensable means to whatever security they could hope for. If it seemed despotic, it was still "the true pattern of divinity," as King James I of England called it; gods are naturally autocratic, their realm is never a republic. No popular uprisings against the king are recorded in the long history of Mesopotamia either. However remote and awful in his majesty, the king still ruled by legitimate authority, not naked force. Absolute monarchy represented government by consent of the governed.

The governed had as well some good practical reasons for grateful consent. Although in time the kings would take to war in order to win personal glory, at first they brought peace, law, and order. In Egypt they maintained permanent garrisons on the frontiers; in Sumer they organized defenses against both rival cities and surrounding barbarians. They suppressed internal feuds, the otherwise interminable disputes over water rights. For all the inequities of distribution, they made possible a higher standard of living on the whole, a greater measure of the effective freedom that comes with security and abundance. They saw to it that most of the surplus wealth of the community went into productive enterprise, typically boasting of their public works, not their conquests; an early pharaoh had himself depicted "cutting the first sod" of a new canal, a Sumerian king proudly put his royal stamp on the bricks of his drainage system. As typically they boasted of their feats as lawgivers or restorers of justice. Far from simply exploiting or oppressing the masses, they in fact provided the chief protection for

c*

the masses against predatory priests and nobles; there is ample evidence that they were generally more public-spirited than were the wealthy class. And among them were some wise statesmen. In Sumer they made the first known effort at international law, a king being called in to arbitrate a boundary dispute between two other kings.

Altogether, the practical success of kingship was amply demonstrated by the immense increase in population in early civilization. Its spiritual success is at least arguable. Inasmuch as publicity went chiefly to royal exploits, in a society where there was no public opinion to speak of, we may doubt the Egyptian legend that the thousands of conscripts were happy as they built the Great Pyramid; yet many may have been happy, or even felt exalted in the service of their god-king.[5]

The common people were less grateful for the king's bureaucracy, which they knew best in the person of the tax collector. Nevertheless, they owed much to it too—as do we. For bureaucracy was the one enduring political legacy of early civilization. It would reappear in every great state to this day, and in all would have a bad reputation; yet it is always indispensable, and is still widely misunderstood. It was at first a revolutionary development. Pharaoh's bureaucracy represented a brilliant social invention: an organization simple by modern standards but the most elaborate that man had yet achieved, and the plainest secret of Pharaoh's success. If it meant slavery to system, this is no less essential to large-scale enterprise; red tape has been called the mother of freedom, as an assurance of orderly procedures and a safeguard against arbitrary ones. And if bureaucracy has everywhere earned its bad reputation (which even in Soviet Russia has made it subject to open criticism), resentment of it commonly misses the mark. Whereas the popular charge is that it is always inefficient, the serious objection is to its impersonal efficiency—for its own appointed purposes. It keeps on remorselessly collecting taxes, enforcing regulations, grinding out orders, without regard either for individual hardships or for larger considerations of the public welfare. The bureaucracy established by the pharaohs, and taken over by later conquerors, was efficient enough to keep Egypt going, through ups and downs, for more than three thousand years. The only institution in the Western world that can compare

---

[5] The kings incidentally earned the gratitude of historians by the pains they took to impress posterity, stamping their signatures on their buildings and leaving records of their exploits. Although their records are typically untrustworthy, and make a rather different impression on us than they intended, they tell us a great deal. At any rate, the kings did succeed in immortalizing themselves.

with it for longevity is a more elaborate bureaucracy—the Roman Catholic Church.

Because of the great irrigation systems that produced bureaucracy, Karl Wittfogel has given the name "hydraulic society" to the kind of absolute monarchy epitomized by Egypt. All the early civilizations were marked by public works on a great scale, as well as monumental architecture in temple, tomb, or palace; the absolute monarch had masses of manpower at his disposal. Such great public works did not appear in classical Greece, feudal Europe, or feudal Japan, but did appear in later states similar to the sacred monarchy, from imperial China, with its Great Wall and its 800-mile-long Imperial Canal, to imperial Rome and the early civilizations of America. As Wittfogel observes, however, "hydraulic society" is not a matter of simple economic determinism. Some states, such as Carthage, Venice, and Holland, developed public works on a considerable scale without establishing an Oriental monarchy, while Ottoman Turkey and Czarist Russia took to Oriental monarchy without engaging in great public works. We are dealing with a basic, recurrent pattern of government that was a logical but not a uniform, invariable development. Its history is intelligible, lawful enough to permit significant generalization, but not to prove any universal historical law.

Immediately it forces a drastic discount of some popular generalizations and laws. As all civilized societies may be divided into haves and have-nots, all history may look like what Marx called it—the history of class struggles. Such struggles have been conspicuous in Western history, beginning with the Greeks. But there was no class struggle of the Marxist kind in the ancient East. We know little about the masses of have-nots if only because they did not actively struggle; while they were evidently class-conscious enough to feel some resentment of their betters, they rose up against the aristocracy no more than against the god-kings. At most there was some conflict within the upper class, usually in the form of intrigue or conspiracy, usually motivated by purely personal ambition. Class struggle appears to be chiefly a luxury of free societies. By the same token, the ancient East confounds the many democratic thinkers who picture history as a continuous struggle for justice and freedom, and habitually remark the "eternal cry" for freedom. Charles Beard lent professional authority to the popular belief: "Since the beginning of civilization there has been a struggle between sheer force and humanity, between the few who have sought dominance by physical might and the many who have sought to protect and govern themselves under customs and rules of their own making." The Grand Inquisitor, alas, was nearer the truth.

The middle class also failed to play the role it has been assigned in much political theory, both democratic and Marxist. Although it has been a major force in Western history, the ancient East suggests that it has no manifest political destiny, as either friend or enemy of freedom, and is not by nature either dynamic or solid. A considerable middle class in Mesopotamia and a growing middle class in later Egypt had little perceptible influence on the political system or the basic structure of the society. The wealthier businessmen might have been complacent enough to agree with their modern spokesmen that economic freedom is the most fundamental and precious of freedoms, but if so they failed to demonstrate any necessary connection between it and political freedom. Even in Mesopotamia, where merchants had more scope for private enterprise, they remained completely subservient, in letters signing themselves "servant of the king." Granted that they were largely dependent on the palace and the temple, their chief customers and the chief source of capital for loans, the fact remains that they did not seek independence through their guilds. Judging by the record, they never dreamed of the axiom of the bourgeois philosopher John Locke, that the main purpose of government is to protect private property.

Hence private property likewise failed to exert either the wholesome or the baneful influence attributed to it in much Western theory. While Pharaoh nominally owned the whole land of Egypt, it appears that peasants might own their little plots, and certainly many wealthy men were large landowners; in Mesopotamia private property and its rights were more clearly defined by law. Such rights constituted an element of freedom. Yet they did not lead to political freedom, become a bulwark of personal freedom, or inspire a struggle to defend or extend freedom. The ideal value and the practical force of private property evidently depend less on any inherent sanctity or innate passion for it than on social custom and political system. In the ancient East men accepted severe restrictions on the rights and uses of property; they were not free to enjoy and bequeath it as they pleased. For the same reason the possession of wealth or economic power did not automatically confer political power, as Marx thought it must and American Federalists thought it should. If the wealthy naturally fared better than the poor in court or palace, they did not control the state or directly wield power—except as the high officials of Pharaoh or the Great King.

Economic power more clearly followed from political power than political from economic.

The issue here is of considerable consequence, especially when we come to later forms of monarchy. Most historians speak of a more or less independent aristocracy under Pharaoh, or describe his regime as a "feudal monarchy." Wittfogel insists that "hydraulic society" was fundamentally different from feudal societies in that the state had "total power" and completely dominated society; it was the only center of power, there being no nobility, guild, church, or any other association strong and independent enough to oppose it. He appears to overstate his case, even with Egypt. The ambitions of powerful landlords seem to have been largely responsible for the collapse of the Old Kingdom, and again for the weakening of the Middle Kingdom. Later pharaohs obviously felt insecure in spite of their divinity; they left many "execration texts," ceremonially cursing their enemies. One left a sad warning to his son: the young god should take care to have no intimates, trust no friend or brother.

Yet the enemies of Pharaoh were chiefly within the palace. Wittfogel at least suggests a sound criterion: "A government is absolutist when its rule is not effectively checked by nongovernmental forces. The ruler of an absolutist regime is an autocrat when his decisions are not effectively checked by intragovernmental forces." In the main this description fits the early sacred monarchies. The only apparent checks on the government or the king were sporadic, uncertain, unreasoned, commonly unprincipled. It seems clear that no class or group maintained a strong tradition of independence, or ever secured any constitutional right to oppose Pharaoh. None had inviolable rights to their rank and property; the highest officials were always liable to peremptory dismissal and confiscation of their wealth, if on charges of malfeasance that like as not were true. We hear of no Magna Cartas, no embattled champions of either ancient privileges or the public weal. Neither did men appeal over Pharaoh's head to a higher law, or to the things that were God's. The immense power of religion was typically on his side.

In later monarchies we may look for other centers of power, as potential centers of freedom. Generally they will be found in the nobility, priesthood, or army, and will mean freedom only for a few. For the common people they will generally mean at most a change in masters, perhaps for better, perhaps for worse. Meanwhile there is no question whatever about the political impotence of the masses in Egypt and Mesopotamia.

With them the chief question concerns their well-being, or more specifically the kinds and degrees of freedom they might enjoy short of any bill of political rights. This brings up an inescapable limitation of all histories of the distant past, which is especially serious in a history of freedom. We are inquiring about the peasant in the villages, the man on the street in Ur, Babylon, and Thebes—the now notorious but long obscure "common man," who throughout history has made up the overwhelming majority of mankind. While we know that he was generally poor in the early civilizations, we must still ask: How contented was he with his lot, or how free in his feeling? What did he think and feel? What capacity and opportunity did he have to express himself? How much desire to choose for himself or to be himself? How much awareness of the possibilities open to him or denied to him? We should remember, of course, that the "common man" is an abstraction, likely to obscure the infinite differences in nature and fortune within the masses of men; but even so it is reasonable to ask about the condition of the masses on the average, on the whole. And we can never answer such questions with assurance. We have only slight and conflicting evidence, and except for the few who rose in the world, we hardly ever hear the voice of the ordinary man. We know him chiefly through the records left by his superiors, who typically had a low opinion of him, and no interest whatever in recording his life for its own sake.

Nevertheless, we can make out some significant developments, especially in the realm of legal justice. Although ancient men scarcely believed that freedom and justice are one and inseparable, as many men now believe, there has always been a real connection between them, beginning with the necessity of law for any effective freedom. Law codes, written or unwritten, confer some rights in the very act of specifying obligations and penalties. If most conspicuously they impose constraints, they also protect the individual against uncustomary or arbitrary constraints. And as ideals of justice grew more conscious, they everywhere tended in theory to promote freedom for the many. The early civilizations made positive advances toward such ideals, in particular through the efforts of kings to protect ordinary men against the abuses of power and privilege.

In Egypt the "Coffin Text" even foreshadowed democratic principles of justice. Here a god announced that he had "made every man like his fellow," made the great floodwaters of the Nile for the benefit of the poor man and the great man alike, and given all men equal access to the kingdom of the dead. On earth Egypt never came near this ideal of equality, but at least the next world was thrown open to common men. In Mesopotamia lawgivers persevered in the efforts of King Urukagina of Lagash, despite the apparent indifference of his god. The idea grew that justice was man's right, not merely a royal favor, and that the gods themselves really approved this right. Hammurabi announced in the preamble to his famous law code that the gods had sent "me, Hammurabi, the obedient, god-fearing prince, to make manifest justice in the land, to destroy the wicked and the evildoer, that the strong harm not the weak." In both lands more than one royal text amplified the warning a pharaoh gave his vizier: "It is an abomination of the god to show partiality." In fact, the god was not yet conspicuously partial even to men: women enjoyed most of the legal rights of men, including some they would not in nineteenth-century Europe and America. In Hammurabi's Babylon they could be judges.

How successful the monarchs were in enforcing impartial justice is much more doubtful, as their many admirable decrees themselves suggest. Remote from the common people in their divine majesty, they could not readily check up on the bureaucracy through which they had to rule. Communications were always better from the top down than from the bottom up; and let us add in fairness that another reason for the absence of real public opinion was the lack of technological means for expressing such opinion, over the entire land. Still, the system by its nature made for partiality and favoritism, when not corruption. "I did not take away a man's daughter nor his field," an Egyptian overseer wrote in a testament that Henri Frankfort was pleased to cite; but this testament clearly intimates that other overseers did help themselves to daughters and fields. One may have similar doubts about the cheerful-looking servants and peasants portrayed on the tombs of the wealthy; the wealthy might need a good case to present to the judge in the underworld, for the records make plain that they were given to oppressing the poor. It is as plain that beatings were a routine official way of dealing with peasants behind in their payments.

At best the royal law codes embodied no idea of equal rights. Rather they explicitly legalized class favoritism, as in Hammurabi's code penalties or damages were carefully adjusted to rank—patrician, plebeian, slave. Plato and Aristotle would later state the logic of his code by arguing that justice consists not in giving equal rights to men naturally unequal, but in giving every man his due. The due of the common man included no inviolable right to life, liberty, or the pursuit of happiness. What freedom he enjoyed was a negotiable asset: he could be sold into slavery to repay his debts. He had a harder time repaying them by free labor because the law fixed wages—maximum, not minimum wages—and was more partial to creditors than to debtors. What he thought and felt about all this remains a matter of conjecture; but the very necessity of conjecture is significant—his thoughts and feelings were beneath record. Oriental monarchies are proverbial for the splendor of their court and the poverty of their masses. There is never any question of the splendor, and it always had to be paid for, out of the sweat and toil, if not the tears and blood of the masses.

At any rate, we must not allow this question of their feelings to confuse the issue of freedom. Granted that the rule of the sacred monarchs was not simply brutal, and may often have been benevolent, it was still despotism. We have reason to believe that at its best it gave the masses of common men ample bread and beer, gave them psychological security, gave them the spiritual comforts of "miracle, mystery, and authority"; but we know that it never gave them political freedom. The degree of personal freedom that neolithic men had enjoyed in the home and the village was further qualified. Many were serfs, all were liable to periodic conscription, all were subject to an absolute power that they could never openly resist or hope to change. The good laws that might protect them from the strong were always proclaimed by the sacred monarch—by "me, Hammurabi." If the laws failed to protect them, they could not demand new laws.

We must accordingly qualify the statement that the sacred monarchy represented government by consent of the governed. The consent was not a reasoned consent, a free choice among known alternatives. It is "revealing," wrote Frankfort, that "during Egypt's long history no attempts to overthrow the existing order were made," but the question remains: What does this reveal? Frankfort saw in it the basic contentment of the Egyptians, a reasonable pride in the achieved stability of an order they believed was divinely maintained. To others it reveals more plainly the ignorance and inertia of the Egyptians, the blind acceptance of an order something less than divine. The ruling principle of obedience in the ancient East could breed the virtues of loyalty and fortitude, the wisdom of patience and resignation, the exaltation of self-surrender; yet it always looks slavish because it was unreasoned obedience, to an arbitrary authority. Ultimately it reveals the basic irrationality of the whole system. The "thrilling" Egyptian ideal remarked by Frankfort—the ideal of a perfect harmony between man and the divine, symbolized in the person of Pharaoh, incorporated in an immutable society that he and he alone maintained—might thrill us more were it not for one objection. What the Egyptians believed was preposterous.

For such reasons whatever freedom of thought and speech was permitted in the sacred monarchies made little difference. Apparently there was little official censorship or thought control. Some men speculated freely, even daringly, about the gods; in Egypt some skeptics were bold enough to doubt even the life to come. ("Behold, no one who goes over there can come back again!"—so "make holiday" and "let thy desire flourish.") Men could also voice their complaints about corrupt or oppressive bureaucrats. If they could not openly denounce the sacred monarch himself, they could at least appeal to him and covertly criticize him. Apart from the many grave robbers who took to desecrating the royal tombs, the recorded behavior of the subjects of the god-king often suggests that he was in practice regarded as a fallible mortal, not a divinity. Yet there was no need of laws prohibiting fundamental criticism of the monarchy, because there was little if any such subversive thought on principle: as a divinely ordained institution, it was immune to searching inquiry or criticism. There were no treatises whatever on political theory or public affairs. The rare adventurers in thought proclaimed no conscious ideal of adventure, of free inquiry, or of free criticism.

By its nature "hydraulic society" was a closed society. The degree of social mobility it permitted did not prove dynamic. Commoners who rose in the service of Pharaoh rose by his favor, which was most surely won by servility; he was unlikely to honor vigorous independence of spirit. Hence whatever new blood got into the system failed to change it, or to stir fresh initiative. The sacred monarchy could never realize its ideal of a static, immutable order, but it could and did effectively resist change in its basic structure so long as it was able to resist external powers. Its natural fate was stagnation.

3. The Effects on Creativity

Since to us there is a depressing monotony in the outcome of the early adventures in civilization, and the later adventures in imperialism, we might in justice begin by stressing again the creative achievements of the sacred monarchies—all that they passed on to other peoples, and finally to us. What came to look like stagnation might first be called stability. For all the turmoil in Sumer, its people maintained their way of life for a thousand years. The Egyptians, once more, maintained theirs much longer. The tenacity with which they clung to the basic forms of their culture, through the periodic breakdowns of their government, may be viewed as a tribute to the creativity of their founding fathers.

The most conspicuous remains of the Old Kingdom, the pyramids, have given some lovers of the Greeks the impression that the Egyptians were always morbidly obsessed with the life after death; but actually the early Egyptians were not at all morbid. As one might suspect from their material achievements, they were a practical, bustling people, devoted to all the goods of this life—goods they believed they could take with them into the next life. If they had a mystical attitude toward nature (or "Thou"), it did not deter them from aggressively exploiting its physical resources. Medical texts that came down from them have a matter-of-fact spirit verging on the scientific. In this spirit they achieved their amazing technological feats, which the Greeks would never match, nor even the Romans surpass. The Great Pyramid —the only one of the Seven Wonders of the ancient world to survive— was a marvel too in the expertness of its builders, the 2½-ton blocks of stone being dressed and fitted with a joint of only one-fiftieth of an inch, and laid out in sides over 750 feet long with an error of only a few inches. And in keeping with its survival, the great bulk of what we owe to Egypt was the work of the Old Kingdom.

We know it best by its art. If all that pertained to Pharaoh soon became conventional, initially art was animated by a humanistic as well as a daring experimental spirit. The sculptured figures of the early pharaohs are almost lifelike, not yet pretentious or forbidding in their majesty. Naturalism is more pronounced in secular sculpture (for example, the well-known statues of the Scribe and the "Village Mayor"), and especially in the scenes of everyday life depicted in tomb art. These reveal an unmistakable love of nature and of life, with a playful, exuberant fancy that makes as unmistakable the freedom and spontaneity of art in the Old Kingdom. Its craftsmen likewise developed the exquisite minor arts of Egypt—in textiles, ceramics, metals, wood, and semiprecious stones—by which mundane life was made ever more elegant and refined. To what extent common men shared in all this gaiety and civility we cannot know; but the upper classes seem to have enjoyed to the full a gracious, genial, urbane way of life, in one of the golden ages of culture.

In speculating on what inspired the remarkable creativity of the early Egyptians we must give some heed to their own answer—the gods. At least their gods gave them "immortal longings," if of a rather low order; we would not have the pyramids and all the tomb art were it not for their primitive conception of the afterlife, which required that the body of the dead be preserved from destruction and all its future needs be amply provided for. But we cannot really credit the gods with this brilliant achievement, least of all as we respect the religious spirit. Men had been worshiping much the same sort of gods long before the Old Kingdom, to no such effect, and now had received from them no new tables. The devout may wish to believe that the One True God blessed the early Egyptians with a measure of illumination and grace, but if so they caught only the faintest glimpse of his spiritual interests. From first to last the religion of Egypt was grossly materialistic. It remained a quest not of God but of the miraculous, by which men might get their own way in this life and the next, and the quest produced an ever-increasing mass of incoherent belief and inconsistent practice as new gods were added but all the old ones kept on; the pantheon came to include at least two thousand illiterate deities, mostly in subhuman, animal form. No more was Sumerian civilization due to loftier religious aspiration, or any clear measure of divine grace. Its gods were still sharply limited in power, knowledge, and virtue, and in their service of these gods the Sumerians had purely mundane motives, since they had no immortal souls to save. Their temples appropriately served as banks, charging high rates of interest.

The early kings, however, do deserve much of the credit for the cultural achievement. They were themselves creative as architects of peace and order, builders of the administrative system that provided the necessary wealth, leisure, and security. The greater kings might very well have been a positive inspiration, a lift to the whole community. And whether or not they inspired genius, they at least had the wit to discover and employ it. As one early pharaoh set the extraordinary Khufu-onekh to work on a pyramid, so another had as vizier Imhotep, the first known physician. In carrying out their public works, moreover, the kings built up even more durable knowledge. Pharaoh's officials worked out the ancestor of our solar calendar of 365 days by carefully recording every year the height of the Nile flood, getting the average over a century. The palace school was a major center for the acquisition and transmission of such learning, especially in astronomy and mathematics, which would eventually reach the Greeks, and through them us.

The kings themselves might obscure the credit due them as patrons, in that civilization by its nature requires and provides for much more individualism than is likely to appear in royal annals. Egyptian tradition makes it plain that Pharaoh's architects were proud of their work, as their masters were of them; we know a number of them by name. The tomb art of the nobles strengthens the impression that the creativity of the early kingdom owed to a considerable degree of individualism and personal freedom, in a state not yet highly centralized or weighed down by bureaucratic tradition. In the cities of Sumer the signs of an independent spirit are as clear. A poem concerning the great hero Gilgamesh, for example, records that about 3000 B.C. a popular assembly in Erech voted to fight for independence against the overbearing king of Kish; and the tradition of freedom was still alive six centuries later, in the time of King Urukagina.

In Egypt an independent spirit became more noticeable following the collapse of the Old Kingdom, about 2200 B.C. The shock of this failure, and of the century or so of anarchy that followed, jolted the Egyptians out of their complacent optimism. While some became skeptics and took to a frank hedonism, others groped toward loftier ethical values, ideals of social justice that anticipated the prophets of Israel by a thousand years. There were glimmerings of a potential cornerstone of freedom, the idea of the sanctity of the individual. The afterlife was made more moral as well as more democratic; the dead now had to face a last judgment, earn their paradise by good conduct. One commoner, the prophet Ipu-wer, even dared to treat Pharaoh as a fallible human being, and openly to criticize him.

Yet he is the only such heretic on record in the whole history of Egypt. The Middle Kingdom that restored order settled down into the old pattern of the sacred monarchy; it became more rigid as Pharaoh grew stronger and ruled through a growing bureaucracy. He now relied more on human than divine power, in particular on military power. Senusret III, of the dynasty that founded the Middle Kingdom, heralded the new royal style: "I have set up my statue on the frontier, not that ye should worship it but that ye should fight for it. I am the King, and what I say I do." Little came of the new thought, in any branch of culture. A people who had displayed great native ability failed to profit from adversity, or to meet the challenge to their basic institutions. They failed again when the Middle Kingdom collapsed in turn, about 1800 B.C., and the land was overrun by the rude Hyksos. The outraged Egyptians finally summoned the energy to throw out the invaders, a couple of centuries later, but about all they learned from their humiliation was that they were no longer securely isolated, in a world growing more cosmopolitan; the pharaohs of the New Kingdom took to imperial adventure, in the course of which they grew more arrogant and oppressive. Exposure to cosmopolitan influences stimulated no lasting major innovations in thought or culture. In the less secure land of Mesopotamia, meanwhile, new peoples had replaced the Sumerians, building kingdoms that we shall glance at later; but they retained the basic forms of Sumerian civilization, including the sacred monarchy, and created relatively little of enduring importance.

The significant fact remains that almost all the great achievement of both Egypt and Mesopotamia came in the early centuries of their history, long before the end of the third millennium B.C. Thereafter, through the second millennium and well into the first, their peoples contributed much less to the life of the spirit or to the powers of man. And as we may give the sacred monarchy much of the credit for the early achievement, so we must hold it largely responsible for the blight that settled on creativity. The art, the thought, and the learning of both lands were devoted primarily to the service of the gods and god-kings. The wise men and the holy men all worked to sanctify the status quo, inculcate the supreme necessity of "miracle, mystery, and authority." The story is more significant because this was to be the typical career of the Oriental sacred monarchy down through the Ottoman Empire: an early period of cultural achievement, more or less brilliant but usually brief, followed by a long period of stagnation or decline, during which luster was largely confined to the ceremonies and trappings of the royal court.

Such religious advances as were made in Egypt and Mesopotamia were still not clearly made under divine auspices. The idea of a supreme god, corresponding to the Great King, was strengthened by imperialism as the tribal god of conquerors replaced the gods of the conquered and took on a universal aspect in ruling over mixed peoples. The imperial Amon of Egypt, grafted on the old sun-god Re, was never able to get clear of the labyrinthine confusion of Egyptian deities, or in particular to supersede the immensely popular Osiris of the underworld (Egyptians were willing to put up with some glaring contradictions for the sake of a double guarantee of immortality); but

Marduk of Babylon superseded the Sumerian pantheon. Loftier stand-ards of social justice also led to a more ethical religion, as men sought to hold the gods to these standards, and in Egypt they were connected with the doctrine of the Last Judgment, later to be taken over by Christianity. Otherwise these lands passed on to the higher religions chiefly a prehistoric heritage, including the Mother Goddess and the dying god, together with a mass of popular myth and ritual.[6] Neither land itself developed a higher religion or any conscious ideal of spirit-ual freedom. Egypt in particular developed instead a flagrant corrup-tion; here the masses were more consciously exploited by the priesthood than by the monarchs, just as they had been in the Sumer of King Urukagina. The sacred monarchy naturally tended to dis-courage the growth of spirituality, as of intellectual freedom, for it identified the cause of religion with the cause of the state, keeping it a worldly success religion. The god-king or heaven-sent king was un-likely to be a spiritual type himself or to inspire truly religious adora-tion.

The most striking exception to this rule, Ikhnaton of Egypt, finally proves the rule. He was indeed striking as an iconoclast, a revolutionary figure in the history of religious thought. He not only set up his sun-god Aton as a universal god but tried to destroy the old gods, hacking the name of Amon out of inscriptions. Although scholars are still debating the purity of his monotheism and its possible influence on Judaism, he at least transcended the traditional religiosity and had a genuinely spiritual vision. Whereas Amon, "the hidden One," could be approached only by priests, the new temples of Aton were open to the sky, free from secret rites, and the famous hymn to Aton was as free from the crude anthropomorphism of the old solar myths and their dragon monsters. Yet Ikhnaton himself was still Pharaoh—a god whom his subjects had to worship. Characteristically he tried to impose his new religion by imperial force; he initiated the unfortunate para-dox that monotheism, commonly regarded as the highest type of religion, was to inspire much more persecution than any other. He had as little notion of the brotherhood of man as of religious freedom, showing no concern over the lot of his subjects, which contemporary records indicate was especially hard in his time (c. 1350 B.C.). In any

---

[6] The influence of Babylonian—or ultimately Sumerian—mythology on the Old Testa-ment is now well known. Less well known are such legends as that recorded by Ham-murabi, telling how as an infant he was found floating in a basket in a drainage ditch, and adopted by a gardener. Moses was one of a number of semi-divine heroes to follow his example in getting started in life.

case his "Amarna revolution" was an utter failure. As his successor took the name of Tutankhamon to emphasize his devotion to the old god, the temples to Aton were all razed, the name of Ikhnaton was in turn obliterated everywhere. The violent revulsion against his sacrilege strengthened the hold of the old-time religion, and the power of the priesthood. The priesthood devised some new forms of magic (for example, selling passports to the hereafter that got around the moral requirements for admission by issuing verdicts of acquittal in advance), but out of its ranks never came an apostle of popular enlightenment or of either social or religious reform. Prophets were as unheard of in Mesopotamia.

A new style of art that came in with Ikhnaton's attempted revolution, veering toward realism, had a more lasting influence, but failed to inspire a really new start. More apparent was an increasing ostentation, as art became more blatantly a mode of royal propaganda and pharaohs strained for the colossal in statue and temple. Most conspicuous was the essential sameness in the art forms of Egypt throughout its history, the despotism of its formal conventions, symbolized by the rigid, frontal, staring attitude of its sculptured pharaohs. A similar despotism in Mesopotamia accentuated a natural consequence of the sacred monarchy. Art could continue to flourish after a fashion under this monarchy, which always had need of it for purposes of splendor, but the fashion was set and severely limited by these purposes. There was little idea of art primarily for beauty's sake, still less for the community's sake or the artist's sake. It had to obey the canons fixed by its patrons: proud monarchs, who had to be represented much bigger and better than life, and a naturally conservative priesthood, bent on maintaining the ancient forms of religiosity. In Egypt the conventions seem more artificial and monotonous because scenes of common people and everyday life could still be represented in a naturalistic, even playful style. In Mesopotamia the relatively large, independent merchant class and the bustling city life might lead one to expect an art freer, more realistic and animated in style, if also more bourgeois or plebeian; but in fact it became even more rigidly bound by convention than Egyptian art.

We may therefore wonder about the personality of all these anonymous artists, who had so little chance to express it. We cannot assume that they were necessarily irked by the canons they had to obey. Especially in Egypt, they illustrate the possible advantages of a fixed tradition: working in a ready-made style, they concentrated on execution, and while turning out much mediocre work, maintained a high average level of competence. They indicate that freedom is not absolutely essential to art, as also that art does not necessarily promote the cause of freedom. Yet many must have had more potential individuality than they revealed, greater gifts than they could realize; and some may have suffered consciously. They also indicate that a measure of freedom is essential to a vital art. They did their finest work in the minor arts and crafts, which were not so tightly bound by convention; some could work for the bazaar or free market. In the major arts their masterpieces stem chiefly from the early period, when there was most freedom and spontaneity, and from such periods as Ikhnaton's, when some innovation broke in.

So they recall a writer of the Middle Kingdom who complained that he could say nothing new—"not an utterance that hath not grown stale, what the ancestors have already said." Architects could at least go on creating monumental forms in imperishable stone, workers in the minor arts could achieve triumphs in technique. Writers, expressing thought more directly, suffered more from the limitations of the prevailing mentality.

While nothing that has come down from the writings of the Sumerians is a masterpiece, their literature was at least a promising beginning. Varied, wide-ranging, and sometimes lively, it had flashes of humor, even satire—potential modes of emancipation. Not much came of the promise, however. The peoples who succeeded the Sumerians honored them by making their language the first "classical" language, no longer spoken, used only for high learned, literary, and religious purposes; and dead languages are poor mediums for a living literature. For well over a thousand years the scribes went on copying Sumerian texts. They polished and amplified them, giving a more finished form to such works as the Epic of Gilgamesh, but they did not go on to create a distinctive literature of their own. The failure of Egypt to produce a distinguished literature, or any epical work, may seem more surprising; for even while the writer of the Middle Kingdom was complaining how hard it was to say anything new, no poet had yet celebrated the glorious achievements of the Old Kingdom, yet written the epic of Menes. Still, this is not really surprising. Invincible Pharaoh, doing everything singlehanded, would not lend himself to dramatic epic. He would also tend to discourage realism, humor, and satire; there is little trace of humor in Egyptian literature, though the earthy, pleasure-loving men of the Old Kingdom must have been addicted to it. Religious exaltation was as foreign to the spirit of Pharaoh in the later kingdoms; the famous Pyramid texts are little more than magical incantations. Hence the glory of Egyptian literature, the Hymn to Aton, came when the heretic Ikhnaton momentarily succeeded in breaking through the fixed forms of thought. Thereafter writers returned to the utterances of the ancestors, without complaint. Some others must have been conscious of the staleness, unhappy about it; but the incubus of the sacred monarchy is most apparent in the many more who seemed content to go on repeating.

The scribes suggest other considerations of wider, deeper import. For the professional historian one in particular is disagreeable—the historical influence of formal education. The establishment of a system of education usually follows the great creative period of a society, and usually works to discourage further creativity. Teachers are seldom innovators, schools as seldom nurseries of new thought or freedom; "academic" is generally the right word for them. Sumerian schools, designed primarily to train scribes for the economic and administrative purposes of temple and palace, included some literary training, but it consisted in copying, memorizing, and imitating the classical texts. With this tradition of learning by rote they established other traditions that would endure to modern times, notably the poorly paid teacher. Although Mesopotamian scribes were well prepared for some of the tasks that awaited them, such as the appalling monotony of copying royal inscriptions over and over again, they were scarcely trained for creative thinking. Egyptian schools also supplemented their basic curriculum with some training aimed at the formation of both mind and character, an ideal of wisdom that was essentially worldly and foreshadowed the Greek ideal of the whole man; only it too was a conservative, ultraconventional training, which bred a complacent sort of smartness.

This was not very smart for the worldly purposes of the pharaohs. Copying texts that they were proud to claim as the work of the Old Kingdom, the scribes built up myths of a grossly exaggerated antiquity, a false past; but they added very little to empirical knowledge and skill. The genius of the Egyptians, and its limitations, may be epitomized by their early discovery of how to determine the volume of a truncated pyramid—"the masterpiece of Egyptian geometry," according to George Sarton. In two thousand more years of building and calculating they found out nothing better.[7] Similarly about the only important technological discovery they made after the Old Kingdom was glassmaking; they kept using essentially the same tools, without improvements. Perhaps the most ingenious among them were the tomb robbers, who managed to locate and plunder about 99 per cent of the carefully concealed burial chambers of the divine pharaohs and their relatives. Otherwise the technological rut helped to confirm the illusion of the Egyptians that their society was immutable, and to ensure their inability to get out of their social and political rut.

The embryonic scientific spirit that made possible the technological feats of early civilization had no real chance in the thickening atmosphere of miracle and mystery. Learned men serving the palace and the temple continued to have very practical, materialistic motives as they sought to predict and control the course of nature, displaying a tireless industry in the collection and systematization of their data; but they continued to seek control by magical means, and their most elaborate science was divination. They became the more devoted to magic, however, because they were a privileged class, largely exempt from the vulgar doings and makings that might have sharpened their empirical sense. The oldest known work of philosophy, the *Instructions of Ptah-hotep* dating from the Old Kingdom, gave this advice to youth: "Be not proud because thou art learned; but discourse with the ignorant man as with the sage. For no limit can be set to skill, neither is there any craftsman that possesseth full advantages." The later scribes taught a different kind of wisdom. They boasted of the exalted status that came with literacy, advising the youth to "put writing in thy heart, so that thou mayest protect thine own person from any labor and be a respected official"; they looked down on artists and craftsmen as well as peasants. In more commercial Mesopotamia, where literacy was more widespread and more devoted to the purposes of business, it was still a sign of privilege, and the highest privilege was in the service of the gods or their appointed monarch. In both lands scholars were set apart by their mastery of a "higher learning," of an honorific or esoteric kind. They established the aristocratic tradition that through

---

[7] Sumerian genius made a more influential contribution that had a more anomalous fate. The Sumerians discovered the virtues of the number 12 for calculation, in its divisibility, and made it the basis of their weights and measures instead of the obvious 10, derived from the number of fingers. Their system spread all over the world. But with the discovery of decimals 10 became a better basis and outmoded the work of the bright Sumerians. Among the antiquated relics of their system is our dozen and the twelve English pence to the shilling.

the centuries to our own time not only distinguished but divorced high learning and culture from useful knowledge and practical activity.

On all counts they call for some reconsideration of fashionable ideas about the role of an elite, as custodians of culture. Democratic culture, it is often said, suffers from the want of a privileged elite. The custodians in the ancient East indicate how culture may suffer as much from privilege, in particular how the pursuit of truth may suffer, and why the best criterion of intellectual progress may be the extent to which knowledge is diffused in a society. Another reason for the stagnation of early civilization, at any rate, was that the masses could contribute little or nothing but their manual labor. Illiterate, trained only to obey or follow orders, they could scarcely make the discoveries and inventions that learned men were professionally incapacitated to make. Commoners who did rise in the social scale, like the self-conscious scribes of Egypt, were apt to be the least imaginative or curious as they aped the intellectual and literary manners of their betters.

Those who cherish the humanistic ideal of self-realization may now reconsider as well the unparalleled "success" of Egypt. By the criterion of sheer endurance, or the stability prized by many political philosophers, its history is truly remarkable. By the criterion of cultural achievement its success is more doubtful; John Wilson, a sympathetic historian, concludes that in view of its size, wealth, and longevity it made relatively slight intellectual and spiritual contributions. By simple human standards, in terms of the worldly well-being sought by the Egyptians themselves, its success is still more doubtful. There is no question of the sorry failure of its ideal during the long centuries of decline to the humiliating end. The Egyptians submitted to a distinctly harsher rule by Pharaoh, to a notoriously corrupt bureaucracy, and to a still more corrupt, immensely rich priesthood, presiding over temples that came to own one out of every five subjects of Pharaoh, and owned the souls of the rest through their possession of the ritual magic necessary for admission to the next world. The Egyptians lost the gaiety, the confidence, and the independent spirit of their forefathers, in the briefer period of the Old Kingdom. They lost sight of the ideals of social justice they had glimpsed during the Middle Kingdom. They became slavishly resigned, devoted to an ideal of "silence." Their only hope was the next world.

The end of their nominal freedom came with conquest by Assyrians, Chaldeans, and Persians, but the failure of their ideal was apparent even in the imperial grandeur of the New Kingdom. I repeat the conclusion of a previous study: "The divine pharaohs now acted like mere supermen, vain and vulgar. They plastered Egypt with inscriptions boasting of their prowess, pictures showing them defeating whole armies singlehanded, while rows of little Egyptians cleaned up the little enemies. By this time the little Egyptians symbolize an utter absurdity: that men should consent to live and die to feed so colossal a conceit. . . . It is fitting that the most enduring works of Egypt remain the pyramids. They are monuments to the majesty of her ideal, and to its basic absurdity; to the promise of her beginnings, and to its curse. They failed even in their primary purpose as sacred houses for the dead, for they were always desecrated by robbers. They served chiefly to inspire the Egyptian masses to endure—blindly, without question, without need." Or with absolute need, I might now add; for the Egyptians were utterly dependent upon a politico-religious order that had deprived them of the capacity, opportunity, and incentive for the realization of any other potentialities.

Chapter Three	*THE SPREAD OF*
	CIVILIZATION

1. The Ways and Means of Diffusion

Ideally, wrote Whitehead, civilization means intercourse by persuasion instead of by force. Its actual historic meaning has been more complex. The early civilizations employed force much more extensively and systematically than had the neolithic barbarians; the villager naturally tended to be a settled, peaceful type, as most primitive food growers still are. With organized warfare civilization promoted the growth of slavery—the major threats thereafter to the freedom of whole peoples. It also promoted intercourse by persuasion, but for unidealistic reasons: the chief means to such intercourse was commerce. The expansion of civilization, with its mixed blessings, was due to both methods; and both had unintended results.

The immediate stimulus was the need of raw materials. The Egyptians recorded how they "smote the wretched nomads" in and about Sinai, where they got the bulk of their copper, and smote other peoples in regions producing gold. Otherwise they did not engage in large-scale war and conquest until late in their history, since they were largely self-sufficient. In needier Sumer empire came much earlier, under Sargon; he boasted of conquering lands rich in metal and timber. Such imperialism led to the establishment of new cities and outposts that radiated the influence of civilization, inspiring barbarians to imitate it—and before long to assail and plunder in turn. The "Hun" entered history early. Meanwhile undramatic commerce was having considerably wider and deeper influence. It fostered an enterprising spirit, rational calculation and resourcefulness, literacy and knowledge—potentially more freedom of mind. Similarly it stimulated barbarians, who were persuaded to produce the needed raw materials in return for manufactured goods, and with these picked up some cultural goods, new ideas, arts, and skills. Excavations reveal the rising level of culture along the trade routes, in ever-widening waves. Only these influences were not simply peaceful either. The goods most desired by the barbarians were metal weapons and personal ornaments, which went mostly to the chieftains and medicine men, and tended to make them more militant and covetous. We cannot know how the leaders persuaded or coerced their followers into producing a surplus for trade; but the rise to civilization again meant the rise to power and privilege of the few, at some expense to the many.

The waves of diffusion from the Near East are indicated roughly by the later appearance of agriculture, pottery, metallurgy, and writing in other regions of the world. Eastward, the impulses that helped to stimulate the growth of the Indus Valley civilization eventually reached China. Here rose the Shang kingdom, with its capital at Anyang, at a date variously estimated from 1800 to 1400 B.C. The Chinese (who are inclined to prefer the earlier date) like to think that their culture is wholly indigenous, but it seems fairly certain that their ancestors indirectly owed much to Near Eastern peoples they had never heard of. Later we shall consider the distinctive civilization of their own that they developed, in particular under the influence of Confucius. Our present concern is the westward course of civilization, about which we know a great deal more.

Thus in Syria we can follow every stage of the growth of Byblos from a fishing and farming village to a civilized city. It was the main port for the export of the cedars of Lebanon to Egypt, which was content to leave it independent; in exchange its people were as content to adopt much Egyptian culture. Mesopotamian influences also pervaded Syria, but were still more marked in Asia Minor to the north. In this land of mineral wealth colonies of Assyrian merchants were settled by 2000 B.C.; their business records tell of regular caravans crossing the Taurus Mountains. Anonymous, still illiterate peoples had come up in the world some centuries earlier, in such widely separated localities as Alaja in central Anatolia (later the heart of the Hittite Empire) and Troy II on the Dardanelles (the second city from the bottom in the mound containing the famous nine Troys). By trade, no doubt supplemented by plunder, they accumulated enough wealth to enable their chieftains to live like kings in palaces, and to be served by skilled goldsmiths; their palaces and tombs have yielded exquisite works of art. Schliemann, the discoverer of Troy, was so dazzled by the golden hoard he found in Troy II that he thought it was King Priam's treasure, and the citadel-town was at least civilized enough to anticipate the fate of Homer's Troy, being destroyed by a great conflagration some thousand years before it.

The processes of diffusion are clearest in Europe, where a great many prehistoric settlements have been excavated. Neolithic peoples came in and gradually moved on, along such routes as the Danube Valley; later they were followed by metalworking peoples from Asia Minor, come to exploit the mineral resources of the Balkans. We may postpone consideration of their activities until we take up the story of Western civilization, for at this time they had little if any reciprocal influence on the heartland of civilization, the main stage of history. The point to emphasize now is that, except for Minoan Crete, Europe was always behind the metropolitan Near East, and the farther from it the farther behind. For a long time, the wave of diffusion was a series of successively lower levels of culture, extending from commercial towns on Aegean islands to neolithic villages in the far north, where forest peoples were just beginning to take to agriculture.

The dates for mainland European prehistory are still tentative and approximate. In their pride some European scholars have maintained that their ancestors achieved a Bronze Age culture before 2500 B.C.; more cautious scholars set the date up to a thousand years later. No estimate is really flattering to the early Europeans. If they were working metals by 2500 B.C., they made slow progress in the next millennium or so, whereas if they started much later they made a more respectable showing, but were still pretty slow to get started. The "Nordic people" that some German scholars manufactured out of the mixed neolithic peoples and cultures in the north were among the most backward. (Scandinavian scholars have generally not endorsed the Nordic myth.) Outside of Greece, in short, Europe was scarcely a cradle of freedom. Certainly its mixed, scattered peoples had no common consciousness, or sense of high mission. Its chief magic was not its blood but its mineral riches, in particular its amber from the Baltic region, prized for magical purposes. The "Amber Route" through Europe is marked by hoards of metal weapons and ornaments, apparently intended for the barbarian market.

The European peoples did have a potential advantage, however, in their remoteness from the Oriental sacred monarchies and their lack of a common culture. The many scattered peoples, with their different tastes and traditions, might stimulate the ingenuity of merchants and metalworkers. The latter in fact began designing distinctive types of tools, weapons, and ornaments; Europe at least gave birth to the safety pin. And on the island of Crete a people did take advantage of the opportunities provided by a new world. Here the Minoans built a civilization that might be called European, not Asiatic.

2. *The Minoan Civilization*

The earliest known inhabitants of Crete were neolithic peoples, presumably come from Asia. In the third millennium B.C. newcomers who brought metal, during waves of migration that populated the whole Aegean world, were evidently Asiatics too, certainly not Aryans or Hellenes. They seem to have come directly by sea, since they left no clear trail in southern Europe. Those who settled on the southernmost island of Crete had to be seafarers of boldness and skill, and as such they soon began to grow civilized through commerce; they were carrying on an active trade with Egypt as early as the Old Kingdom. They took advantage of the vine, the olive, and the fig, for the cultivation of which the Mediterranean region is especially well suited, and which readily yielded a surplus for trade. They also built up a bronze industry, profiting from their central location; the tin needed for bronze seems to have come largely from central and western Europe, as little was available in the Near East. By the beginning of the second millennium palaces had risen in Crete, at such cities as Knossos and Phaestos, under the rule of chieftains who were to become known by the generic name of King Minos. The growth was presently ended by disaster, through invasion or civil war that everywhere laid low the palaces; but by 1700 Minoan civilization was on the rise again, to maintain a maritime empire for several centuries, reach the height of its brilliance, and deeply impress mainland peoples.

It naturally owed a good deal to Egypt and Asia. The principal deity of the Minoans, the Mother Goddess, was attended by the lions and the symbolic double ax that figure so prominently in Hittite art, and go back to the Sumerians. Their earliest written script, which scholars have only recently begun to decipher, appears chiefly on clay tablets, as in Sumer, and their language may have had affinities with Akkadian, the language of Sargon. Excavations in Syria have indicated that not only their metallurgy but their palace architecture derived from the mainland. Yet such debts only accentuate the striking differences between Minoan civilization and all earlier or contemporaneous civilizations. It was distinguished by a free, humanistic spirit the more remarkable in view of its antecedents. Somehow the Minoans escaped from the prevailing bondage to "miracle, mystery, and authority."

Thus their art was not dominated by religious or royal themes. They built no great temples or tombs, no colossal statues of gods or kings— none of the Oriental monumental forms that are so impressive, and finally oppressive. Their only great building was the palace, and this was not designed primarily to awe. The main one at Knossos was more like a big household than an imperial palace: a complex of storerooms, workrooms, and living rooms, including royal apartments and a Throne Room, but not isolating the royal family. It was airy, bright, commodious, exuberant with color, opened to sky and countryside by wide terraces. Minoan architects were concerned chiefly with livableness, not size or splendor. They took pains with ventilation, sanitation, and especially drainage; their drains were a marvel of technical skill and ingenuity, unequaled in antiquity or in the early centuries of Europe. King Minos enjoyed more comfort and ease than Louis XIV ever knew at Versailles.

The frescoes in the royal palace more directly manifest the humanistic quality of Minoan art. Instead of depicting the awful majesty of gods and god-kings, or commemorating royal triumphs, they depict the life of nature and civil society, freshly observed and joyously felt. They include scenes of handsome, slim-waisted youths and maidens engaged in bull-leaping, groups of bare-breasted "Parisiennes" holding animated conversation. Similarly Minoan sculptors never strained for grandeur but confined themselves to small figures, making lovely statuettes in ivory and faïence; their subjects range from goddesses to naked little boys. Ornamental art displays the same fresh, lively fancy, pottery in particular having a variety and grace lacking in the Orient, where it had become a routine industry. Minoan artists were limited, to be sure, by their preference for the dainty, and they failed to outgrow some crude conventions, such as a full-face eye on a face in profile; but they were never so bound by convention as were Oriental artists, and they seem to have known much more joy in creating.

How the Minoans managed to win their freedom of spirit may be better understood when their language is better known (though the clay tablets they left will no doubt turn out to be chiefly business records, as in Sumer). Meanwhile we at least have some clues to the conditions of their freedom. They got their start in independent towns or city-states, as did people all over the Aegean world; from first to last their civilization was more distinctly urban than the Egyptian, and more largely based on commerce and industry than the Mesopotamian. They were the first people to trade extensively by sea and to realize the advantages of seapower, which was to be so important in the rise of Greek and later of European civilization; it gave them at once independence and the stimulus of constant intercourse with other peoples. Living by their wits, they apparently held craftsmen in much higher esteem than did Pharaoh's bureaucracy, and encouraged them to be inventive. (It was in Crete that Greek legend placed Daedalus, the master craftsman.) A large, prosperous middle class played something like the role it would in European history. The handsome vases and house furnishings of ordinary merchants, in small provincial towns, testify that wealth and culture were widely diffused, while innumerable personal seals suggest considerable individualism.

One reason why religion never dominated Minoan culture as it did the Sumerian and Egyptian was perhaps that the Minoans were less dependent on agriculture. No temples are found anywhere in the early Aegean world. Although figurines reveal that the Mother Goddess was there from the outset, she was probably not much interested in trade. That she became the patron deity of Crete may well have been due not only to the power of age-old tradition but to more gracious ways she learned under genial Mediterranean skies. If her lions were reminders of her fearsome possibilities, the many charming representations of her, the gaiety of her worshipers, and their evident love of nature intimate that she was primarily a queen of love and fruitfulness. She encouraged her worshipers to play and to inaugurate festival games—to become, indeed, the first known people to make play an art and a national pastime. Homer would describe a ballet on the "dancing floor" that Daedalus had made for fair Ariadne in Knossos: the floor of the court theaters found in Minoan cities, and found nowhere else in the ancient world before them. The Mother Goddess also helps to explain why Minoan women enjoyed much more freedom than women would in classical Greece. They took an important part in religious ceremonies, flaunted their charms at public festivals, and engaged in sports together with men. King Minos had no Oriental harem.

Although the Cretan Zeus of Greek legend was a dying god, the male partner—if any—of the Mother Goddess in Crete was not prominent. The male principle, however, was by no means ignored, and it was distinctly less gracious. King Minos himself was a priest-king, representing the Bull. He was the Minotaur incarnate—an image found everywhere on the palace walls. As such he had a dread aspect, the memory of which was preserved in Greek legend: he demanded victims, and got some of them by raiding Greece. In delivering Athens from the ravages of the Minotaur, the legendary Theseus most likely reflected historic fact, in that the sea empire of the Minoans must have meant more or less tyranny to the subject peoples. Probably it meant some oppression to the Minoans themselves. Toward the end of their history King Minos of Knossos seems to have won control of the island by subduing the princes of other cities; the loss of independence no doubt rankled. The many tablets found in the storerooms and workshops of his palace imply an imperial bureaucracy, which likewise may have been resented by merchants in other cities.

But at least King Minos assured law and order, and for some time so splendid a security that the later cities built no defensive walls. Greek legend credited him with ridding the Aegean of piracy, which would later become a curse again. It made him a symbol of justice too; upon his death he would still carry on in Hades as a judge of the dead. And though the nature of his administration is uncertain, the evidence strongly suggests that it was not despotic. Crete was dotted with bustling towns—according to Homer a hundred of them, swarming with multitudes—in which little business men continued to thrive and to adorn their homes with lovely works of art. It seems clear that the Minoans generally enjoyed more personal liberty than any other civilized people since the early days of Sumer.

With the peasants it may well have been different. As usual, we know little about their condition except that there must have been a multitude of them too. They contributed to the thriving commerce by producing wine and olive oil for export, replenishing the many huge jars found in the palace. And as usual they endured when, about 1400 B.C., Knossos and all the other cities of Crete were suddenly destroyed by foreign invaders. Thereafter Egyptian records make no more mention of the "Keftiu." The settlements that eventually reappeared on the ruined sites were much poorer, adorned by no great palaces, no frescoes, no notable art of any kind. Possibly the peasants were not surprised or merely appalled by the abrupt end to the gaiety and luxury, for they may have suffered from rulers intent chiefly on ease and pleasure; art connoisseurs make out the familiar signs of decadence in the late unwalled cities. Anyhow the peasants clung to the Mother Goddess. Fifteen hundred years later Plutarch observed that the Cretans called their country a "motherland," not a fatherland.

Much more of Minoan tradition endured, however. It had been a major influence on the Mycenaean civilization that grew up in mainland Greece about 1600 B.C. The Mycenaeans were ungrateful, as it was apparently they who leveled the cities and palaces of Crete, but in ending its brilliance they did not end its influence. By virtue of what they had learned from it they were able to take over its Aegean empire and its trade. When a couple of centuries later they in turn went down before rude invaders from the north, the Dorian Greeks, and the whole Aegean world entered a dark age, enough Minoan culture survived to preserve it from complete barbarization. The Phoenicians came in to carry on its tradition of sea trade; excavations at Ugarit, in their land of Canaan, have shown that they knew "Caphtor" as the great center of arts and crafts. The Hebrews, who were deeply indebted to the literature of Canaan, also knew of Crete.[1] They were more directly influenced by the Philistines, who long dominated Palestine, and whom ancient tradition traced to Crete—"the remnant of the island of Caphtor," according to Jeremiah.

Most important by far was the Minoan contribution to the later Greeks. The extent of this contribution we cannot know for sure, though we may have a better idea when Minoan records have been translated; but that it was a significant influence seems certain. Mycenaean culture, which unquestionably owed a great deal to Crete, passed directly into Greek tradition. The Mycenaeans were Homer's Achaeans —the conquerors of Troy, and the national heroes of all Hellas. The flowering of Hellas may be viewed as an unconscious Renaissance.

At least the similarities between Minoan and Greek civilization seem too striking to be merely coincidental. Like the Minoans, the Greeks rose in independent towns, on trade by sea, with the benefit of the art and learning of more ancient peoples. As they rose they displayed much the same delight in music, poetry, dance, sport, and festival games, and much the same humanism and freedom of spirit. Because of this freedom Greek culture is properly considered an independent development, as almost certainly the Greek ideal of political freedom was; yet Greek legend points to deep continuities—and the core of historical fact in this legend, once regarded as mere fable, has been repeatedly

---

[1] It is believed that the name of their Jordan probably comes from the Cretan word for river. Homer mentions the "Iardanos" in Crete.

demonstrated by archaeological discoveries. So Homer had memories of "broad Knossos," which had been destroyed centuries before his time, and was unearthed only in this century. The kind of unique "dancing floor" he described would be used for the staging of Greek choral dramas. Delphi traced its musical and poetic contests back to Crete; a Cretan, appropriately, was the first winner of the prize for the cithara and sacred song. Even the unplayful Spartans believed that their rules for physical education had come from Crete.

The famous discipline of the Spartans may remind us that the Minoans evidently grew soft, felt too secure without walls. When catastrophe struck Knossos, they seem to have gone down praying instead of fighting; the complete confusion in which the Throne Room was found, with scattered ritual vessels apparently in the act of use, suggests that King Minos had hurried there to play the Minotaur. But the poverty of Spartan culture, the dearth of art and civility in its disciplined prime, may dispose us to forgive the gay, high-spirited, free-living Minoans, who for many centuries had been much more enterprising than the Spartans ever became; who with their love of art and sport had yet the energy, skill, and valor to build and maintain a greater empire than Sparta ever won; and who left memories of a gracious way of life that other Greeks cherished, whether or not they had been directly stimulated by knowledge of it. Crete might truly be called the cradle of Western freedom.

3. The Coming of the "Aryans"

A different kind of link with Western history was forged by an unknown people who about 2000 B.C. invaded Anatolia, the high central plateau of Asia Minor, and conquered what they called the land of the "Hatti." From this they got their name of Hittites, recorded in the Old Testament. The biblical writers had no idea of their historical importance, for although they built up an empire mighty enough to overthrow Babylon and later to fight Egypt to a standstill, it went the way of all empires. It had disappeared from human memory by the time the Greeks spread over Asia Minor, and it came back to life only in our own century, when its capital was excavated at Boghazköy. Scholars who then succeeded in translating its native language made a startling discovery: the Hittites were an Indo-European speaking people—the first to appear on the historic scene.

Some centuries after their entrance, another people, who called themselves Aryans, invaded and conquered northern India; their descendants became Brahmans, the ruling caste of India. Toward the beginning of the first millennium a related people took over the land of Persia, in time to make it the seat of a great empire and to give it its modern name of Iran ("Airyana"). Meanwhile other Indo-Europeans had settled in southern Europe, including peoples who were to become famous as the Greeks and the Romans. Still others—Celtic, Germanic, Slavic—would spread all over Europe. Together they have dominated Western history to this day. Almost all the major languages of Europe belong to the Indo-European family.[2]

Plainly we are dealing with peoples of major importance, especially in the history of freedom. So we need at once to dispel much popular confusion. We are not dealing with an "Aryan race," endowed with an inborn genius for freedom. The whole family of Indo-European languages presumably derives from a parent tongue, but this tongue is unknown; the family includes offshoots and blends, in-laws rather than direct descendants; and whoever the speakers of the parent tongue were, their linguistic offspring were of different racial types by the time they entered history. In strict usage, "Aryan" is applied only to peoples who called themselves so, notably those who established themselves in India and Persia. It does not apply to the Germanic peoples, some of whose scholars fondly appropriated the term to christen their native genius. Neither is it certain that the Indo-Europeans were originally Europeans. The "Battle-ax folk" in prehistoric northern Europe, who have been considered the possible fathers of the race, came in from the east. (The battle-ax itself seems to have appeared earlier in Anatolia.) Scholars now prefer southern Russia as the most probable homeland of the Indo-Europeans, but do not rule out the possibility of central Asia.

Certain of their characteristics, however, are well established. They were inlanders, since they borrowed from other peoples the word for "sea." Everywhere they entered as illiterate herdsmen, growing some grain but living mainly off their cattle. The Aryans in particular brought with them the horse, the taming of which was perhaps their chief immediate contribution to civilization; they became pioneers

---

[2] The chief exceptions are Hungarian, Finnish, and Esthonian, belonging to a group called Finno-Ugrian. Another curious exception is Basque—unrelated to any other known language, and the only linguistic survival from prehistoric Europe.

in cavalry and light-wheeled chariotry. All were more warlike than the sedentary agricultural peoples in the lands they invaded or conquered, and all had an aristocratic society, in which chieftains were prominent. Their chief gods were sky-gods, among whose favorite associations were the thunderbolt and the storm. Being pastoral rather than agricultural peoples, they made little of the Earth Mother or her dying lover-son.

As barbarians and warriors, the Indo-Europeans may be said to have had a natural inclination to freedom—for themselves. As rulers, they showed no inclination to extend its blessings. Typically they established an aristocracy of warrior lords above a mass of peasant serfs—a pattern that left a lasting imprint on European history to this century. (*Freo* in Anglo-Saxon means both "free" and "noble.") In the Near East they soon took over the basic pattern of the sacred monarchy, and in India the Aryans developed the caste system, the ultimate in the closed, unfree society. Only in the Mediterranean world, where the Minoans had set rather different precedents, did they advance the ideal of political freedom that is reputedly natural to the Indo-Germanic genius. Neither did they have any manifest cultural destiny by virtue of their blood or their language. The Germanic, Celtic, and Slavic peoples in Europe neglected to become civilized until late in their history. For more than two thousand years the only Indo-European peoples to make significant history were those who entered the civilized world of the ancient East, and exchanged their language for a superior culture.

Yet they had the strength and the wit to make this exchange. Rapid as their expansion was, they were much less destructive than later nomadic barbarians, such as the Huns and the Mongols, and they proved more capable of ruling the lands they conquered. They also realized more fully certain advantages implicit in their pastoral culture. The Indo-Europeans did have a kind of native freedom of spirit that could enable them to play a major role in the history of freedom.

Aside from the hardiness, vigor, and courage natural to warriors, pastoral peoples are typically more independent and enterprising than agricultural peoples. They are less bound to the soil and to a life of toil; they are much less submissive than peasants, obeying their chieftains out of loyalty rather than mere docility; they are freer to think for themselves, and to lift their thoughts. In the Indo-Europeans this difference in spirit was most marked in their religion. Unlike the Earth Mother, who so often dwelt in caves, their sky-gods were typically associated with light instead of darkness, being known as "the Bright Ones." While some, such as Mithra and Indra of the Aryans, were to achieve considerable importance in religious history, all had spiritual possibilities as "high" gods. They also had loftier ethical possibilities than the amoral Mother, who encouraged a degrading obsession with phallus or fertility rites, and characteristically was served by temple prostitutes and eunuch priests. If the sky-gods were disposed to be as fierce and arbitrary as the storm, or as their warlike worshipers, they were disposed as well to sanction the warrior virtues of courage and independence, the tribal ideals of loyalty and honor. But more important at this stage were the very limitations of early Indo-European religion, the lack of real devoutness. These barbarians seem to have been relatively casual about their gods, even though the Sky Father was a Thunderer. They did not live in fear, instead asserting their own power and their own virtue, refusing to submit tamely to the forces either of nature or of other men.

All this we know best from their poetry. When the Indo-European peoples became literate, they typically recorded their ideals in epics— from India and Greece to Ireland and Scandinavia—which reflected their early "heroic age." In these they as typically celebrated not the success of the hero, nor any magical power he got from the gods, but the unconquerable spirit that made him superior to his fate. It was commonly a tragic fate, befitting a mortal always aware of his mortality. They drew imagery from the key inventions of man to emphasize the inexorable necessity to which man is subject: from pottery and clay the brittle pot into which the gods mold him, from the loom the goddesses who spin his fate, from the wheel the invariable cycle of his life. Even so the upshot was never despair. The ultimate stress was not on the impotence of man but on the power and the dignity of his spirit.

This imaginative freedom, together with an aptitude for learning from their more civilized subjects and neighbors, helped the Indo-Europeans to realize the ironic mission of rude conquerors. Such conquest is at first a setback to civilization, commonly inaugurating a dark age. In time it may result in a progressive society, as the vigorous invaders disrupt crusted traditions and then add something of their own when they take to civilized ways. Conquest is not an ideal way, still less a certain one, to prevent stagnation and promote creativity. But since civilization grew up in Sumer and Egypt it has usually been the prelude to new growths.

4. The Growth of Empire

In building the first empire known to history, Sargon of Akkad set the pattern for almost all later ones. He was king of the Akkadians, a Semitic people who had long lived on the borders of Sumer; empire has usually been the work of new peoples breaking in on the civilized world. After bringing all Sumer under his dominion, he marched out to conquer other lands and by his military exploits became a legendary hero, who like Alexander the Great was celebrated in saga and romance for many centuries after his empire collapsed. It lasted only a century— longer than Alexander's, but not so long as most. Although its collapse may be attributed to the pardonable inexperience of his successors, it was the natural fate of empire.

This is an artificial state, lacking the organic unity of a society, held together by force rather than the mystique of the early sacred monarch. Through the spoils of conquest and the exploitation of its subjects it may achieve a splendor that dazzles later generations, but that immediately may inspire other rude peoples to invade it, and that always tends to corrupt its rulers. Emperors take to ostentation and bombast, parading the godlike powers and abilities for which their subjects feel no spontaneous reverence. They also have to depend on professional armies, which generally came to include mercenaries; ambitious generals would then take part in the intrigues and conspiracies within the ruling class. The masses of common people might be trusted to remain submissive, but not to strengthen the empire by active devotion. To win the loyalty of subject peoples, the semblance of a vital unity, calls for a wisdom that has been rare in conquerors, and rarer in their successors.

During the second millennium B.C. in the ancient East, new peoples periodically reorganized and invigorated old societies. The gods usually profited from their ambitions; any temple destroyed during the course of conquest would normally be rebuilt on a grander scale. Men might profit too, after the initial devastation and misery. The best of the new rulers brought order and security over wide areas that might have been suffering from strife or misrule; they built new cities and roads, strengthened and expanded the economy, produced more wealth than they had at first destroyed. Although none displayed anything comparable to the originality of the pioneering Sumerians, they built up

D*

kingdoms of some note in cultural as well as military history. Nevertheless, they may be dismissed summarily in a history of freedom. All the newcomers settled down into the invariable pattern of the sacred monarchy; the word "freedom" or "liberty" does not appear in the index of even the most sympathetic studies of them. The major developments in the second millennium, the first age of empire, may be sufficiently indicated by a brief survey of two peoples—the so-called Babylonians and the Indo-European Hittites.

The Babylonians were another Semitic people, first known as the Amorites ("Westerners"), who under the great Hammurabi again united the land of Sumer and Akkad, not long after 1800 B.C. Ruling from Babylon, hitherto an insignificant town, they made their capital one of the most famous cities of history. Their works were less original than they seemed before the Sumerian achievement was well known, but even so the Babylonians approached the ideal mission of newcomers in an antique land. Hammurabi's law code was a distinct advance, remaining the most orderly, rational, and comprehensive code in all antiquity before Roman law. Merchants as efficiently systematized commerce, carrying their law and their bookkeeping methods to other lands. Scholars made Babylon a brilliant center of culture too; it hummed with literary activity as they set about collecting, recording, and digesting the whole rich heritage they had come into. In preserving this heritage, for the benefit of the later Hebrews among others, they added some elevated ideas of their own. (In their version of the Flood myth, for instance, the goddess Ishtar bitterly rebukes the great god who sends the flood, concluding her protest against the indiscriminate slaughter with the statement "On the sinner lay his sin"—an ideal of justice that the authors of the Old Testament would take many centuries to reach.) Of particular importance were their contributions to mathematics and astronomy, inaugurating the tradition that would make the Babylonians the most famous astronomers of antiquity, and the Greeks their eager pupils. They systematized all the available learning of their time.

Only they did their work too thoroughly: for the next thousand years the scholars of Mesopotamia would do little but copy it. And though the Babylonians might have gone on to more independent work of their own, had not disaster struck the dynasty of Hammurabi about 1600 B.C., their promise was doubtful. They were not creating an original literature or art. In their pursuit of knowledge they were still on the wrong track, and showed no signs of suspecting it. Still seeking primarily to discover the will of their inscrutable gods, they spent less time and thought on empirical inquiry than on the arts of divination, especially through the examination of the liver—a superstition that spread all over the ancient world, much faster than their scientific discoveries. (Among the many peoples who took to peering at livers for omens were the Etruscans, teachers of the Romans.) Babylonian astronomers and their progeny had no reason for surprise or dismay when their remarkably precise calculations proved much less influential than the astrology associated with the later Chaldeans in Babylon.

The conquerors of Babylon were the Hittites, who destroyed it so completely that the land went into darkness for a century or so. It was a pointless destruction, inasmuch as their kingdom was a thousand miles away; the folly of such conquest was emphasized shortly afterward by a long period of anarchy in their own land. Yet this people was to write one of the more honorable and significant chapters in the history of the second millennium. Less brilliant than Babylon, their empire more clearly foreshadowed a new era.

Entering Asia Minor from regions unknown, the Hittites had become the major power in western Asia. In the anarchy following the sack of Babylon they were dominated by the new kingdom of Mitanni, in which an Aryan dynasty ruled an Asiatic people known as the Hurrians, but shortly after 1400 B.C. they rose again under Suppiluliumas, the greatest of their kings. He broke the power of Mitanni, recovered the lost provinces in Asia Minor, conquered Syria, and won such repute that the widow of an Egyptian pharaoh (almost certainly Tutankhamon) asked for one of his sons to replace her husband. His successors maintained the empire, holding their own against imperial Egypt. In 1286 one of them fought the mighty Ramses II at Kadesh in Syria—a celebrated battle in which Ramses boasted that he "broke the back of Hatti forever," as usual almost singlehanded, but which was at best a draw and more probably a defeat, since he immediately retreated.[3] Some years later another great Hittite king, Hattusilis III, signed a treaty of peace with Ramses, the first major treaty in recorded history. The Hittite Empire remained a world power until its sudden overthrow about 1200 B.C.

To culture it made no contribution worth mentioning. The Hittites borrowed from surrounding peoples the basic arts and skills of civiliza-

---

[3] Among the Hittite allies listed in Egyptian records were Homer's Dardanians—the first mention of these "Trojans."

tion, even their religion. Their characteristic weather-god, Teshup, was Hurrian; for the rest, the "thousand gods of Hatti," and the myths, rituals, and magic that went with them, were a primitive conglomeration lacking distinctive character or spiritual potentiality. Unlike later Indo-Europeans, they wrote no epic to commemorate their heroic age, and left no poetry of any sort. They came nearest to a style of their own in their monumental sculpture, which at best has a rude kind of grandeur but is hardly one of the great styles. Their massively fortified capital of Hattusas (modern Boghazköy) was a center of power, never a center of high culture comparable to the Babylon they wantonly destroyed. Their primary achievement was political.

This was a fairly impressive achievement, however, and may warrant the pride of the European scholars who have seen in it the first manifestation of Indo-European genius. The Hittite conquerors did not rule by brute force alone. They organized their kingdom on a feudal basis, granting local autonomy to the subject peoples, and seeking to win their loyalty by equitable treatment. While requiring annual tribute from the vassal princes, they represented this as a contractual obligation, solemnized by oath; the Hittite king regularly reminded the vassal of the good service for which he was indebted to his overlord. If an ungrateful vassal balked at paying homage or tribute, the king took pains to communicate his grievances before setting out to war. "Up now!" he would conclude his diplomatic preamble. "Let us fight, and let the Weather God, my lord, decide our case!" For the Hittite kings were not themselves gods, or at first even godlike. The early kings seem to have been something like constitutional monarchs; their authority was limited by the *pankus,* a council of nobles or warriors that supposedly represented the "whole body of citizens" and could sentence to death a criminal king. Later kings who were not so limited were still not so despotic as most Oriental monarchs. They issued laws more humane than those of earlier peoples, based more on a principle of restitution than of retribution; Hittite law was unique in its emphasis on due process, the surprising pains taken to ascertain all the facts in a case. The Hittite royal annals were as novel in their relative sobriety and straightforwardness. While the scribes naturally put a good face on the royal record, they were content with a bald prose, they recorded defeats as well as triumphs, and in boasting they were never so blatant and preposterous as the authors of the imperial propaganda of contemporary Egypt.

Hence the Hittite kings played a leading role in a major development of the latter part of the second millennium—what has been called the first era of internationalism. The monarchs of Egypt, Babylonia, and Mitanni, the three great powers in the Near East before them, kept up a steady diplomatic correspondence, addressing one another as not only equals but brothers, and cementing their friendship by exchanging gifts and princesses; they sowed the seeds of the universalism that was most nearly realized in the religion of Ikhnaton. When Suppiluliumas destroyed the power of Mitanni, he took over its place in the concert. He made as numerous treaties as conquests, and justified the conquests as "liberations" of lands from the rule of Mitanni, declaring that these lands thereupon "rejoiced" exceedingly. We may doubt their rejoicing, yet applaud this sign of something like a decent respect for the opinions of mankind. More clearly statesmanlike was the famous treaty that Hattusilis III made with Ramses of Egypt: a "good treaty of peace and brotherhood that shall create peace between them for all time," and that was in fact kept until the end of the Hittite Empire seventy years later (a better record than the average for European powers). All we know of the vainglorious Ramses gives reason to believe that this statesmanship was primarily the work of the Hittite monarch.

A further reason is another remarkable document left by Hattusilis, a kind of autobiography. In this he briefly recounts his triumphs, won with the aid of the goddess Ishtar to whom he had dedicated himself, but chiefly he justifies his usurpation of the throne from a brother who had tried to destroy him. After long suffering he had rebelled against his brother, "not sinfully" but openly, with the usual appeal to the verdict of heaven: "Up now! Let Ishtar and the Weather God pass judgment on us." Again we may doubt his entire truthfulness, or even the judgment of Ishtar; but again we should first remark the novelty of such political conscience—a reasoned defense of his conduct by an absolute monarch, who called himself a servant of his god, and who felt obliged to explain himself to his people, as if he were their servant too. His unique autobiography might do for the epic that the Hittites failed to write.

Yet we cannot regard the Hittite Empire as a landmark in the history of freedom. The repeated uprisings of its vassal princes, and of peoples on its fringes, intimate that its rule was not considered a blessing. It owed its success most obviously to its military strength. More revolutionary than its political wisdom was a new weapon it perfected—the light two-wheeled, horse-drawn chariot; and the Hittites borrowed this invention from the Aryan-led Hurrians. Their government grew less novel when they failed to solve the besetting problem of monarchy—the problem of succession. Their early, more or less limited kings chose their successors, as well as most of their high officials, from the "Great Family" of their privileged kinsmen, and they therefore had to contend with palace intrigue; the most ambitious or disgruntled members of the Great Family became disposed to assassination. After the early kingdom collapsed, succession was made hereditary, and though this familiar, if arbitrary method worked better, it had familiar consequences: the Hittite monarchy became more like the Oriental sacred monarchy. Thereafter we hear no more mention of the *pankus*. The Great King took the title of My Sun, borrowed from Egypt and Mitanni, and with it took on an aura of divinity; although not deified until his death, he was "beloved of the god" and acquired superhuman powers. There is no evidence that these powers made him more beloved by his subjects.

There is no evidence either of brutal tyranny or flagrant corruption; so perhaps our parting word should be a tribute to a relatively modest, plain-speaking people who made little conscious effort to strut before posterity. A noble class, owning large estates and presumably supplying chariots, may well have maintained their traditional ideals of honor and valor; ordinary townsmen were liable to forced labor but otherwise were free citizens; though some peasants were bound to the soil, serfdom appears not to have been the rule; and though slaves were by law worth only half what freemen were, they were legally persons. If together the Hittites did not develop a brilliant, gracious, or refined culture, they may have enjoyed a decent way of life, under kings who spoke naturally and directly to their people. But in any case neither the best nor the worst in them lived after them. However wise or humane their rule, it had no apparent direct effect on later political history. Their writings preserved memories of the deeds of the great Sargon, a thousand years before; none of their own Great Kings survived in legend, either as statesmen or as conquerors. The peoples who succeeded to their rule in Asia Minor revealed no awareness of a unique political legacy. The Hittites were remembered only by readers of the Hebrew Scriptures, in such stories as that of Uriah the Hittite whose wife Bathsheba was coveted by King David; and these gave the impression that the people who had built an empire were only a small tribe of mercenaries, living in Palestine by the uncertain grace of the Hebrew kings.

This ignominy was at least in keeping with the end of the Hittite Empire. There had been repeated signs of weakness underlying its vigorous rule, for its strongly fortified capital of Hattusas had been sacked more than once by semibarbarous peoples. When last rebuilt its fortifications were more imposing than ever, with a double line of massive walls, and great towers flanking the gateways and projecting all along at intervals of a hundred feet; but even so it again fell to barbarians, who about 1200 B.C. destroyed it for good. The Hittites would have taken no comfort from the thought that their rude conquerors included, and probably were led by, another Indo-European people—the Phrygians.

At about the time that Hattusas fell, Troy fell to Homer's Achaeans, the Mycenaeans. (According to Homer, the Phrygians were allies of the Trojans.) "The Isles were restless," wrote the Egyptian scribes, "and no land stood before them, beginning with Kheta"—the Hatti. Egypt managed to throw back these "Sea Peoples," but they flooded over other lands. Philistines settled in Palestine, giving their name to the region. Cities were burned down all over Asia Minor; almost every excavation shows a charred layer dating from this period. The contagion spread to Babylonia, where the Kassites—the successors of Hammurabi's dynasty—were overthrown. Meanwhile other Indo-European peoples were pressing behind the Sea Peoples. Within a generation or so after the fall of Troy, Mycenae was destroyed by the Dorian Greeks.

All this restlessness signified no stirring of new ideals, nor quest of freedom; everywhere the invasions inaugurated another dark age, which was to last for several centuries. Yet they also heralded a new age in history. By all odds the most revolutionary contribution of the Hittites was one they failed to exploit: a barbarian people in their realm learned how to work iron. Their kings treated the new metal as a kind of precious stone, more valuable than gold, turning down Pharaoh when he asked for a present of the royal stuff. Possibly it helped to topple their empire, as legend had it that the Sea Peoples were "men of iron"; they might have learned the secret from barbarian mercenaries of the Hittites. It is certain, at any rate, that some of the newcomers were using iron by the next century. It is also appropriate; for the new metal had revolutionary possibilities that new peoples could best realize.

Chapter Four

THE FERMENT OF THE FIRST MILLENNIUM B. C.

1. The Iron Age

Because of the relative scarcity of copper and especially of tin, the bronze that gave its name to the first age of metal had remained very costly. No ordinary man could afford metal tools of his own, much less weapons. Thus in Egypt peasants continued to use flint and stone implements for many centuries after the establishment of the Old Kingdom. Iron, however, is far more common; so once men had learned an efficient method of working it, metal would at last become cheap. It opened up immense economic possibilities beyond the growth of a large new industry. With good cheap tools, production of all kinds could be increased, in agriculture and in other industries; trade would be stimulated, in staples as well as luxury goods. There was in fact such a boom in the first millennium, as evidenced by the growth and spread of population. The boom then stimulated further inventiveness. An unprecedented number of new tools were fashioned, among them spades, tongs, shears, and planes, while oxen were made to work corn mills and olive crushers. At least two inventions may be called epoch-making—the simple alphabet and coinage. These were primary means to realizing the revolutionary social possibilities of the Iron Age.

As the costly bronze had kept metal weapons and tools in effect a monopoly of the ruling class, iron was potentially a great democratic force. It was a boon to new peoples ambitious to rise in the world, for they could arm themselves more readily, hope to meet on more even terms the armies of Great Kings. Hence more small states arose, possible laboratories for experiments in popular government. Above all, iron was a boon to the little man. Able to possess his own metal tools, he might now become an independent farmer or artisan, thereby providing more opportunities for small merchants too. A growing middle class, accustomed to individual enterprise, might grow critical of ancient traditions that impeded such enterprise, and the sacred monarch therefore look like what he does to us—a despot. Some peoples did away with kingship.

The Phoenicians, who anticipated the new age by living chiefly on trade, were inspired by commercial needs to invent their alphabet shortly before its dawn. Although related peoples on the Syrian coast probably contributed to the invention, the Phoenician alphabet became the most popular and influential; it spread all over the Mediterranean world during the Iron Age. Old peoples naturally clung to their familiar, sacred, clumsy hieroglyphs and syllabaries, which their priests and scholars kept using down to the Christian era, but newly literate peoples as naturally preferred the much more economical and efficient alphabet. Common men could now easily learn to read and write, little artisans and merchants to keep their own accounts. The aristocratic monopoly on learning might be broken.

The Greeks, who most fully exploited the democratic potentialities of the alphabet, were also quick to exploit the invention of coinage, about 600 B.C., which they credited to the Lydians, founders of a new kingdom in Asia Minor. Replacing bars of metal, standardized coins facilitated trade and encouraged industry, but the Greeks helped out with a more revolutionary innovation—small change. Early coins, of silver and gold, had been in denominations too high for the daily transactions of the poor; with small change the little man could buy and sell little things, in small quantities. As Gordon Childe observed, he was no longer condemned to eat his wages. Small producers were encouraged to produce cheap goods for a growing market, and so to swell the tendencies to individualism.

The little man would very soon discover the proverbial evils of money. He suffered from mortgagers and usurers, often being enslaved for debt; here and there the Iron Age engendered bitter class struggle. At this stage in the history of freedom, however, the important point is that the little man now could and did struggle. And his ambiguous condition reflected a deeper ferment, because of which the first millennium became a major turning point in history. The increasing social mobility, with increasing trade, promoted more cosmopolitanism, while

the growing individualism led to more self-consciousness, more awareness of possibility and choice. All this entailed more possibilities of
uncertainty and insecurity, tension and conflict, from which traditional
loyalties and sanctities might suffer; but by the same token it might
emancipate and revolutionize thought. By all odds the most important
creations of the millennium were new intellectual or spiritual values,
represented by the emergence of philosophy, science, and the higher
religions. They amounted to the discovery of Man, of Nature, and of
God.

Now, the Iron Age is among the most striking illustrations of the
importance of material, economic factors in history. At the same time
it is as conclusive a refutation of any pure economic determinism. The
discovery of how to work iron was not itself economically determined;
it was made by barbarians, not by civilized peoples whose economy
called for it. Once made, it created the possibility of new productive
forces, then of new institutions and creeds; but different peoples responded to these possibilities in different ways. Only a few peoples,
indeed, realized the revolutionary potentialities of the Iron Age. First
of all we must note that it did not revolutionize life in the heartland
of civilization. The Hittites signaled the response of the old peoples,
who had not made this key discovery, who generally failed to appreciate its possibilities, and who even banned the use of iron in religious
rituals—symbolizing their fidelity to an archaic way of life.

Egypt was too far gone in slavish piety to be rejuvenated. It could
muster up some military power when no other empire was strong (as
under Sheshonk, the biblical Shishak), but it could summon no spiritual or cultural energy. Iron did not even come into common use in
Egypt until late in the seventh century—hundreds of years after
"barbarians" had taken to it—and then largely because of Greek
influence. While some other peoples at about this time were groping
toward loftier religious ideals, Egyptians were reverting more fervently
to the mysteries of Isis and Osiris, prehistoric fertility cults that had
been made over into magical means of personal salvation. In Mesopotamia, always more restless and active, there was a response of sorts
in the rise of the Assyrian Empire—the first great power to emerge
from the dark age following the invasions of the Sea Peoples. But the
notoriously cruel Assyrians exploited chiefly the ugly possibilities of
the Iron Age, in the creation of military engines, the anticipation of
mechanized warfare, and the development of military power to plunder,

destroy, and enslave. If they illustrated the destructiveness that is liable to attend creativity, finally they illustrated again the blight of the sacred monarchy.

They may first be credited with some cold-blooded achievements. While by their systematic cruelty they thoroughly earned their reputation as the Scourge of God, won immediately by destroying the northern kingdom of Israel, they possibly furthered God's purposes in other unconscious ways. They not only conquered but learned how to organize and administer a large empire, thus preparing the way for the much greater Persian and Roman empires, and thence for the whole series of empires—Byzantine, Sassanian, Arab, Seljuk, and Ottoman—that were to rule this region down to our own century. In brutally carrying off and transplanting captive peoples, they advanced the cosmopolitan tendencies of the age. Their kings were careful to foster commerce, the lifeblood of civilization, and made one important contribution to technology about 700 B.C. Sennacherib built the earliest known aqueduct to supply his capital with water—a device that would make it possible for other great cities to grow up in the arid Near East. They were also pious enough to preserve the heritage of literature and learning handed down by the Babylonians. The Assyrian kings, notably Ashurbanipal, built great libraries and brought many scholars to court to translate the classical texts into the vernacular. The "Age of Ashurbanipal" (669-626), which left us as well the finest Assyrian sculpture, has been compared to the Renaissance in Europe.

But the comparison emphasizes how far the Assyrians fell short of any emancipation of the human spirit. Their chief contribution to the life of the spirit was their elaboration of demonology, which helps to explain their atrocities; they were themselves hounded by the religious fears they brought to other peoples. Otherwise they were remarkably unimaginative. Their learned men were mere copyists, still copying the texts of the Sumerians, adding no speculations of their own.[1] Their humorless art likewise adhered to tradition; though the animals in the sculptured reliefs of Ashurbanipal are depicted with exciting vigor, the human figures are as stiff and forbidding as they had been since the end of Sumer. The great Ashurbanipal himself brings us back to the Assyrian role as Scourge of God. In his last years

---

[1] When the Babylonians made their Marduk the supreme god, they revised the cosmological myths of the Sumerians to give him an appropriate role in the creation. When the Assyrians moved in their Ashur in his stead, they simply recopied the Babylonian tablets, substituting his name for Marduk's, and doing a careless job at that, here and there overlooking the old god.

he was woefully oppressed and mystified by the evil days that had befallen his kingdom and himself—a holy king, who "did well unto god and man, to dead or living." We find it easy to understand the evil days, harder to sympathize with the holy king. In 612 B.C. his capital of Nineveh was utterly destroyed, the kingdom extinguished, and the Assyrians disappeared from history, more quickly than any other prominent people before or after them. They might have gone into utter oblivion had not the lesser victims of their abominable cruelty included the Israelites.

The native Chaldean Empire that briefly succeeded to the rule of Mesopotamia, and that in Nebuchadnezzar provided another Scourge for God's chosen people, was brilliant enough to make Babylon one of the Seven Wonders of the ancient world. (The Assyrians had preserved the Babylonian magic number seven.) It gave no promise of a fresh development in culture, however, grew politically rotten in a very short time, and offered only a feeble resistance before falling to the Persian Emperor Cyrus the Great, in 539 B.C. Its fall marked the end of the long era in which Egypt and Mesopotamia had dominated history in the Near East. The future belonged to newcomers on the ancient scene. Eventually these too succumbed to its tradition of "miracle, mystery, and authority"; but first they displayed some creativity, pointed toward the greater changes to come.

2. The Persian Empire

The secret of success in the first millennium was still not clearly race or blood. A kingdom of the Indo-European Phrygians that toward 800 B.C. emerged in the heart of Asia Minor, replacing the Hittites, showed enough signs of originality to influence the Greeks, whose tradition made them the inventors of music; but in the seventh century their kingdom was overwhelmed by new barbarians from Europe, the dread Cimmerians. An Asiatic people, the Lydians, now carried the torch in Asia Minor; after a desperate struggle they succeeded in driving out the Cimmerians, and then built up a strong kingdom with a brilliant capital at Sardis. Upon subduing the Greek cities in Ionia, they took so enthusiastically to Greek culture that little is known of their own original culture beyond their reported invention of coinage. This helped to enrich their kingdom, and to shorten its life. Although the last of their kings, the fabulously wealthy Croesus, held his own against the covetous Aryan Medes, who had been largely responsible for the overthrow of the Assyrian Empire, he was less successful against their kinsmen, the Aryan Persians. Sardis fell to Cyrus the Great in the mid-sixth century. With these Persians the imperial possibilities of the Iron Age were at last fully realized.

They had been living in Iran for some centuries, giving no signs of a high destiny. Like other Indo-Europeans, they maintained an aristocratic society based on a largely pastoral economy, featuring the horse. Before the rise of the Medes their land was split up into independent princedoms, none of which had reached the level of civilization in neighboring Mesopotamia. The Medes formed a state that must have had much influence on the later Persian state, but almost nothing is known about it except that it was short-lived. Immediately it was the genius of Cyrus that gave the Persians their historic destiny: welding them into a nation, he proceeded in one generation to conquer a greater empire than any before his time. Under his grandson Darius it extended from the Nile and the Aegean to the Indus, embracing considerably more than the heartland of civilization.

The early Persian emperors were not only great warriors but great rulers and builders. They succeeded in administering their vast empire by setting up provinces under satraps, who were directly responsible to the king and were kept under supervision by annual inspectors. They ordered the imperial economy by issuing a uniform coinage, while also standardizing weights and measures, and further stimulated trade and industry by building a network of roads, lined with caravanserai and supplied with relays of horses; one was the famous 1,700-mile "Royal Road" from Sardis to Susa, their capital. Darius regally displayed the economic unity and strength of his empire by importing from all over materials for his new palace at Susa—gold from Sardis, cedar from Lebanon, oak from India, ivory from Ethiopia, etc. Commerce reached as far as the Danube and the Rhine, where Persian coins have been found. The prosperity of the early empire was such that real wages were doubled in Babylonia.

More important, the Persian emperors deliberately fostered the cosmopolitan spirit of the age. Where the Assyrians had massacred or enslaved, Cyrus the Great was the most magnanimous of conquerors. To the Babylonians he announced himself as a liberator, not a conqueror, and everywhere he proved himself by generosity to his new subjects, respect for their gods and their customs. Isaiah even hailed him as a Messiah for restoring to Palestine the Israelites who had been carried off into captivity in Babylon. His successors were less magnanimous but still tolerant, even accepting Aramaic as the universal language of their empire for business purposes.[2] Perhaps they realized that such liberality was good for business, and certainly they knew that the Persians had much to learn from their more civilized subjects, whose arts and skills they freely adopted. While Persian art achieved some distinctiveness, it was a cosmopolitan product that reflected Scythian, Assyrian, Hittite, Egyptian, Babylonian, and Greek influences. For all such reasons it has been said that the Persians created a world civilization, not merely an empire. The degree of unity they achieved, or of loyalty among their subjects, was apparent in the army of Xerxes that invaded Greece—a host made up of contingents from many diverse peoples, including Greeks. When Alexander the Great conquered the Persian Empire and then dreamed of setting up an empire that would be a brotherhood, or "union of hearts," he was more likely to have got this idea from the Persians than from his tutor Aristotle.

Above all, the Persians heralded a revolutionary new era through their great prophet Zoroaster. Apparently born in the sixth century B.C., he preached the aristocratic morality of the Indo-Europeans at their best, but preached it in the name of Ahura-Mazda, a much more spiritual deity than any of them had yet conceived. As the Zend-Avesta, the sacred book of Zoroastrianism, is a hopelessly incoherent, fragmentary collection of much later writings, his gospel is somewhat uncertain, and may not have been the pure monotheism celebrated by still later admirers; at least his royal disciple Darius recognized other gods besides Ahura-Mazda, considering him only the greatest god. But Zoroaster clearly did attack the reigning polytheism, denouncing the old tribal gods as evil spirits, and as clearly attacked the still more ancient tradition of magic and idolatry. He preached a purely ethical service of Ahura-Mazda, a god of truth and light. Man's duty was by his own free will to aid the supreme god in his constant struggle with the powers of darkness and evil, led by Ahriman. This struggle would finally end in the triumph of righteousness, with heavenly rewards for the faithful; but man had to earn his afterlife by a strenuous moral life on earth, not by passive obedience, ritual appeasement, or any

---

[2] The success of this Semitic language—later to be spoken by Jesus—is a tribute to intercourse by persuasion instead of force, for the Aramaeans never created a great empire. It remained the standard language of all Semitic Asia except Arabia until the rise of Mohammed, who as an apostle of force unfortunately complicated the moral. Arabic then replaced Aramaic.

mode of miracle and mystery. In particular he had to be truthful—a virtue for which the Persians won a wide reputation.

By implication Zoroaster's dualistic gospel made human history much more meaningful than it had seemed in earlier civilizations. With their essentially static view of the universe, the Egyptians had no word for history in our sense; and while the Mesopotamian peoples all knew that the gods ruled history and misfortunes were due to offenses against them, they never knew the nature of their offenses—their kings always did their anxious best to divine the will of the gods. Zoroaster gave man a clear purpose and incentive: he linked the human drama with the cosmic struggle between good and evil, which would have a positive denouement. Some historians have accordingly seen in the early Persian emperors not only a high sense of mission but a new theory of history, containing the germs of the invigorating idea of progress. As a self-proclaimed liberator, Cyrus the Great implied that he was bringing in a new order, better than the venerable past. Darius also implied that he was remaking history by emphasizing that he was "an Aryan, having Aryan lineage," with nothing but pure intentions. "Says Darius the king: By the favor of Ahura-Mazda I am of such a sort that I am a friend to right, I am not a friend to wrong; it is not my desire that the weak man should have wrong done to him by the mighty; nor is it my desire that the mighty man should have wrong done to him by the weak. What is right, that is my desire. . . . I am not hot-tempered. What things develop in my anger, I hold firmly under control by my will power."

Still, it is possible to read this as Oriental bombast, not simple truthfulness. The proclamations of the Persian emperors were not wholly new, after all; one can find something like them in Hattusilis and Hammurabi—for that matter as far back as King Urukagina of Lagash. In any case these antecedents recall that the new order did not last long. About the style of the later Persian emperors there is no question: it is the old bombast. Under them the mighty man did not have to worry about possible wrong done to him by the weak. Their desire for the right was not overriding, their temper or their whim was generally much more apparent than their will power. They had reverted to the old order of the sacred monarchy, with a vengeance— a literal vengeance on those who might dispute their claim to be King of Kings.

The outcome of the Persian Empire was scarcely surprising. The Persians had grown up in the shadow of the sacred monarchy, and the great majority of their subjects knew no other form of government. The oldest known Persian writing is a royal proclamation: "This land of the Persians which I possess, provided with fine horses and good men, it is the great god Ahura-Mazda who has given it to me. I am the king of this land." The theme of me and God may not inspire truthfulness or fidelity. The gift of Ahura-Mazda was somewhat besmirched as early as Cambyses, the son of Cyrus the Great: he secretly had his brother assassinated, inaugurating what was to become royal Persian routine, and he ruled as a despot. Following Darius, Xerxes showed more vigor than he is generally given credit for, because of his fiasco in Greece; yet the Persian Empire lived primarily off the achievements of Cyrus and Darius, aided by the feebleness of the Egyptians and Babylonians. Xerxes was the last emperor to lead the army in person. The imperial rule of his successors was enlivened chiefly by harem intrigue, conspiracy, and assassination. The satraps became increasingly corrupt and insubordinate, some of them virtually independent. The one emperor who for a time restored unity, Artaxerxes III, succeeded by dint of slaughtering several dozen of his brothers and sisters.

This pattern of degeneration, which would be repeated in subsequent empires down through the Ottomans, seems to have been more sordid and brutal under the Persian than earlier regimes. One reason, perhaps, was the weakening of traditional sanctities by the ferment of the Iron Age. Men could respond to the genius and the magnanimity of a Cyrus, but otherwise they might not really believe that there was anything divine about the royal autocrat before whom they had to prostrate themselves. Thus Persian monumental art, inspired solely by the service of the Great King, became exhausted within a century; the later kings would only build meaningless palaces in which to squander their wealth. For the same reason the kings might be more openly opposed, as they were by satraps. The nobility, the army, and the priesthood now had more independent influence or potential power. Absolute monarchs in all the later empires in this region would have to contend against such opposition from within the ruling class.

In the Persian state, however, opposition to the Great King did not yet rise on grounds of clear principle, in the name of constitutional rights. While in Zoroastrian theory law was immutable, in fact the king alone issued law; even nobles were subject to execution at the royal whim. If as Aryans the Persians had an independent spirit, they enjoyed no political freedom. And with the failure of their new political order they proved incapable of creating any other new values. They contributed nothing of importance to poetry, empirical knowledge, or technology. Outside the royal palace and harem they clung to their aristocratic virtues, but they lost sight of the teachings of Zoroaster. The famous Magi restored the old polytheism and its magical accessories, with a fanatical insistence on doctrinal and ritual purity that anticipated the Christian horror of heresy, and that made them a symbol of Oriental wisdom. Ahura-Mazda, the god of truth and light, proved less influential than Ahriman, the Evil Spirit. Ahriman became Satan—a prince of lies who had little power against the almighty Jehovah of Israel, but who acquired immense power in later Christendom and spread more darkness than he himself knew.

Even so, the remarkable constructive achievements of Cyrus and Darius, in confronting a task of unprecedented magnitude, were by no means wasted effort. Their groundwork remained—the frame and basis of *cosmopolis*. We may accordingly be grateful even for the failures of the Persians. They stimulated the wonderful achievement of Athens, which became the leader of the Greek world after its heroic resistance to the hosts of Xerxes. Later they drew the Greeks into the ancient East in the wake of Alexander the Great, stimulating the Hellenistic achievement that educated the Romans and the early Christians. All owed more than they knew to the work of the magnanimous Cyrus.

3. The Phoenicians

"Whoever cultivates the corn cultivates righteousness," said Zoroaster. In keeping with Aryan tradition, he praised agriculture above commerce; and it may indeed be better for building character. Commerce, however, is more likely to produce a lively intelligence. The Greeks were an obvious case in point, but so were an earlier pioneering people in the Iron Age—the Phoenicians.

Appearing on the coast north of Palestine by the middle of the second millennium B.C., the Phoenicians lacked the Greeks' advantage of geographical and cultural distance from the heartland of the sacred monarchy. They were subject to the power as well as the tradition of the ancient civilizations, by now given to imperialism; we first hear of them when the Egyptians invaded their land. Nevertheless, they had the wit to rise to the challenge of the narrow coastal plain on which they lived. Like the Greeks, they went to sea and took full advantage of the possibilities of commerce. They became the most adventurous sailors of antiquity, reaching and passing Gibraltar before the first millennium; later their Admiral Hanno would explore the whole coast of Africa—a feat attempted by no Europeans until two thousand years after him. By trade they built up their famous cities of Tyre and Sidon, taking over the Mediterranean when the Minoan and Mycenaean sea empires collapsed. By the bold, hardy spirit displayed in their seafaring they weathered the anarchy of the dark age and maintained their independence in little Phoenicia for some centuries. They helped to educate both the Israelites and the Greeks, even apart from their supremely important invention of the alphabet.

As early as 1000 B.C. the Phoenicians began planting the colonies that radiated their influence throughout the Mediterranean world. Some went as far as Gades (Cadiz) in Spain; others settled in Cyprus, Malta, Sicily, Sardinia, and North Africa. These colonies were not military or trading outposts, but permanent independent settlements by men seeking their fortune, or crowded out of the little homeland by rising population. Although they had cultural and sentimental ties to the mother city, as pioneers in a distant land they began fashioning a different kind of state better suited to their business enterprise. While the mother cities in Phoenicia retained their traditional kings (such as the King Hiram who made an alliance with King David of Israel), many or most of the colonies became republics of a sort. Among these was Carthage in north Africa, the last and the greatest of the colonies of Tyre. It built up a sea empire that gave serious trouble to the Greeks, and much graver trouble to the Romans: a power great enough to threaten the main course of Western history.

Carthage was probably founded toward 800 B.C., when civilization was emerging from the dark age in hither Asia. Although little is known of its early history, it apparently recognized its star in the city of Tartessus in Spain. (This may have been the biblical Tarshish, for which the stiff-necked Jonah sailed when the Lord told him to go to Nineveh; whereupon he learned his lesson in the belly of a whale.) Tartessus had grown rich, powerful, and famous on its metal industry, particularly its monopoly on tin, brought in via the Atlantic. In the sixth century it was destroyed by the Carthaginians, who then took over its monopoly, blocked Gibraltar, and spread stories of the terrors of sailing in the Atlantic. In the next century Carthage was halted in Sicily by the Greeks, who won a decisive battle, but it kept on growing. It was about the greatest commercial and industrial city of the time when it began its life-and-death struggle with Rome, on which depended the mastery of the Mediterranean world.

Carthage owed its power to its political institutions as well as its commercial enterprise. Aristotle, who discussed its constitution at some length, called it a democracy. More precisely, it was an aristocratic republic like later Venice, ruled by merchant princes; or in other words, an oligarchy. Aristotle noted that its elected magistrates were generally chosen for their wealth, and that while popular assemblies could freely discuss and oppose matters brought before them, a council of elders first decided what these matters should be. He added that the Carthaginians escaped the evils of oligarchy, in particular class war, by sending the poor away to colonies, where they could enrich themselves. A modern democrat might add that, unlike the Oriental monarchies, they had established the tradition that government was a public affair. On the record, at any rate, the merchant rulers of Carthage had not only the qualities of energy, initiative, resourcefulness, and daring that have come to be associated with private enterprise, but more political genius than landed aristocracies have typically shown; they could be more enlightened or astute because as merchants they were accustomed to methods of persuasion rather than mere force. Aristotle was especially impressed by the fact that Carthage had never had a revolution or been ruled by a tyrant. He concluded that its constitution was "justly celebrated," one of the best he knew.

He was no democrat, however—he also had high praise for the constitution of Sparta. Other Greeks were shocked by the venality and corruption of the rulers of Carthage; another apparent reason why it had no class war was that the merchant princes bribed the common people to acquiesce in their policies. And crisis finally exposed the characteristic limitations of the business spirit that had made the city rich. In the Punic Wars with Rome, Carthage had the advantages of considerably more wealth and manpower, and in the great Hannibal more brilliant generalship; Rome had better soldiers and more public spirit. Carthage depended on mercenaries and subject peoples to do its fighting, while selfish interests ruled at home. Following Roman success, the patriotic Hannibal initiated reforms that drastically limited the power of the oligarchs; whereupon they turned on him and forced him out of the city. Their eventual reward was the utter destruction of Carthage, as a generation or so later the Romans decided to end its history.

At the end the Carthaginians did fight with desperate courage, some half a million of them perishing in the final siege. As so often with the defeated in history, we cannot do them full justice: we do not have their side of the story. We know them chiefly through alien Greek and Roman sources, which except for Aristotle are almost uniformly critical. Still, it is significant that they left no record. The material evidence from excavation lends support to the harsh judgments of the Greeks and Romans, on a people whose first and last objective was wealth.

The early Phoenicians were famous for their luxury goods, especially their purple fabrics. As Homer's heroes got their choicest possessions from Tyre and Sidon, historians once magnified Phoenician influence on early Greek art, but it is now clear that the art of the Phoenicians was largely derivative and had little independent influence; while manufacturing wares for export, they made their wealth mainly as carriers and middlemen. The later Carthaginians were famous for none of their wares. Their art was imitative and undistinguished, and it got poorer as increasingly they imported instead of copying Greek goods. Although almost all their literature is lost, there is no sign of poetry, drama, or philosophy. They were fervently, even fanatically devoted to their Lady of the Heavens, Tanit, but without any appreciable elevation or emancipation of spirit; she long sanctioned human sacrifices and never inspired any prophet comparable to those of their fellow Semites in the land of Canaan. Altogether, about all that mankind owes to Carthage is some slight technical improvements in shipbuilding and warfare, and the word "gorilla," brought in by Admiral Hanno. The only Carthaginians who are well known are Hannibal and the mythical Queen Dido of Virgil—both tragic figures, in a national drama otherwise lacking the dignity of high tragedy.

The Greeks, it might be added, were still more enterprising than the Carthaginians, better at their own commercial game. Carthage did not issue coinage until the fourth century B.C. and it never developed a banking system comparable to that of Rhodes or Alexandria. One apparent reason for its relative sluggishness was that it had fewer independent merchants and artisans; trade was largely monopolized by a small oligarchy, as it had earlier been by the Phoenician kings, in the ancient Oriental tradition. But chiefly the Greeks point to a trite conclusion. Through a measure of freedom the Carthaginians won considerable wealth and power, the material means to the good life; and with that their speculation ended. The Greeks, no less interested in wealth and power, were deeply concerned as well with the ends of freedom, the question what is the good life.

4. The "Axial Period"

From the outset of civilization, as we have seen, man remained blind to what now seem the most obvious implications of his epoch-making achievement. He had made an elaborate world of his own, splendidly walled, furnished, and adorned; yet he was still not a self-conscious maker, really aware of his own powers or his freedom to create for his own purposes. He had acquired a great deal of empirical knowledge, about agriculture, astronomy, medicine, metallurgy, mechanics; yet he had no sound idea of how he had got this knowledge, no explicit idea of natural causes or natural law. He had provided much more opportunity for the gifted individual, created more need of individual enterprise; yet he had not declared the value of individuality, the right to personal freedom, or the need of independence of spirit. He had transcended the tribalism of prehistoric man, in heterogeneous cities and then in empires, even attaining an era of internationalism; yet he had little or no concept of universality, or of mankind. In his religion, as in his magic, he gives the impression of having answered the first and last questions before he consciously asked them. Although there must have been many scattered individuals who grew self-conscious and under stress asked searching questions, as we know some Egyptians did after the collapse of the Old Kingdom, the significant thing is that we know hardly any of their names or their works. It was not until what Karl Jaspers has called the "Axial period," from about 800 to 200 B.C., that man realized the implications of civilization, and can be said to have discovered his humanity.

The immediate sign of a revolutionary change in his mentality is the great names that have come down from this period. Almost all the well-known names before it are the names of kings and conquerors, and of their gods. Now we hear of great individuals of a very different kind: Zoroaster, Buddha, Confucius, and Lao-tse; Amos, Jeremiah, and Isaiah; Homer, Thales, Solon, Aeschylus, Socrates, Plato, and a hundred other Greeks. Together they represent the most extraordinary creative era in man's history between the rise of civilization and the rise of modern science. This era made a mark on every great society thereafter, and provided the standards by which we judge all previous societies.

It seems more extraordinary because of a mysterious coincidence. The most influential of these pioneers all appeared in or about the sixth century B.C., independently, in widely separated lands, without any apparent influence on one another. This was probably the century of Zoroaster in Iran, certainly of Buddha in India and Confucius in China; in Palestine the prophetic movement now culminated in Jeremiah and Deutero-Isaiah, who gave Israel its loftiest visions of the One God; and in the Greek world appeared Solon, the great lawgiver, while Thales and his successors gave birth to natural philosophy and science. There would seem to have been some deep ground swell. But if so, it remains mysterious: it did not affect most peoples. Say that man had at last come of age, as he was bound to, he did so only among a few peoples of diverse and relatively recent antecedents. Call in the Iron Age and its increasing tensions, and these still elicited radically different responses. The mere fact that the creativity was extraordinary indicates that it was not clearly determined by the common material conditions of life. It was rather the plainest demonstration of the power of genius, the difference that great men may make in history. The pioneers of the sixth century were indeed Promethean.

Outside of Greece the major outcome was the emergence of the higher religions—Zoroastrianism, Hinduism, Buddhism, Confucianism, Taoism, and Judaism. These embodied virtually all the basic religious ideas on which man has lived ever since. The differences among them are so fundamental that one cannot believe in all of them, but even men who believe in none of them may agree that these religions deserve the name of "higher."[3] All moved away from the immemorial tribal gods and nature gods, toward more universal, spiritual conceptions of deity or the cosmic order. Their primary concern was no longer the material success of the nation or the assurance of good crops, but the spiritual welfare of man. They offered visions of some Good beyond

---

[3] I should emphasize that my concern here is not the metaphysical question of the truth of any religion, but only the empirical question of its effects on freedom. As orthodox Christians are likely to think that the truth revealed by Jesus was unique and entire, I might remark that the gist of his gospel was of course drawn from the prophets of Israel. The only really novel idea added by Christianity was that God had deliberately sacrificed himself in order to save man.

the flux of earthly life, rescuing man from his long obsession with food and phallus. They proposed different ways of treating the powers above, but ways alike more amenable to his ideal purposes. Their service of deity was far from mere servility.

The advance represented by such loftier spirituality is plainer because it signified as well a growth of rationality. Thought was much freer, more conscious, and more critical. Above all, it was no longer governed by myth. In Buddha, Confucius, and the Greeks the emancipation was specifically philosophical; but prophets and philosophers alike repudiated the universal practice of magic, or any merely ritual way of dealing with nature or deity. The higher religions gave much more intelligible, moral content to the ancient idea of the sacred. All sought to educate man, enlighten him, elevate him by insisting on righteousness instead of rites, the ideal instead of the idol. They introduced universal ethical ideals, based on the tacit if not explicit assumption of the brotherhood of man. It is hard to do justice to such once novel teachings because they may now seem elementary, platitudinous; but this in itself proves the great difference that the higher religions have made in man's thinking.

Although none preached a gospel of individualism, indirectly they did much to emancipate the individual. By discrediting the external forms of ritual religion, they led the way to some inner relation with deity that might stir a consciousness of selfhood, or of personality. They conferred a spiritual independence and responsibility on the individual, a moral obligation to serve the god or to seek the good that was yet a free choice, up to him. While preaching the good will essential to the maintenance of any social freedom, they fostered a respect for the spirit in man that seeks truth and goodness, and that might therefore claim a right to freedom. Judaism taught that he had been created in the very image of God. Hinduism even proclaimed a divinity within man, a oneness with the soul of the universe that was his birthright, and that made superfluous any special revelation by God or covenant with him: the individual was directly attuned to the infinite and the eternal.

The prehistoric myth and magic came back, of course, and with them the as ancient tribalism, or heavenly favoritism. The higher religions created a much wider gap between the lofty spirits and the masses of simple worshipers, whose needs were tended or exploited by conservative priesthoods. From now on we must always keep in mind the obvious but often neglected distinction between ideal religion, as represented by the founders and their truly spiritual followers, and established or historic religion, as represented by worldly churches with vested interests in "miracle, mystery, and authority." But if only because religion is always degraded or corrupted by worldly success, and never succeeds in rooting out either primitive idolatry or tribalism, it is necessary to remember that the higher religions began as literally subversive, revolutionary movements, and that they retain revolutionary potentialities. Their founders all defied universal, timeless tradition, when they did not—like Buddha—attack point-blank the tyranny of reigning superstition. None offered any mere "opiate for the masses."

Immediately, however, it is necessary to dwell on the fundamental divergences from the outset of the Axial period. If the awakening resulted from some deep, common experience, Israel flatly denied a universal experience by claiming a unique divine revelation. Elsewhere the new modes of rationality and spirituality were more freely available to all mankind in theory, but they took mutually exclusive forms. The Far Eastern religions were at their purest godless by Judaeo-Christian standards in that they rejected the ancient belief in personal gods, and conceived of no Being who was concerned about man and demanded worship. Within these religions, the World Soul of Hinduism differed as radically from the Heaven of Confucius as both did from the Jehovah of Israel, while for Buddha there was apparently no God at all. As for Greece, its philosophers never reached a basic agreement on the cosmic spiritual reality, if any. Conceptions of the essential nature of man and the good life varied as widely. He might or might not have an immortal soul; his chief duty might or might not be to serve the heavenly powers; his highest good might come from fulfilling himself in the natural world or from scorning this world. Only the Greeks discovered natural law in a scientific sense. Almost everywhere the basic pattern of the sacred monarchy would recur, with attendant myths; but otherwise we can no longer generalize so freely about a basic mentality as we can in the ancient East.

Such divergences became more pronounced in the course of time, amounting to estrangements. Israel and especially Greece lead us to the basic theme of East and West—for a student of human freedom the most important theme that emerges from the Axial period. The great societies that embraced Hinduism, Buddhism, and Confucianism were indeed diverse; but at this stage we may lump them together, and postpone detailed consideration of them, for a simple reason. Apart from the invariable corruptions, none of these higher religions fostered the growth of a free society. None inspired a conscious ideal of freedom.

Buddha, the boldest of the Eastern thinkers, makes plainest the reasons why they failed to promote any such cause. He based his gospel on the evil of life in the natural world, unrelieved by flattering hopes of a benevolent Creator or by any promise of heavenly rewards in a life to come. The way to escape this evil was to suppress all natural desire; the highest goal for man was Nirvana, a kingdom of no world. Buddha accordingly offered man what he called "Deliverance," what is commonly known as "spiritual freedom," or what I should call peace of mind. This may be considered a higher good than ordinary freedom. (Today it seems to be what many free Americans chiefly crave, and enjoy only with the help of tranquilizers.) Still, its essence remains a freedom *from* desire to carry out earthly purposes, or to realize the common garden varieties of freedom. Although Buddha taught in a spirit of compassion and love, his Way naturally bred an indifference not only to ideas of political freedom but to energetic efforts at social reform. Buddhism then became the first great missionary religion, traveling all over the Far East, and in the process taking on all the popular accessories of a salvation cult—heavens and hells, saints and devils, holy water, rosaries, relics, etc.[4] Buddha himself was worshiped as a savior-god, in defiance of his plain teaching that he was a mortal pointing out a way of salvation available to men by their own unaided efforts. But if many of his worshipers, especially in China, took a more cheerful view of earthly life, no great apostle or Buddhist church ever led a popular struggle to improve the social, political conditions of this life.

In Buddha's native land of India his religion failed to last, giving way to the older religion of Hinduism, but by a different approach this aspired to a similar goal of tranquillity through nonattachment. The approach was mysticism: an immediate, intuitive sense of the World Soul, an immanent spiritual reality behind all the transitory or illusory appearances of the material world. This was accordingly an ineffable kind of knowledge, beyond ordinary sense, reason, or logic; one could enjoy the supreme experience of unity with the Eternal only by escaping the world of the senses. Because mysticism raises obvious intellectual difficulties, in particular the question how or why the timeless

---

[4] It strikingly anticipated the ritualism as well as the ethical idealism of Christianity, the next great missionary religion. As James Ferguson noted, "The Buddhist kept five centuries in advance of the Roman Church in the invention and use of all the ceremonies and forms common to both religions." One striking difference is that no war has ever been fought in the name of Buddhism.

World Soul gives rise to an illusory temporal world, and because mystics often feel impelled to utter the sublimely unutterable truth, India produced a rich philosophy and literature. Schools gave different answers to the problem of bridging the gulf between the ideal and the natural world, and to the question of what attitude to take up to this world. But the weight of Hindu thought, supported by the testimony of Indian history, was a substantial agreement on the unimportance if not the unreality of the temporal world, and the supreme importance of nonattachment to it. Similarly the self that most thinkers agreed was the ultimate reality was not the person or the individual known to Westerners, but an impersonal medium or spiritual receiving set, which in becoming attuned to the World Soul lost all consciousness of individuality.

Hence Indians never wrote history, which perforce takes place in time and is made by persons. Although they developed a theater, they never wrote tragedy either; this was literally taboo. If the appearance of evil was hard to account for, it could only be apparent, another temporal distraction from the "real" spiritual reality; the wise and holy men were indifferent to it on high principle. And so they logically remained indifferent to the wretched poverty of the teeming Indian masses. From their tranquil ranks came no indignant prophets, social reformers, or apostles of freedom. The conspicuous earthly counterpart to Hindu spirituality was the caste system that India maintained for well over two thousand years—the most consistent, sustained effort in all history at a static, closed society, or at the ideal of complete acceptance of one's social status and earthly lot. A by-product of both was the degraded superstition of the Indian masses; the Brahman caste was content to leave them to the magical devices that helped to keep them content. Since the Axial period, no other great society has been so priest-ridden as India, whose popular piety is still symbolized by its sacred cows.

In China the teaching of Confucius was very different, and raises more complicated issues. He was by far the most humanistic of the great Eastern teachers, not at all otherworldly. While respecting "Heaven," a kind of impersonal moral order that governed the universe, he was concerned primarily with establishing a harmonious human order on earth. As a truly impartial order, Heaven called for no worship or propitiation (no popular temples were dedicated to it), but at that the piety of Confucius was tempered by a degree of skepticism. "We don't know yet how to serve men," he told a questioner, "how can we know about serving the spirits?" Hence he advised men to "respect spiritual beings, but keep them at a distance." He kept them at a proper distance even in emphasizing the importance of *li,* or ritual and ceremony. Ritual, especially in the form of ancestor worship, was a primary means of maintaining social unity and harmony; and with Confucius it involved some conscious make believe, a measure of the playfulness that Huizinga dwelt on in *Homo Ludens*—possibly the best means of realizing whatever truth may be embodied in myth and ritual. He was so worldly and sophisticated, indeed, that Christopher Dawson, speaking as a Christian, has declared that Confucianism as a religion "is unintelligible to us by reason of its very rationality."

Similarly Confucius was devoted to an ideal of culture in the Greek sense—the conscious cultivation of human nature. As an apostle of harmony he eschewed any radical dualism of body and soul, any idea of radical opposition between man and nature, or Heaven. He took an essentially optimistic view of human nature and earthly life, basing his ideal social order on ethics instead of law, and his ethics on the cultivation of natural sympathy and natural piety instead of stern commandments and rigorous discipline. His creed was singularly free from both dogma and intimidation by anxiety or fear. And in keeping with his breadth and liberality of spirit, it had democratic implications that were explicitly stated by Mencius, his foremost disciple. "In a nation," Mencius wrote, "the people are the most important, the state is next, and the ruler is the least important." As a "Son of Heaven," the Chinese emperor ruled by a mandate from Heaven; but Mencius declared that the people might justly rebel, or "change the mandate," if he abused it.

Yet Confucian China remained a sacred monarchy, much like all the others. There was no legally constituted authority apart from the emperor to define or restrict his mandate from Heaven. In practice he could be removed only by assassination or civil war, and this resulted only in rule by a new Son of Heaven, never in a new political order. The people's right to revolution was less than nominal: there was not even a word for *rights* in classical Chinese. Later Confucianists argued that the emperor could be punished only by Heaven, though on earth it appeared to be as remiss as all other gods. China remained basically true to Confucius, or at least truer than any other great society has been to its avowed religion; but thereby it demonstrated that in spite of his liberality of spirit he had much to do with its failure to become a free society.

His primary objective was order and stability, not freedom. He was profoundly conservative—in his own words, "a transmitter, not a maker, believing in and loving the ancients." The ancients in fact had their way, to a greater extent than he perhaps realized or intended. The ritualism he encouraged opened the door to all their magic, the prehistoric superstition that has run riot in China to this day, swamping as well the mystical religion of Lao-tse. Like the ancients, too, Confucius subordinated the individual, for the sake of harmony and stability stressing not his rights but his duties—to the ancestors, the father, the emperor. He taught a gracious way of life, but one that found little room for personal enterprise and initiative, any spirit of quest or adventure, any searching curiosity or dissent. If his creed was too rational and worldly to deserve the holy name of religion by Christian standards, it was not rational enough for basic intellectual purposes, or in particular scientific purposes. It stimulated no such free inquiry and criticism, or such rational studies of nature, history, and politics, as the Greek contemporaries of Confucius were embarking on.

The troubles of these Greeks, however, recall us to a familiar theme —the costs of the Axial period. We may anticipate some of the problems created by the realization of new possibilities, apart from the much greater gulf between the choice spirits and the common people. The loftier visions were not simply visions of harmony, peace, or joy. The growing rationality might lead to growing disagreement, the profounder questioning to deeper disquiet, and both to a growing awareness of ultimate uncertainty. If assured of his spiritual kinship with God or cosmos, man might yet feel less at home in the natural world; the higher religions mostly tended to sever his bonds with nature, disrupt the deep unity he had felt in worshiping the Mother Goddess and her ever-dying, ever-resurrected son. His spiritual independence might make him feel lonely and insecure, more anxious for magical means of personal salvation. His spiritual responsibility might induce feelings of guilt and sin, or fears of an Almighty more despotic than the always limited nature deities and tribal deities; he might have less confidence in his natural powers of intelligence. Having a clearer knowledge of good and evil, he might have a deeper sense of his imperfection or get the notion of his Fall. All such tendencies may be considered good for his soul; but they would not necessarily give him more effective freedom, in the only life he can ever be sure of.

| Chapter Five | # THE UNIQUENESS OF ISRAEL |

1. The Early History of the Hebrews

Among the Semitic peoples who as early as Sargon's Akkadians became prominent in ancient history were a group known as the Apiru or Habiru. Throughout the second millennium they appear in documents from the major lands—Egypt, Mesopotamia, Syria, Asia Minor. Usually they appear as troublemakers, nomadic or mercenary raiders. Among them, it seems highly probable, were the people destined to become known as Hebrews. So we might be warned at once against popular generalizations about the "Semitic character." While the Hebrews were desert nomads, Semitic Amorites were building the great city of Babylon, Semitic Phoenicians were taking to the sea. Other Habiru groups settled down to become Moabites, Ammonites, Amalekites, Edomites, Midianites—idolaters showing no sign of religious genius. Some remained nomads, perhaps surviving as Arabian tribes who today are still living in regions where Herodotus named and placed them. The Hebrews themselves would clamor to their tribal god for a king, so as to be "like all the nations." They would get their wish and become much like other nations, at least the little nations around them. But they would also develop a unique character and culture, as different from the Babylonian and Phoenician as from the Aryan. As a nation they would share the fate of all the others, meet their end more quickly than many. As a people they would survive all the others, and make a deep, lasting impress on Western history. They would become troublemakers in a profounder sense and on a much greater scale, both inspiring and obstructing the growth of freedoms that they themselves hardly enjoyed.

Immediately they give trouble to the historian by their one great enduring work, the Old Testament. Archaeological research has demonstrated the factual basis of a great deal of biblical history, which scholars were once inclined to regard as essentially mythical or legendary. Nevertheless, it is not trustworthy history, if only because of its religious inspiration. The authors of the Old Testament treated all serious matters—social, economic, political, military—in religious terms. A secular historian has to discount or at least reinterpret their account of their past.

There is no question, however, that the Hebrews entered history as herdsmen, like their patriarch Abraham living in tents. Their pastoral society was strongly patriarchal; the authority of the father corresponded to that of the thoroughly masculine God they would come to worship. As shepherds rather than horsemen, they were not so warlike or aristocratic as the Indo-Europeans, but they had a comparable independence of spirit. They early came under the influence of more civilized peoples, from whom we now know they borrowed some of their myths. Their own legends had it that Abraham came from Ur in Sumer, where he could have seen the Tower of Babel and heard of the Flood. Quite possibly they spent some time in bondage in Egypt, as a people is unlikely to invent such humiliating stories about its past; they may have been enslaved when the Egyptians threw out the Hyksos. (One recorded Hyksos chieftain was named Jacob-el.) Here they perhaps picked up the custom of circumcision that later helped to make them a "peculiar people."

In any case the Hebrews certainly entered Canaan in the thirteenth century B.C. As certainly their invasion of the "Promised Land" was not the triumphal procession narrated in the Book of Joshua; excavations confirm what may be gathered from the Book of Judges, in which cities and kings supposedly destroyed by Joshua crop up again. Although they leveled some cities, including Jericho, they settled in the hill sections of central Palestine, where they maintained themselves with considerable difficulty. Their promised land was mostly a poor land, "overflowing with milk and honey" because it was better suited to goats and bees than to the raising of crops, and it became poorer for their coming; the early Hebrew settlements in excavated mounds are much inferior in culture to the Canaanite towns below them. They were still primarily a pastoral, not an agricultural people. Their later prophets would hark back to the purity of the simple pastoral life of the ancestors, but it was not in fact idyllic. As Judges itself makes clear, the ancestors kept warring on one another as well as on the Canaanite city-states, neighboring Habiru tribes, and the Philistines on the coast: "Everybody did what was right in his own eyes." Often they had to submit to the right of the Philistines, who had a monopoly on iron. During this troubled period they became known as Israelites instead of Hebrews. (The last biblical reference to the Hebrews occurs in a battle between the Philistines and the Israelites, and suggests—somewhat confusedly—that the Hebrews had been fighting on the wrong side.) They did not dominate the land until they became a nation under King David, about 1000 B.C. All along they had been aided by the irruption of the Sea Peoples, for while this gave them the Philistines to contend with, it left no strong imperial power in the region.

There is more question, however, about the religion the Hebrews brought with them into Palestine, especially about the teachings of Moses. He was so rare a type of cultural hero that even skeptics may agree that there must almost surely have been a great leader behind the legendary figure presented in Exodus; some powerful personality made an indelible impression on the people in the Wilderness. Moses may well have been born in Egypt, as his name is Egyptian (meaning "child"), and he might have been influenced by Ikhnaton, though this seems less likely; Ikhnaton's religion had been largely confined to the royal court.[1] But just what Moses taught will remain forever a matter of conjecture, given the hopeless confusion of lofty ethics, tooth-for-a-tooth secular law, and prehistoric taboo in the different versions of the so-called Mosaic law recorded in Exodus. And whatever he taught, it is clear that the settlers in the Promised Land were by and large still attached to an essentially primitive religion.

They worshiped their god Yahweh (Jehovah) at "high places" marked by immemorial stones. He was a purely tribal god. The "covenant" that the patriarchs made with him, as described in Genesis, was a kind of contractual agreement profitable to both sides: in return for their exclusive devotion, he agreed to devote himself exclusively to them. He fulfilled his share of the bargain by showing no concern whatever for the rest of mankind except to slaughter them when they got in the way of his own people; so Moses could exult, "The Lord is a man of war!" The devotion he demanded in return involved the

---

[1] When Freud argued, in *Moses and Monotheism,* that Moses imposed the religion of Ikhnaton on the "stiff-necked" people, and that they finally murdered him for his pains, he got around this difficulty by assuming that Moses had been an Egyptian noble. Historical scholars are more impressed by the essential difference between the personal God of Israel and the sun-god of Ikhnaton.

E*

familiar modes of propitiation, flattery, and ritual etiquette. Like most gods, he loved the savor of meat and insisted on regular offerings of it: "None shall come before me empty-handed." He gave considerable trouble because he was as fallible and moody as other gods, often "repenting" what he had done, sometimes regretting that he had ever made the bargain in the first place; in wrath or dismay he slaughtered many of his own people too. In all this one can make out the potentialities of the later monotheism. The patriarchs adhered to the contract, worshiping no other gods; Yahweh continued to take an intense personal interest in his people, while never showing the least interest in having affairs with other gods or even goddesses; and he was already unique in having deliberately "chosen" his people. But simply to appreciate the religious growth of Israel—not to mention the tremendous historic drama of the "local god who made good"—one must note that its early religion was no more spiritual or edifying than most primitive religions.

With the establishment of the kingdom began the history that made the Israelites more "like all the nations," and finally more unlike them. The differences are much more important; but to understand and appreciate them, we must again first dwell on the likenesses. Yahweh initiated the new phase when he responded to the clamor of the people by appointing a king, Saul. The independent Israelite tribes had been governing themselves by a kind of primitive democracy, under a council of elders; now they were united in an embryonic sacred monarchy. In later Europe defenders of the divine right of kings would never weary of repeating that God himself had ordained kingship.

Although the tragic career of Saul is one of the great dramas recorded in the Old Testament, his divine sponsorship might have seemed unclear had he not been succeeded by the outlaw chieftain David. David became a truly great leader, worthy of comparison with the heroes of the greatest nations. He began his long reign (c. 1005-965) as a conqueror, destroying the power of the Philistines and subduing other neighboring peoples. As a ruler he was still more impressive, creating a strong kingdom out of rude, quarrelsome tribes, in a land that under the more civilized Canaanites had never been united. He organized a professional standing army and a professional bureaucracy. He set up a national capital at Jerusalem, hitherto an obscure town, where he inaugurated a great building program by erecting a palace and planning the Temple that would make it a spiritual capital as well. For such purposes he had to employ Phoenician architects, engineers, and craftsmen; Israel would never develop a notable style of its own. But he started it on the road to civilization, and himself cultivated the one art in which it did distinguish itself: he was a poet and musician, very possibly the author of some of the Psalms that were attributed to him. In general, Canaan under King David at last began to look like a promised land.

Unfortunately, it was a quite expensive promise. David's bureaucracy included the inevitable tax collectors. Yahweh himself was displeased at the census David had taken, to count the heads of all his subjects for administrative purposes. Even apart from the heavy taxation, the gain of national independence entailed a loss of personal freedom: every Israelite was now liable to forced labor, without compensation. The costs of monarchy became plainer under David's son Solomon. As Harry Orlinsky observed, David was fortunate in that his good lived after him, "his evil was interred with Solomon's bones."

Solomon ruled as a full-fledged Oriental despot. He ascended the throne in the customary manner by getting killed an older brother who had a possibly better claim to it; he was helped by harem intrigue, which continued to feature the history of Israel. Although he made concessions to the false gods of his many foreign wives and concubines, he earned his reputation as a holy king by building the Temple of Jerusalem in magnificent style, even if the style of his imported architects. He also earned his reputation for Oriental splendor; excavations, as of his huge stables at Megiddo, prove that it was a real splendor. He carried through the whole building program of David, adding some grandiose ideas of his own. The costs matched his ideas: to finance his Temple alone he had to impose terrific taxes, conscript many thousands of his subjects, and turn over twenty Galilean towns to King Hiram of Tyre. Only a few could evade the costs, through the corruption of his officials. The immediate outcome of the reign of King Solomon, who became another symbol of Oriental wisdom, was calamitous. A revolt that began in his last years grew into an open rebellion upon his death in 925 B.C. It permanently split the kingdom in two, ending whatever chances the Israelites might have had of maintaining their independence.

Their chances were slim at best, since empire was on the rise again. The northern kingdom of Israel, with its capital at Samaria, managed to hold out until 722, then falling to the bloody Assyrians; they carried off the lost ten tribes (whom European scholars would identify with the American Indians). The little southern kingdom of Judah huddled around Jerusalem until 587, when the Babylonians finished razing its cities, destroyed Solomon's Temple, and carried off into captivity most of its remaining upper class and its artisans. The political history of the kingdoms need not be detailed. Both wrote some bright pages under able kings, and at the end both put up a desperate, heroic resistance. Chiefly they hung on by more or less astute diplomacy, paying tribute to greater powers or playing off their enemies against one another, when not against their fellow Israelites. The important point is that the religion of Israel grew out of almost continuous national crisis, and finally national catastrophe.

Meanwhile the prosperity achieved under David and Solomon had had the familiar social consequences. In the earlier towns there had been no pronounced inequality in wealth and power; excavations disclose larger and smaller houses but nothing like the palaces in the Cananite towns before them. In the kingdom rising prosperity was enjoyed chiefly by a few and led to an increasing gulf between the haves and the have-nots. The masses bore the brunt of Solomon's oppressive taxation; many must have been worse off than their nomadic ancestors. Thereafter Israel was rent by the bitter class feeling of the Iron Age. That this failed to break out into open class war was not due to political enlightenment or reform. As in other Eastern nations, the poor were simply powerless when not spiritless, the more so because the high priests were generally not on their side.

The social law of Israel also was much like that of other nations. It retained some ancient provisions dating from the nomadic days, borrowed others directly or indirectly from the codes of the Canaanites, Babylonians, and Hittites or Hurrians. It was in some respects more humane than these codes, in others harsher, but on the whole it embodied no loftier conceptions of personal freedom or social justice. Like the others, it legalized slavery. It differed principally in that God was made its author, not merely its inspiration; so later Europeans and Americans could argue that slavery had divine sanction. Similarly God confirmed the inferior status of woman, befitting the unseemly manner of her creation out of man's rib by a kind of afterthought. Although women could get divorce in Egypt, only men could under the law of Palestine.

As we approach the great prophets who emerged from this background, it is well to keep in mind that they did not represent the nation of their time. The common habit of contrasting the average practice of our own time with the loftiest thought of other ages may be good for our souls, but it is not conducive to historical understanding. The prophets were so eloquent in indignation and exhortation because Israel was not devoted to the proper service of God as they conceived it. Rich and poor alike had the same material interests as other peoples, or ourselves. They were always attracted to the gods of their more prosperous or powerful neighbors, since these gods appeared to take better care of their people. (Solomon himself had worshiped Astarte in his old age.) They sometimes stoned the prophets, as they would later crucify Jesus. The greatness of Israel stemmed not from its consistent idealism, but from its capacity for spiritual growth.

2. *The Unique Ideals*

You are a Canaanite, the prophet Ezekiel told Jerusalem, and had an Amorite for a father, a Hittite for a mother (16:3). The Promised Land of the Israelites was indeed a great crossroads, where they could draw on a cultural wealth to which all the major peoples before and around them had contributed. Research has steadily magnified their indebtedness to the Canaanites in particular, beginning with their Hebrew language, a dialect they adopted in Canaan; the Old Testament is full of allusions to Canaanite verse and echoes of Canaanite legend. Yet research has also made clearer the striking difference between prophetic Judaism and all other contemporary religions, especially those of their neighbors. The Old Testament describes as "abominations" the characteristic religious practices of the Canaanites. The Israelites would have nothing to do even with the great fertility goddesses, though they had particular need of fertility when they took to agriculture in their arid land. Neither were they seduced by the still more attractive Egyptian idea of a heavenly afterlife. Toynbee has said that the region about Syria became the major birthplace of the higher religions because it was a meeting place for various civilizations. The genius of Israel was displayed chiefly in all that it deliberately rejected from these civilizations.

The great prophets, the men primarily responsible for these rejections, were themselves a unique type. The early prophets of Israel were a familiar breed of soothsayer and wonder-worker. Like their fellow magicians in all the other nations, they were professionals, apparently organized in bands or guilds; King Jehoshaphat could summon four hundred of them to divine God's will about a military project. Like Elijah, they passed on their mantle, or taught their trade, to successors. In the eighth century B.C., however, appeared Amos—the herald of an altogether different tradition. The new prophet was strictly an individual. While always speaking in the name of the Lord God who had called him, he impressed himself upon the community by the power of his thought, his passion, his personality. He never pretended to be a miracle man. No more did he pretend to mysterious powers of divination when he "prophesied" doom—he was merely talking plain religious sense. One of a long line, he was still no professional and taught no successor, for he had no magical tricks to teach. He came to denounce "false prophets" of the old popular type, the wonder-workers. He might denounce the high priests of Israel as well.

A major theme of the prophets, beginning with Amos, was social injustice—the oppression of the poor, to which the high priests were typically indifferent. To "explain" their teaching by the tensions of the Iron Age is only to accentuate their uniqueness. The poor were oppressed in all the nations, at all times; in Israel alone did prophets arise to protest vehemently in the name of God. If Zoroaster preached that God demanded only righteousness, and many a God-sent king, from Hammurabi to Darius, had proclaimed his intention of protecting the poor against the rich and powerful, none expressed such indignation at unrighteousness, none insisted so uniformly and absolutely that men live up to their avowed belief in justice. Nor can any later religion, indeed, match the prophets of Israel. Few Christian saints cried out insistently against social injustice. St. Thomas Aquinas could write very calmly about the naturalness of serfdom, while even gentle St. Francis stressed mainly the blessings of poverty—blessings that a saint may appreciate, but that few of the poor can.

The prophets were as radical in their denunciation of ritualism, their scorn of the universal practice of offering sacrifices. They chose to ignore Yahweh's plain demand for burnt offerings in the Mosaic law. Jeremiah went so far as to say that he had not actually made any such demand (7:22). Micah summed up their repudiation of all the traditional hocus-pocus of ceremonial worship: "What doth the Lord require of thee, but to do justly, and to love mercy, and to walk humbly with thy God?" For this reason too the prophets came into conflict with the priesthood of Israel, which like the priesthoods of all nations was much concerned with rites and forms.

But the priests might join them in opposition to kings who tolerated the worship of alien gods, or any violation of the covenant with Yahweh. Kingship in Israel departed from its Oriental prototype. One account in the Book of Samuel has Yahweh giving his people a king as a boon, which at the time of David he no doubt seemed. (Some of the Psalms indicate that in annual ceremonies the king played a role harking back to the ancient dying god, a bringer of fertility.) Another account in Samuel represents Yahweh as giving in to popular demand in disgust; he warns the people of all the oppression that will come with kingship, but since they will have it, so be it. In either case, however, the king was in no sense divine or eligible for deification. Neither was his power absolute; he was always subject to a higher law, not of his own making and not even his business to interpret. He could be openly denounced on principle. David himself had been rebuked by Nathan for his sins, which the authors of the Old Testament do not conceal. The whole career of the most revered of Israel's kings was narrated with a realism to be found in none of the royal annals of the ancient East.

In making its unique history, Israel was also the first people to write something like real history. For the prophets had introduced a novel theory of history—a consistently ethical interpretation of it. All the other nations knew that the gods ruled it, and that human success depended on pleasing them. Only the prophets spelled out God's pleasure in intelligible moral terms, and declared flatly that failure in particular was due to human evil. In effect they made not God but man responsible for history, put his future squarely up to him. When they foresaw the approaching national disaster they did not resign themselves or content themselves with dire prophecies; they attacked the policies of the kings, exhorted and denounced more vehemently than ever. When disaster struck, first one kingdom and then the other, they stuck to their guns. They made no excuses about the superior power of the Assyrians and the Babylonians, saying simply that Israel was being punished for its sins. It was right that the people should suffer; it would be enough if a "saving remnant" were left to carry on. And when they offered the hope of a Messiah who would restore Israel, it was always with the proviso that Israel repent of its sins and obey the commandments of its God.

This idea of a Messiah, which was to be so fateful for Western history, represented an entirely new religious possibility. To be sure, he was to be a human Messiah—usually a descendant of the house of David. The prophets did not entertain the sublime, or presumptuous, idea that God himself would act as Redeemer, take upon himself the sins of the people; they had long rejected the old notions of a ritual scapegoat or any such ceremonial means of relieving man of the responsibility for his own sins. If even so the idea of a Messiah looks like an obvious kind of wishfulness, of a weak, oppressed people, there were many such peoples—and none of them dreamed such a dream as this. For although the prophets assumed that he would restore the material prosperity of Israel, he became a symbol of peace and justice too. He gave a deeper spiritual meaning to the historic process: God would fulfill himself in man's history, not in the endless cycles of nature.

For such reasons the prophets eventually arrived at a pure monotheism. As a tribal god, the early Yahweh had not denied the existence of other gods; even in the Ten Commandments he had only demanded in jealousy that no other gods be put before him, i.e., that he come first. The prophets' moral interpretation of history required what their feeling told them, that he could have no possible rival. He must be the Almighty, the one and only ruler of man and the universe. Deutero-Isaiah was the first to state this explicitly and emphatically. "Thus says the Lord" of Isaiah again and again: "I am the first and I am the last; besides me there is no god. . . . Before me no god was formed, nor shall there be any after me. I, I am the Lord, and besides me there is no savior."

This monotheism may be considered the logical outcome of not only the growing universalism of the Iron Age but the whole religious development of antiquity—the sky-gods, the supreme gods of conquerors, the universal sun-god of Ikhnaton, the Ahura-Mazda of Zoroaster; yet the God of Israel was again strictly unique. The creator of all mankind, he was himself a Person—not a mere personification of the sun or any other natural force. He was absolutely transcendent, wholly out of this world, with nothing of the old nature deities about him, and no supernatural intermediaries to distract attention from him. He had no rival whatsoever, no Evil Spirit such as Ahura-Mazda had to struggle with. Later on the Israelites learned of Satan, to whom there are several references in the Old Testament, but the greater prophets did not dream that any power could oppose their Almighty.[2] For his sake they renounced all dalliance with the oldest and most popular deities of the East, the Mother Goddess and her lover-son. Under Christianity the familiar supernatural cast would come back—the

---

[2] Satan's most prominent appearance, in the Book of Job, is not as the Lord of Evil but as a kind of prosecuting attorney for God, residing in heaven with him. He does not appear in the Garden of Eden, where Christians have read him into the serpent.

Dying God, the Mother, Satan, angels and demons, saints as intermediaries, kings with divine rights; but this only emphasizes that
prophetic Judaism was the purest monotheism that man had yet
known, or would know again until the rise of another prophet, Mohammed.

There remains the most obvious contribution of the prophets—the
Old Testament. Without them it might have become a great work of
ancient literature; the Israelites started writing the Pentateuch at least
two centuries before Amos, displaying a natural genius as poets and
storytellers. But the prophets made the Old Testament one of the
very great creations of the human spirit. To them it owes its elevation,
directly in their own writings, indirectly in revisions of earlier writings
and the inspiration of later ones. They give it an exalted meaning that
survives all the futile, exasperated controversy over its literal truth:
the history of an extraordinary spiritual quest and growth. They were
not themselves seekers of God—they spoke with impassioned certainty;
yet they were religious revolutionaries. Whether or not they were
speaking the true word of God, they were plainly contradicting many
a word that he had supposedly spoken through Moses. They transformed an ordinary tribal god, as ferocious as most and less civilized
than many, into a universal God of righteousness, even of love. Although they were still thinking mainly of Israel, not of all mankind,
in their spirit later Israelites could draw out the universal implications
of their teaching. Jesus would exhort in the name of the same God,
in the same radical spirit. "It hath been said, An eye for an eye, and
a tooth for a tooth: But I say unto you . . ." and so he went on rejecting
sayings of the old Yahweh, to preach a more explicit gospel of brotherhood.

The prophets did not have the last word, however, in the Old Testament. The Scriptures were edited, canonized, and sealed by priests,
in a rather different spirit. The priests were concerned primarily with
a strict observance of the Law—a ceremonial as well as moral Law.
They could give the impression, remarked by Frazer, that the creation
itself was merely a prelude to the institution of the Sabbath; at least
the Sabbath is much more prominent than a sundry law reading "Thou
shalt love thy neighbor as thyself." The Law was designed to keep
Israel a "peculiar people," set it apart from all the other nations. Probably it did much more than the prophets to hold the people together
during the long centuries of dispersion and persecution that awaited
them. But it was scarcely a mode of emancipation, a stimulus to further

quest and growth. The Sacred Book became a closed book, subject to endless annotation but sealed against fundamental analysis or criticism. Christians took it over and then sealed their own testament in the same authoritarian spirit. They bring us to the question of its ambiguous role in the history of Western freedom.

3. *The Issues of Freedom*

A writer of books must stand in awe of the Bible if only because it would appear to be the most influential book in all history; countless millions more copies of it have been printed than of any other book. A student of freedom cannot long stand in simple awe, or ever regard it as a single work with a single main tendency. The legacy of Israel to the West is so mixed that every generalization about it needs to be qualified. It involves the incalculable powers of religious inspiration, in stirring love and hatred, hope and fear. It includes such important but generally forgotten simplicities as the weekly day of rest, which many Protestants decided must be a day of no play. It has been thoroughly confused by coming through Christianity, which in diverse and contradictory ways has supplemented, modified, distorted, and obscured it. While officially recognizing Judaism as the source of their religion, Christians soon came to ignore its independent claims, to scorn it as the religion of those who had rejected and crucified Jesus, even to forget the fact that Jesus was a Jew, constantly quoting Jewish Scripture as he preached to his fellow Jews. Yet this fact alone makes plain the immense importance of Israel to the West. It points immediately to some positive contributions to freedom of mind and spirit.

To begin with, these resembled the contributions of all the higher religions that emerged in the Axial period. The God of the Prophets could free men from the ancient obsessions with fertility, the ancient compulsions of idolatry, the ancient delusions about magical or ritual means of achieving their earthly purposes. He could nerve men by the moral responsibilities he placed upon them. Demanding only righteousness, he was a God they might get along with by rational means. Popular religion in the West, as all over the world, would return to idolatry and the immemorial ritual methods of propitiating deity; but Christians would at least be less disposed to peer anxiously at livers, to believe that the stars ruled their destiny, to relapse into the unreasoned determinism of the ancient East. Vulgar superstition could never remove the need of righteousness.

More important, however, were the contributions stemming from the uniqueness of Israel. Of these the most positive was its ideal of social justice, or in effect freedom for the poor. Neither Greece nor Rome produced men comparable to the prophets of Israel. Their impassioned indignation, echoed by Jesus, gave the Western world a potentially more dynamic "program for discontent" than any other civilization has had. Hence even godless revolutionaries have paid tribute to them as the first great social reformers, the creators of the social conscience of Western man. The spirit of the prophets burned most fiercely in the Hebraic Karl Marx. Perhaps the strongest proof of their influence is the main reason why it may be overlooked—that their once radical teachings have become pious commonplaces. So too with their implicit ideals of equality and fraternity. Their immediate message was only the equality of all Israelites in their Covenant and before their God— it was not the brotherhood of all men; but it would conduce to such brotherhood as their God became concerned with all mankind. Jesus taught in their spirit, often in their own words. Because of all the Christian cant about these ideals we may forget that any ideal that inspires cant is a live force, just as dishonesty pays only because men are generally honest.

The moral earnestness of the prophets was intensified by a view of earthly life that also entered Christianity, and that made much more earthly difference than we are likely to realize until we consider other great societies. Buddhism and Hinduism, once more, alike taught the wisdom of nonattachment to the natural, temporal world, which they branded either as evil or as unimportant, even unreal. In the West Platonism spread similar ideas, and many Christians would be seduced by this kind of spirituality, or lofty contempt for God's creation. But more typically Christians would take this world very seriously, as the prophets always did. In creating the world, the God of Genesis had repeated seven times that "it was good," and after creating man had called it "very good." The prophets could not believe that evil was inherent in the very nature of the world. Evil was man's doing—and it was man's business to overcome it, here and now, in the only world there was for him. Life on earth was wholly real, and should be as earnest.

The prophets accordingly took time with an entire seriousness. In their view human history had purpose and goal—it was never mere vanity or meaningless cycle. They quickened an active spirit by keeping the future open and refusing ever to foist history on Fate or Chance. During the prolonged national crisis they would not permit the people to subside into the fatalistic resignation of Egypt, into the Mesopotamian kind of anxiety over the will of inscrutable gods, or into any Oriental mode of passivity. They denied the people as well the loftier kinds of religious escape, into rapt contemplation or mystical communion; in preaching God's truth they did not pronounce it ineffable. Man's duty was always clear, and it always called for strenuous moral effort. His goal was a high goal worthy of his best effort. As the prophets dreamed of the restoration of the kingdom of Israel, their image of the future included material success, the ideal of Carthage; but ultimately their ideal was a kingdom of triumphant righteousness.

Implicit in their moral theory of history was a political theory congenial to liberals: the main object of the state was to secure justice, not mere power or prosperity. Also implicit in it was an assumption necessary for ideals of freedom—a respect for the power and the worth of the human spirit. A god who laid such purely moral responsibilities on man was asserting the dignity of man, and might make him proud of his humanity. The prophets themselves proved this dignity, and the real power of the human spirit, by keeping steadfast as the national catastrophe approached, maintaining their faith both in God and in man's responsibility. And though their main concern was the covenanted community, not the individual, the later prophets began to assert the moral rights of the individual. They rejected the traditional belief—enshrined even in the Ten Commandments—that the sins of the father are visited upon the children unto the third or fourth generation. In the days to come, said Jeremiah, "they shall no longer say: 'The fathers have eaten sour grapes, and the children's teeth are set on edge.' But every one shall die for his own sin; each man who eats sour grapes, his teeth shall be set on edge." Ezekiel had God himself announce that "the son shalt not suffer for the iniquity of the father," but that he would judge "every one according to his ways." They were literally unrealistic: children do suffer from the sins of the fathers, as the national catastrophe itself proved. Nevertheless, they were affirming a principle that is essential to a rational morality, and to any claims of individual freedom.

Although the humility of the prophets is more conspicuous, their kind of pride has been obscured by the Christian doctrine of Original Sin and the traditional stress upon man's natural depravity. They all knew well enough that man was disposed to be sinful, but they knew nothing of the Fall of Man. None of them ever mentioned it—nor did Jesus himself.[3] They were more aware of the proud idea that God had created man in his own image. And though the prophets also stood too much in awe of God to be apostles of freedom, their heretical role suggests another latent source of freedom in the legacy of Israel. The humility of Israel was shot through with a kind of willfulness that would reappear in the Puritans, the most Hebraic of the Christian sects.

One may see a spirit of independence in the patriarchs, who set the terms of the Covenant with Yahweh and demanded a great deal of him. Certainly their "stiff-necked" descendants complained often and loudly when he seemed to be scanting his side of the bargain. The prophets and later priests made still heavier demands on God as they extended his moral responsibilities, insisting that he reward righteousness. History was so intensely meaningful because they assumed that God's whole concern was man. All along, moreover, there was some spirit of questioning in Israel, some resistance to authority. It appeared most obviously in criticism of the high priests and the God-sent kings, but it could touch God himself. Even the prophets at times almost complained of his stern justice, intimating that Israel had suffered enough. Job is the classic example of such independence of spirit, which comes through in spite of some pious mistranslation by Christians (just as they introduced a "virgin" into Isaiah, to prepare for Mary, where the Hebrew text had only a "young woman"). In the English Bible Job expresses a conventional piety: "Though he slay me, yet will I trust in him." What Job actually said about God was: "Behold, he will slay me; I shall not survive; nevertheless will I maintain my ways before him." Even so, he got into the Old Testament, to trouble later readers by maintaining his ways and forcing the problem of evil. Dostoyevsky was one of many to be profoundly impressed by

---

[3] Even the old Yahweh who expelled Adam and Eve from the garden said nothing of original sin. His expressed motive was only a jealous fear: "Behold, the man is become as one of us, to know good and evil"—so, lest he also eat of "the tree of life" and become immortal too, Yahweh drove him out of Eden in a hurry. It seems necessary to repeat such commonplaces when Karl Barth, the most dogmatic but best known of modern theologians, never mentions this verse in the course of his elaborate "Christological" interpretation of the Old Testament, in which he emphasizes the Fall. He also ignores the silence of the prophets and Jesus on the Genesis myth. His whole interpretation may strike some as more fantastic because it is based on the premises that the Bible is the *only* source of true knowledge of God and man, and that human reason is wholly incompetent to judge this truth.

Job—and impressed much more by his searching questions than by the Lord's evasive answer, not to mention the trivial happy ending appended by later priests.

The blend of humility and pride is most striking in the portentous idea of the Messiah. Humility made imperious the need of a Messiah, as it intensified the torment of Job over the sufferings of the righteous: Israel did not dream of personal immortality or rewards in heaven. Although many later Jews embraced this dream, the authors of the Old Testament hoped only for the survival of the community on earth. The old Yahweh had made it clear in the Garden of Eden that he did not want man to eat of the tree of life and "live for ever," and the great prophets were never so proud as to believe that they might join their transcendent God. Israel was spared only the fear of eternal torture in Hell, as Yahweh would never permit a Satan either to lord it "for ever" over a realm of his own. But the prophets therefore required more of God in this life. In anticipating a Messiah they were more willful than both the Greeks and the later Christians, for they were demanding heavenly justice *on earth*. Their image of the ideal future, which became the great white hope of Israel, accordingly foreshadowed the modern idea of progress. Unlike other peoples, or the earlier authors of the Eden myth, they placed Utopia in the future, not the past. Some writers have seen a "charter of human freedom" in the vision of Micah: "Neither shall they learn war any more. But they shall sit every man under his vine and under his fig tree."

How much this Hebraic spirit contributed to the dynamism of the Western world it is impossible to say. Christianity confused this issue too by insisting on personal immortality—an image of a heavenly future that might stimulate more active effort in this world, or that might disparage this world, inspire men chiefly to seek a private salvation in another world. Berdyaev expressed a common Christian attitude when he deplored the arrogance of Israel's insistence on justice on earth: "There is a resistance to God, an arbitrary assertion of a purely human justice and truth." A follower of the prophets might find more arbitrary and arrogant the Christian assertion that man is fit to join God in heaven, enjoy an eternity of bliss. In any case, as Berdyaev recognized, the spirit of modern reformers is closer to the spirit of the prophets. The Western faith in progress has been centered on the good life on earth.

Yet the immediate inspiration of this novel faith was scarcely religious. It was a secular faith that arose with the rise of science—a kind of worldly knowledge in which the prophets expressed no interest whatever. They never conceived of a steady, indefinite improvement of man's life by man's own efforts. While always requiring moral effort, they believed only that God in his own good time would send a Messiah, acting like the *deus ex machina* in Euripides. Their image of the ideal future was hardly a logical historical consequence of the past, still less of the dreadful present they knew. It was pure myth. Their spirit was essentially hostile, indeed, to such worldly interests as science. The authors of the greatness and the uniqueness of Israel, they also point to the reasons why its legacy was a major hindrance to the growth of freedom, even the source of the fiercest opposition to it. For the prophets never actually wrote any charters of human freedom. The simple truth is that they were not in the least concerned about freedom—political, intellectual, or religious.

We may dismiss briefly the failings that Judaism had in common with all the major religions, such as the ritualism and legalism that crept back in spite of the teachings of the prophets. The much-abused Pharisees were in this respect no worse than Christian churchmen, who soon began stressing the forms and ceremonies that Jesus had scorned. They were considerably more liberal, in fact, tolerating wide differences in opinion and welcoming some unorthodox ideas, such as resurrection in a life to come; and at their worst they never permitted the pagan idolatry and superstition that have run riot in Christianity to this day—the worship of saints, images, holy relics, etc. Similarly Israel cannot be blamed for the royal autocracy blessed in Christian as in all other religious traditions. Early Christian emperors got this idea directly from the Oriental tradition of sacred monarchy, with the anticipatory sanction of St. Paul. Later Europeans who cited the Old Testament in support of the divine right of kings neglected to note that, excepting Solomon, Israel never permitted its kings to entertain such exalted ideas of their God-given authority and majesty as were held by the "Sun King," Louis XIV. The prophets provided more texts for resisting royal arrogance by their stress on a higher law.

Our concern here is rather with the distinctive elements of Judaism that made it illiberal on principle. The most obvious of these was its claim of a monopoly on religious truth—an exclusiveness that was taken over by Christianity and Mohammedanism, and distinguishes them from all the other major religions of man. From first to last, Yahweh announced that he was a "jealous God" who would tolerate the worship of no other gods. He grew more intolerant as he developed from a local into a universal god, and still more when Christians achieved a political sway that had been denied to little Israel. Such exclusiveness might seem becoming, even necessary to a belief in the One True God, were it not that the most pious men in other high religions have taken for granted that the limited human mind would have partial, variable conceptions of the divine mind, and that it is blasphemous to scorn beliefs sacred to other good men. In Israel, as in later Christendom, the exclusiveness came down to simple bigotry: an unreasoned belief, founded on tribalism, fortified by a provincial ignorance of most other creeds, and especially in Christendom maintained by threats of dreadful punishment for unbelief or mistaken belief. In any case it meant a plain denial of religious freedom. At their most heretical, or in their martyrdom, the prophets never argued for anything like freedom of conscience. The word "conscience" does not appear in the Old Testament.

What does appear is the ugliest legacy of Israel—fanaticism. Religious fanaticism was another of its major innovations in the history of man. It stemmed from the fierceness with which the prophets denounced all dalliance with other gods, and it flourished on a kind of innocent absolutism in their gospel. They spoke "from the heart," with a flaming, unreasoned conviction. In simple men their faith might appear as simple credulity, and encourage positive irrationality. It passed into Christianity as an authoritarian faith, which could flame into a murderous hatred of men of different faith when it acquired political authority.

Again the simple truth is that the great prophets were by no means philosophers. They had no such concepts as "nature," "natural law," or "natural rights"; the only law they knew was based not on a cosmic order but on the decree of a personal deity, the God of Israel. They had as little concept of "man" except as a servant of the Lord. Such questions as they raised never touched the existence or the nature of God. Had they encountered a philosophical skeptic—a type virtually unthinkable to them—their answer to his questions could only have been the question of the Psalmist: "Canst thou by searching find out God?" They could never appreciate the possible values of doubt, the humility of doubt, for they were not themselves inquirers or seekers of the truth. While they clearly introduced new conceptions of God, as clearly they were not asserting the claims of reason or directly appealing to reason. Instead of demonstrating, they exhorted and denounced. They did not appeal either to mystical intuition, or even to religious experience. They simply laid down the new law, in the name of the living God. Under the influence of Greek rationalism Christianity went on to develop an elaborate theology; yet efforts to rationalize or liberalize its faith have always been opposed by fundamentalists, thundering out of an authoritarian tradition. And the fundamentalist always has a strong case. The truth of Christianity, as of Judaism, finally rests not on reason but on revelation—the seemingly irrational claim that the Creator of all mankind revealed himself only to a small, obscure people, which means that to this day he has failed to reveal himself directly to the great majority of mankind.

As the source of this revelation, the Bible became the major barrier to the growth of freedom in thought. Writings that had been freely edited by anonymous priests over centuries, and that were then supplemented by diverse writings attributed to various apostles, were pronounced to be the infallible word of God himself. The possession of such a book, which gave early Christianity an immense advantage over rival mystery cults, gave later Christianity an inexhaustible source of inspiration, and of confusion, bitter controversy, and bloody conflict. One can hardly begin to say how much inspiration untold millions of men have got from so great a book, the more because of their belief that it was the very word of God. One can point more easily to a great deal of tangible mischief done by this belief. Any Sacred Book tends to hamper intellectual and religious growth by sanctifying the ignorance and prejudice as well as the lofty aspiration of its time, limiting when not discouraging or prohibiting free inquiry and criticism. The Jewish-Christian Bible was a more imposing bulwark of obscurantism because it was held to be divinely inspired in a very literal sense, by a jealous God who demanded unquestioning faith and obedience. Inasmuch as God's word was often unclear or seemingly inconsistent, a free rein was given to fancy in metaphorical or allegorical interpretation, but no freedom was permitted to critical judgment on fundamentals. When the growth of knowledge made it apparent that God or the Holy Ghost was also careless of history and ignorant of science, the Bible became a more positive embarrassment to truth seekers. "Freethinkers" were by definition irreligious men, not only mistaken but wicked.

The Old Testament in particular was a mine of harsh texts, for as the record of a religious growth extending over many centuries it naturally contained many relics of a barbarous past. In the savage religious wars between Protestants and Catholics any atrocity could be justified by citing a God who had ordered Saul to slaughter every man, woman, child, and beast in an enemy town, and then punished him for sparing a few. Scores of thousands of old women were burned to death on the authority of as plain a biblical text: "Thou shalt not suffer a witch to live." Orthodox religion became the center of opposition to moral as well as intellectual enlightenment. Men entrenched themselves behind the Bible to fight against almost every major cause in the history of Western freedom—freedom of conscience, democratic government, civil liberties, the abolition of slavery, equal rights for women.

Apart from his jealousy, the God of Israel had despotic tendencies inherited from the fierce old Yahweh, and from the whole religious tradition of the ancient East. Sometimes he was represented as a Father, who could be loving but was always a symbol of stern authority. Much more often he was a Lord or King. Men were typically his "servants" —not the mere "slaves" they had been of Marduk, but subject to the same demand for absolute submission, the same insistence that they existed only to serve him. He could be as arbitrary and unaccountable as Oriental despots, or the gods of Sumer, and once he became almighty was less disposed to permit any question of his ways. Thus he never bothered to answer Job's questions about justice, the undeserved sufferings of the righteous; speaking out of the whirlwind, he merely boasted of his mightiness, though there had never been any question of his power. Nevertheless, Job abjectly humbled himself in the dust. In all the Old Testament there is no Promethean rebel against tyranny. The dominant spirit of Israel was the spirit of Eli when he was told that he and his family were to be destroyed because of the sins of his sons: "It is the Lord; let him do what seems good to him."

If this spirit may be called a sublime humility, it is unlikely to encourage intellectual or moral independence. It too entered Christianity, with the arbitrary God of St. Paul. As the old Yahweh had deliberately hardened the heart of Pharaoh in order to afflict the hapless Egyptians with more plagues, make a more flamboyant show of his powers, so Paul concluded that he was deliberately refusing grace to the stubborn pagans and Jews, choosing to save only a few; and so the appalling idea of predestination was passed down by Augustine, Mohammed, Luther, and Calvin. Today some religious thinkers still glorify an unaccountable God. Not only Karl Barth but the gentle Nicolas Berdyaev has written that men have no right to assert their own standards of truth and justice, or to hold God up to the loftiest ideals they can conceive.

Such difficulties have been aggravated because the God of Israel and Christendom is pre-eminently a Person, given to strong emotion. In reforming the old Yahweh, the prophets often made him kind and compassionate—the God of love taken over by liberal Christianity. More often they stressed his severity and wrath—the awful kind of majesty that made him a God to be feared, as he would also be in Christian tradition. (As Tertullian wrote, "How are you going to love unless you are afraid not to love?") It did not occur to them that jealousy and wrath might seem unbecoming emotions for an Almighty God, and a doubtful way of either exhibiting or inducing wholehearted love; God all too plainly was angry with Israel in their day. Hence it is possible to find more fear than joy in the faith of Israel, as the Puritans certainly did. (Crane Brinton has remarked that there is very little laughter in the Old Testament—except as mockery, "laughing to scorn.") Its language had no word for "religion"—only the expression "the fear of God" to designate the true religion. One may then argue that a God of Wrath, a religion of fear, is more realistic, better suited to both the facts of life and the needs of man; for only a very lofty thinker, far removed from the realities of history and everyday life, could conceive that God simply loved his creatures. But our concern here remains freedom; and fear does not emancipate the spirit. If a healthy degree of it is essential to simple prudence, a man is not free to think and do his best until he has overcome it. If religious fear is likely to make him work harder to save his soul, it is as unlikely to make him struggle for more freedom, for himself or for others.

For all these reasons we must qualify even the contribution of Israel to the cause of social justice. The prophets did not attack the institution of slavery or the inferior status of women. They proposed no concrete measures of reform, made no efforts to change the social or political system of Israel in order to assure more equity. In their own time they accomplished little if any improvement in the lot of the poor—certainly much less than was done for the poor of England by the Utilitarians, led by the unsaintly Jeremy Bentham, who worked for specific legal reforms. In the long run the most important thing is doubtless the burning ideal, not the new law; yet a historian must add a reservation. The prophets set the tradition that would be followed by Jesus, and after him by St. Paul, the Church Fathers, the medieval saints, and countless clergymen—preachers of the ideal who made little or no effort to reform the social, legal, or political system. The tradition survives in the common saying that it does no good merely to change institutions: you must first make over the hearts of men. The historical fact remains that all this preaching—the many centuries of earnest work on the hearts of men—did little to improve the earthly condition of the poor until more secular-minded men set about changing institutions and laws. A believer in democracy is obliged to assume that institutions count for something.

He must discount, too, the prophets' moral theory of history, apart from the narrow legalistic interpretation of it imposed by the priests who edited the Old Testament. Together with their dream of the Messiah, it illustrates the great possible value of myth, even the social necessity of myth, since man can never live by reason alone; but it also illustrates the necessity of reason for criticizing the myth. The prophetic idea that history is God's judgment on men will always seem plausible, as men are always sinful enough to warrant their disasters, and it will always seem apposite, as men can never be reminded too often of their moral responsibilities. Born of a desperate crisis, it may seem especially pertinent in our own age of crisis. Yet a theology of desperation is not clearly a sound norm for civilization. We have intellectual responsibilities too, and these oblige us to recognize that the prophetic view of history was strictly unrealistic. Israel itself may well have suffered more from its fanatical devotion to its jealous God—as in later times it unquestionably did—than from its concessions to alien gods. In any case the prophets had a very limited understanding of history. Like all the peoples before them, they had no concept of scientific truth, no clear criterion for distinguishing fable from fact. They had as little idea of natural causes, physical or social, or any "chain of events," such as the Greek Thucydides analyzed. Except for their moral judgment, they made no clearer distinction between remediable and irremediable evils; the failures of crops and of kings were alike God's judgment on man. So they dreamed that a descendant of the House of David would restore the kingdom, little realizing that David had brought upon Israel the problems that plagued them, that the wise Solomon had aggravated their problems, and that a new kingdom would face them all over again. They were primitivists, idealizing the simplicity and the mythical purity of the lives of their pastoral ancestors.

Ultimately the lofty historical theory of the prophets accentuates the narrowness of the Hebraic tradition that was incorporated in Christianity, and that long contended against the Greek humanistic tradition. They did not have behind them as rich a native culture as did Confucius and Buddha. They were indifferent to almost all except the religious values of civilization: to not only the wealth, comfort, and ease but the arts and sciences, the graces and skills—the material and spiritual goods from which had sprung the evils they denounced, but which had made possible their own lofty visions, far beyond the spiritual reach of the patriarchs. In severing the bonds between nature and man, their utterly transcendent God had drawn a curtain over the natural sources of knowledge, beauty, goodness, and joy. They had little more intellectual curiosity than the author of the myth of Eden, which represented the desire for knowledge of good and evil as a fall from grace, not the rise of man. In their passion for righteousness they had little idea of excellence for its own sake, or of virtue as its own reward. They did not promote the kind of freedom that comes with reason, disinterested love of truth, breadth of interest, hospitality or generosity of spirit.

Their spirit passed into St. Paul, who scorned the foolish wisdom of the Greeks and could see no earthly good except the life "in Christ." It was as apparent in Pope Gregory the Great, who is commonly credited with laying the spiritual foundations of Western civilization, in another period of desperate crisis. It continued to crop up, as in the medieval suspicion of curiosity about the natural world, St. Bernard's denunciation of Peter Abelard, Luther's revulsion against the Renaissance, the Puritan hostility to art. Even so I judge that the Hebraic tradition has not seriously obstructed the creativity of the Western world. Early in the Middle Ages men took eagerly—as had David and Solomon—to the worldly interests that the prophets ignored or scorned; and soon they were intoxicated by the foolishness of the Greeks. I also judge that the prophetic ideal of social justice had a deeper, wider, more abiding influence than their negations, and that many such unsaintly reformers as Bentham were more indebted to them than they realized. It is impossible to calculate with any precision the dual effects of Judaism, or by simple addition and subtraction to come out with a definite sum. But at least there is little question, I believe, that the growth of freedom in the Western world owes much more to the Greek than to the Hebraic spirit.

4. *The Later History of the Jews*

When Cyrus the Great ended the Babylonian Exile and ordered the restoration of the Temple in Jerusalem, many of the Israelites preferred not to return to their impoverished homeland, but to remain in brilliant, wicked Babylon, where they had begun to prosper in trade and industry. Only an ardent minority welcomed the gift of Cyrus and set about rebuilding the Temple. These established a theocratic state, under the rule of a high priest, in which the people came to be known as Judaeans or Jews instead of Israelites. They remained subjects of the Persian Empire, however, and after its fall to Alexander, subjects of the Hellenistic Seleucid Kingdom. In the second century B.C. they rebelled under the Maccabees, setting up an independent kingdom, but in the next century they came under the dominion of Rome. As Roman subjects in a minor province of the empire, they brought upon themselves more national disasters. One of the bloodiest of insurrections ended in the utter destruction of Jerusalem in A.D. 70. When two generations later the benign Emperor Hadrian thought to build a temple to Jupiter in the desolate city, thus to restore something of its former religious glory, the Jews rose up in a still bloodier and more fatal rebellion. All Palestine was devastated, a million Jews were killed or enslaved. As a nation, they had no more influence on history until this century.

Nevertheless, their later history deserves an epilogue, even apart from its intrinsic interest in the record of an extraordinary people, and from the many great men they were to contribute to Western civilization. It throws more light on Judaism, its influence on Christendom, and the issues of freedom. For terrible as were the national disasters, they had profoundly ambiguous consequences. In some respects they proved to be a blessing, materially, culturally, spiritually. In other respects they brought on a much deeper tragedy than the immediate terrific cost in blood and tears.

The Jews prospered in the Diaspora following the fall of Jerusalem to the Babylonians. They continued to spread after the end of the Babylonian captivity; they were esteemed as colonists by the Hellenistic kings, who moved them into new cities and granted them special privileges. They developed capacities for handicraft, trade, and finance for which they had had little scope in their own little kingdom. One sign of their prosperity is that a people who probably numbered less than a million when Jerusalem fell had grown to from four to seven millions by the time of the Roman Empire. Culturally they profited still more from foreign rule and association, discovering capacities for art, thought, and learning that neither the prophets nor the high priests had been disposed to encourage.

Most interesting and significant were their associations with the Greeks. They began rubbing elbows with the Greeks in Babylon, where the fanciful may speculate on an imaginary conversation between Pythagoras and Ezekiel. Athenian coins became the main currency in fifth-century Palestine and inspired the first Jewish coins, on which were represented sacrilegious human figures as well as the owl of Athena. During the Hellenistic era Greek influence became much more marked. It inspired at least one Jewish poet to write a tragedy in Greek form about the Exodus; it may have contributed to the critical spirit of Job, as it more likely did to the vein of Epicurean skepticism in the Book of Ecclesiastes; and it even stimulated deliberate efforts to fuse Judaism and Hellenism, notably by the high priest Menelaus. Above all, it led to the translation of the Torah into Greek, in Alexandria toward 250 B.C.—a unique event in the ancient world, which made the Jewish Scripture the only Oriental scripture available to Greek-speaking peoples, and gave Christianity an inestimable advantage over other Oriental religions. In Greek Alexandria the Jews later produced Philo, their first major philosopher, who anticipated Christian theology by his efforts to interpret Scripture in the light of Greek philosophy. (He was pleased to believe that Moses had been the first real philosopher, and that Plato had learned Platonism from Jewish sources.) Behind Philo lay the chief Greek contribution to Judaism—the high regard for learning that the Pharisees incorporated in Jewish tradition by establishing schools everywhere. Hence in later Europe the "peculiar people" would produce so many brilliant mathematicians, scientists, and philosophers that they acquired a reputation as a peculiarly intellectual people, with a passion for learning that is no more apparent in the Old Testament than are the gifts that in America enabled them to dominate the entertainment industry.

The Hellenistic Greeks had in turn shown some interest in the Jews, tending to idealize them as a "philosophical race" who were free from the decadence of the "modern" world, and who had preserved the early purity of religion; they linked the Jews with the Persian Magi and the Indian Brahmans as a people led by priests and obeying a divine law.

Thus the Stoic Clearchus made them descendants of Indian philosophers and had one of their sages giving Aristotle experimental proof of the Platonic doctrine of immortality. Presumably Greeks were among the many proselytes to Judaism before the Christian era, and there might have been more had they not been repelled or embarrassed by the requirement of circumcision, a theme for derision among their womenfolk. Meanwhile their legends about the philosophical race, which seem to have been inspired especially by the Jewish habit of discussing religion in their synagogues, point to still other ways in which many of the erstwhile Israelites profited spiritually from the national disaster.

Dispersed all over the ancient world, they might realize more fully the implications of universalism and individualism in the teachings of the later prophets. Many gave up Yahweh, who on the face of it had let his people down badly, and became assimilated with other peoples, losing their identity as Jews; but others met the challenge by reaffirming the faith of the prophets. It was during the Exile that Deutero-Isaiah proclaimed the loftiest conceptions of the One God and of the ideal mission of Israel, which through its sufferings would lead all peoples to a knowledge of God, and to an era of universal peace. (His writings take up chapters 40-66 in the Book of Isaiah.) If few were capable of sustaining so sublime a vision as this, foreign rule at least tended to make many fall back on the inwardness of the prophets. When Jerusalem was destroyed again, Johanan ben Zakkai said simply that henceforth the Jews would have only God and his Law, but this would suffice. It sufficed better because there was no longer a high priest or a rich priestly aristocracy ruling from the Temple. The self-sufficient synagogues that replaced the Temple put more stress on conduct, and might escape the ancient spell of miracle and mystery that came over the later followers of Jesus. Then persecution further strengthened the Jewish community, as it had the early Christian community. Christian violence and atrocity gave them no reason to believe that their religion was inferior, and helped them to practice the brotherhood that Christians merely preached.

Still, the Jews had brought on this persecution by their own violent intolerance. Their historians recorded a fateful story. King Jehu lured all the worshipers of Baal in Israel into their temple, by false promises of a religious celebration, whereupon he proved his holy zeal by having them all massacred in cold blood (2 Kings 10). The immensely influential Book of Deuteronomy, supposedly found in the Temple some years before the destruction of Jerusalem by the Babylonians, endorsed such zeal: it made out that God had commanded the extermination of all the previous inhabitants of the Promised Land. The national humiliation that followed did not make the people humbler or simply purify their faith. It naturally tended as well to warp and embitter them, narrow and rigidify their faith. Their Psalms are full of variations on the theme of hatred and vengeance. The characteristic response to the humiliation was summed up in Psalm 137, beginning with its beautiful lament "by the waters of Babylon," and ending with a curse on Babylon: "Happy shall be he who takes your little ones and dashes them against the rock!"

The unique religious growth represented by the prophets soon came to an end as the prophet gave way to the priestly editor, then to the annotator. The priesthood that ruled Judah after the Exile, and gave the sacred writings their final form, was concerned primarily with tightening and enforcing the Law set down in Deuteronomy, which required strict obedience to elaborate ritual regulation and taboo—the most detailed prescription in religious history. Such literal-mindedness had an ironic consequence, later leading to the inclusion of some unorthodox books in the sacred canon because of supposedly holy authorship. (Thus the great Book of Ecclesiastes and the sensual Song of Songs—pure love poetry rooted in an old fertility cult—were admitted because King Solomon was believed 'to be their author.) But immediately the legalism intensified the ancient tribalism of the Jews, making them literally a peculiar people, uncivil on principle. An incidental penalty was that they could not sit down to eat with Gentiles, who served food that was not kosher. More portentous was the ban on intermarriage with Gentiles; Ezra, the greatest of the early priest-rulers, ordered all Jews with foreign wives to divorce them. This policy may well have been necessary to enable the people to maintain their identity, but it helped to make the Old Testament a primary source of the racism that developed in the Western world—most conspicuously among Protestant peoples, who based their faith directly on the Bible.

In Palestine, meanwhile, such piety led to a fierce revulsion against all Hellenizing tendencies. This precipitated the revolt of the Maccabees, who celebrated their success in regaining independence by executing the Hellenizing high priest Menelaus. Their kings soon grew more intolerant, slaughtering thousands of liberal Pharisees. In 63 B.C. their reign was ended by a civil war, which Pompey settled by making Judah a Roman province. Although the Roman-appointed King Herod presently rebuilt the Temple on its most magnificent scale, in the course of an ambitious program of public works, he was hated not only as a despot but as a patron of Greek culture. The common people resented such civilized interests much more fiercely than they ever had oppression by the wealthy. So there arose the Zealots—a party committed to violent, uncompromising opposition to alien rule and alien influence. They massacred not only thousands of Gentiles but many of their more temperate fellow Jews, and eventually led the suicidal rebellions in Palestine, at a time when Roman rule was growing mild, the rest of the Mediterranean world was enjoying an era of peace hitherto unknown, and a Jewish sage observed that only the Romans kept the Jews from swallowing one another alive.[4]

Still more fatal in the long run was the dream of the Messiah. Although Deutero-Isaiah had suggested that as the emissary of a universal God he would lead all nations to the millennium, the prophets mostly proclaimed that he would assure the triumph of Israel over all other nations. Isaiah himself repeatedly lapsed into a crude tribalism. ("Behold, I will lift up my hand to the nations, and raise my signal to the peoples; and they shall bring your sons in their bosom, and your daughters shall be carried on their shoulders. . . . With their faces to the ground they shall bow down to you, and lick the dust of your feet.") If this obsessive delusion is pathetically understandable in view of the long subjection of Israel, it nevertheless reduced Judaism to a worldly success religion, on a primitive plane of success. The Messiah became a symbol of jingoism. The later apocalyptic writers, like many of the Psalmists, gloated over the prospect of the humiliation of other nations, the prostration of all peoples before Israel.

With the coming of Jesus, the dream ended in nightmare. Their tradition had not prepared the Jews, of course, for the claim made by his followers that he was the Son of God—a pagan idea they might be forgiven for rejecting, more especially because according to the Synoptic Gospels Jesus himself had not clearly made such a claim. But a further difficulty was the spirit of the Zealots. If they might have

---

[4] His observation might remind us that the Old Testament preserved some evidence of a humane, civil spirit that survived the long era of bigotry and fanaticism. The lovely short story of Ruth was written in protest against Ezra's blanket condemnation of foreign wives. (It was included in the historical section because its author had made her out to be the grandmother of David.) The humorous short story of Jonah ends with a plainer message of charity, as God spares even the repentant Assyrians—a message often overlooked because orthodox readers mistake the unimaginative Jonah for one of the prophets, and semi-sophisticated readers worry over whether he could really have lived in a whale's belly.

understood this Messiah when he said that he came to bring not peace but a sword, they could not accept him when he counseled submission to Caesar, even to turning the other cheek, and himself submitted to the ignominious fate of crucifixion. Messianic delusions inflamed their hostility to his followers. So the Jews made possible his triumph by driving Christianity out into the Gentile world, where it could take on pagan culture and become an imperial religion; but they began the persecution for which they would be repaid a millionfold.[5]

Altogether, both the glory and the tragedy of Israel may be traced to the singular idea cherished by its people—the exalted, conceited, preposterous idea that they and they alone were God's chosen people. Although other nations had rejoiced in the belief that their tribal gods were the mightiest and would bring them success in war, none had made such exorbitant demands on their gods or professed such extravagant contempt for the gods of other peoples. Only Israel believed that it had a special covenant with the Ruler of the Universe. In spite of the universal implications of their teachings, every one of the prophets insisted on the divine favoritism early affirmed by Amos: "You only have I known of all the families of the earth." This tribal conceit inspired the greatest works of Israel, as it brought out the best in Yahweh too, and it enabled the people to endure when they were scattered over the face of the earth, despised, oppressed, subjected to a more prolonged martyrdom than any unchosen people has ever had to endure. But it never endeared them to their neighbors. They antagonized tolerant Greeks and Romans long before they antagonized the as intolerant Christians. Resolutely, heroically, perversely, fanatically, the chosen people then chose national suicide.

Christians were in this respect less peculiar, as they had made no literal covenant with God and could mingle more freely with the uncircumcised, sit down to a table that was not kosher; but they were no less arrogant and exclusive. Salvation was through Christ alone, they alone were true followers of Christ. This conceit inspired great works in them too; it did much to liberate the extraordinary energy

---

[5] The Sect recently discovered through the Dead Sea scrolls has complicated but not basically altered the tragic story. Calling themselves "the poor," they seem to have anticipated much of the teaching of Jesus, in particular his role as a suffering Messiah, and so have encouraged the speculation that he was originally one of them. If so, however, he rebelled against them too. They were even more devoted to ritual purity than were the Pharisees, and they were more intolerant, being required "to hate all the sons of darkness." There was no room in their creed for charity to good Samaritans, publicans, or sinners.

of the medieval world. Yet it was always a menace to the freedom of all other peoples, from the early pagans and Jews to the "natives" of colonial empires. It split Christendom itself into warring sects, each claiming that it alone knew the true service of a jealous God. It produced the appalling record of Christian persecution—by far the bloodiest, cruelest record in all religious history. Christendom made it plainer that it is sacrilegious for any people or sect to consider itself the elect of God, above all when it professes a belief in a universal God.

| # THE UNIQUENESS OF GREECE

1. The Birth of Freedom

Like the Israelites, the Greeks were keenly aware of their difference from other peoples, whom they called "barbarians," and so were as prone to tribal conceit; but there all likeness ends, and Western history begins. The Greeks had a more reasoned, civilized sense of their difference, based on culture rather than divine favoritism. As early as Herodotus, moreover, this was a conscious difference between East and West. They confused its issues, to be sure, by an artificial geographical distinction between Europe and Asia, idealizing a "Europe" that is actually a promontory off the great land mass of Eurasia, and that had not yet been arbitrarily separated from it by running a line down the Ural Mountains. They dreamed up a mythical conflict between Europe and Asia, beginning with the Trojan War; Herodotus reported that the Persians attacked Greece in order to avenge the defeated Trojans. (Whoever they were, these Trojans had certainly never heard of either Europe or Asia.) Yet the essential distinction they made was cultural. Greeks were free men, living under laws of their own making; "barbarians" were peoples willing to live without freedom, obey without reason. The life in freedom as we know it in fact began with the Greeks.

In general, they made the most radical break with the tradition of "miracle, mystery, and authority." Like Buddha and Confucius, their great spokesmen typically spoke in their own right as men, not as prophets with divine credentials; but the Greeks kept on thinking for themselves and exploring further possibilities. Of all the peoples who contributed to the spiritual ferment of the Axial period, they alone

145

developed an open society in keeping with the new modes of thought. They alone set up a conscious ideal of freedom and rose to political freedom. In Athens they established the first important democratic state.[1]

A particular clue to their uniqueness is a saying of Anaxagoras: "All things were in chaos when Mind arose and made order." More than any other ancient people, the Greeks put their trust in Mind, or reason. While elaborating one of the greatest mythologies, they achieved the greatest measure of freedom from the myth. By rational inquiry they endeavored to explain miracle and dispel mystery, to rationalize the authority of both the gods and the state. Their curiosity grew into a passion for understanding. Thinking for themselves instead of appealing to ancient authority, they began to think about thinking too; they established rules of reasoning, means to systematic thought. In time some even became conscious of their ignorance, and of the possible wisdom of doubt. They realized the diverse possibilities and the ultimate uncertainties that are the necessary condition of freedom of thought; for if man knows the absolute truth about God, the universe, and his own condition, there is little room for inquiry, as little reason for countenancing dissent.

By the same token the Greeks discovered Nature too. They sought to explain the natural world in its given terms, and to deal with it by rational instead of magical means. They were the first people to become clearly aware of natural causes, the conditions of empirical knowledge; arriving at the concept of natural law, they laid the philosophical foundations of science. The knowledge of such necessities, which immediately sets a limit to man's freedom but ultimately enables him to gain more power, helped to emancipate the Greeks from bondage to magic, and strengthened their disposition to feel at home in the natural world. Unlike Hindus and Buddhists, they sought wisdom and happiness by fulfilling and perfecting nature, not by escaping or suppressing it.

For with nature they had discovered human nature—Man. They were also the first people to become fully conscious of man as a maker.

---

[1] In this chapter I am substantially repeating the account of the Greek achievement that I gave in *The Uses of the Past, The Loom of History,* and *The Spirit of Tragedy.* Having reviewed this achievement three times, I must confess to a little weariness as I set out once again. I can only add that my present context has called for considerable additional materials and some shifts in emphasis, but has given me no reason to revise my basic judgments. Further study of the first millennium B.C. has deepened my conviction of the supreme importance of the Greeks in the history of freedom.

Realizing that laws and political institutions were man-made, the Greeks were freer to make them over to suit their own purposes. They set about creating their supreme work of art, which was the perfection of man himself. They set up their characteristic ideal of *arete*, or all-around excellence, while on their national shrine at Delphi they inscribed their characteristic motto—Know thyself. And with this growing consciousness of the powers and possibilities of man emerged the self-conscious individual. The higher religions of the first millennium all offered the individual a measure of spiritual autonomy, in means to inner peace or freedom from anxiety, but the Greeks gave him more actual autonomy in social life, through self-respect and opportunities for self-realization by other means than self-abnegation or service of the gods. He could more freely cultivate his natural gifts and fulfill his natural desires. He began expressing himself in lyric poetry, dwelling on his personal joys and sorrows instead of the affairs of gods and god-kings. He might even stand out against the community on principle, as Socrates dared to do.

Because of all these discoveries, the Greeks were remarkable for not only the brilliance and originality but the range and diversity of their achievement. No other culture of the first millennium was so many-sided. Their much-celebrated art, though distinctive enough, was perhaps the least novel of their creations. Their literature was unparalleled in its variety, ranging from lyric and epigram to epic, and including such new forms as comedy and tragedy. Their philosophy was likewise by far the most varied and comprehensive; while the Indians devoted themselves chiefly to metaphysics and theology, and the Chinese almost entirely to ethics, the Greeks speculated on all the basic problems of thought. They alone went on from natural philosophy to extensive achievement in science. They made history too a branch of rational inquiry, instead of royal annals or religious propaganda. The many basic terms they contributed to our lexicon—history, physics, geometry, geography, logic, theology, ethics, politics, aesthetics, etc.—testify to the literally extraordinary range of their thought.

There remains a significant exception: the Greeks did not develop a higher religion. Although their philosophy would be a major influence on Christianity, they themselves produced no man comparable to Zoroaster, Buddha, Confucius, and Deutero-Isaiah, or later to Jesus and St. Paul. It might be said that they made their chief contribution to religion by their worldly failure, on which Christianity flourished. We shall presently have to study this failure, which for lovers of

freedom is as depressing a story as any in history; and we shall then
have to qualify all these initial tributes. But first it must be said that
what made possible the distinctive achievements of Greece was its
essential humanism. While its Olympian gods amiably lent a hand,
they did not lead the way. The man Homer had put them in their
place; Thales founded natural philosophy by not calling them in to
explain the world; Solon got no tables from them when he gave Athens
new laws; Aeschylus taught them the ideals of justice that the Greeks
had worked out for themselves; Socrates set out on his quest of wisdom
without invoking their aid. Presently we shall have to consider, too,
the issues raised by this humanistic spirit; but the immediate question
is how and why the life in freedom began.

It is well now and then, Emerson remarked, to take a look at the
landscape from between one's legs. As the glorious Greeks have come
down in our tradition looking much like their sculptured gods, all
radiant and serene in the "miracle" of their achievement, and as we
nevertheless know that they lost their independence in convulsions of
ungodly behavior, we might well begin with an incongruous perspective on this miracle. Their own poet Hesiod offers such a perspective.
Living at the dawn of Greek culture, in the eighth century B.C., he
mistook it for a twilight, calling his era the Iron Age. This would have
been an accurate name for it except that to his primitivistic way of
thinking it represented the last stage in degeneration from a supposed
Golden Age—a myth that would haunt Greeks to the end of their
history. In *Works and Days* Hesiod dwelt on the thankless, toilsome
life of the farm, but still described it as the "natural" life for man;
he denounced the folly of taking to trade and going to sea. Wise in
the ways of taboo, he was a son of Boeotia, an agricultural region proverbial among the Greeks for stupidity, where his father had migrated
from Cyme in Asia Minor, an Aeolian city also proverbial for stupidity.
Strabo reported that for three hundred years the Cymeans had levied
no tolls for the use of their port, got no revenues of any kind: "It was
late before they perceived that they inhabited a city lying on the sea."

Meanwhile other Greeks were thriving on the folly of trade in Ionia,
a region a little to the south of Cyme. They had very early got on to
the idea of a city lying on the sea, and no doubt had levied as high
tolls as the traffic would bear. The Ionians were known for their
smartness. Although it did not endear them to the Greeks in "Europe,"
it enabled them to build up such celebrated cities as Miletus, Ephesus,
Smyrna, Samos, and Chios. And it was in these busy seaports in Asia

that the Greek genius began to flower. The great fathers of the arts and sciences—Homer, Thales, Pythagoras, Herodotus, Hippocrates —all came from Asia Minor.

But who were these Ionians? We know only that their antecedents were obscure, mixed, and more or less inglorious. When shortly after the Trojan War (*c.* 1200 B.C.) Homer's Achaeans were overwhelmed by barbarian Dorians pouring in from the north, survivors evidently made a stand or found a refuge among related peoples elsewhere in Greece, as in Attica. Under continued pressure, some of their descendants presently began migrating to Asia Minor. Among these emigrants were Aeolians (as at Cyme), who got their name from a word meaning "variegated." The Ionians liked to think that they came from Athens, and most probably some did (though later Athens was not proud of them), but they too had no common ancestry, even no common language; Herodotus, a Dorian from Halicarnassus to the south of them, noted four different dialects in Ionia. While they had had to do some fighting to gain a foothold, their own legends suggest nothing like a crusade or a Heroic Age. Like the Hebrews, they profited from the confusion of the dark age, the absence of any strong imperial power in the region. Very little is known of the two or three centuries during which they established themselves. As they were proud of their Homer and the Heroic Age he celebrated, they might not have appreciated Macaulay's comment on the much more significant kind of history they were making during this period: "The circumstances which have most influence on the happiness of mankind, the changes of manners and morals, the transition of communities from poverty to wealth, from ignorance to knowledge, from ferocity to humanity—these are, for the most part, noiseless revolutions."

The mongrel Ionians at least make clear that the secret of Greek success was not race or blood, except for the possible advantages of mixed blood. Those who founded Miletus—destined to become the greatest of their cities—unwittingly exploded the racial myth, for according to their own legend they brought no wives along and settled down with Carian women whose menfolk they had slain. They did have some advantage, however, in their Indo-European ancestry. The Greeks everywhere brought with them their sky-gods, patrons of vitality rather than fertility, who encouraged a fearless expression of their own virtue and power, and to whom they felt closest when they were most fully realizing themselves, not humbling themselves. As they settled down they came under the spell of the local fertility gods and

F*

goddesses, who had ruled the countryside since times immemorial; these chthonian deities would live on side by side with the Olympians, even breed with them, in a quite illogical if not unseemly manner. But the gods of light remained the national gods of Greece. Homer would purify the ancestral religion, realize its ideal possibilities, in the greatest of the Indo-European epics; while the peasant Hesiod tried to enlighten the Olympians about the needs of the poor.

The Ionians also make clear that the natural environment was not the key to the Greek achievement, inasmuch as not only the Cymeans but earlier and later peoples alike failed to make of it what they did. Nevertheless, it too afforded some real advantages. Ionia was a beautiful land, with fertile river valleys and coastal plains under bright skies. Relatively barren mainland Greece at least yielded the olive and the vine, the Mediterranean staples, and it was a still more beautiful land, bathed in brilliant sunshine. The Greeks responded to their radiant setting in their art and their outdoor life.[2] They were stimulated as well by the challenges of their environment, which nowhere made life easy. In Asia Minor they had established themselves in scattered outposts on a kind of frontier, surrounded by alien peoples and supported by no mother country; and as they prospered they sent out colonies, to repeat the experience. In rocky Greece, mostly ill-suited to agriculture, they could prosper only by trade and industry. Everywhere they took to the sea, in defiance of Hesiod; almost all their greater cities were seaports. Only the Spartans consistently disdained commercial pursuits, and they were the least creative of the Greeks; though unfortunately we must keep in mind that they triumphed over the brilliant Athenians.

Meanwhile we are recalled to the legacy of Minoan Crete. Although

---

[2] In *Civilization and Climate* Ellsworth Huntingdon has explored the influence of climate on history, arguing plausibly that while it is not the most important determinant, it is the most fundamental one. Historians have tended to neglect its influence if only because it is so obvious; in deciding—by ways often not too clear—what are the "important" events, they may forget that nothing is more important than sunshine. They may also forget the simplicities that strike any traveler. One who has visited Greece and the Aegean islands can readily understand how the Greeks might have been stimulated by the dazzling beauty of their surroundings, especially by the distinctness of contours and intensity of colors, to create the kind of art they did; while a traveler to the gaunt, sere Anatolian plateau may better understand why the Hittites never developed a gracious art and culture. Yet geography and climate are plainly only conditions, not causes of cultural achievement or freedom of spirit. Countless peoples have failed to respond notably to beautiful surroundings or invigorating climate. When Hippocrates observed that fertile soil and mild climate made Asiatics more gentle and affectionate but also more torpid and cowardly than Europeans, he overlooked the fact that none of these adjectives fitted the Ionians.

we cannot know, once more, just how much the Greeks owed to the lively Minoans, their memories of their predecessors disclose that they did not have to start from scratch. In any case, they followed the Minoan example. The plainest reason for their worldly success was their commercial enterprise, involving the "base mechanic arts" that their philosophers would later look down upon. The Ionian cities fully exploited their location on the sea, as well as river valleys leading into the interior. They built merchant fleets to compete vigorously with the Phoenicians for the eastern Mediterranean market, and by 700 B.C. had largely won this trade war; Egypt presently allowed them to take over the city of Naucratis in the Nile Delta as a trade center. Now they were also beginning the great colonizing movement that over the next two centuries was to dot the Mediterranean and Black Sea coasts with Greek cities. They were about to demonstrate more clearly than either the Minoans or the Phoenicians why commerce, for all its unideal motives, might promote the growth of freedom more than did the rise of the higher religions. It was not only giving them the wealth and leisure for cultural pursuits but directly stimulating their intelligence, advancing their knowledge, sharpening their wits, fostering habits of rational calculation and speculation.

In particular, it had carried them into a greater, older world. The dawning of high culture in Ionia—the period in which, it is often said, the modern Western world was born—is known to archaeologists as the "Oriental period" of Greek culture. Like the Minoans before them, the Greeks borrowed heavily from the technology, art, and learning of the ancient East, while borrowing as well from other parvenus—their alphabet from the Phoenicians, coinage from the Lydians, the flute from the Phrygians. Thales, Pythagoras, Herodotus, Democritus, and other Greek pioneers kept traveling to Egypt and Babylon to acquire more learning. That the older peoples took over little in return made more apparent the peculiar genius of the Greeks, which lay not merely in native originality but in their curiosity, adaptability, and openness of mind. If they profited from their Indo-European tradition, they profited much more by their relative freedom from sacred traditions.

Hence the Greeks were the first people to take full cultural advantage of the cosmopolitan era. Hellenic culture became so rich because it was so many-faceted, not so pure or purely "classical" as most of its admirers have made out. Embracing forms and contents picked up from many diverse sources, it remained open to diverse, inconsistent, unclassical influences. Plato, whom many have regarded as the supreme Greek, might be called the most "Oriental" in his otherworldly kind of spirituality. In his *Laws*, which propose strict regulation suggestive of a Committee on un-Greek Activities, he also reminds us that most of his fellow Greeks did not live by the Apollonian ideal of poise, restraint, "nothing to excess." We may better understand and honor this ideal if we remember that the Greeks were an unusually energetic, restless, turbulent people, given to excess. We might expect as much from their extraordinary creativity—such creativity does not make for harmony or serenity. Had they actually been devoted to the classical ideal they might have enjoyed a longer, happier history; but they would never have made so brilliant a one.

Above all, the Greeks were the first people fully to realize the revolutionary social possibilities of the Iron Age, with its cheap tools. Their rise in the world was marked by the rise of many small, independent farmers, merchants, and artisans. Individual initiative and enterprise might now count as much as noble birth, and shake off the traditional fetters of priests and kings. The growing spirit of individualism was dated by one Aristonothos, who about 700 B.C. signed his name on a vase he made—the oldest known such work in existence. Upon the invention of coinage, the Greeks not only hit on the idea of small change but made more use of money than other peoples did to reduce serfdom and forced labor. For the first time in history common men now had a real chance to save, build up an individual surplus, and solidly improve both their economic and their social status. And whether consciously or no, the Greeks seized on the idea of contract implicit in money transactions among free men. Contract—a rational agreement—began to displace fixed status and unreasoned tradition as the basis of their most characteristic political institution, the *polis* or "city-state."

Classical in its proportions, the *polis* was another source of unclassical confusion and excess. Thus "Ionia" was only a geographical term, denoting an area where a dozen separate cities competed or fought with one another; it never denoted a nation. Neither did "Greece." Because Greek philosophers soon began talking of universals and eternal essences, immutable forms of Being, we may forget that Greek culture was rooted in local, temporal communities, highly unstable forms of political being. Their devotion to the *polis* was the most obvious reason why the Greeks eventually lost their independence. Yet this *polis* was an essential condition of their freedom in the great classical period. As they spread all over the Mediterranean world, they did not build an imperial state, a bureaucracy, or anything comparable to the "hydraulic" societies. Instead, they learned to govern themselves in intimate little cities, grew more accustomed to being their own masters. They developed their independent spirit in these independent city-states, where there was no remote sovereign and government was a visible public affair.

All such conditions still do not fully explain the brilliant achievement of the Greeks. It would be futile in any case to seek the "real" or "ultimate" cause of this achievement, since such causes are unknown even in physics, the most exact of the sciences; but their kind of achievement is least amenable to strict determinism. The most significant thing about them is that somehow they became *conscious* inquirers, critics, and creators. If all their thought was perforce historically conditioned, it was highly individualized and diversified, no simple product or reflection of the "historical process," and it then reacted upon this process. From the outset of human history genius played an incalculable part; but the free-spirited Greeks now force such questions as how much power conscious ideas and ideals may have in shaping society, how much difference philosophy, literature, and art may make in the march of events, how much influence the great pioneers in thought may wield on the masses of unthinking men. If we cannot answer these questions either with assurance or precision, we can no longer disregard them. Unconscious, involuntary determinants may have greater force than mental determination; but in the Greek world this is too plain to be ignored.

2. Homer: The Distinctive Mentality

"All men's thoughts have been shaped by Homer from the beginning," wrote Xenophanes. This was an impressive tribute to a minstrel-poet, inasmuch as Xenophanes was a philosopher and deplored Homer's influence. No doubt he overrated it: the thought of ordinary Greeks was shaped by much older traditions, which always lurked in the depths of their minds. Yet he was substantially right. Homer was a primary source of all that was most distinctive in the Greek mentality; his epics were in a real sense the Bible of Hellas. As far as records go, the history of Greek freedom begins with this minstrel—not with any great statesman, thinker, or prophet.

Hence it begins in a further anomaly. The Greeks knew nothing at all about the man they revered above all others. By way of his biography they had only conflicting, more or less preposterous fables; even the torpid Cymeans could put in a claim that their city was his birthplace. Modern scholars have conducted exhaustive philological and historical researches, only to deepen the uncertainties about the first great writer in the Western world. It is not even certain that there ever was a man Homer. Although most scholars now believe in him, some still maintain that the *Iliad* and the *Odyssey* were written by different poets, others that both were the work of a flock of anonymous minstrels or redactors. They disagree as widely about his time, placing him anywhere from the eleventh to the seventh century B.C. Nevertheless, their controversies need not detain us. It is certain enough that he (or they, whom we might as well keep calling Homer for convenience) lived in the Ionian period, writing out of a tradition that preserved memories of the Mycenaeans, but writing as a spokesman of a new society.[3] The Greeks themselves never doubted the existence of their Homer. And if we may discount the contribution of the man, we cannot disregard the influence of the works that came down in his name. Possibly the man only expressed ideals already shaped by his predecessors; but at the very least he gave them such memorable expression that they became the national ideals of Hellas, made the Greeks aware of what united them and distinguished them from all other peoples.

Even Plato, his severest critic, testified to the depth of Homer's influence. Mind you, he wrote scornfully, here is the poet lauded as "the educator of Hellas"; but he had to deal with the unholy educator because most Greeks had taken him to heart. All their artists had long been representing the gods as the glorified human beings he pictured, and according to Herodotus, had been the first to name. Other writers, notably Aeschylus and Sophocles, were proud to acknowledge their indebtedness to him. He was nowhere more revered than in Athens during its great days; here his epics were recited by relays of minstrels

---

[3] Excavations at Mycenae, which was never more than an insignificant town after its destruction by the Dorians, have confirmed the accuracy of some of his pictures of Mycenaean life. They have also stamped other details, such as temples with cult statues, as unmistakably Ionian. In general, Homer's Troy resembled a Greek *polis* more than it did either Mycenae or Troy VII—the layer in the mound of Troy now identified with Homer's city.

at the great national festivals, and became the core even of formal education. Alexander the Great, perhaps his most ardent pupil, took the *Iliad* along as he set out to overthrow the Persian Empire, and inaugurated his crusade against "Asia" by ceremonies at the shrine of Homer's Troy. Later the Roman conquerors too came under his spell. As they took over the Greek world, in the process going to school under the Greeks, they learned that his Trojan hero Aeneas was the father of their race; and in the *Aeneid* Virgil tried to do for them what Homer had done for the Greeks. Under Roman rule the Greeks continued to revere their great educator. Dio Chrysostom reported that in a colony he visited on the distant borders of the empire, almost all the people still knew the *Iliad* by heart, and cared to read nothing else.

More important, however, was the indirect, largely unconscious influence of Homer. Much of his spirit persisted under new forms as the Greeks went on to build a society quite different from his own. For his primary virtue as an educator was his liberality or breadth. Neither prophet nor conscious pedagogue, he exemplified an imaginative and intellectual freedom that might still inspire the Greeks when they were learning new lessons in new schools.

To begin with, he helped immeasurably to make art the mode of emancipation that it ideally may be. In all the great societies before Greece, art had had some such effect as a creation of man's own spirit, an expression of his mastery; yet it everywhere became most obviously a conservative force, serving primarily the interests of high priests and god-kings, immortalizing the reigning superstitions and delusions, sanctifying the tyranny of the status quo. With Homer it still served immediately the interests of an aristocratic class—he showed no concern over the lot of common folk; but he expressed much more than class interests. One reason for believing that there was a man Homer, and that he was a maker, not merely a transmitter, is his unmistakable superiority over his traditional materials. As an aristocratic minstrel, celebrating the exploits of heroes who aspired chiefly to the winning of fame and plunder on the battlefield, he recorded a good deal of slaughter in gruesome detail, to the gushing out of blood, brains, and bowels. In his own right he was much wiser and more humane than his warrior-heroes, stating explicitly his dislike of Ares, the god of war and "enemy of mankind," and displaying an urbanity uncommon in heroic epics. As uncommon was his artistic mastery of his materials. Granted a good deal of sprawl and repetitiveness, he maintained a firm grasp of his main theme and achieved an exceptional clarity in design as well as detail. His epics represent an astonishing triumph over the kind of fabulous confusion and extravagance that run through the Babylonian Epic of Gilgamesh—another traditional poem, which had behind it a thousand years of thought and artistry.

In a historical view, the most significant triumph is Homer's treatment of myth. We cannot be certain just how seriously he took the mythology that fills his epics, but we do know that he was selective, and so by implication critical. He suppressed many barbarous myths that were popular in his time, as is known from other sources (including Hesiod). He openly disdained some ancient beliefs, for example when Achilles expresses his contempt for the raging river-god with whom he has to fight in crossing the Scamander. In particular Homer ignored the most venerable deities in his world—the fertility daemons, the mother goddesses, and the dying gods, including Dionysus. If his attitude toward his own Olympian gods remains uncertain, this suggests more strongly that he used myth freely for both poetic and religious purposes. Unlike all the Eastern peoples, including the Israelites, he in effect possessed the myth, was not possessed by it. He thereby made the traditional mythology a potential treasury instead of an intellectual nuisance. It became something of a nuisance for philosophers, while it might befuddle ordinary Greeks, who were like to mistake fable for fact; but the great tragic poets handled it with the imaginative freedom of Homer, to suit their different poetic purposes and express their different religious thought.

Another sign of such freedom is the basic realism and rationality of Homer. As he peopled a world virtually free from black magic and taboo, so he banished the evil spirits that plagued Eastern peoples, the monsters that Gilgamesh had to struggle with. Some fearful creatures begin creeping back into the *Odyssey,* the later of the epics, and at all times his heroes have to reckon with the unpredictable gods; but essentially they live, fight, and die in the natural world. While plenty of mystery remains in this world, Homer's men do not depend upon miracle or magic in dealing with it, nor anxiously consult oracles. Having paid their ceremonial respects to the gods, they choose and carry out their own purposes, sometimes even in defiance of the gods. Hence the later philosophers who attacked the religion of Homer still owed a great deal to his freedom from superstitious awe, which cleared the way for rational criticism. Xenophanes could go on to conceive of a supreme god "not like mortals either in form or in thought," and make his famous epigram that if donkeys could speak they would describe God as a superdonkey—an epigram that one cannot imagine coming out of Israel. Although no philosopher himself, Homer had also heralded the professional "lover of wisdom": his wise Odysseus marks the transition to an age of sophistication and enlightenment.

Modern readers may take for granted and therefore overlook as remarkable a sign of Homer's emancipation—his humor. All the ancient societies must have had folk humor (or so in humanity we must hope), and they may have had professional comic writers, but their serious literature has scarcely a trace of humor; presumably it was beneath the majesty of god-kings, or the dignity of scribes. Homer is the first great writer clearly to indulge in it. Moreover, it suggests not merely playfulness but detachment, a kind of philosophical reserve, for it is most pronounced in his treatment of the gods. He anticipates the irreverent comedy of Aristophanes in farcical scenes of the gods brawling and bawling on Olympus, or getting "knocked all over the place" by their father Zeus. Zeus himself provides comic relief in the *Iliad* as he makes a fool of himself on Mount Ida, seduced by the blatant wiles of Hera, itching all the more when she coyly reminds him how shameless it was to make love in so public a place.

Such scenes might make one wonder whether Homer really believed in these mythical gods at all. If most ancient peoples were not so uniformly solemn about their gods as the Israelites were, they never made such open fun of the gods as this. Hence some critics have deplored the intrusion of so blasé a spirit in the Bible of Greece. At least it brings up the glaring deficiencies of Homer's religion, in an age that elsewhere was about to give birth to higher religions.

His Olympians were not spiritual beings, of course—only glorified men and women. Apart from their notorious philandering, with mortals as well as with other deities, their behavior was often scandalous even by human standards. They could act like the fools and bitches they called one another. In their dealings with men they were arbitrary and capricious, or consistent only in their rank favoritism. Although their overlord Zeus was beginning to show some concern for justice, he still liked to put on tyrannical airs, flaunt the illusion that he was all-powerful, if only because his jealous wife and unruly children kept showing up the illusion. The Olympians were accordingly as unsatisfactory for philosophical as for ethical purposes. They could answer none of the first and last questions because they had not created this world, and were no more responsible for the condition of mankind than for the life of nature. When the Greeks began to conceive of One

God, a truly spiritual being, they tried to name him Zeus, but the name could never stick: aside from difficulties in living down his adulterous past, the feudal lord of Olympus was hopelessly unqualified for any universal responsibilities. The most that can be said for the Olympians in this regard, I again conclude, is that they make plainer the real progress of the human spirit; for no civilized man today would ever dream of worshiping them.

Yet in their own day they too represented a clear progress. In a historical view, one may have much more respect for Homer's Olympians, and appreciate in particular their contributions to the cause of freedom. For one thing, Homer brought order out of the age-old religious chaos by reducing the gods to a well-defined family and putting them in their place on Mount Olympus.[4] As a group they could compensate for their individual caprices and shortcomings; each had his own special interests and different favorites among men, so that every individual or community might count on the devotion of a congenial deity. Most important, Homer made a great advance simply by creating the gods in man's own image. The divine was no longer identified with natural forces, no longer symbolized by stone, snake, or bull, but was identified with humanity, represented in ideal human form. Only by fully realizing his humanity, the spirit that distinguishes him from the brute world, can man attain to true spirituality. And as Homer naturally created the gods in a Greek image, he endowed them with his own civilized qualities. If they were temperamental and sometimes spiteful, they were generally gracious, essentially reasonable, never so savage as the old Yahweh in his jealous or wrathful moods. They could smile, as Yahweh never could. By according them a decent respect, men could hope to maintain decent relations with them.

For the Olympians had the virtues of their defects. Relieved of all cosmic responsibilities, they lived at ease on Mount Olympus, feast-

---

[4] The story of their mongrel antecedents, which has been worked out in considerable fascinating detail by modern scholars, is summarized in my *Loom of History* (pp. 83-86). Here I should repeat only that the innumerable illicit love affairs of the Olympians were not due to simple wantonness. As the Greeks moved into old lands, they were generally too pious, or too politic, to kill off the local gods and goddesses; and the most convenient way of domesticating these deities was to make them offspring of the Olympians. As the father of the blessed gods, Zeus naturally worked hardest in this cause of international good will. Admittedly he gave no signs of embarrassment in acting the part of heavenly bull, but at least he sacrificed whatever chances of domestic peace he may have had. His wife Hera, originally a mother goddess who had been forced into marriage with him, could never forgive him all his affairs with nymphs and goddesses.

ing, laughing, going to bed at night; so their worshipers did not have to live in constant fear of them, or of the dark. Relieved in particular of responsibility for the crops, which were taken care of by the hard-working fertility daemons, they became associated with the beauty and joy of nature, the radiance of sun and moon, the passion of the Greeks for light. ("Make the sky clear," prays Ajax in the *Iliad*, "and grant us to see with our eyes. In the light be it, though thou slay me!") Glori-fied human beings, the gods could be further educated and civilized; they became primarily civic gods, patrons of culture. Unable to assure private salvation, they encouraged a rich communal life, fostering all the arts. Never almighty, they showed some jealousy in their demand for the customary ceremonial attentions, but they could not be so fiercely intolerant as Yahweh, and they never declared that man's whole duty was to serve them. They authorized no sacred book, no rigid dogma, no powerful priesthood, no authoritarian church. They left the Greeks free to inquire, pursue truth, explore other ideal possi-bilities, aspire to a full life of their own. Both the limitations and the values of Homer's Bible may be summed up in the statement that it was no Bible at all in the Christian sense, and that he gave the Greeks no word for either "God-loving" or "God-fearing."

Now, the heavenly Olympians never really lorded it over the Greeks. The chthonian gods remained popular, and in time grew more so; Apollo, the favorite Olympian, had to admit Dionysus into the national shrine at Delphi, though Homer had denied him admission to Olym-pus; and more gods poured in from the East, to bring back the religious confusion that Homer had reduced to order, and to belie the alleged Greek genius for classical simplicity, clarity, and harmony.[5] We shall have to keep returning to the fantastic conglomerate that constituted Greek religion. Nevertheless, the Olympians were a vital force in classical Greece. They were intimately associated with the patriotism that was its living religion, especially in Athens, presided over by Athena. Indirectly they made possible the whole rich life of the *polis* by the freedom they permitted—a freedom that could hardly have been achieved if the chthonian gods had had it all their own way. They had an enduring influence in the essential humanism of the Greek spirit,

---

[5] A sufficient example is Smyrna, which had perhaps the strongest claim as Homer's birthplace. The cults here came to include Zeus in several of his sixty-odd manifestations, Asclepius, Dionysus-Briseis, his mother Semele, the Sipylene Mother, the Ephesian Artemis, the Syrian Atargatis, the Egyptian Isis, Nemesis, Tyche, Hestia, "Lady-Moon," the river Hermes (though Homer had ridiculed river-gods), and even Homer himself, who never gave the least hint of pretensions to divinity.

the abiding belief that man is closest to the divine when he is at the height of his own powers. They proved their own virtue even as they began fading out of the scene. Although displaying some understandable resentment of their rivals, especially the newcomers from the East, they retained their dignity, retired in good order, and made do with the heavenly sinecures they were pensioned off with. The blessed immortals died a natural death. Their creator, who had been indulgent of their foibles, might have rejoiced in the thought that they did not have to be killed.

Indeed Homer might even have foreseen their death. Although he declared them immortal, he had a deep sense of mortality, he could be ironical about the gods, and in any case he may have felt in his bones that they too were subject to the universal fate. Certainly the story got around that Zeus might eventually be overthrown, as he had overthrown his father Cronus. And Homer at least knew that Zeus was subject to Moira—a mysterious, shadowy, but inexorable Necessity governing both gods and men; more than once the father of the gods lamented that he could not save his favorite heroes from their preordained fate. Moira could suggest to later philosophers the idea of natural law, or a lawful universe. Meanwhile it points to the profounder implications of Homer's Bible.

In his basic realism, Homer had an acute sense of necessities, or the inescapable limits to human freedom. Again and again he returns to the sad truisms about mortality, the generations of men that pass like the leaves and are gone forever. As insistently he repeats that no man can escape the fate in store for him. He knows that character has much to do with fate, but as a realist he also knows that on earth there is much sorrow and no clear justice. Although one may gather that Moira is in some sense a moral law, and that like Zeus in some moods it authorizes the punishment of evildoing, it is not a divine intelligence or a divine purpose, and is in no sense a benevolent Being concerned with man's welfare. It may seem a harsher necessity because it is utterly impersonal, requiring Zeus to forgo his compassionate impulses. And the fate of man is the more tragic because Homer offers no hopes of a heavenly life to come. Death is not even the peace of sleep. Hero and common man alike end in Hades: a ghostly underworld not yet set up for eternal torture but dreadful enough for heroes, whose shades are aware that they are only shades, and can never hope to enjoy any of the goods of life. During the classical period only a few Greeks dreamed of heaven. Homer's tragic view of life runs through classical literature, most notably the tragic drama of Athens.

One might think that such pessimism ought to be paralyzing, fatal to ideals of freedom. Even so sophisticated a poet as W. H. Auden declares that the world of Homer is "unbearably sad," because nothing whatever comes of human joy and suffering, they have no meaning beyond the feeling of the moment. Yet on the face of it Homer and his audience did not find the human condition unbearable. Out of their joy and suffering came the brilliant culture of Greece, beginning with his great epics, and the conscious ideal of freedom. Among the most distinctive and original creations of the Greeks, indeed, was the literary form of tragedy, which they mastered during the golden age of democratic Athens. None of the Eastern peoples before them wrote tragic drama, nor did any of the great Eastern societies after them; until this century it has been written nowhere except in the relatively free Western world. The apparent paradox is only apparent; for great tragedy can be written only by men who are free in mind and spirit, no longer slaves to "miracle, mystery, and authority." In this view Homer's *Iliad* represents a momentous declaration of spiritual independence. It was an assertion that on these "unbearably sad" terms, without supernatural aid or consolation, man could not only accept but celebrate his condition, triumph over his destiny.

Here again the Babylonian Epic of Gilgamesh serves to accentuate the world of difference in the sovereign spirit of Homer. The supreme literary achievement of the Mesopotamian peoples, it often expresses eloquently a comparable sense of man's hard lot, unrelieved by hopes of life eternal. Its main theme is the hopeless quest of immortality by the godlike hero Gilgamesh. At first unafraid of death, resolved to cheat it by winning undying fame through his heroic exploits, he finds it unbearable when his boon companion is killed; so he wanders the earth seeking some supernatural means of escaping it. His failure is embittered by apparent success: at the bottom of the sea he at last finds a plant that magically rejuvenates, only to lose it on his way home when he pauses for a swim in a pool and leaves it on a bank, where a snake carries it off. We leave him weeping in the thought that he has spent his heart's blood merely to enable snakes to escape death by sloughing off their old skins—a jeering irony that might seem to deepen the tragedy. Actually it is a trivial, illogical ending, which evades the tragic issue. It implies that mortality is not the inalterable law of man's being but only a dirty trick of fate, due to a miscarriage of magic. It signifies that the Babylonians never found a dignified way of facing up to the common fate, never realized an ideal that could sustain and ennoble man in spite of this fate.

By contrast the *Iliad* ends with the heartbreaking lamentations of the Trojans over the loss of their hero Hector; but it ends with dignity, without snakes or jeers, on a lofty plane where sorrow is both deepened and exalted by thoughts of the magnificence of Hector. He had known that he was fated to die in this war, and when his doom was upon him he had still asserted his unconquerable spirit: "Yet I pray that I may die not without a blow, not ingloriously." His slayer, Achilles, knows that he too is doomed: his goddess mother had told him that he would certainly be killed if he remained in Troy, whereas if he went home he would live at ease like a lord. Nevertheless, he chose to remain: better a short heroic life than a long inglorious one. When on trial for his life, Socrates would cite the example of Achilles in preferring death to the surrender of his living ideals. We may add that the spirit of the heroes is quite irrational, since fame will do them no good whatever in their graves; and at that it may not seem spiritual enough to those who demand eternal rewards in heaven. To Homer it sufficed. Although at times he made fun of the immortal gods, he never mocked his heroes. The ancients noted that he "praised almost everything"— all the natural goods of fruit and flower, sport and game, art and song; but most of all he praised the heroic spirit.

Hence we must drastically qualify the notorious "fatalism" of Homer, as of most of his pupils. His heroes are never simply resigned to the fate they talk so much about; they know plenty of fear, sorrow, and dismay, but never simply despair. Keenly aware that man is subject to greater powers, they still assert their own power, their freedom to win glory. Never masters of their fate, they are always captains of their soul. Indeed, they are almost without parallel in their superb self-confidence. They are never crippled in body or broken in spirit. Secure in their own virtue, they suffer as little from anxiety over the future as from guilt over the past. No evil spirits haunt them, no dark omens obsess them. As H. V. Routh observed, fate itself was a defense against fear—the hero could not be robbed of life before his destined end; and the greater heroes could be killed only by their peers, usually with the aid of a god—it took a god to kill them. In their pride and sense of mastery, Routh concludes, they represent "the most consistent and successful attempt yet made by man to realize his own grandeur and freedom."

Later Greeks were generally less self-confident. Many would believe that the gods were like the old Yahweh who destroyed the Tower of Babel—jealous of any independent human achievement, disposed to regard any human pride as presumption. "The power above us," Herodotus remarked, "suffers none but himself to be proud"; and the tragic poets of Athens dwelt repeatedly, remorselessly, on the punishment of *hubris*. Yet neither Herodotus nor the poets counseled mere submissiveness or humility. Like Homer, they still respected the proud hero, still affirmed the power and the dignity of the human spirit. However reverent or fearful of the gods, Greek writers and thinkers retained the basic faith of Homer in man's power to choose and hold to his own ideal purposes. To the end they continued to bank on his native capacities for the pursuit of truth, goodness, and beauty.

Thus Socrates spoke of heeding the voice of the daemon within him, or what we might call the voice of God; but the ideal he died for was the pursuit of wisdom and righteousness on earth, not the service of God or salvation in a life to come, and in his teaching this was an ideal that man could attain by his own efforts, without the help of God. So was the good life as Plato conceived it. Aristotle went further, asserting that pride was "the crown of the virtues" and warning against undue humility, as both "commoner and worse" than vanity. Epicurus, more oppressed by the evil of necessity, nevertheless declared, "There is no necessity to live under the control of necessity," and added that freedom is "the greatest fruit of self-sufficiency." Even the Stoics, with their sad wisdom of resignation and their ideal of freedom from all desire, were still proud; for they still taught that man could win this freedom by his own powers of reason and will, without supernatural aid. And at the end even the Neo-Platonic mystics, taking off on the flight "from the alone to the Alone," got there on the wings of the human spirit, rejoicing in a feat that required no special gift of divine grace.

To later Christians, beginning with St. Paul, such self-reliance seemed the deadly sin of pride. Their eventual triumph is a reminder that while the Bible of the Greeks helped to get them into trouble, it proved to be not a very good one for times of trouble, or at least not for ordinary Greeks. Our immediate concern, however, is Homer's contribution to their ideal of freedom; and it calls for a different note about these ordinary Greeks. Although he showed no interest in commoners, from whose ranks none of his heroes came, he helped to prepare for the freedom they enjoyed too.

Directly he pictures an aristocratic society ruled by kings, in which the common people have no more real voice than they do in the feudal councils on Mount Olympus; a shadowy popular assembly that shows up on some important occasions serves only to ratify the decisions made by the rulers. Now and then the great king Agamemnon may even assert that he gets his right from the gods—a venerable idea that Homer's star Macedonian pupil, Alexander the Great, would help to revive. Yet in Homer's world it was already archaic. The greatest king is never a god, and is not actually regarded as a divine agent; he may be openly defied, as Achilles defies Agamemnon. Neither is he remote or awful in majesty; like Odysseus, he may work with his men, even work with his hands, and he owes his prestige chiefly to his prowess as a hero, not his royal blood. Above all, he is no absolute monarch, able to rule as he pleases. He is expected to obey "Themis," a law not of his own making, and to treat his subjects as followers, not as slaves. He never commands unquestioning obedience, which no true Greek outside of Sparta would ever regard as a primary virtue. The shadowy popular assembly at least foreshadows the novel Greek idea that government is a public affair.

Altogether, a people brought up on Homer would not necessarily develop democracy; but neither would they naturally accept the despotism of the ancient East, or think of prostrating themselves before their rulers. Unlike the Egyptians and the Babylonians, they might understand what Bury meant when he wrote that the legendary Lycurgus of Sparta was not a man—"only a god." They might reverse the historic process in Sumer, where "kingship descended from heaven" on cities that had had popular assemblies and a word for "freedom."

3. *The* Polis *and Its Culture*

Although the Phoenicians and other peoples formed city-states, the Greek *polis* became strictly unique. It stands out so conspicuously in the history of human freedom that it calls for an immediate word of caution: uniqueness is not easy to understand. We have nothing quite like the *polis* today, not even a precise name for it. The conventional translation "city-state" is misleading. It was different from our city, as it took in some surrounding country and involved no sharp distinction between countryman and man on the street; and it came to much more than the modern state, while also somewhat less. Its constitution, said Aristotle, was a "mode of life." This was a very open mode, literally and figuratively, but again quite different from the American way of life. Because it contributed so much to the growth of freedom we need to be wary of foisting our own notions of freedom on it—and also to keep an eye out for the usual anomalies.

Knowing nothing of its origins and early history, beyond its original meaning of "citadel," we may nevertheless presume that the growth of the *polis* was largely unplanned. The emigrants from Greece who established themselves in Asia Minor must have had war leaders, if not kings in the Mycenaean tradition; there were still kings in and about Ionia as late as the seventh century B.C. Their disappearance seems to have been due more to economic development than to any revulsion on principle against the idea of kingship: as the Ionians prospered in trade and industry, feudal war lords gave way to busy merchants. When the curtain begins to rise on Greek history, at any rate, we do not hear of popular rebellions against kings. Instead we hear of conflicts between an oligarchy and the common people—in Miletus, for example, between parties known as the "Wealthy" and the "Handworkers." Such class conflict would continue to the bitter end of Greek history, but immediately it led to a new kind of government: one based on neither ancient custom nor military power, but on some kind of compromise in the common interest. Later Greeks had some reason for their fond belief that the *polis* as they knew it had been established deliberately in order to secure justice.

During the early stages of this struggle appeared the "tyrants," uncrowned monarchs whose title is also misleading. They were not simple despots; the Greek word for them was at first not a bad word. Generally they came into power as champions of the common people, when not elected by them. Now recognized as the first professional politicians, they signified that government was already a public affair. Some were great statesmen; two of them—Pittacus of Mytilene and Periander of Corinth—were honored by inclusion among the traditional Seven Wise Men of Hellas. Among the accomplishments of Periander was the abolition of debt slavery, a custom accepted in Israel as everywhere in the ancient East. Still, rule by tyrants could readily become tyranny in the modern sense. It was a passing phase in the history of the *polis*, here and there intermittently repeated, but nowhere generally accepted. All Greek thinkers agreed that it was the worst form of government.

That they never agreed on what was the best form is a sign of the freedom of Greek thought, but also the beginning of difficulty in understanding the *polis*. This was not a particular form of government, nor by any means necessarily a democracy. Short of a sacred monarchy, the *polis* might have almost any form; generally it veered toward aristocracy or oligarchy. The essential idea was rule by law: law based on public consent, and binding on both rulers and ruled. It was a principle of constitutionalism, limiting political power by law, denying rulers any right to arbitrary rule. In the ancient East law had been laid down by great kings, in the name of the gods; men generally accepted and obeyed it in much the same spirit as they accepted the weather—they could do no more about it. In the *polis* law was made by Solons, citizens working in the public interest; the Greeks accepted its constraints because they had thought about it, grown fully conscious of it, and recognized it as the essential means to not only security and order but equity, liberty, and all the goods of civic life. They revered no hero or god more than they revered their great lawgivers.

Solon, the greatest of the early lawgivers, was perhaps the first to state explicitly the principle of rule by law from which stems the Western tradition of freedom under law. In 594 B.C. he was made a special magistrate by the rich and poor of Athens to settle their bitter conflict. He averted the threat of civil war by new laws that made concessions to the poor, canceling their debts, prohibiting their enslavement, exempting them from direct taxation, giving them some voice in electing magistrates and some means of holding the magistrates to account. He balanced such concessions by refusing to divide up the estates of the wealthy and by preserving their greater power, since they bore the brunt of taxation; he excluded the poor from public office, providing that magistrates should be chosen from the upper class. Hence Solon did not set up a full-fledged democracy. Neither did he put an end to class war; continued agitation made most of his specific reforms short-lived. But he did effectively establish the principle of government by rational consent, in the interest of all, instead of government by privilege or by force. His constitution made Athens a model for other Greek cities.

If as usual we cannot wholly explain this political achievement of the Greeks, we can again make out some of its conditions. The most apparent was the very smallness of the *polis*. Only a few of the "great" cities of the classical world had as many as five thousand citizens, which Plato considered the ideal number; and though citizens did not include women, children, slaves, or foreign residents, the cities were still small enough to be intimate communities. Men who knew most of their fellows by sight, possibly even by name, might get into the habit of discussing public affairs. Such habits were stimulated by growing enterprise and calculation in commerce, and especially in Asia Minor by the openness of a kind of frontier life in a new world. In their many scattered cities the Greeks accordingly developed a wide variety of political institutions, which enabled them, or in their competition almost obliged them, to reconsider their system of government, anticipate the study of comparative government. As they sent out more colonies they had more opportunities to improvise and experiment. In general, the idea of growth and change, as well as struggle, was implicit in the very nature of the little *polis,* as it was not in the great settled states of the ancient East. If the early Greeks aspired to the stability that Plato and Aristotle prized above freedom, the conditions of their life hardly permitted it.

But the key remains the essential rationality that was apparent as early as Homer—however he came by it—for other peoples living in small city-states had not produced Solons. In his own person Solon exemplified Aristotle's definition of law, as "intelligence without passion"; himself an aristocrat, he disappointed some of his followers by refusing to set himself up as a tyrant. With the principle of rule by law arose the *Logos* in philosophy, the rule of Mind; the *polis* may have suggested to the early philosophers the idea of a lawful universe. At any rate, the Greeks began linking Moira with Dike, or justice. Some, including Solon, appear to have anticipated the later Stoic doctrine of "natural law" that passed into Roman law and thence into Western political tradition: a cosmic moral law or universal principle of justice, above all man-made laws, and the criterion of their justice.

This was not clearly the prevailing belief, however. Most Greeks seem to have regarded justice as "natural" only in that it derived from the nature of man, not the nature of the universe. Or more precisely, it suited the nature of Greeks: "barbarians" were obviously content to put up with arbitrary rule. The jealous independence of the *polis* precluded any deep, widespread faith in a universal moral law above it—it was always a law unto itself. For similar reasons it was much more than a modern state, and its ideal theory quite different from modern democratic theory. The Greeks never made a clear distinction between the state and society, or drew up bills of rights protecting "the people" against the state, because the *polis* was virtually indistinguishable from society or the people, embracing all their major interests and constitut-

ing their highest interest. They were not so much citizens with abstract
rights as members of a community with status, as in a family. Their
lexicon had no word, indeed, for the "individual" or the "self." They
made no clear distinction either between the ethical and the political,
still less between things that are Caesar's and things that are God's.

The *polis* could not actually realize this ideal unity and self-
sufficiency, of course, and even its ideal had essential limitations, which
will concern us later. Meanwhile we must note that, like its gods, it
had the virtues of its defects. Apart from the realism they imbibed
from Homer, the Greeks had some reason not to believe in a cosmic
principle of justice or in divinely sanctioned laws. Such laws do not
necessarily make for freedom, or even for justice; in the ancient East
they had supported rather the principles of absolute authority and unquestioning obedience—and would continue to do so, to the benefit
of the privileged few. Above all, the Greeks had good reason for their
devotion to the *polis*. If it gave them no inalienable rights as individuals, it fully provided for all their major interests. It built the temples
to the gods, built and maintained as well the theater, the gymnasium,
the market place, the open-air centers of social life. It staged all the
great annual festivals, which were at once religious, patriotic, and
recreational. Civic life was literally a commonwealth. It was precisely
in and through the *polis* that the Greeks developed their richly varied
culture, and the individual came to have more scope and incentive for
self-realization than he had ever had before.

For in spite of its domination of society, the *polis* was by no means a
totalitarian state. Sparta became such a state, but for this reason Sparta
was singular; the normal *polis* was an open society. It permitted freedom of thought and speech, especially in debate of public affairs, and it
gave the individual ample freedom in his private life. It encouraged
competitiveness in all fields, stimulated the individualism that led vase-
makers to sign their wares (and incidentally made Greek vases eagerly
sought and imitated all over the ancient world). It stimulated an excessive individualism, in fact, with the blessing of Homer. His heroes were
devoted to an ideal of personal honor and fame, not a patriotic ideal;
Achilles could nurse his injured pride by sulking in his tent, refusing
to aid his fellow Greeks against the Trojans, and incur no feeling of
guilt or public charge of disloyalty. Later Greeks idealized patriotism
so insistently because so many of them still put their personal interests
first; they produced perhaps the most distinguished list of traitors in
history—headed by Athenians. For such reasons too the *polis* was

eventually a political failure. But in culture meanwhile it had proved a brilliant success.

Directly, it promoted the civic art of Greece, in which patriotism and an ambition for personal glory could work hand in hand. The early tyrants were patrons of culture, and they set the tradition that would be maintained to the end of the *polis* by initiating programs of public works, in order at once to honor the gods, to beautify the city, and to provide jobs for the poor. The Greek temple was a monument to civic pride as much as to the patron deity. Typically crowning the citadel or some eminence, always built with an eye chiefly to its exterior, it was never set apart from the community, and never designed for mysterious rites in inner sanctums available only to high priests. All the major architectural works, with all the statues in and about them, were civic works, in a real sense of, by, and for the people. There were no great private mansions, as no imperial palaces or tombs. Content to live in modest homes, the classical Greeks lavished much more of their wealth and genius on their civic centers than had any people before them.

By the same token, art achieved in the *polis* an autonomy it had never enjoyed in the civilizations of the past. It was no longer a servant of rulers or priesthoods. While religion continued to provide the subject matter of most art, its inspiration grew more and more nominal— just as it was certainly not the primary inspiration of Homer's epics; in sculpture the real cult was the human form. No longer bent to magical ends, art was free to develop its own magic for its own ends. Its freedom was reflected in the myths about artists and poets (such as Marsyas, Linus, Arachne, and Orpheus) who like Daedalus were destroyed for indiscretion or *hubris*. Among the many reminders of the price the Greeks paid for their freedom, this theme nevertheless emphasizes the novelty of their self-consciousness as creators, for it is found rarely if at all in the mythologies of peoples before them.

How much influence this art had on the daily life and the national history of the Greeks we can never know. Neither can we take for granted that it had simply a wholesome influence; it did not conspicuously improve their morality, and it might have intensified their rashness or their jealous provincialism. But given the deep needs it evidently satisfied, and all the energy that went into it, the burden of proof lies on those who would deny it any real influence. One who knows the modern industrial city, or the ordinary American small town, has reason to believe that a daily acquaintance with beauty has

some uplifting effect on the human spirit, and that a habitual acceptance of drabness, trashiness, and ugliness is not conducive to self-
realization or freedom of spirit. The wealth of civic art in Greece
stimulated creative impulses, rather than the possessive impulses to
which the immense material resources of the modern world have been
largely dedicated; and presumably most thoughtful men would agree
with Bertrand Russell that the best life is that in which creative impulses play the largest part, possessive the smallest. At least the *polis*
clearly had something to do with the joy in creation and the zest for
life that are so much more evident in Greek art than in most Oriental
art before it; and these are absolute goods, good in themselves—ends as
well as means of freedom.

In literature the supreme creation of the *polis* was Athenian drama,
which we shall consider in due time. Indirectly, however, it made possible another distinctive expression of the free Greek spirit—lyric
poetry. Sappho wrote of her purely personal emotions, her passion for
her girl students, by which she unwittingly immortalized her native
island of Lesbos; while Anacreon celebrated his love of wine and beautiful boys, with as little concern for the gods of the *polis*. The kind of
individualism they exemplified was more explicit in Archilochus, whom
the Greeks ranked second only to Homer.[6] "No man would enjoy very
many delights who heeded the censure of the people," he wrote; and
he even admitted cheerfully to having run away from the battlefield,
thrown away his shield, to save his neck: "Hang the shield! I'll get another just as good." Here Archilochus was far from declaring the rights
of the individual on high principle or from asserting the claims of
conscience; a moralist may remark that his self-indulgence amounted to
license, not liberty. Nevertheless, a historian must remark that his bold
defiance of convention revealed the exceptional freedom of mind that
the Greeks had attained through the *polis*. Men thinking for themselves, no longer bound by tribal custom, might rise to rational, impersonal conceptions of truth and goodness.

So in fact they did. The most enduring, historically important work
to come out of the *polis* was natural philosophy. It may have been
coincidence that Thales of Miletus was a contemporary of Solon of
Athens, but there was none the less a logical connection between the
conscious ideal of rule by law and conscious theory about the universe.

---

[6] The few extant fragments of his poetry give little idea of the greatness they saw in him.
They only remind us that the great bulk of Greek art has been lost, as most of the imperishable works of man perish—unless pains are taken to preserve them.

In any case, the first clear sign of natural philosophy remains the statement of Thales: "All things are made of water." It is difficult now to appreciate how astonishingly bold and original this simple, erroneous statement was. Whereas men over the ages had explained the universe in mythical terms, for magical purposes, Thales was trying to explain it in natural terms, for rational purposes. He was not denying the gods, to be sure, for he also said that "all things are full of gods," in some sense that is unclear. Mythological notions likewise influenced the logic of his successors, Anaximander and Anaximenes; philosophers are still debating the precise meaning of their key terms, such as the "Boundless" that Anaximander made the essential reality of the universe. Yet there is no question that the mode of thinking of these men was essentially rational, their purpose genuinely philosophical rather than magical, their primary concern the nature of the world rather than the nature of the gods. The statement of Thales does herald the emancipation of mind that Renan hailed as "the only miracle in history."

Knowing the costs of this miracle, in permanent confusion and uncertainty over first and last principles, let us at once repeat that the bold statement of Thales was, fittingly, erroneous. Philosophers would ever after seek the essential reality, and never agree on it. The emancipated mind would assert its omnipotence, elaborate more systematic forms of delusion, tyrannize over thought by claims of finality. It would seek cosmic law and order at any cost, and first of all sacrifice the wealth of appearances, the natural possibilities inherent in copiousness and variety, change and growth. In the interest of some metaphysical superreality, it would often degrade the actual temporal world in which ordinary man enjoy their freedom, granting this world at best a low order of reality. While forever failing to demonstrate conclusively the absolute, universal, eternal truths that it typically asserted, it would as typically assert that no other kind of truth can really do for man. It would often constrain both the theory and the practice of freedom, in ways that must concern us from now on.

Nevertheless, philosophy would also work to keep thought both active and free, if only because of the endless disagreement among its practitioners; and our immediate concern is a genuine emancipation of mind, a growth of critical thought necessary to the maintenance of conscious ideals of freedom. By their essential appeal to reason, the Greek pioneers in philosophy provided a corrective for its occupational excesses. If their thought was still colored by myth, they did not claim the supernatural authority of the myth, but argued in ways that invited rational criticism. When later thinkers claimed an intuitive or semi-mystical knowledge, they still had to demonstrate it. It is now difficult, too, to appreciate how far these pioneers advanced, unless one can realize that they started from scratch, without a vocabulary, a method, a logic, or philosophical tools of any sort. They had first to discover their very problems, and in the process they succeeded in asking almost all the basic questions. They discovered as well the fundamental idea of proof, proceeding to develop rules of deductive reasoning, set up standards of logical consistency. Lacking a public, they created all the essential means to a public, aboveboard kind of discussion and argument.

In short, mind was not only emancipated but disciplined, as it could never be by myth alone. And Thales himself prepared for the most objective kind of discipline, which would have the most revolutionary consequences. He became famous for having foretold an eclipse of the sun (on a day now fixed as May 25, 585 B.C.); he had hit upon the natural cause of a heavenly event that had always stirred superstitious awe or anxiety. How clearly or fully the early philosophers generalized the concept of natural cause and natural law is uncertain, as their works have disappeared, but they at least pointed toward the premises of science. This "miracle"—the realization that natural events are not miracles—became quite explicit in the Hippocratic writings on medicine. "It seems to me," declared a student of epilepsy, "that the disease is no more divine than any other. It has a natural cause, just as other diseases have. Men think it divine merely because they do not understand it. But if they called everything divine that they do not understand, why, there would be no end of divine things."

The obviously practical concerns of Greek medicine may help to explain how philosophy got started. Although the Greeks initiated another hoary tradition by a story that Thales fell down a well while gazing at the stars, he too could be quite practical. All the rest we hear about him has to do with his technological feats, his contributions to navigation, his shrewdness in business—his worldly interests as a citizen of busy Miletus, the leading commercial city in the Greek world at his time. As later Greek philosophers set still another tradition by their aristocratic aloofness from such vulgar practical interests, recent historians have dwelt on the neglected material factors and economic motives that may have stimulated philosophical speculation. Gordon Childe explains it as a natural product of the Iron Age—a new intellectual tool forged by the new society resulting from iron tools.

Prehistoric art: bison from Lascaux

Ziggurat at Ur   *Courtesy, The University Museum, Philadelphia*

Sumerian royal jewelry from Ur
Courtesy, The University Museum, Philadelphia

Victory tablet of King Narmer: Old Kingdom, Egypt   *Courtesy, Cairo Museum*

"Village Mayor": Old Kingdom
Courtesy, Cairo Museum

The Great Sphinx   *Courtesy of TWA*

Throne of Tutankhamon, from his tomb at Thebes
Photograph by Harry Burton, The Metropolitan Museum of Art

The Last Judgment before Osiris
Courtesy, The British Museum

Statue of Ramses II at Luxor
Photo by Pinney, from Monkmeyer

Code of Hammurabi, the "god-fearing" prince   *Courtesy, The Louvre*

Business records from Babylon
Courtesy, The Metropolitan Museum of Art, Gift of Matilda W. Bruce, 1907

Ruins of Babylon   *Courtesy Underwood & Underwood*

Throne room in the Palace of Minos, Knossos
Courtesy Royal Greek Embassy, Press & Information Service

Assyrian King (Ashurnasirpal) on a lion hunt   *Courtesy, The British Museum*

Obelisk of Shalmanisu III with picture of captive Israelite king, John
Courtesy, The British Museum

Late Hittite sculpture   *Courtesy, The Metropolitan Museum of Art, Rogers Fund, 1943*

The stables of King Solomon at Megiddo (reconstructed)
Courtesy, The Jewish Museum, New York. (Frank J. Darmstaedter)

King Solomon's temple (cross section of a reconstructed model)
Courtesy, The Jewish Museum, New York. (Frank J. Darmstaedter)

The Moses of Michelangelo
Courtesy, The Metropolitan Museum of Art, John Taylor Johnston Memorial Collection

The spoils of Jerusalem, from the Arch of Titus in Rome

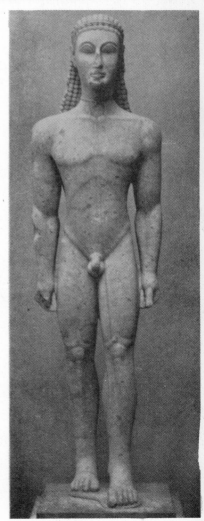

Archaic Greek sculpture: "Apollo type" from the seventh
century, B.C.   *Courtesy, The Metropolitan Museum of Art,*
Fletcher Fund, 1932

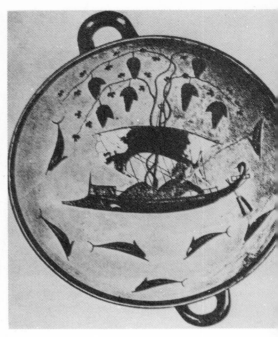

Attic vase of the sixth century: Ajax and Achilles throwing dice   *Courtesy, Vatican Museum*

Attic cup: Dionysus in a boat   *Courtesy, Glyptothek Museum, Munich*

Acropolis of Athens   *Courtesy of TWA*

Athena mourning
(5th century)
Courtesy, Acropolis
Museum, Athens

The Death of Socrates, painting by Jacques
Louis David
Courtesy, The Metropolitan Museum of Art,
Wolfe Fund, 1931

Hermes of Praxiteles
Courtesy, Olympia Museum, Athens

Benjamin Farrington emphasizes still more the technological interests of the early philosophers, arguing that their speculations were based on observation and experiment, and were guided when not inspired by the new techniques of the age. Others add that the universal medium of money, by which all kinds of goods are reduced to a single value, may have suggested the idea of a single reality behind the multiple appearances of the world. It is at least clear that the early Greek thinkers were by no means aloof from the workaday world. Thales could more easily transcend the supernatural because he and his fellow Milesians were so much engrossed in the business of the natural world, while his contemporary Solon, as we shall see, laid the economic as well as political foundations of Athenian greatness.[7]

Yet practical utility was not clearly the direct inspiration of philosophical speculation, nor technology the guide to its development. It is surprising enough that philosophy began in Greece as an inquiry into the nature of the universe, not the condition of man or the will of the gods, but it is more surprising because this metaphysics served no practical need. To technology the brilliant Ionians made relatively slight contributions. They never developed the habit of systematically applying their knowledge, or of checking their thought against observation and experiment. By such methods they could not have proved anyway that all things are made of water or of air, but as the philosophers went on to develop rules of reasoning they remained weakest at inductive logic, the drawing of general conclusions from observed particulars. As for the Iron Age, philosophy may be viewed as a natural response to the new social tensions, but no more than prophetic Judaism or Ionian lyric poetry was it an inevitable response. The plainest condition of its birth was the remarkable freedom of the *polis*. It came directly out of the heads of independent thinkers: of highly original individuals who under common social, material conditions thought up different theories about the universe—theories alike only in being singularly uncommon, and of no apparent social utility.

The miracle that took place in Ionia was not merely the emanci-

---

[7] That philosophy was no virgin birth should also remind us that Thales, its "father," was not a godlike genius who suddenly blazed on the scene, out of nowhere. Half Phoenician himself, he had behind him not only the learning of Babylon and Egypt, the cosmopolitan life of Ionia, and the rationality of the Homeric tradition, but almost surely other nameless, forgotten men who had begun to speculate before him—the indispensable lesser men who contribute to the great movements, but are overshadowed by the geniuses and rarely get into the books. They help to explain why Thales did not make a tremendous impression on the Greeks, and why even Aristotle could think that "true philosophy" had begun with the Magi and the Chaldeans.

pation of mind from the delusions of magic and miracle. It was as significantly an emancipation from purely practical thought, as from common sense. Like art, thought too now achieved autonomy. Philosophy soon got too remote from practice and ordinary experience, indeed, and so became liable to delusions of "pure reason"; but the important point remains that men had discovered a new realm of possibility, beyond the workaday world, and were consciously creating new problems instead of myopically stumbling over them. They had given birth to "theory"—potentially a powerful instrument of thought, but originally a word meaning "sightseeing." So when Thales wondered what the world was made of, he was simply being curious. His answer was of no practical use to him whatever, and would have been of no more had it been nearer the truth; it simply satisfied his curiosity. If it fed his vanity too, he nevertheless symbolizes the beginning of the disinterested pursuit of truth for its own sake. As a practical man who was able to foretell an eclipse, this stargazer just possibly had some glimmering of the tremendous practical importance that such scientific inquiry would eventually have. In any case, his own supreme importance is as a herald of the scientific spirit.

This is still a rare spirit, even in a civilization that rests on the findings of science. It must have been rarer in classical Greece. Many Greeks seem to have been curious, and especially in Ionia disposed to entertain or at least to tolerate the bold speculations of the philosophers; we hear of little or no popular outrage about them until much later in Athens. But we hear of no popular excitement either. The legend about Thales tumbling into a well suggests that ordinary Greeks had much the same attitude toward philosophers that ordinary Americans do, regarding them as impractical fellows, and had no more passion for the pursuit of truth. There is no evidence that the rise of natural philosophy had any decisive, immediate influence on Greek history. Although Thales was listed among the Seven Wise Men, no one spoke of him as the Educator of Hellas. His fellow Ionians spurned his wisdom when he urged the cities to band together in self-defense against the advancing Persian Emperor Cyrus; instead they fought separately and fell the more quickly, thus losing their independence. Thereupon the Ionians did not embark on a more eager pursuit of wisdom or truth. Much more conspicuous than the "popular movement of enlightenment" that Farrington sees in Ionian philosophy was a popular religious revival that swept the Greek world in the sixth century—a revival of faith in prehistoric nature deities, especially

Dionysus. This gave the Greeks a kind of ecstasy that they could get from neither philosophy nor the Olympian gods, but it represented no more spiritual than intellectual enlightenment.

In a longer view, however, the birth of philosophy in the Greek *polis* looks as significant as the birth of higher religions elsewhere. Immediately it may have made some difference in Greek history in so far as it was associated with the growing idea of rule by law. Probably it made more difference as metaphysical speculation broadened into science, religion, and ethics. Pythagoras launched the extraordinary idea that number was the key to the universe—an idea that was to have a tremendous career in science—but immediately he inaugurated the tradition of otherworldly idealism, including the belief in an immortal soul, that led to Plato.[8] Xenophanes went from city to city attacking the religion of Homer, denouncing popular beliefs as mere superstitions, most likely to little immediate effect; but the awareness of superstition—the idea that there was such a thing—kept spreading. By the time of Periclean Athens philosophy pervaded the whole climate of opinion, to some extent—however unknowable—shaping the mentality of political leaders, especially Pericles himself, and seeping down into the mentality of the man on the street. Its positive influence on Greek history may still be discounted if only because philosophy was new, and did not become embedded in tradition and formal education until the Greeks were on the point of losing their political independence, or control of their history; much of their most influential philosophy, as of Plato and the Stoics, was plainly a response to their political failure. Yet its influence on later Western history was incalculable in both senses of the word. Greek philosophy became deeply embedded in Christianity, and thence in the whole cultural tradition on which Western civilization grew up. It is engrained even in the common sense of the practical man who distrusts "mere" theory—especially in America, the first great nation to be founded on conscious theory. Out of the philosophical tradition that may be traced to Thales of Miletus came both modern science and modern democracy.

Through much the same sort of miracle, anomaly, and contradiction we may reach a similar conclusion about another enduring by-product

---

[8] The followers of Pythagoras bring up another anomaly, as they were probably the first to know that the earth is a sphere and to anticipate that it is a planet. Believing that the "real" world was spiritual, they had a passion for supernal harmony and simplicity, and a contempt for mere matter and flesh; yet they contributed more than the Ionian materialists to an understanding of the structure of the physical universe.

of the Greek *polis*—the study of history. Herodotus, the "father" of history, was certainly no comet blazing out of nowhere. Behind him were Ionians known by name, such as Cadmus and Hecataeus of Miletus, who had made history a rational inquiry. Of the writings of Hecataeus we have almost nothing but a simple, sufficiently astonishing statement: "I write what I deem true, for the stories of the Greeks are manifold and seem to me ridiculous." No such statement as this can be found in all the extant literature of the ancient East. Its scribes had merely recorded annals of their kings, chronicles lacking the least critical analysis, and though the scribes of Israel kept a more sober record, they still distorted it by their naïve faith that success or failure was due merely to the proper or improper service of Yahweh. Herodotus too was much impressed by the jealousy of the gods, who seemed bent on destroying great men just because they were great; yet he treated history essentially as an affair of, by, and for men. Most unusual, he set about inquiring into the manifold stories not only of the Greeks but of other peoples as well.

He was still far from being a profound analyst of causes and consequences, or of the means and ends of Greek freedom, the central theme of his *Persian Wars*. Neither was he a scientific historian: he had no idea of "laws of evidence," no clear method for sifting facts out of legend or fable. Although he periodically warned his audience that he did not feel obliged to believe all that he had heard and was reporting, he evidently did believe some of the ridiculous stories of the Greeks. Nevertheless, Herodotus was a remarkable pioneer. He was the first to profit fully from the stimulus of diversity in the many little city-states, and especially from their commerce with the greater world of the ancient East. He traveled all over the known world "for the sake of learning, for the sake of inquiry." With his lively intelligence, eager curiosity, and breadth of interest he had a still more exceptional dispassionate spirit, which enabled him to be fair to the "barbarians." In this respect no philosopher was wiser than he, no religious prophet freer from tribalism. He was perhaps a better educator in history because he had no preconceived standards, knew no laws, and so tampered with the evidence less than some modern systematizers of history do.

Only again we must add that in his own time he was not hailed as a great educator. Greek historians had little if any influence on the history made by the Greeks, little if any more on the serious thought of the day. Herodotus represented the Persian Wars as primarily a struggle to preserve Greek freedom, or to make the world safe for the

Greek ideal; but he wrote, of course, after these wars and did not give the Greeks this ideal. Thucydides then analyzed the failure of the Greeks in the disastrous Peloponnesian War—after the event, too late for them to profit by his thought even had they been in a mood to do so. While most Greeks had a deep reverence for the past, the most thoughtful generally continued to display a severely limited understanding of it, and little real historical sense.

But again the Greeks had started something of real and lasting consequence, an essential means to self-knowledge, and to any hope of escaping the tyranny of the past. If historians may be inclined to exaggerate its consequence, out of professional pride, the study of history has had plain enough influence on actual Western history. It becomes plainer when one adds that it has not been simply a wholesome influence, or a pure boon to the cause of freedom. Most of the history taught in schools has been national history, presented in a nationalistic spirit; it has saddled peoples with false images of their past, which are more dangerous than sheer ignorance of it. As this comment implies, however, the study has also become much broader and more sophisticated. By now it has made possible a clearer, fuller consciousness of the world drama we are all involved in. The understanding it gives certainly does not guarantee the solution of our problems, but as certainly there can be no hope of solution without some such understanding.

So we might conclude with another tribute to Herodotus. By his travels he learned an awareness of the power of custom, or culture, that would remain rare until the rise of modern anthropology. "If one were to offer men to choose out of all the customs in the world such as seemed to them best," he observed, "they would examine the whole number, and end by preferring their own." In fact, very few would examine the whole number, with anything like his dispassionate interest. The Sophists in Athens did something of the kind, only to acquire an evil reputation; most classical Greeks continued to generalize provincially about barbarians, while their loftiest philosophers erected temporal Greek customs into laws of nature or eternal forms of Being. Herodotus himself usually ended by preferring the customs of the *polis*, but his preference was not mere prejudice. He might be called the father of universal history, as of the history of freedom.

4. The Golden Age of Athens

In his Funeral Oration, delivered in 431 B.C., Pericles proudly asserted that Athens was a democracy, favoring the many instead of the few. Athenians were free men, able to live "exactly as we please." They enjoyed their freedom under laws of their own making, which assured "equal justice to all" regardless of class; class was no bar to merit, nor poverty to public service. Pericles went on to state the essential premises of the democratic faith, beginning with a trust in common men. Athens believed that "ordinary citizens, though occupied with the pursuits of industry, are still fair judges of public matters." Unlike other nations, it regarded public discussion not as an impediment to action but as "an indispensable preliminary to any wise action at all." Unlike Sparta in particular, it threw open the city to the world, freely admitting aliens, and it enforced no rigorous discipline, allowing its citizens to live as they pleased because it trusted to their native spirit more than to "system and policy" (or one might now say, to security regulations). It assumed that free men would respect the law, and in defense of their city would prove as manly and brave as the Spartans, who from their cradles had been trained only to fight and to obey.

Pericles presented his oration in the first year of the fatal Peloponnesian War between Athens and Sparta, the subject of our next chapter. As Sparta won this war, we are reminded at once that the democratic faith is strictly a faith, and a risky one. Yet the Funeral Oration remains one of the most important documents in the history of freedom, as the first manifesto of democracy. The Greek *polis* was not typically dedicated to equal suffrage and equal rights. Self-government is an arduous, time-consuming business, for which ordinary men have no natural passion or need; of the greater cities, only Athens developed and maintained a full-fledged democracy. And Pericles affirmed that democracy was what had made Athens great. As free men governing themselves, the Athenians were not only public-spirited but enterprising, resourceful, versatile, able to cultivate "refinement without extravagance and knowledge without effeminacy." They had made Athens "the school of Hellas" as well as its greatest power. Nor was this a mere boast thrown out for the occasion, Pericles insisted—it was "plain matter of fact."

Although his picture of Athens was undoubtedly idealized, there is no doubting either its essential truth. In plain fact Athens had become the cultural capital of all Hellas, and would remain so long after its humiliating defeat—remain forever the great symbol of the glory that was Greece. We may be struck chiefly by all that Pericles neglected to boast of, beginning with the many masters and masterpieces it had produced. He took for granted a burst of creativity that now seems the most extraordinary in all history. For in this one century, out of a city-state numbering only a hundred thousand or so people, came such men as the builders of the Parthenon, the sculptor Phidias, the tragic poets Aeschylus, Sophocles, and Euripides, the comic poet Aristophanes, the historian Thucydides, and the philosopher Socrates, together with such upcoming youngsters as Plato and such visitors as Herodotus, Anaxagoras, and Democritus, attracted by the liberality and the brilliance of the city—names than can hardly be matched among the hundreds of millions of Americans in our own history. And if in view of this contrast democracy cannot be considered the sole or sufficient cause of Athenian creativity, it unmistakably had much to do with it. Pericles spoke even more truly than he knew. Boasting over dead soldiers, he prepares us for a history that fully illustrates the costs of freedom, but most strikingly demonstrates its values.

The history begins with legends of a great king, Theseus, who federated Attica and established a democracy—legends that refer back to Minoan and Mycenaean times, but actually were spun and embroidered after Solon's time. Until the sixth century Athens had been an insignificant city, well behind the Ionians in wealth, power, and culture, and not up to mainland Corinth either. Solon started its growth by introducing not only his constitutional reforms but a new economic policy. Whereas Athenians had been trying to grow their own food in the relatively poor soil of Attica, Solon encouraged them to concentrate on olive oil and wine for export, and then to import the needed grains. To ship the oil and wine, they began manufacturing vases, competing with Corinth for the Aegean market. By the end of the sixth century their potters had captured this market; they were turning out the exquisite Attic vases admired in modern museums. The vases also prepare us for incongruities: the Greeks themselves never took them very seriously as works of art, considering them only household ware, while their philosophers disparaged the mechanic arts that fashioned them. The potters belonged to a growing middle class that helped to weaken the power of the aristocracy and to support

Solon's policy of moderation, the Delphic wisdom of "nothing to excess"; this classical wisdom was immediately a product of class struggle, not of formal philosophy. At the same time, the enterprising businessmen of Athens were good enough pupils of Homer never to make a religion of business or to proclaim it the main business of life, the main proof of Athenian greatness.

As they prospered, the Athenians displayed an openness to change that was a tribute to the wisdom if not the intention of Solon: they adhered to his basic policy, and felt free to change his laws. The great lawgiver was followed by Pisistratus, a tyrant, but another moderate and a supporter of the popular cause; he weakened aristocratic control of religion and its attendant privileges by encouraging popular cults, especially the festival of Dionysus, out of which grew Athenian drama. When his more autocratic, contentious sons took over his rule, the Athenians got rid of them and thereupon, near the end of the sixth century, adopted a thoroughly democratic constitution. This was primarily the work of Cleisthenes, another aristocrat who like Solon refused to become a tyrant.

Cleisthenes did away with the ancient four tribes that had been the seat of power and privilege, replacing them with ten tribes created on a purely territorial basis, for the sake of representation on public committees. In thus rationalizing government, breaking with tribal tradition, he incidentally helped to liberate the individual from the patriarchal family or clan, with its narrow loyalties and rigid obligations; in time sons might be relieved of responsibility for the crimes of the fathers—an issue taken up by Aeschylus. Immediately Cleisthenes enfranchised all Athenians by removing property qualifications for suffrage. The supreme authority became the popular assembly, which all citizens could attend. Major officials were either elected by popular vote or chosen by lot; the major law courts amounted to popular juries. If aristocrats might be expected to dominate proceedings in council, court, or assembly by virtue of more leisure or oratorical skill, the majority still had the last word. The principle of equal voice, equal rights, was firmly established. Pericles later assured the equal participation of the many poor by introducing daily pay for the thousands of jurors chosen every year.

Now, such political rights were by no means extended to the whole adult populace. They were denied to women, of course. Although some recent scholars have questioned the traditional view that the Athenian woman was little more than a household slave, she certainly had a less honorable status than Minoan women had enjoyed, and outside the home had no profession except as dancing girl or courtesan. In his Funeral Oration Pericles remarked that her greatest glory was to be "least talked of among the men, whether for good or for bad"; and as all over classical Greece there were shrines to the Companion, none to the Wife, so the only known woman of distinction in fifth-century Athens was Aspasia, the mistress of Pericles. Democracy itself had something to do with the lowly position of woman in the freest society yet known: busy in the home, she could not readily participate in the active public life. Meanwhile Athena helped women no more than the Virgin Mary later would, for she was primarily a man's goddess and no longer a bringer of fertility.

Similarly political rights were denied to the many resident foreigners, and the many more slaves. Although the foreigners were no despised minority (like many "alien" groups in modern society), they had no say in the government. Slaves were not treated harshly either except in the local silver mines of Laurium, where they were worked like draught animals. Otherwise the best than can be said for the Athenians in this respect is that they were no different from other peoples of their time, that most of them were hard workers in field or shop, not slaveowners or the supercilious men of leisure idealized by Plato and Aristotle, and that their "Old Oligarch" complained of the "extraordinary" license granted to slaves, who could dress and live like pure-blooded Athenians. The slaves made it plainest that classical ideals of justice and freedom were not founded on any concept of the "natural rights" of man.

Yet as far as it went, Athenian democracy was a much purer democracy than any civilized people before it had achieved, or than any is ever likely to achieve again. Its citizens were not merely represented in their government—they actively participated in it. Apart from attendance at the popular assembly, which met once a month, they served on the administrative councils and in the law courts. They served more often because members of the councils, like elected officials, were chosen annually and were not eligible for re-election; and every day a new chairman was chosen by lot. (The one exception to the ban on re-election was the office of general; it was as a general that Pericles remained in power over a number of years.) Hence every Athenian might expect to be a public official at some time during his life, and at any given time perhaps a quarter of them might be engaged in public work, including soldiering and public building enterprises.

H*

There were no professional administrators, legislators, judges—no bureaucrats of any kind. Athenian democracy amounted to government by amateurs. As such it might not be the best kind of government for the people, but it was literally government of and by the people. It best illustrates what Aristotle meant when he defined man as a "political animal": not an animal who joins a political party and conscientiously votes every other year or so, but one who participates naturally, freely, fully in the life of a *polis*.

Athenian democracy was shortly put to a severe test by the Persian Empire. Having suppressed an Ionian revolt stirred up by Miletus, the great Emperor Darius sent an army to subdue the troublesome Greeks on the mainland; it was repulsed by the Athenians, virtually unaided, at the battle of Marathon in 490 B.C. Ten years later the Emperor Xerxes himself led a huge host into Greece, marched on Athens, and sacked the city; but he failed to crush the spirit of its people. Several years before, when they had hit on a rich new vein in their silver mines, they had followed the advice of their statesman Themistocles, using this godsend to build a powerful fleet instead of squandering it on bonuses for every citizen. Now, as an army led by the Spartans retreated, they took to their ships and the nearby island of Salamis. Under the command of Themistocles, they here destroyed the Persian fleet in a great naval battle. This time they were aided by allies, but the Athenian fleet played the leading role, as Athenian determination had from the outset, and as it continued to do until the Persians were driven out of Greece for good a year later. In view of the golden age of Athens that followed, the battle of Salamis is surely one of the most decisive battles in the history of freedom.

Immediately it marked a significant contrast between the Athenians and the brilliant Ionians. Although the Ionians made some heroic stands, especially in Miletus, they displayed less political energy and less ardor for liberty. Following the defeat of Xerxes, to whose armada they had contributed a hundred ships, they rebelled against the Persians again when the Athenians and Spartans sent a fleet to their aid, and this time they regained their freedom; but before long they began succumbing again, to Persian intrigue and bribery rather than force of arms. More often than not they were ruled by tyrants, installed and maintained with enemy aid. If all along they generally prospered under the mild rule of the Persians, their creativity suffered; during the fifth century they produced relatively few great men or works. So Athens under Persian rule might have kept turning out its exquisite vases; but it could hardly have created the drama of Aeschylus, built the Parthenon, become "the school of Hellas."

Much more striking, and fateful, was the contrast between Athens and Sparta. The Dorians who invaded the region of Sparta in the Peloponnesus not only had maintained the original custom of Indo-European conquerors, living as warrior-lords above a mass of peasants, but had fixed the status of the peasants as "helots" or serfs. In the eighth century they conquered the neighboring Greek region of Messenia and reduced its populace to serfdom too. By then they were a small minority who had to put down repeated revolts; so to maintain themselves they evolved the celebrated constitution that was later attributed to the legendary Lycurgus. From the age of seven, every Spartan male was brought up in public barracks, trained to serve the state as a soldier until the age of sixty. He was forbidden to engage in agriculture, commerce, or any other profession; the state allotted him sufficient land, with helots to work it. With its professional standing army (the only one in Greece) Sparta had kings to serve as generals, magistrates to rule at home, a senate of elders to offer counsel, and an assembly to shout approval—not to debate. The Spartans accordingly became famous for their iron discipline and their valor, as exemplified when they fought and died to the last man at Thermopylae. Other Greeks found it hard to understand their way of life or to label their constitution, which was democratic in that all Spartans were "peers"; but they generally admired Sparta as the ultimate in absolute rule of law, which was yet by common consent of its citizens. Later Greek philosophers, prizing above all order and stability, were most impressed by it, since it had maintained its caste system for several centuries. Plato incorporated much of its system in his *Republic*.

We may be more impressed by the irony that in denying freedom to the masses of helots it denied personal freedom to the Spartans themselves. They could call nothing their own, neither their property nor their souls. (A visitor at their public mess remarked that now he understood why they had no fear of death.) They were more profoundly enslaved by a training that smothered any impulses to creativity, prevented any intellectual or cultural development; it sharpened the wits of adolescents only by training them to spy on and murder restive helots. In the seventh century, when Greek culture was dawning, Sparta produced some art and poetry worthy of this culture. In the fifth century, the golden age of Athens, it produced nothing whatsoever; the local archaeological museum has naught to show for this century, or for the next two. By this time the rulers of Sparta had become aware that any kind of commerce with other Greeks might be subversive. They were suspicious of all foreign visitors, expelling them when there seemed to be danger of contamination by foreign ideas, and they kept Spartans at home, sending them out only on military campaigns, forbidding them even to compete at the Panhellenic games. As they won the Peloponnesian War, historians are still dwelling on the moral and spiritual failings of democratic Athens, its sins of pride; but the moral they draw would be more wholesome if the discipline of proud Sparta had not been as utterly barren in fruits as immoral in purpose and inhuman in method.

Economists have also passed severe judgments on the Athenians for squandering so much effort and wealth on such unproductive enterprises as the Parthenon. "The works of Pericles served no economic purpose but that of display," wrote one; "they could not be realized in money, or exported to other lands, or utilized for the production of more wealth. The skill and treasure devoted to them were permanently sunk; their construction afforded a means of employing the people, but when completed they provided no employment for industry and no incentive to trade." Other economists today might view them with suspicion as incitements to "creeping socialism." Some Athenian aristocrats anticipated these charges, attacking the reckless extravagance of Pericles. The common people who supported him were doubtless prejudiced by selfish interests: they welcomed the employment. At any rate, the fact remains that the Athenians did devote a larger share of their surplus wealth than any state before or after them to works of art designed for the whole community, not for kings or the rich. The thrilling remains on their acropolis dispose most men to forgive their extravagance, and at least force a significant question: Freedom for what? To what end? And if this question is forever debatable, the Athenians at least did not give the trivial answer that the chief use of freedom is to accumulate wealth, more material means to a still unspecified end.

The source of their inspiration is likewise somewhat dubious, perhaps, inasmuch as it was not clearly the religious idealism suggested by all the temples and statues with which they glorified their acropolis. In its development the Athenian state had moved from a tribal-religious to a rational, secular basis. Although it retained a religious aura from deep-rooted attitudes and more especially from Athena, who was always on Athens' side, conventional Greek piety still required only ceremonial respect, not an ideal service of the god. The plainest inspiration of the Athenians was pride in their own achievements, beginning with their glorious victory over the Persians. If most of them were not so casual or skeptical as Pericles, who neglected even to mention the gods in his Funeral Oration, they still did not credit Athena with their victory any more than with their democratic constitution. Certainly Apollo had little spiritual influence on them: from his national shrine at Delphi his oracle had discouraged resistance to the Persians, predicting their victory, and he continued to play rather shady politics, usually favoring the Spartans. The very popular Dionysus, on the other hand, inspired no great temples or statues. Although Pisistratus had favored his cult for political reasons, Dionysus himself had no known political interests and no strong ethical ones; he offered his worshipers chiefly a spiritual freedom of sorts, including the freedom of unclassical excess. He did not directly inspire, either, the great tragic dramas that were performed at his annual festival.

These dramas, the most distinctive creation of Athens, may or may not have had an appreciable influence on its history; but they must concern us as the grandest expression of its living faith, the grandest response to its history. Apparently sprung from the annual ritual drama of the dying, resurrected god that for untold centuries had been performed all over the ancient East, Greek tragedy took on a philosophical content that basically altered its meaning and purpose. Performed under the eye of Dionysus, it was no longer a magical rite or means to supernatural power; the tragic poets never invoked his aid, never sought communion with him, never held out the slightest hope of resurrection or life immortal through him. They were still deeply concerned with the issues of mortality, the welfare of their community, but they endeavored to promote the civic welfare by wisdom instead of by miracle. Aeschylus led the way by returning to the tradition of Homeric epic, seeking to give lofty expression to the national ideals, or consciously to elevate these ideals. He created the incomparable theater of Athens: a theater representing the whole *polis,* attended by most of its citizens, held on a major civic occasion, concerned with the most vital civic issues. His popularity in his day attested to a remarkably high level of literacy and taste in the Athenian citizenry (later Aristophanes could even base a comedy on a critical debate over the relative merits of Aeschylus and Euripides—a theme simply unthinkable in popular drama today); but he had made it a level of high seriousness. After the great age of Athens, dramatists would

never again have the habitual privilege of addressing their whole community, on so great an occasion, in so hallowed a form, with such freedom to speak out of their loftiest thought and deepest feeling.

The most deeply religious of the tragic poets, Aeschylus was also
the most ardently patriotic. In his masterpiece, the *Oresteia* trilogy, he
sounds almost Hebraic as he insists that Zeus is just, evil comes only
from men, wrongdoers are inexorably punished—even unto the third
or fourth generation of their descendants. Yet unlike the prophets
of Israel, he was speaking in his own right as an Athenian, not in the
name of a God who had called him. Zeus had not given Aeschylus
such ideas—it was Aeschylus who was educating Zeus. And in *Eumen-
ides,* the concluding drama, he offered a radiant new vision. The
Furies who had been hounding Orestes, representing the old-time
religion of fear and the old tribal code of a tooth for a tooth, give way
to the civilized Olympians, "divinities that face the sun." Athena
emerges as the patron of the Athenian ideals of justice, reasonableness,
and civility, the "sacred" art of persuasion instead of rule by force.
Athens, she tells the Furies, is "the city of the just," devoted above all
to rule by law. She refers the case of Orestes not to Zeus but to a jury
of Athenian citizens, and when it is deadlocked she casts the deciding
ballot in favor of Orestes, or of rational, supratribal principles of
justice. The *Oresteia* has been called the *Divine Comedy* of Athens;
but it ends with a paean to Athens rather than to Zeus, a prayer that
Athens will remain true to her ideals of justice and civility. It expresses
the exalted patriotism of a poet who had fought at the battle of
Marathon, and who on his legendary epitaph asked to be remembered
only for his valor in this battle.

Still bolder was his *Prometheus Bound*. Here Zeus appears as a
brutal tyrant—much worse than the Zeus of Homer—bent on destroying mankind. Against him and his ministers Force and Violence stands
Prometheus, "the high-souled child of Justice" who had saved man in
defiance of Zeus, and is now ready to endure ages of torment rather
than repent and submit to him. As an out-and-out rebel against tyranny,
even when divinely sanctioned, Prometheus was a radically new type
in world literature. The possibility that he may have inspired the
Book of Job accentuates his uniqueness. Job gives up his bold effort
to understand the arbitrary ways of Yahweh; his drama ends in an
unconditional surrender, to a Voice that says nothing at all about
justice. Prometheus never wavers in his insistence on justice by rational,
human standards; the trilogy introduced by his drama apparently

ended in a reconciliation with a Zeus who came to accept these stand-ards.[9] Job became a symbol of patience, Prometheus a symbol of unconquerable spirit.

The idea of religious progress implicit in both these trilogies is in *Prometheus Bound* linked to a singular theory of human progress in general. Whereas Hesiod had made popular the myth of a Golden Age in the past—the kind of Eden myth found among most ancient peoples—Aeschylus anticipated the scientific account of man's origins. Once upon a time, Prometheus tells the Chorus, men had been witless creatures living in holes in the ground, knowing nothing, having eyes that saw to no purpose. He had not only brought them fire but taught them to yoke animals, build houses with bricks, dig up minerals, make ships, and with these technological arts and skills he had taught them writing, mathematics, astronomy, medicine. He had led them, in short, from savagery to civilization. Most likely Aeschylus conceived this outline of history as myth or metaphor, not scientific history; but in any case its implications are distinctive, and lead to the heart of the Greek achievement. It amounts to a paean to the humanistic values of civilization, ignored by the prophets of Israel. And the god who ostensibly created these values—the Bringer of Light—was again the poet's own idea. The historic Prometheus had been a primitive fire-god, who in Athens became the patron of some appropriate trades and by Hesiod was endowed only with cunning: he tricked Zeus into accepting the worst parts of the animals sacrificed to him by man, but gave no sign of any passion for justice or capacity for Christlike martyrdom. Aeschylus created him in his own Athenian image. This Prometheus was unlike the typical gods of the past, who had taught men chiefly duties, chiefly for the sake of their own proper service. His crowning gift to man, appropriately, was "blind hopes," that man might cease to live in fear of death, or of the gulf between him and the immortals.

Sophocles expressed a similar humanism more directly in a famous Chorus of his *Antigone*:

> Numberless are the world's wonders, but none
> More wonderful than man. . . .
> O clear intelligence, force beyond all measure!

---

[9] The two other plays have been lost but fragments suggest such a reconciliation, which was the usual ending in Aeschylus. At least the Zeus of the bad old days had to be re-formed before he could play his role in the *Oresteia*.

Many a pious moralist has contrasted this pride in man and his works with the humility of Israel: "What is man, that thou are mindful of him?" Actually, however, the contrast is not so simple. Like Homer, Sophocles had a humble enough view of man's fate—indeed, a darker view. No Homeric hero had to endure so terrible a fate as his Oedipus Rex. No great hero in all Greek tragedy illustrates so dreadfully the recurrent, almost obsessive theme of *hubris*. "It was above all Sophocles," writes E. R. Dodds, "the last great exponent of the archaic world-view, who expressed the full tragic significance of the old religious themes in their unsoftened, unmoralized forms—the overwhelming sense of human helplessness in face of the divine mystery, and of the *ate* that waits on all human achievement—and who made these thoughts part of the cultural inheritance of Western man."

Still, even this pessimism may be called proud, for it implies that man deserves a better fate. We sympathize with Oedipus, the apparent victim of the gods; we must wonder about the nature of these gods, who predestined the appalling fate he did his best to escape. What Sophocles thought about them is uncertain—much less clear than most critics make out, inasmuch as they differ widely in their accounts of his religious beliefs.[10] They differ, too, in their accounts of Aeschylus and Euripides; the clearest certainty is that the tragic poets themselves had diverse ideas about the gods and the human condition. The whole question brings us back to the uniqueness of Greek tragedy, and its significance in the history of freedom. There was no real tragedy in the ancient ritual dramas, nor in the later Christian mysteries, because there was never any question about their import or doubt about their outcome, which was always pure triumph. Greek tragedy typically ends in acceptance or reconciliation, on various terms; but wherever it ends, it begins as a profound inquiry into the human condition, a recognition of painful mystery. It begins in doubt, not faith. It questions the powers that be, by human standards. Like Oedipus Rex, it seeks the truth that may make man free, or make him mad: "I will know who I am." It is itself a manifestation of *hubris*—as God taught Job.

---

[10] Interpretations range from a pious, god-fearing Sophocles, who taught that man must always humble himself, before gods who are always right, to a defiant Sophocles, who in spite of the implacable gods insists on the dignity of man and glorifies above all the heroic spirit. The disagreements are widened because conventional critics tend to identify Greek piety with Christian piety, and unconventional critics to identify Greek skepticism with modern agnosticism. "My" Sophocles is a pupil of Homer, essentially as humanistic; but here it is enough to note the actual uncertainties about his religious beliefs. By common consent he is never so explicit as Aeschylus.

The spirit that created it was accordingly long smothered in Christendom—no prophet or saint has ever written tragedy; but with the emancipation of the Renaissance it would reappear. Hamlet would testify most eloquently to both the values and the penalties of the kind of spiritual freedom represented by tragedy.

In the *Antigone* of Sophocles, a value of particular historical significance has been obscured by pious moralists of a different stamp. Seeking always to read into Greek tragedy a justification of the ways of god to man, they have insisted that its heroine was properly punished because of her excessive pride. So it may have seemed to ordinary Athenians too: a mere woman was refusing to obey the law, defying the state. But this is precisely what makes Antigone significant: she deliberately chose death in obedience to a "higher law" above the state. While Aeschylus had proclaimed lofty ideals of justice, he proclaimed them in the name of Athens, and he suggested no serious conflict with its actual laws, or with the reigning ideal that a man's highest duty was to serve Athens. Sophocles here dramatized such a conflict. Antigone was a martyr to her conscience—a word still unknown to the Greeks, as to the Israelites. She foreshadowed the martyrdom of Socrates, with whom the explicit ideal of freedom of conscience begins to emerge, for the first time in history.

As a tragic poet, Sophocles knew that this was no simple issue either. "O fate of man, working both good and evil!" went on the famous Chorus in *Antigone* that chanted the wonders of man's spirit:

> When the laws are kept, how proudly his city stands!
> When the laws are broken, what of his city then?

The drama of Sophocles, which never ended on so triumphant a note as the *Oresteia* of Aeschylus (God Bless Athens!), reflected the costs of Athenian democracy, in internal and external strife. As an old soldier who had fought at Marathon, Aeschylus wrote in the glow of the triumph over the Persians, an era of glorious promise. The younger Sophocles knew this promise, having danced as a boy in the victory procession; but he lived through the fatal Peloponnesian War. He leads us to the still younger Euripides, who knew directly only the aftermath, and almost all of whose plays date from the period of the war.

As a freethinker, a bitter critic of the Olympian gods, often a critic of his fellow Athenians too, and generally a heretic in his treatment of both the traditional materials and the traditional form of tragedy, Euripides was notoriously the most "modern" of the tragic poets,

anticipating Ibsen. Relatively unpopular in his own day, he represented a type now fashionable but in his own day new—the artist
as conscious rebel. He was a friend of the Sophists, who similarly represented a new type of philosopher; they were professional educators, self-
conscious intellectuals setting up as critics of traditional belief and
behavior. With Euripides they are still controversial figures. In our
worried age they are commonly cast as the intellectual villains in the
tragedy of Athens itself: rationalists who undermined its ethical ideals,
impious humanists who declared that "man is the measure of all
things," relativists who taught that justice was merely a matter of
convention and law nothing sacred—skeptics when not downright
cynics, who "questioned everything and believed nothing."

They were in fact ambiguous troublemakers, who in their day probably did Athens more harm than good, but in the long run did her
much credit. Although the Sophists are known chiefly through the
writings of Plato, their inveterate enemy, they clearly prepared the
way for his master Socrates. At worst, they raised fundamental questions that had to be faced sooner or later. Their skepticism involved
something all too rare in the history of thought—a clear, honest
recognition of the limits of human knowledge. The cause of freedom
in particular has suffered much less from such admissions of uncertainty than it has from impassioned claims to certainty in matters not
in fact positively known, not to mention the patent falsehoods that
most men have held for truth throughout history. And the Sophists
clearly made some positive contributions by their critical, skeptical
spirit, beginning with the demonstration of falsehoods. By their awareness of convention—the power of custom recognized by Herodotus—
they exposed some provincial beliefs, as when Antiphon shocked pious
conservatives by denying that there was any "natural" difference between Greeks and "barbarians." One might wish that they had taught
Plato more than they did about such provinciality.

The critical spirit of Euripides, whom we know much better than
we know the Sophists, certainly sprang from no mere nihilism. As
plain as his cleverness was a serious aim to free men from delusion,
ultimately a positive idealism loftier than that of the traditionalists he
outraged. He was the first known writer of importance to attack the
institution of slavery and to uphold the cause of women. In *The Trojan
Women* he wrote the first major literary protest against the barbarities
of war. He attacked the Olympian gods for the same reason that he
debunked the traditional heroes: they sanctioned such inhumanity,

fell far short of civilized ideals. If at further expense to grandeur, he democratized tragedy by introducing the language of everyday life, he was the first to give common men a dignified role in it. Altogether, he no doubt earned his indictment for impiety: by respectable, conservative standards he unquestionably did tend to corrupt the youth of Athens. But so did his friend Socrates.

Looking back to the *Apology* of Socrates, we may at first see only the obvious magnanimity that places it among the noblest works of man. We know that he was not at all impious: he surely did believe in the gods in some "higher sense" that that of his accusers. We know too his complete integrity, proved by his willingness to die for his belief. He taught that men should seek first and last not wealth, power, or fame but the improvement of their soul, the spirit in man that seeks truth and goodness. As he professed no certain knowledge of an immortal soul, he taught the loftiest pagan ethic of goodness for its own sake, virtue as its own reward: "No evil can befall a good man, either in life or after death." He was the very model of a philosopher: a humble inquirer who was always reasonable, never fanatical, and wiser than others in remarking that he knew that he knew nothing; yet a dedicated inquirer who had absolute faith in the reality of truth, justice, and goodness. His fervor was tempered by his habitual irony (as in his profession of ignorance), and the rare freedom of philosophical humor and reserve. We know that he started Western man on the endless quest of wisdom and virtue through self-knowledge.

And so we may forget how literally revolutionary was a simple statement of Socrates in the *Apology:* "The unexamined life is not worth living." This is another landmark in the history of freedom. Like the teachings of the unholy Sophists, it represented a defiance of convention, of traditional piety, of the wisdom of the ancestors. It asserted that not authority but moral freedom was essential to moral order. As it got Socrates into trouble, so it will still get men into trouble, with themselves as well as with others. For once men begin examining the ideas they live by, there is no telling what they will come out with; the only certainty is that respectable ideas are in jeopardy. Still, this is what freedom of thought means—and why it has been uncommon in history.

More specifically, Socrates was the first martyr to the ideal of freedom of conscience. To Lord Acton, devout Catholic though he was, this was the very essence of freedom: "the assurance that every man shall be protected in doing what he believes to be his duty against the influence of authority and majorities, custom and opinion." With Socrates the ideal was at once clouded and ennobled by his reverence for law. In the *Crito* he rejected an opportunity to escape prison and the decree of death, arguing that it was his duty to obey the laws of Athens, laws to which he owed his education and his very existence; he did not argue that every man ought to have the legal *right* to do what he believes to be his duty. Yet he had flatly refused to hold his tongue, stop his heretical teaching. He asserted that he would not bow to authority and majorities, would not be bound by custom and opinion: he would live and die by the light within. And though he spoke of obeying a "daemon" within him, his stand was essentially different from the stand of the prophets of Israel. He did not maintain that this daemon was the living God of Greece, or any absolute supernatural authority. Socrates spoke as an individual, in effect for the individual.

His memory lived on, to make his martyrdom the most notorious blot on Athenian democracy. But that it lived on suggests a further tribute to the democracy. His fellow Athenians soon recognized the greatness of Socrates and felt the remorse he prophesied; tradition has it that his accusers were punished. Thereafter they carried on his habit of free inquiry and open discussion; centuries later their philosophers listened curiously to the subversive doctrine of a wandering Jew named Paul. At that, the Athenians had had some good excuse for silencing Socrates. To allow the individual to set his private conscience above the public law is always dangerous, inasmuch as conscience, alas, is not infallible or incorrupt. Socrates was the more dangerous because he was an ardent educator, every day seeking out the youth and attracting an eager following. He was not only scornful of public opinion but apparently critical of democracy itself, leaning toward aristocracy.[11] While he did not condone the "Rule of the Thirty"—aristocrats who took over Athens at the end of the Peloponnesian War and massacred many democrats in a bloody reign of terror—he had some close friends and pupils among them.

Most obviously, Socrates was a victim of the national disaster that

---

[11] It is uncertain to what extent he held the beliefs attributed to him by his pupil in the *Republic;* scholars are still debating where Socrates leaves off and Plato begins. The uncertainty, however, should not obscure the unmistakable difference between the Socrates of the *Apology* and the aging Plato of the *Republic,* or especially the *Laws.* This Plato prescribed an unexamined life for all but the rulers, rigorously censoring poetry and music as well as religion. He took a stand much like that of the Grand Inquisitor, on principles that would clearly justify the execution of Socrates.

ended the golden age of Athens. The city would recover from its defeat, and as the "school of Hellas" attract some more great artists and thinkers; but the end of the war marked the end of its real glory. Shortly before, Euripides had left for Macedon, the land of the future, where he wrote his masterpiece *The Bacchae* and died in voluntary exile. At about the same time Sophocles had died more appropriately at home, leaving as his last testament the sublime *Oedipus at Colonus* —the last great tragedy that Greece would write. Here there is only to add that in its fall—by its failure—Athens produced still another masterpiece. This was the history of the Peloponnesian War, by Thucydides.

Like Herodotus conscious of a high theme, Thucydides wrote with much more moral earnestness, but his history is therefore the more remarkable for its objectivity and restraint. His effort at impartiality would be admirable if only because he was himself a victim of the war, exiled from Athens for twenty years after a failure as a general (a fact he mentions casually in a single sentence, with no effort at self-defense). What makes it significant is his conscious scientific intention. He took great pains to get at the facts, collect and check up on all the available evidence, by consulting actors and eyewitnesses on both sides. He was more critical than Herodotus of the manifold fables of the Greeks, explicitly discounting or rejecting their traditions in the light of rational analysis. He deliberately refrained from all "romance," even though aware that its absence would detract from the popularity of his work; he was content if his history would prove useful to "those inquirers who desire an exact knowledge of the past." In particular he went much further than Herodotus in his inquiry into underlying causes, and his consistent view of them as natural causes, in the Hippocratic tradition; he did not shoulder off on the gods the burden of explanation. He was a world removed from the historians of Israel. The story he has to tell is a very dark one; but it constitutes one of the great works of the Athenian Enlightenment, another of its major contributions to freedom through self-knowledge.

Before taking up this story, however, we must note a significant omission of Thucydides. He went to such pains, denied himself the gratifications of popular applause, because he believed that the Peloponnesian War was "the greatest movement yet known in history," and that a true account of it would therefore be "a possession for all time"; yet he had very little to say about the greatness of Athens that alone made it momentous, of concern for all time. In this chapter we have considered only a few of the representative works of Athens, done nothing like full justice to its unparalleled creativity. Thucydides mentions none of its great works. Excepting Pericles, he mentions none of its great men either. He devotes only a few sentences to the Persian Wars, and to the brilliant period between Salamis and the outbreak of the Peloponnesian War: this whole passage was not "historic" enough to an Athenian who had come to take it for granted. One would never guess from his history that throughout the fateful war, sometimes with the enemy camped outside their walls, the Athenians carried on the rich cultural life that made their city the school of Hellas. They kept on adorning their acropolis, attending the plays of Sophocles, Euripides, and Aristophanes, listening to Socrates and the Sophists, speculating about everything under the sun. They even put on *The Trojan Women*—an impassioned denunciation of Athenian atrocities. (It was produced after their brutal assault on the neutral island of Melos, described by Thucydides.) They might have fared better had they devoted all their thought, energy, and wealth to the life-and-death struggle with Sparta. As it was, the glory and the tragedy were inseparably linked to the end.

| Chapter Seven | *THE FAILURE OF CLASSICAL GREECE* |

1. The Immediate Causes

The Peloponnesian War that broke out in 431 B.C., only fifty years after Salamis, and then raged on through brief intermissions until the surrender of Athens in 404, was by modern standards a piddling affair. In the account of Thucydides it sometimes seems ludicrous, the more so because of his grave, dignified manner: a story of crucial, savage campaigns that may be preceded by sophisticated debate, held up by oracles or festive games, terminated by a hasty setting up of trophies or silly disputes over who won—altogether giving the impression, I have remarked, of high-spirited, precocious schoolboys playing a stupid, vicious game. Yet this war was as momentous as the Persian Wars. Immediately it marked a fatal disaster for Athenian democracy; in a longer, broader view it signaled the failure of the Greeks as a whole, or of the first great historic adventure in the life of freedom. It is freighted with much more ominous significance than the Persian Wars, and calls for much closer attention.

The main outlines of the tragic drama are plain enough. Following the defeat of the Persians, Athens formed a confederacy to protect the Greeks against further assaults, in particular by maintaining a fleet; the smaller cities that could not afford to contribute ships paid in an annual sum of money to a federal treasury, set up on the holy island of Delos. Athens soon began laying down the law to its allies: refusing to allow them to secede, transferring the treasury from Delos to Athens, eventually using some of the funds for its own civic purposes, such as building the Parthenon. The Delian League in effect became an Athenian empire. Meanwhile Sparta, alarmed by its power, had built up a confederacy of its own with the help of Corinth, a bitter trade rival of Athens. Incidental wars between cities grew into general wars between the rival confederacies, culminating in the Peloponnesian War. Battles were fought all over the Greek world, for a long time to no lasting effect because the Spartan army dominated the land and the Athenian fleet controlled the sea. The turning point came in 413, when a great Athenian armada was utterly destroyed at Syracuse in far-off Sicily. Thereafter Athens managed only to prolong a losing battle. It gave up when the Spartans destroyed its last fleet in the Dardanelles, not far from Troy.

The immediate reasons for the failure of the Greeks are as plain. In his Funeral Oration Pericles told the bereaved Athenians that loyalty to one's country, death in its cause, outweighed all defects that a citizen might have as an individual. Local patriotism remained the highest good for the brilliant Greeks. Through Homer they had acquired a common consciousness as Hellenes, by the commerce and industry on which they flourished they had become increasingly interdependent, and in the national emergency of the Persian invasion many had managed to make common cause; yet they never had the wit to form a lasting union. They remained split by jealousy, continuing to war on one another. So the greatest movement in all history known to Thucydides was not the extraordinary flowering of Athens—it was only another war.

Worse, it was not a war fought on high principle, to make the Greek world safe for freedom or for any ideal whatever. As Thucydides himself saw it, it was a sheer power struggle, sprung from selfishness, greed, and ambition. It began disgracefully with a wanton attack by Thebes, which had collaborated with Xerxes, on its little neighbor Plataea, which had stood firm against the Persians. As the war went on, its savagery was intensified by class war within the cities. Oligarchs everywhere supported the Spartans, democrats the Athenians; and extremists on both sides took charge, butchering their enemies, crushing the moderates between them. In a famous passage Thucydides tells how the whole Greek world was demoralized by greed and lust for power. Frenzy passed for manliness, perfidy for loyalty, while prudence was branded as cowardice or treason, honesty became the badge of simpletons.

Still worse, "the school of Hellas" itself gave lessons in folly and infamy. When Pericles died, early in the war, the Athenians turned to demagogues; his successor Cleon played Machiavellian politics. According to Thucydides, their leaders became not merely callous but cynical, openly proclaiming that might makes right. He has it that the Athenians attacked the unoffending island of Melos merely because it wished to remain neutral, punishing it by slaughtering all its men of military age, enslaving its women and children. In this spirit they invited disaster by as wanton an attack upon Syracuse. It appears that Athens became hated as a tyrant city, and the demoralized Greeks looked to mindless Sparta as the liberator of Hellas.

Now, recent history has made this drama still more portentous. The whole world is engaged in the effort at which the Greeks failed, seeking to establish a United Nations and to avert a war that would be infinitely more catastrophic. It is split into two hostile camps, alike in their jealousy of their national sovereignty. America is cast in the role of democratic Athens, Russia of totalitarian Sparta. It is easy to draw lessons for America from the failure of Athens: the dangers of a short-sighted realism that depends on wealth and power more than on principles and ideals, or at their expense; of a self-righteousness that tends to alienate allies and to deny neutrals the right of neutrality; of the corruptions of materialism, self-interest, and business as usual; of the demagoguery that feeds on the insecurity and anxiety underlying complacence, and distracts the nation by witch-hunts. Americans might heed the wisdom of Pericles, who warned the Athenians that they had more to fear from their own blunders than from the enemy.

But it is too easy to draw such lessons. It may be seriously misleading even though—or even because—they are obviously salutary lessons. For democratic America is quite unlike Athens, revolutionary Russia still more unlike ultraconservative Sparta. The drama today not only is being enacted on an immensely greater stage, by an immensely larger cast, but involves radically different issues and principles. Our very awareness of much greater complexity, and much more terrible danger, is another significant difference. The youthful, parochial Greeks had little such historical consciousness. They could see the Peloponnesian War only as a struggle for the independence of their own little *polis*, not as the great national crisis that we can perceive, still less as the crucial test of Greek freedom or the Greek way of life. Thucydides, who did have some such sense of crisis, could still say that nothing very important had happened before his time, and so could hardly appreciate all that was at stake. Given our much greater knowledge, wider experience, fuller awareness, we need immediately to qualify the obvious explanations and judgments of the failure of the Greeks.

The traditional accounts of classical Greece, in which the Apollonian ideal suffuses the whole culture with composure, balance, harmony, sanity, "sweetness and light," at this point become profoundly unjust to the Greeks; for the idealists can account for their failure only in terms of some abrupt change or radical corruption. It appears that a glorious people all of a sudden went rotten. Then we may hear of the sins of selfishness and pride: an old story that is always pertinent, but so old and familiar that it explains little, and simplifies a great deal. For these are quite unoriginal sins, common to all great societies at all times, and perhaps most conspicuous in societies on the rise. What people or nation was humble, meek, unselfish, or indifferent to worldly goods as it came up in the world? Not America, surely; but as surely not ancient Greece either.

There remain other plain reasons for the failure of the Greeks. To begin with, they were pioneers in the free, open society. They were engaged in a much riskier enterprise than the settled societies of the ancient East, one that by its nature guaranteed instability, and bred internal as well as external threats to their security. Their excesses were understandable in view of their exceptional creative energy, which is naturally turbulent and destructive of traditional sanctities, but they were more understandable because as pioneers the Greeks had no historic landmarks to guide them, no long tradition to steady them, no time-tested institutions to support them. In particular they had no precedents for a democratic federation. Scattered as they were all over the Mediterranean world, they could not in any case have readily formed a United Greek States, but there were ideal reasons too for their failure to unite. As Kitto observes, they knew of a great state, the Persian Empire, and naturally they wanted none of it; nor would they want to be represented by anybody in a remote parliament—they knew all the advantages of the intimate *polis* and were used to governing themselves.

At the same time these restless, ambitious youngsters were subject to the ancient traditions of violence and war. The Peloponnesian War was by no means a corruption or a break with the past. The dazzling Greeks had always been given to war, not on behalf of ideals of justice or any cause holier than independence; war was a major concern of the walled *polis*. No important thinker ever questioned its legitimacy or took up the problem of militarism. Similarly the Greeks took piracy for granted. Solon made provision for it in his laws; Thucydides still considered it quite legal, as did Aristotle a century later. Hence we must discount somewhat Thucydides' account of the demoralization of the Greeks. If they evidently grew more cynical or savage, they nevertheless had no high tradition of unselfish idealism, or of devotion to any cause beyond the *polis*. They had not risen as a man when Athens heroically withstood the Persian hosts, but had looked to self-interest; many had sat out the war, many others fought for the Great King, and all along oligarchs and would-be tyrants were ready to sell out to him. Within the *polis* the Greeks had long known violent factionalism, bitter class struggle. Civil war often broke out for the most trifling reasons; in his *Politics* Aristotle noted at least four revolutions, including one in holy Delphi, that started over quarrels about a marriage. The responsibilities of freedom never became engrained habits as they have in established democracies today.

And so we might make some allowance even for the Athenians, the freest and most brilliant of the Greeks, whose poets and architects gave immortal expression to the classical ideal, and whose unclassical character was summed up by Thucydides: "They were born into the world to take no rest themselves, and to give none to others." Historians are still more likely to do some injustice to the defeated when they favor the cause of the defeated, for they must find some good reason why the right side lost.[1] They pay tribute to Athens in judging it by higher standards than they do mindless Sparta, but in harping on its obvious sins they tend to slight another obvious reason for its defeat—the historical accident of the plagues that devastated it early in the Peloponnesian War, killing off about a quarter of its people. Among the victims was Pericles, the great leader who otherwise might have led it to victory. Thucydides noted that the plagues had much to do with the demoralization and recklessness of the Athenians.

At that we may also discount somewhat his account of how the liberator of Hellas became a "tyrant city." Though it was not so simple as his admirers often make out, he was clearly hostile to Athenian democracy and sometimes misleading; thus Melos, which he describes as an unoffending neutral, was in fact a friend of Sparta, once sheltering its fleet. Like almost all classical thinkers, he paid little attention to the Greek economy, and so ignored the economic necessities—due to the wisdom of Solon—that made the imperialism of

---

[1] A popular historian has said, for example, that "no people in history has been more tyrannical and cruel than the Athenians at certain moments." Possibly he considered Hitler's Nazis too recent to belong to "history," but even so he might have remembered that the Athenians did not torture men to death as did many other peoples, including medieval Christians.

Athens not simply a matter of lust for power. Seapower was vital to Athens because it was dependent on grains imported from the Black Sea region; it needed to maintain control of the sea in self-defense against the still-mighty Persian Empire. Had it allowed other cities freely to pull out of the Delian League, as some soon started to, this would certainly have dwindled if not broken up. It could hardly hope, either, to allay the jealousies of Sparta and Corinth by sweet reasonableness. As it was, the "tyrant city" remained generally popular with the democratic parties in other cities. In the depths of its supposed degradation it was still providing an audience for Sophocles, Euripides, and Socrates.

In any case, it was not simply democracy that failed. Conservative scholars have often dwelt on the shortcomings of the common people of Athens, as a classic example of what happens when the "lower classes" dominate government; but all the excesses reported by Thucydides were as rife among the aristocrats, who everywhere generally sided with Sparta. Athenian aristocrats made repeated efforts to betray their city to Sparta; and when they came into power, at the end of the war, they imposed a much more atrocious tyranny than had any of the demagogues before them. They were as lacking in wit as in idealism, for they might have known that victorious Sparta would have nothing to offer Hellas, not even security for themselves. Its famous discipline had only selfish ends, which in victory soon became corrupt. Sparta sold out to the Persians the Greek cities in Asia Minor, in return for Persian aid in its wars on other Greeks. There was no mourning in Hellas when, within a generation after its victory, its power was broken by hitherto inglorious Thebes. Meanwhile the Athenians remained proud of their democracy, which they restored and maintained through the fourth century.

There remains another obvious fact: the faith that had made Athens great did not die, any more than did the faith that made Israel. The forms always die, wrote Croce, die in men's arms; so "the universe darkens before their gaze, and the only history that they can relate is the sad one of the agony and death of beautiful things." The Greeks could appreciate this kind of poetic history, since they wrote as well as made tragedy. But as Croce added, the spirit behind the forms does not die, history is still the history of life. The Greeks could appreciate this too, though not so vividly. They had a deep sense of mortality, of impermanence, of time as the enemy of man and all his works; and they could never have dreamed that their spirit would live on in such a civilization as ours. As their inheritors, we owe it to them to consider more deeply the issues raised by the tragic outcome of their adventure in freedom.

2. *Interlude: The Deeper Issues*

Although factionalism and war may sufficiently account for the political failure of the Greeks, and certainly speak louder than their words, their brilliant achievements in thought invite not only a harsher judgment of their folly but a study of the underlying reasons why they should have known better, and did not. The most familiar analyses of their failure have generally started out from Thucydides. One plausible theory has it that their living faith was corroded by individualism and rationalism, as represented most conspicuously by the impious Sophists; these movements undermined not only the traditional wisdom of moderation but the traditional sanctities, the essential belief in objective principles of justice. Another theory, recently made popular by Arnold Toynbee, has it that the Greeks all along lacked the religious beliefs essential to idealism: they worshiped Man, and so were doomed to discover his insufficiency. For a student of freedom the difficulty remains that individualism, rationalism, and humanism were the plainest conditions of the distinctive Greek achievement. Later they were as plainly linked to the growth of freedom in the Western world; and all history suggests that they are indispensable conditions of a free society. Although they may be united with a faith in a divine power, this faith alone has never produced such a society. Freedom lovers will always disagree on the sort or the degree of individualism, rationalism, and humanism that is desirable; but they can never afford a blanket condemnation of the basic principles.

Now, in general the new ways of thought and life cultivated by the Greeks naturally generated confusion, tension, and disharmony. In the normal course of events, many men would resist these ways, many more would fail to keep up with them, and the society as a whole would fail to accommodate them adequately. The new aspirations and energies might run wild for want of clearly defined, approved channels of expression. Pericles was pleased to say that the Athenians trusted more to their native spirit than to "system and policy"; but however versatile and resourceful their spirit, they might have done better with more system and more definite policy. For the freedoms he boasted of were mostly unsupported, as uncontrolled, by strong institutions, clear principles, or deeply engrained habits. They had grown out of class war, through shifting compromises, and were exposed to shifting interests. They were protected by no professional jurists, no professional public servants of any kind. There was no system of public schools in Athens to prepare the young for life in a democracy, no higher education at all until the Sophists came along. There were no organized political parties to formulate policy, channel differences of opinion, or effect compromise by alternate rule. The Greeks had especial need of wise statesmen, and produced some notable ones; but they did not produce enough of them, or have any reliable means of keeping them in power.

In particular, the individualism of the Greeks was more likely to become reckless and lawless, or simply selfish, because it was neither sanctioned nor disciplined by any explicit democratic or religious principle. It was rooted in the Homeric tradition of personal fame and glory and was nourished by habitual competition, as much in art and athletics as in business, but everywhere off the battlefield with little team play. (Lovers of Greek art may forget that the great tragic poets competed annually for a prize, being ranked 1-2-3 and also-rans, and that victors in the Olympic games whom Pindar honored by odes stood out still more because there were no second or third places, as no team scores.) On the one hand, the individualism was tempered by little sense of strictly moral responsibility, or in particular of altruism. The classical Greeks came closest to such a sense in their insistence on patriotic duty, but this duty was more practical than ethical, a means chiefly to tribal victory; the patriot was not morally responsible to God or mankind. On the other hand, there was as little clear sense of the rights of the individual or the sanctity of the person. He could not be held up to a clear ideal of altruism if only because there was no word for him, or for "ego." There was no place for him in the civic temple, no article about him in the laws of the *polis;* the constitution of democratic Athens never included a Bill of Rights. The unconcern for civil liberties, or for the person as a person, was typified by the institution of ostracism: any Athenian could be exiled for ten years if a sufficient number of his fellow citizens considered him a menace, or for any reason wanted him out of the way. If some dangerous aristocrats were thus ostracized, so was the celebrated Aristides the Just, and so might have been Pericles; in any case the banished man had no legal recourse. Here was one reason for the commonness of treason in classical Greece, long before its "demoralization."[2]

The marked individuality of the Greeks, and the considerable freedom they usually enjoyed in private and civic life, may obscure an essential feature of their *polis* that calls for caution in generalizing about their individualism. For however understandable reasons, they never specifically delimited the authority of the state. They were not so explicit, to be sure, as some worshipers of the modern nation-state. (They would have blinked at Mussolini's credo: "All for the state; nothing outside the state; nothing against the state.") Still, they failed to formulate a principle of individual rights against the state, or freedom from it. They walled off from it no major domain, such as religion; they set no ethical goods on principle above the good of the state. Aristotle would mention the problem of the good man in the bad state, only to drop it at once—without mentioning Socrates. Like most classical thinkers on record, he worried much more over the bad man in the good state, and saw the chief danger as not too much interference but too much freedom.

The issue of Greek rationalism is more complicated. There is little question that some of the later Sophists tended to undermine the foundations of traditional morality. In their cleverness they taught chiefly the art of how to win arguments, "make the worse appear the better case," and justified such practice by asserting that morality was merely self-interest, justice merely the interest of the stronger. As they were evidently popular with the bright young men of Athens, they must have been of some aid and comfort to the unprincipled, especially the political leaders who had adopted a policy of Machiavellian realism —a kind of realism that pure rationalists are prone to. When most serious, furthermore, the Sophists attacked on principle any absolute standards of right and wrong. It can be argued that men generally need to believe in the absolute truth of their moral principles, and that only religion can surely give them this conviction. Fifth-century Greece, Henry Bamford Parkes concludes, demonstrates "the inadequacy of rationalism alone as a guide for human life."

---

[2] It is also another possible explanation of why the Athenians lost the Peloponnesian War. They turned on the licentious but brilliant, energetic Alcibiades, relieving him of his command in the armada against Syracuse. They had good reason to distrust him, as he later proved his unscrupulousness by betraying both Athens and Sparta; but facing possible exile, he had some reason to look out for his own interests first. He had the precedent of the great hero Themistocles, who after Salamis left Athens and lived off the bounty of the Persians.

Yet religion "alone" is clearly as inadequate for a free society; so it must be repeated that without rational inquiry and criticism no society can maintain a conscious ideal of freedom. If the Sophists demonstrated the perils of such criticism, the traditionalists of Athens demonstrated more emphatically that piety is no certain bulwark of liberty; it was they—not the bright, corrupt young men—who sentenced Socrates to death for impiety. The perils have been magnified, moreover, because of a popular fallacy immortalized by Plato (a more respectable kind of rationalist). As he attacked the Sophists on the grounds that the cause of truth and justice required a belief in fixed, absolute standards, so thinkers today often attack all relativists, asserting that the cause of freedom and democracy likewise requires such a belief. Actually, there is no logical reason why a relativist may not prefer a free society; more logically, he ought to be liberal in his views—as most of the Sophists apparently were. (Protagoras in particular seems to have defended the ideals of democracy and human rights.) Neither is there any logical reason why an absolutist should prefer democracy, or justice conceived as equal rights. Throughout history most absolutists have been authoritarians, hostile to the cause of freedom and democracy—as Plato himself distinctly was.

In any case, the evil reputation of the Sophists raises another fundamental question: How much influence did they actually have on the popular mind? As always, we cannot be sure; but just because of the remarkable pioneering achievements of the Greeks, we may assume that there was a considerable gulf between the intellectual leaders and ordinary men, even in highly literate Athens. Thus some historians say that by the time of Euripides most Athenians were skeptics, as might be expected from all the intellectual ferment; but the fact remains that Euripides was unpopular, and once was indicted for impiety. Protagoras was expelled from Athens because of a skeptical treatise he wrote on the gods, and so was Anaxagoras for such teachings as that the divine sun was only a hot rock. Aristophanes won popular applause (and repeatedly the first prize) by attacking all these "intellectuals," especially Socrates, anticipating the attitude of modern American conservatives. Lovers of free Greece are embarrassed, indeed, because such witch-hunts are known to have occurred nowhere except in Athens. Immediately the indictments point again to a defective rationale: free as thought usually was, there was no clear, avowed principle of freedom of thought and speech. Ultimately they suggest that if the rationalists were influential enough to frighten conservatives,

Athens may have suffered more from a positive irrationality.

We are always likely to forget how much prehistoric superstition survived in the mentality of the brilliant, precocious Greeks—even the greatest Greeks. It is written all over the work of Hesiod, whose science of agriculture includes warnings against "overstepping taboos." It crops up unexpectedly in the loftiest passages of the poets, such as Aeschylus; in his bold vision of human progress he noted rhapsodically that not the least of the great blessings Prometheus had brought to man were "the ways of seercraft," the arts of divination. The classical Greeks always depended on these arts, consulting omens and oracles in every emergency, filling the national shrine of Delphi with monuments to their credulity. One instance brings up still another unwholesome reason why Athens lost the Peloponnesian War. The general Nicias, who succeeded the impious Alcibiades to the command of the armada against Syracuse, was about to give up the fruitless campaign and sail for home when an eclipse of the moon occurred. Had the Athenians heeded Anaxagoras, the rational philosopher they banished, they would have known that eclipses are predictable events having natural causes. Nicias knew it was a dread omen, consulted his soothsayers, and heeded their warning: the armada must stay on in Syracuse for thirty days. So it stayed on, to be annihilated, and virtually to assure the defeat of Athens.

Despite the growth of philosophy, such irrationality was more pronounced in fifth-century Athens than in the society pictured by Homer. One apparent reason was that the rise of democracy brought popular religion to the surface: the common people had never been really emancipated from magic or miracle, clinging to primitive beliefs that the aristocratic Homer ignored. Another apparent reason was a growing anxiety or dread, perhaps reflecting an insecurity due to the continual wars, which made it harder for the Greeks to know themselves and be themselves. Its symptoms include the popularity of "cathartai," experts in ritual purification, but they appear in the greater writers as well. They are foreshadowed by the powers of darkness that begin to reappear in the *Odyssey*. In Herodotus the gods are much more jealous and pitiless than Homer's Olympians, and they are no less pitiless in the thought of some other writers who made them concerned with justice. Now they punished not only evildoers but the descendants of evildoers—spreading a notion of hereditary guilt that was unknown to Homer, and that discouraged ideas of personal rights and responsibilities. Worse, guilt commonly took the form of *miasma*, a pollution due to no conscious moral offense. A terrible example was the *Oedipus Rex* of Sophocles. Homer's Oedipus was no outcast, continuing to reign after his dreadful, unwitting offense was discovered; whereas in Sophocles' drama all Thebes has been afflicted with blight and plague because of a defilement that the gods had preordained, that Oedipus had done his best to avoid, and that the unhappy Thebans knew nothing of.[3] Euripides was indignant at such divine injustice, but the more indignant because most Athenians took it for granted that innocent and guilty alike must suffer from *miasma,* and did not hold the gods up to rational moral standards.

We are accordingly brought back to the basic anomalies of Greek religion. The thesis that the decay of Greek morals was due to a decay of religious faith is always seductive (even though, to judge by the writings of traditionalists in every age, religion and morals have been decaying steadily all through history). It always remains hard, however, to size up the actual state of religion and morals in any given society: to determine how deep the religious faith went, how much it affected social behavior, or how generally and how far men lived up to their professed ideals, religious or ethical. It is especially hard with fifth-century Greece and its medley of spiritually incompatible Olympian, nature, and mystery gods, backed by a mythology that included many grotesquely indecent, absurd fables. Again we may be baffled by the mentality of even the greatest poets—as when we hear that Sophocles entertained the new snake-god Asclepius in his own home, until a suitable shrine could be prepared. At any rate, the specific question is to what extent this incongruous religion had buttressed or promoted ethical idealism, in particular the ideals of justice that were flouted during the Peloponnesian War. The evidence remains conflicting; but I judge that chiefly it gives reason to doubt a close connection.

Homer, the educator of Hellas, had certainly not taught a faith in divine or cosmic justice. Hesiod fathered a different tradition when he affirmed that the gods were just, even making Zeus over into a "farseeing" guardian of the rights of the poor and oppressed. Solon sometimes spoke in the language of Hesiod, as did some other poets, and men also spoke of the universal law of Dike—Eternal Right. But in spite of this education the Olympians were still not clearly given to moral indignation during the great age of Athens. Aeschylus said in

---

[3] This whole development, which exemplifies a long-neglected aspect of the Greek mentality, is outlined in *The Greeks and the Irrational*, by E. R. Dodds.

so many words that his ethical religion was unconventional: the chorus in the *Agamemnon* that declares the gods to be just, and evil to be solely the work of man, also declares, "Far from others I hold my mind." Among those others was Herodotus, the historian of Greek freedom. While the more analytical Thucydides dwelt on evils due solely to men, he represented irreligion as a symptom rather than the cause of demoralization. The Greeks, he observed, were deterred by "no fear of God or law of man"—implicitly distinguishing, not identifying, divine and human law. The stancher defenders of the old-time faith were most shocked by ritual sacrilege or impiety in thought, not unrighteousness in behavior. In Athens they whipped up popular feeling against Alcibiades by the charge that he had mutilated the Hermae, statues of a prehistoric deity, thereby indicating that most Athenians still revered their ancient idols, were not wholly corrupt after all, but were not very spiritual either. And everywhere the violent class war seems to have raged with little appeal to the gods. We hear of no great leader, political or spiritual, denouncing social injustices as an offense against them.

The plainest value of Olympian religion for the purposes of a free society remains not the positive faith or inspiration it offered, but the relative freedom from "miracle, mystery, and authority." If its essential humanism represented the sin of pride, it had nevertheless made possible the most distinctive achievements of the Greeks; had they taken the Hebraic view of man, they could not have set up their ideal of culture. If it had much to do with their shortcomings as well, these were not, after all, very different from the shortcomings of godlier peoples, including the Israelites. And as with their rationalism, the Greeks suffered from not only the excesses but the limitations of their humanism.

Given the many signs of superstitious anxiety, one must qualify Toynbee's thesis that the Greeks worshiped Man. Until near the end of the fifth century the very word for "human" did not convey the idea of man's superiority over the brute world, but distinguished him from the divine: he was a frail mortal being. Their greater writers never allowed the Greeks to forget the gulf between man and the often jealous immortals, or to stake everything on the "blind hopes" that Prometheus had given them; none had anything like the fierce pride of Dante, say. The choruses of Greek tragedy, which usually express a prudential "citizen ethic," repeatedly warn against human presumption. It was the much-abused Sophists who began to dignify

man, rather than merely heroic or excellent men; yet in making him
"the measure of all things" they were still not being simply proud, for
thereby they were declaring the limitations of his knowledge, as in
his inability to get certain knowledge of the gods. They were in some
respects humbler than their critics, emphasizing that the Greeks knew
much less about man and his works than they thought they did. Least
of all was Euripides a man-worshiper. Among his most characteristic
tragic themes (as in *Medea* and *The Bacchae*) was the terrible power
of passion, the irrational in man. His rare compassion was excited
by as rare indignation against the apparent injustice of the gods, but
more especially by the inhumanity of man to man. And his protests
against war and slavery imply another reason why most classical Greeks
failed in reverence for Man: they had no clear conception of Man
apart from the *polis*. As they lacked a declared principle of respect
for the person, or the rights of man as man, so they had still less sense
of crimes against Humanity than of sins against God.

Thus the Funeral Oration of Pericles, which never mentioned the
gods, was no paean to human dignity either. Democracy, he boasted,
had made Athens a model for imitation by other Greeks; and he might
have added that it made Athens disposed to support democratic parties
in other cities—for diplomatic reasons. But he never suggested that
Athens had a mission to defend democracy, much less to spread its
blessings. He expressed nothing like the sense of high dedication in
Lincoln's comparable Gettysburg Address: dedication to a supra-
national cause of liberty and equality, that government of, by, and for
the people should not perish from the earth. The manifest destiny of
Athens was to maintain its own greatness. Pericles asserted a proud
faith in Athenians—not in man, nor even in Greeks.

At that, his hopes may now look modest. While the Greeks had no
idea of original sin, they had much less faith in human potentialities
than Westerners have had. They had no faith in progress, of course.
The unique vision of human progress in *Prometheus Bound* gave no
hint of continued progress in the future; the most that Aeschylus
apparently hoped for was that Athens would stay true to the laws
already on the books. Lacking anything like modern science, the
Greeks could hardly dream of indefinitely improving their earthly
condition. But neither did they bank on the possibilities of growth,
the powers of freedom, realized in their own history. While celebrating
Mind as the source of man's dignity, the means to the good life, they
did not conceive it as a dynamic power, a means to transforming their

world; none of the many revolutions in their cities sprang from revolutionary principles or programs. The turmoil of their open society induced rather a yearning for a static, closed order, corresponding to the classical forms of their art and appearing in the common admiration of the Spartan state. The Greeks grew more fearful of the change they had once welcomed, more disposed to assume that the natural tendency of change was always for the worse. In time the main end of Mind would become peace of mind.

Perhaps the clearest index to the limitations of the classical Greek spirit is Heraclitus, the philosopher who most truly reflected the basic conditions and costs of the Greek adventure in freedom. He was one of the few major thinkers to regard change as an essential reality. ("One cannot step into the same river twice.") For him being was endless becoming, permanence lay only in the order and regularity of change. Similarly he saw the life of man as perpetual tension and strife. "It is the opposite that is good for us"; good can be known only through evil, justice only through strife, harmony only through "an attunement of opposite tensions, like that of the bow and the lyre." The one known philosopher to reject the traditional wisdom of moderation or limit, he pointed toward the tension between the Apollonian and the Dionysian spirit that was one key to the actual achievement of the Greeks. Yet Heraclitus was no more a crusader for freedom, experiment, and adventure than any other philosopher. He apparently did not regard change as potential growth. He held out no promise of a better future, advocated no program of action to make it better. For him, one gathers, the main use of Mind was more to contemplate change than to effect it or direct it.

Even so, Heraclitus recalls us to the exceptional range, variety, and originality of Greek thought. It is not at all surprising that these fledglings failed to realize fully and to respond successfully to the challenge of their pioneering achievements. The wonder remains that they dared and achieved so much, with such relatively limited material and intellectual resources. My point is simply that in justice to them, and to the issues of freedom, we must remember that the conditions of their extraordinary achievement included inexperience, immaturity, considerable ignorance, and an ancient legacy of violence, superstition, and dread, as well as the inevitable costs of freedom.

3. *The Response of the Philosophers: Plato and Aristotle*

As Hegel remarked, the owl of Minerva (or Athena) begins its flight with the approach of twilight. The owls in the century following the fall of Athens were the immortal Plato and Aristotle, the supreme symbols of Greek wisdom; but even so one may be depressed by their kind of wisdom, may sense in it the growing dusk and chill. Both Plato and Aristotle were much less impressed by the achievements of Athenian democracy than by its debacle. Both repudiated the ideals expressed in the Funeral Oration of Pericles; democracy to them meant chiefly mob rule, a prelude to anarchy or tyranny. Both were much more concerned about order and stability than freedom and creativity. At the same time both failed to learn the most obvious lesson, the insufficiency of the little *polis.* Their foreign policy still came down to war, not federation or union—the war that was still going on among the Greek cities, until all fell under the domination of Macedon. In this view their political thought was a symptom of the failure of the Greeks, offering neither a feasible solution for their contemporaries nor an inspiring ideal for those who cherish freedom. And so one may be still more depressed by the reflection that their works became the recognized classics of Greek political thought, the models for Western political thinkers. Considering their thought as a whole, they became the most influential philosophers in Western tradition, for centuries revered as symbols of radiance rather than twilight. Attaining an authority such as they never did in the Greek world, they often served as bulwarks of an authoritarianism foreign to the genius of Greece in its prime.

Yet their works were indeed monuments to this genius. However dubious their political ideals, Plato and Aristotle remain the fathers of political philosophy: the first known thinkers to think through its issues systematically, to get down to basic principles beneath practice and convention, and to offer a coherent, comprehensive theory of the state. This effort was in keeping with their whole philosophical enterprise, which led them to ask all the basic questions. And on every one of these questions they had something fruitful to say. Whatever its effects, their own thought was remarkable for its freedom—its range and mobility, boldness and suggestiveness. Essentially it was by no means a departure from Greek philosophic tradition, but a highly impressive culmination of it. Their aim remained enlightenment and emancipation, by running reason through all the major interests of man; their method remained open, their style lucid, their tone civil. A student of Western freedom must reckon with them in any case; but simply as he deplores tendencies they represented he must first of all acknowledge that their immense influence was a tribute to the fertility and vitality of their thought.

We may take our cue from the philosophical idealism for which Plato is most famous. Coming out of a native tradition going back to Pythagoras, it may have been suggested by his teaching that number was the key to the universe. As numbers were mental constructs, immaterial and immutable, that somehow defined the order underlying the appearances of the physical world, so Plato speculated that the "real" world is spiritual, a suprasensible realm of eternal forms or essences which only the mind can perceive, and of which the physical world is only a shadow or imperfect copy. Such idealism has profoundly ambiguous implications. It has led many thinkers to debase the natural world in which men must carry out their purposes, to divorce the ideal from natural possibilities of truth, beauty, and goodness, and to declare that the human spirit is forever an alien in the only home it can surely know. It can also be a mode of liberation, as it was to the enthusiastic Platonists of the Italian Renaissance and to many poets and thinkers thereafter: a declaration of spiritual independence from the vanities of the passing show, and an assurance that man's ideal aspirations, his loftiest visions of the Good, are bills of spiritual rights written in the constitution of the universe. Immediately, however, the ambiguities lead us to the heart of Plato—or more precisely, to the different Platos that have moved men in the West, in ways that he could never have anticipated, and often might have disapproved.

His famous theory of Ideas was only a speculation, developed in several of his earlier dialogues. Plato did not build on it in his later works. In *Parmenides* he returned to it only to dwell on the basic objections to it, such as the problem of how to connect the eternal, perfect Ideas with the temporal world of imperfect appearances. One reason why his thought is so richly suggestive is that he never developed a complete system, or at least refused to commit himself to one in his writings. Although he grew more doctrinaire, especially about politics, his thought remained a quest, his main concern not Platonism but philosophy. He was true to his faith that "we shall be better and braver and less helpless if we think that we ought to inquire than we should have been if we indulged in the idle fancy that there was no knowing and no use in seeking to know what we do not know."

The spirit of inquiry was emphasized by Plato's characteristic medium—the Socratic dialogue. If it could grow perfunctory and mechanical, interlocutors acting as mere stooges for Socrates, it could also give freer play to the exceptional literary gifts that make Plato one of the most readable of philosophers, and one of the few who can be reread with pleasure as well as profit. In any case the dialogues presented his thought in terms of a public discourse, kept it rational in frame even when mystical or mythical in content. They are always debates about the debatable, in which alternatives to his own theories are necessarily pointed out. Sometimes they are inconclusive, implying a measure of skepticism or ironic reserve—the puzzlement that he said philosophy had begun in, and that is needed to keep it alive.

In this spirit Plato set up his Academy, which was to last for some nine hundred years. It was an institution of high importance as the first real university by modern standards, and incidentally about the only lasting institution developed by classical Greece. Founding it to meet the need of the intellectual training that Athens had failed to provide, and that he later argued should be provided by the state, Plato did not seek primarily to turn out pure Platonists. True to the Greek spirit—and still to the needs of the democracy he despised—he sought rather to teach students to think for themselves. And though his curriculum soon became academic in the disagreeable sense, as he himself considered a knowledge of geometry the first requisite for statesmen, his views are still pertinent for educators in a democracy. He did not believe that the main business of education is to purvey useful information, or to "adjust" students to other unthinking people.

Hence even Plato's authoritarian *Republic* remains a model for discussion, not to say a mine of stimulating thought. While he subordinated the individual to the state, he at least had a lofty conception of the state as a means to the good life. Its proper end was not wealth and power but justice. For Plato the ideal means to justice was now rule by wise men, instead of rule by law, but he was still a good enough Greek to consider tyranny the worst form of government. His philosopher-kings implicitly recognized principles of universal justice, beyond mere expedience, grounded on the nature of man and the requisites for the good life. He foreshadowed the concept of natural law, from which later thinkers would derive a principle of equality that he himself explicitly rejected. Say the worst about his *Republic*, it forces us back to first principles, and should remind us that Israel and the ancient East never produced a work like this.

In such fundamental respects Plato's most famous pupil, Aristotle, was a complete credit to him. Trained in the Academy, Aristotle proceeded to systematize some of his master's doctrines, but he was also stimulated to much fruitful disagreement. His own bent was primarily empirical and naturalistic. He accordingly put Plato's Ideas back into the natural world, where as fixed forms they might mislead scientists until the time of Darwin, but might also be investigated and exploded as they could not be in a supernatural realm. He himself made first-hand pioneering studies in biology, which were unsurpassed until the eighteenth century. Aristotle even stressed a basic principle of development in nature, foreshadowing the theory of evolution. His recognition of a comparable development in Greek philosophy gave him a perspective that might compensate for his want of irony or humor.

In political thought, Aristotle's empirical bent led him to make a comparative study of the many different constitutions of the Greek cities. From this he derived a theory of the state less consistent and neat than Plato's but also less despotically ideal, more reasonable and humane, closer to the realities of community and fellowship. He recognized the values of the family and private property, which Plato sacrificed for the sake of complete devotion to the state. His defense of private property is especially important as the first reasoned case for it on record; his arguments long endeared him to middle-class liberals and are still pretty much the stock arguments.[4] Similarly he adhered to the Greek ideal of rule by law, perceiving the dangers of the absolute power that Plato was willing to entrust to his philosopher-kings; in the Middle Ages his authority was invoked to support the principle of constitutional government. Although no democrat, he could admit that the judgment of the many about public affairs might be better than that of the aristocratic few. He conceived the ideal state as a "mixed" one, including some democratic elements—an ideal that has haunted Western thought to this day.

The fame of Aristotle, however, has been due most obviously to his synthesis of Greek thought and knowledge, ranging from physics and

---

[4] They are that private property gives pleasure, provides an incentive that makes for progress, enables men to be liberal and practice generosity, and is "natural," because backed by the experience of the ages. About commerce, however, Aristotle had little to say except to disparage it as "a mode by which men gain from one another." He looks somewhat uneasy in his historical role as father of economics, for his chief concern was household economy.

metaphysics to ethics, politics, and poetics. It was by all odds the most imposing philosophical synthesis before St. Thomas Aquinas, who was proud to declare his indebtedness to him. Its most famous element was his logic, in particular the syllogism, which crowned the idea of proof that the Greek genius had hit upon, and which dominated Western logic until the past century. That it was commonly handled and taught in a mechanical, uncritical fashion was not Aristotle's fault, but suggests rather the misfortune he suffered in his fame. Early Western thinkers not only mistook his synthesis of Greek thought for universal, timeless truth—they had an almost unerring instinct for seizing on his most dubious doctrines. Thus they made a gospel of his muddled, basically unscientific physics and astronomy, which became a major obstacle to the pioneers in modern science. Until recent times few paid attention to his remarkable contributions to biology.

Still, Aristotle may be held largely responsible for this misfortune. Although his immediate successors in the Lyceum carried on some important scientific research, thereafter the school he founded developed Aristotelianism no more than Plato's Academy developed Platonism. For his synthesis was essentially a closed system, tending more to block than to stimulate further inquiry. He himself remarked that "almost everything has been found out, though in some cases what is known has not been systematized." His logic was not a logic of discovery; it was only a means of deducing truths from accepted premises, and provided no satisfactory means for testing the truth of the premises. Scientific inquiry might have suggested such tests, but outside of biology Aristotle was not a true scientist. In distinguishing between efficient and final causes, for example, he gave the palm to the final causes that cannot be scientifically explored, as the efficient ones may be, and he therefore imposed teleology on physics and astronomy, endowing them with a kind of religious finality. In spite of his biological studies he could commit himself to the strange statement that "Nature makes nothing either imperfect or in vain": in a teleological view Nature becomes something like a deity, and must behave as rationally as philosophers. And as a philosopher he tended to shy away from the implications of his principle of development. Temperamentally Aristotle was averse to fundamental change or growth: he wanted a world that was static, fixed, closed—fit for serene contemplation.

In this respect Aristotle may be considered a thoroughly classical Greek, and his synthesis the complete formulation of the classical cosmos and ethos. But he accordingly exposes the essential limitations of the circumspect Apollonian spirit, and reflects the underlying causes of the failure of the Greeks. We may now take our cue from his celebrated *Poetics*. It is a remarkably original analysis of Greek tragedy, surprising because it treats poetry as an autonomous activity, not a handmaiden of philosophy, morality, or the state; and it is no less surprising for its neglect of the philosophical and religious implications of tragedy, its silence on the tragic sense of life. Aristotle himself had no such sense. His ultimate philosophical ideal was contemplation, of a self-sufficient Absolute, in a world devoid of either comedy or tragedy. As he displayed little sorrow over the tragedy of Athens itself, so he displayed little comprehension of either the conditions of its creativity or the basic limitations of its ideal, and as little awareness of the profound changes that were coming over the Greek world in his own time. His political ideal remained a tidy, self-sufficient *polis*, a tiny replica of the cosmos, and as closed to change.

Similar limitations in the thought of Plato were more pronounced because he was less empirical than Aristotle, more devoted to the intuitive, *a priori*, and absolute. At the same time, he more clearly represented some un-Hellenic tendencies, which immediately indicated a growing split in the Greek soul and eventually would lead the Greek world back to Oriental traditions. In him they took the lofty form of a disposition to an unworldly kind of spirituality.

Now this, once more, was by no means new in Greek thought. The followers of Pythagoras held that the natural, sensible world was a world of "mere" appearances, transient and flawed, far beneath the dignity of the eternal, immutable, perfect reality known to mathematicians. The cult of Orphism that became popular during the religious revival of the sixth century taught that the body was the prison of the immortal soul, and offered various means of escaping this prison; by Plato's time gravestones reveal that many Greeks were banking on hopes of an afterlife. As we have seen, moreover, he did not clearly commit himself to his theory of Ideas. Nevertheless, he had dwelt on this unearthly idealism, disparaged the natural world as a den of mere "shadows." He continued to impose an ideal order on this world, sometimes in plain defiance of observed fact; Plutarch remarked that he made astronomy philosophically respectable by "subordinating natural laws to the authority of divine principles," making the planets behave as he thought heavenly bodies should. As an old man he apparently grew more susceptible to Oriental myth and magic, for instance the Babylonian cult of the Seven Planets that produced the Music of the Spheres as they circled through the heavens. And all along the weight of his thought tended increasingly to degrade the everyday world, the common life, ordinary human nature—the conditions of effective freedom.

Thus Plato lent his authority to the radical dualism of body and soul that would enter Christian thought. In the *Phaedo* he had Socrates argue that the true philosopher is "always pursuing death and dying" —for the sake of his immortal soul dying to the pleasures of the body, the interests of the natural world; and dying, let us add, to the Homeric ideal of all-around excellence, the Athenian ideal of "happy versatility" and the full civic life. A similar dualism of reason and emotion led him to condemn both Homer and the tragic poets, and to become the first known philosopher to be hostile to poetry itself; all poetry was suspect to him because it stirred the passions, "the inferior part of the soul." He was much more supercilious about manual labor, commerce, the crafts, in general all the material conditions of civilized life, which had not been beneath the concern of Solon or Pericles; such activities he considered fit only for slaves and foreigners. On all counts, Plato moved away from the agora and the gymnasium where Socrates had been pleased to talk with all comers; moved to his Academy for an elite. Though still a good enough Athenian to devote his late years chiefly to the problem of the state, he led the withdrawal of Greek philosophy from civic life, into a cloistered world where speculation might be purer and loftier, or more pallid and academic, but in any case was reserved for an elite. He widened the gulf between intellectuals and ordinary Greeks.

Plato's ideal remained harmony, or specifically hierarchical order. By his insistent dualisms, however, he tended to accentuate the actual disharmonies in the Greek world, the split within men between major interests, as between classes. He led, too, a withdrawal from the actual world of flux, uncertainty, and multiformity, seeking refuge in geometrical designs for living as well as thinking. Having degraded the necessary activities of doing, making, earning a living, he evaded the necessities by proposing simply to exempt citizens from such activities —a solution impossible for Athens, or any Greek *polis* except Sparta. As typically he designed an ideal Republic in which harmony was to be achieved by splitting the community into three sharply separated classes of workers, warriors, and philosopher-kings, corresponding to a crude psychological division of man into reason, passion, and animal desires, thus preventing any possibility of real community, or shared goods.

Granted his sincere aspiration to justice and the good life, his sincere aversion to tyranny and arbitrary rule by force, Plato's *Republic* comes down to an argument for absolutism. His ideal is exclusive rule by an elite, unlimited by law, with freedom for none. Although he allows the common people to go about their business and satisfy their appetites, he denies them not only any voice whatever in their government but any educational opportunity to realize the good life as he conceives it; the one other concession he makes to their humanity is the "noble lie" the philosopher-kings will tell them, about how they were born to be drones. For his warrior class he proposes a carefully censored education that will train them only to serve the state, denying them the right to minds and lives of their own, or to any "silly and childish notion of happiness." He permits only his philosopher kings to live the good rational life—though they too must devote themselves primarily to the service of the state. In short, Plato's ideal republic might have been designed by Dostoyevsky's Grand Inquisitor. While it accentuates the failure of the Greeks to distinguish between the state and society, and to provide for the rights of the individual, it makes no provision for the individuality, spontaneity, versatility, and creativity that the Greeks had nevertheless realized in the *polis*. It is ill-designed even to breed more Platos. All that he sacrifices for the sake of perfect order seems more deplorable because even so he did not expect this beehive state to remain stable, but confessed that it would naturally degenerate, in time even revert to democracy, and thence to tyranny.

Plato had other apparent misgivings about his ideal republic. A single sentence in one of his letters might demolish the whole elaborate structure: "Subjection is bad both for masters and for subjects, for themselves, for their children's children, and for all their posterity." In his subsequent *Laws*, however, he settled for a grudging concession, devising a "second-best" state for his incorrigible fellow Greeks. Here he restored the rule by law they were accustomed to, but restored it with a vengeance, making it much more rigorous and drastically limiting the freedoms they had enjoyed. "Those who keep watch over our commonwealth," he had written in the *Republic*, "must take the greatest care not to overlook the least infraction of the rule against any innovation upon the established system of education either of the body or of the mind." Now he took pains to spell out the means of preventing any innovation, prescribing the unexamined life that Socrates had said was not worth living. He simply banished such troublemakers as poets. In their stead he provided a state church with prescribed rites and a prescribed creed, authorizing severe punishments for any infractions of them. Thereby he became the philosophical author of the concept of religious dogma, and so of heresy, and offered the first philosophical defense of religious persecution. The *Laws* sum up the whole story: the "timeless" philosopher had indeed reverted to an age-old ideal—the closed, tribal society.

It is surely easy to understand Plato's disillusionment with Athenian democracy. It is nevertheless important, in fairness both to him and to the Athenians, to remember that as a political philosopher he was by no means a classically serene, poised, balanced Greek, but a casualty of the Peloponnesian War, a bitterly disillusioned man who was unable to put up with ordinary human nature, or especially with the uncertainties and the risks of a free society. It is the more important because he became a symbol of pure idealism, and was the first major example of the potential inhumanity and tyranny of such idealism when it becomes too good for ordinary men and the everyday world. His authoritarianism may possibly have had some influence by indirection on the Roman Church, as it certainly had on much Western political thought; but in any case he posed the perennial issue. "It is not what they want but what is good for them," said Oliver Cromwell, "—that is the question." Plato laid down the law for them because he was sure that he knew what was good for them, and that freedom was bad for them. Later religious and political thinkers (such as Hegel) would add that in complete subjection to authority lay "true" freedom.

On his own age Plato's political thought had little if any influence. He failed in his one venture into active politics, an effort to educate as a philosopher-king the tyrant who ruled Syracuse; presumably his failure deepened his disillusionment, and his addiction to geometry. At any rate, his rigid, tribalistic laws were hopelessly inadequate for an age that was changing in spite of him, moving toward a more open society in a much greater world than the *polis*.[5] At this stage his political thought was significant chiefly as a symptom of the "failure of nerve" that was also to come.

---

[5] An incidental example of his archaism was his concern over the problem of how to keep an ideal *polis* exactly the right size—5,040 citizens. He had added the 40 to make a total convenient for administrators, as it could be divided by all numbers from one to ten; but the trouble was that the citizens might not breed with an eye to such convenience.

This failure was much less apparent in the *Politics* of Aristotle. More temperate, balanced, and pragmatic than Plato, he was openly critical of the inhumanity of his master's *Republic* ("How much better it is to be the real cousin of somebody than to be a son after Plato's fashion!"), and he made only a halfhearted effort to draw up blueprints for an "ideal" state. He was truer to the principle of the mean stated in his complementary theory of ethics. Yet his ruling principles as a political philosopher were substantially the same as Plato's. For him too the main object was "the good of the state, not of the individual." He had no more idea of a right to self-government, also conceiving a well-ordered state as one in which citizenship would not be extended to men who worked for a living with their hands. Concerned with justice in the abstract, he displayed as little passion for concrete rights and liberties; he was as explicit in his defense of slavery as "natural," little troubled by his acknowledgment that not all slaves were in fact "naturally inferior" to their masters. And despite all the empirical wisdom that distinguished his *Politics,* he was usually vague at the critical points of his argument. He failed to define clearly or to examine systematically the elements of constitutional government, the form of "polity" he thought most desirable. While indicating an obvious preference for aristocracy, he was still vaguer on how to institute and maintain it. He had somewhat more to say on rule by a virtuous king as the ideal form of government, especially suited to the interests of the "better class"; but he was as vague on how to get and keep such kings, and keep out less virtuous ones.

Most students of Aristotle have dismissed his remarks on kingship as purely academic. Some have seen in them a prudently disguised defense of his former pupil, Alexander of Macedon, whose unpopularity in Athens eventually forced him to leave his school and seek refuge elsewhere. Possibly, then, he had a glimmer of the new age that was dawning. But if so it was only a glimmer. Although he remarked in passing that if the Hellenic race "could be formed into one state, it would be able to rule the world," he at once dropped the subject, proposing no means of union. His ideal, like Plato's, was still a self-sufficient little *polis,* based on slavery, in which the good life would be open only to a privileged leisure class. This elite might then enjoy his supreme good, contemplation of the Absolute—the Unmoved Mover of the universe, which in its perfect self-sufficiency was utterly removed from all human concerns. The thoroughly unmystical Aristotle was never himself so removed, but in mundane affairs he was no more a man of vision. His *Politics* was already a monument—to the past. It had already been dated by the visions of his pupil Alexander.

| Chapter Eight | *THE HELLENISTIC AFTERMATH* |

1. The Creative Achievements

As by common consent the golden age of Athens was the peak of Greek culture, it follows that the Hellenistic aftermath was a decline. This all too familiar idea of growth and decay, rise and fall, has resulted in considerable injustice to an era that was opened by the extraordinary feats of Alexander the Great, and that was in fact still exceptionally energetic, adventurous, and creative. The injustice was aggravated because until recent times most scholars looked to mainland Greece, especially Athens, where creativity unmistakably fell off; the bulk of the original achievement now came out of "Asia," which revered Athens as the cultural capital of Hellas, but which again took the lead. And the conventional disparagement of Hellenistic culture is the more ironical because it was primarily this culture—not the culture of Periclean Athens—that educated the Romans, molded Christianity, and became the "classical" culture known to later Europe. Hellenistic art and thought had much more direct influence on the Western world than did the great literature of Athens. To appreciate the full importance of this era we must keep in mind, indeed, that ultimately it did mark a decline. It ended in not only the loss of Greek independence but a petering out in almost every field of Greek culture; after 100 B.C. there are few great names, and almost none to match the great Athenians of the fifth century. But to understand this too we must first appreciate the distinctive achievements of the Hellenistic Greeks.

The political history of the period was in its main outlines suitably ambiguous, being at once novel and depressingly familiar. Setting out

in 334 B.C. to destroy the Persian Empire, with an army of only thirty
to forty thousand men, the youthful Alexander the Great completed
the job within four years, and marched on as far as India; but when
he died in 323, only thirty-two years old, his empire at once broke up
as his generals began fighting among themselves. Out of the wars a
number of kingdoms emerged, notably that of the Ptolemies in Egypt
and that of the Seleucids in Asia Minor and Mesopotamia. In view of
Aristotle's dictum that it was almost impossible to govern properly a
large population, the inexperienced Hellenistic rulers did surprisingly
well in administering these kingdoms, creating the necessary bureaucracy and distinguishing themselves as builders of public works. Less
surprisingly, the kingdoms repeated on a larger scale the failure of the
polis: they continually warred on one another. Hence one by one
they succumbed to the rising power of Rome. The wave of the future
was plain by 133 B.C., when the last king of Pergamum in Asia Minor
commemorated his entrance into the hereafter by bequeathing his
kingdom to Rome.

This kingdom had been brilliant enough, however, to make Pergamum known as a second Athens; and it brings up the more enduring
legacies of the Hellenistic Greeks. Although a Macedonian, Alexander
the Great was an ardent Hellenist who took along a copy of his beloved
Homer as he set out to conquer "Asia," and who fancied himself as
"the liberator of Hellas." If mainland Greeks did not recognize his rule
as a liberation, he in fact freed the Greek cities in Asia Minor from
Persian domination, generally restoring a considerable measure of
autonomy, and installing democratic regimes to replace the oligarchs
or tyrants whom the Persians had kept in power. Likewise he had some
idea of a cultural mission. He not only brought along poets, philosophers, historians, and scientists, but started Hellenizing the East by
building many new cities, such as Alexandria of Egypt. The kings
after him carried on his policies, founding hundreds of new cities,
and granting them enough autonomy to maintain the forms and something of the spirit of the *polis*. The tradition of freedom was far from
dead.

The conquests of Alexander accordingly provided a much larger
stage for Greek enterprise. Whereas they had formerly stayed close
to the shores of the Mediterranean, for the sake of security or familiar-
ity, the Greeks now followed in his wake, venturing into a continent.
Though we have little literary evidence of their feelings, the record
suggests that many naturally had no idea of a mere aftermath or twi-

light, but felt rather that they were living in the dawn of an exciting new era. They were stimulated immediately by opportunities for commerce and industry, which they still took to in spite of Plato and Aristotle, and which Alexander had encouraged by turning much of his plunder into a uniform coinage. Outside of mainland Greece, where prosperity declined, the Greeks flourished in the greatest age of business to this time. Despite the constant wars, such new cities as Antioch and Alexandria, and such old ones as Rhodes, Ephesus, and Pergamum, grew much larger and wealthier than the major cities of the classical era. Rhodes in particular took full advantage of the possibilities of the new era. It built splendid harbors, carried on a far-flung commerce, suppressed piracy by a first-rate disciplined fleet, and earned a reputation as the most beautiful and best ordered city in the Greek world.

Above all, Alexander had had a remarkable vision. Soon learning that the Persians he had conquered were not the "barbarians" or the slaves "by nature" that his master Aristotle was wont to assume of all men who were not Hellenes, he began to employ them as high officials, while adding other Asiatics to his army. He himself married a daughter of the Persian Emperor Darius, and encouraged his officers likewise to take foreign wives. "At the sight of these marriages," Plutarch would write, "I should have cried out for joy, 'O dullard Xerxes, stupid fool that spent so much fruitless toil to bridge the Hellespont! This is the way that wise kings join Asia with Europe.'" For Alexander had conceived the idea of making partners of his subjects, to build an empire that would be a genuine commonwealth. At a great banquet, during which Macedonians, Greeks, and Asiatics drank from a common mixing bowl, he offered a prayer for *homonoia*, "a union of hearts." He was the first known ruler to have this vision of brotherhood, centuries before Christ. Thereby he gave the first clear political expression to the loftier ethical and religious ideals realized in the Axial period.

Alexander's dream was premature, of course. His ambitious, relatively rude Macedonians were not ready for it, nor were Greeks brought up in the *polis*. But at least he inaugurated the most cosmopolitan age yet known to history, one in which such ideas could grow and spread.[1]

---

[1] The "Alexander Romance," which began making a mythical figure of him soon after his death, appropriately spread his fame in more than twenty languages, from Greek and Persian to Hebrew, Arabic, Ethiopic, and Turkish. In Egypt he became a son of the god Amon, in central Asia the god Iskander, in Ethiopia a Christian saint, in Arabia Dulcarnain, "Lord of the Two Horns"—a role that got him into the Koran. Immediately he foreshadowed the Emperor Ashoka in India: a conqueror who renounced war and conquest and set about repairing by good works the misery he had caused.

Greek became a universal language, the natural medium for the New Testament. Greek influence stimulated a revival of learning in Babylon, a growth of naturalistic art in Buddhist India, a growth of learning and schooling in Israel. The Greeks in turn grew more broad-minded as they mingled freely with the erstwhile barbarians, in what they now thought of as the *oikoumene,* the "civilized world." Among their leading thinkers were some Asiatics, notably the Phoenician Zeno, founder of Stoicism.

In some important respects Hellenistic society was freer, more open than classical Greece had been. Admittedly the Greek was now less of a political animal; with a few exceptions, in particular Rhodes, the *polis* was dominated by the larger kingdoms. But just because it was no longer so independent, or free to make its own foreign policy, its citizens were no longer so closely tied to it and might be more inde-pendent themselves. The Hellenistic world was full of wandering minstrels, artists, teachers, prophets, philosophers. It provided more opportunity for specialists and professionals, as for Jacks-of-all-trades. The foreigner was no longer an alien, still less an enemy; he might readily become a citizen. Cities were pleased to confer honorary citizen-ship upon distinguished visitors, or sometimes upon the whole citizenry of another city (as Athens did upon Rhodes). If these were rather empty honors, they at least emphasized that Greeks were no longer inclined to agree with Aristotle that "all belong to the state," or that the good of the individual must always be subordinated to the good of the state. The obverse of the cosmopolitanism of the *oikoumene* was a more conscious individualism.

In general, the Hellenistic Greeks enjoyed more freedom of the kind we know today—freedom to go about not only their business but their private affairs. They began forming private associations, for pro-fessional, social, or religious purposes. They took more interest in domestic life, building more comfortable, spacious homes and adorn-ing them with works of art, while their public officials gave more attention to their physical well-being, developing the art of city plan-ning, paving and draining the streets, and bringing water into the home. Similarly, Hellenistic cities provided for education as Athens had not, maintaining public schools. (The best known is the magnifi-cent gymnasium at Pergamum.) This education was aimed primarily at *paideia,* the perfect development of the individual—not the service of the state. And it was now available for girls too. With the growing devotion to family life and the home, women came to enjoy a higher status; the Wife might compete for honor wih the Companion. As queens, women were among the most forceful personalities of the age, down to Cleopatra of Egypt.

The uses made of this freedom were open to considerable question. Hellenistic culture was an uneasy compound of classical, Oriental, royal, and bourgeois elements, molded by professionals (who may also be called mercenaries), in a spirit at once more practical and more rhetorical than that of classical Greece. But first it should be emphasized that the Greeks maintained their tradition of high culture. They still regarded material wealth and power more as means than as ends, and spent a considerably larger proportion of their wealth on embellishing their cities and enriching their civic life than modern Americans are wont to do. The larger cities vied with one another in the splendor of their public works and festivals, thereby running to ostentation, but at least proving an aspiration to more than a high standard of aimless, unthinking living. Smaller cities everywhere maintained their temples, statuary, theater, palestra, stadium, and agora, built in marble or enduring stone.[2]

The least impressive achievement of the Hellenistic Greeks was in literature. Writers culitvated such forms as the epigram, the pastoral, the comedy of manners, the romance, with the new theme of romantic love—forms suited to the new mode of life, but not making for high seriousness. Civic life no longer provided the great issues and occasions that had inspired the drama of Athens. The dearth was most apparent in the most ambitious works, such as the *Argonautica* of Apollonius of Rhodes—an epic much more polished and elegant than Homer's, and as much more pallid and hollow. As a highly self-conscious performance, it pointed to the major contribution of the Hellenistic Greeks, which was simply their preservation of their poetic heritage. This they studied reverently, closely, continuously. They established the first great libraries, as at Alexandria and Pergamum. With these they bred the new types of the literary critic, editor, grammarian—prototypes of the classical scholars to come. Since these can be dreary types, let us

---

[2] The ruins of Pergamum, on a terraced hill, give the most vivid idea of the real splendor of Hellenistic cities. As I have elsewhere remarked, however, the ruins of Priene (near Miletus) are a more striking example because this was an independent city of only a few thousand people. The loveliest works of little Priene now embellish museums in Europe, but the bare remains of its public buildings and its streets enable one to visualize a gem of a city, well planned, beautifully built, and proudly adorned, that could hardly be matched in the much wealthier modern world. Its theater alone might humiliate any town of its size in America.

remember that upon the likes of them depends the transmission of a great heritage, sometimes the recovery of lost or forgotten masterpieces. The letter that may kill the spirit is as necessary to keep it alive.

In art the Hellenistic achievement was comparable, but considerably more original and noteworthy. The idealization of the human form in classical sculpture gave way to an increasing realism and dramatization that current fashions in art brand as decadent; the once greatly admired Laocoön, for example, may now seem too theatrical. There were also unmistakable tendencies to both the grandiose and the rococo; the Colossus of Rhodes bestrode a world of nymphs, Pans, and Cupids. Yet Hellenistic art as a whole may be called more truly humanistic than the art of classical Greece, as it was certainly freer, more individualized, and wider in range. Sculptors represented not only superhuman gods but all classes and types of men, women, and children —a Dying Gaul, an Old Market Woman, a Shepherd Boy; they discovered the possibilities of beauty in forms of the plain, the toilworn, the anguished, even the ugly. They explored new possibilities in the art of portraiture, the free-standing statue, and dramatic grouping with depth. They were at least true to the spirit of their restless, adventurous age, even in their frequent straining for effect reflecting its tension and tumult; their art was a live growth, not an exhaustion. They would have been much poorer Greeks had they merely repeated classical forms and subjects, or aspired merely to the serenity and composure of the statuesque. At that they had some authority for their strained effects, for the painted statues and painted temples on the cluttered acropolis of Athens were by no means so chaste as the time-washed marbles look today.

In science there is no question whatever that the Hellenistic Greeks far outstripped the achievements of their ancestors. Unhappily, laymen are unable to appreciate the work of the giants of this age—the almost incredible brilliance, say, of the mathematician Apollonius of Perge, the founder of conics. Euclid we all know of, as more than two thousand years later we still study his *Elements* in school; but even so, few realize that no other textbook has ever served so long and so many. As few know that this was a golden age of science, the greatest before the seventeenth century in Europe, which provided the basis and much of the inspiration for the European pioneers. Archimedes, one of the mathematical geniuses of all time, also founded the science of theoretical mechanics, in which he was unsurpassed until the time of Galileo. Herophilus of Chalcedon founded the science of anatomy, Erasistratus of Chios the science of physiology; together they prepared the way for Galen, and thus for Vesalius in Europe. Among the geniuses in astronomy was Aristarchus of Samos, who proposed the theory that the sun, not the earth, was the center of the universe, and so emboldened Copernicus to publish his heretical theory. On the premise that the earth was a sphere, Eratosthenes of Cyrene established mathematical geography.

We can do nothing like justice here to all this extraordinary work, but we might pause over Eratosthenes as perhaps the most illuminating illustration of its cultural conditions. He lived in the third century B.C., when most of the greater thinkers were not yet exclusive specialists; while famous chiefly as a geographer, he was also a mathematician, astronomer, philologian, philosopher, historian of science, even a poet. Possibly he had started his geographical studies under the inspiration of Homer, whom he loved and studied closely, and whom Strabo called the father of geography. More obviously his work was a product of the *oikoumene,* a world much larger and better mapped than that known to classical Greeks. As he emphatically rejected the distinction between Greeks and "barbarians," so he was aided by the relative freedom from religious prejudice, as from the presuppositions that vitiated the astronomy of Plato and Aristotle. His calculations of the shape and size of the earth were based on purely naturalistic premises, unconfused by myth. Some of his estimates were astonishingly close (he missed the correct length of the earth's diameter by only fifty miles), demonstrating that the Greeks had learned to make brilliant use of mathematics for scientific purposes.[3]

Most pertinent, Eratosthenes was for some years chief librarian of the Museum at Alexandria. This Museum, founded by the Ptolemies, was a major innovation of the Hellenistic Greeks. Except for the religious brotherhood of the Pythagoreans, and the somewhat cramping auspices of Plato's Academy and Aristotle's Lyceum, scientific research had been carried on chiefly by scattered, gifted individuals. Now it became a co-operative enterprise, at once more open and more highly organized. The Museum was not merely a great library but a research institute, equipped with laboratories and staffed with teachers and

---

[3] One may therefore be pleased to know that even their miscalculations could be fruitful. The philosopher Posidonius later tried to correct the estimates of Eratosthenes, and came out with a much smaller one for the circumference of the earth, which led him to place India much too close to western Europe. This error was piously handed down through Strabo and Ptolemy to Roger Bacon and finally Christopher Columbus, who thereupon set sail more optimistically to find this shorter passage to the East.

technicians; almost all the great scientists of the age studied at it. Here too philologians systematized grammar and punctuation as a means of preserving and accurately transmitting texts. As Benjamin Farrington has remarked, the Museum created the whole technique and tradition of scholarship, inaugurated the "Age of the Textbook"— another dull affair that may not look like a mode of emancipation, but that nevertheless greatly facilitated the growth and spread of enlightenment. It helped both to inspire and to preserve many scientific texts that otherwise would most likely have been lost to the world.

Of much more direct importance, however, was the philosophy of the Hellenistic era. Perhaps its grandest product, this was certainly the clearest, fullest response to both the universalism and the individualism of the *oikoumene*. Now that the *polis* was no longer self-sufficient, civic life no longer the end-all or be-all, thinkers concentrated on the quest for the good life started by Socrates. They took up the problem dropped by Aristotle, how a good man should live in a bad state. They sought freedom and self-sufficiency for the individual, a good life that could be lived apart from the state or under any kind of state. In this quest they ranged through the whole familiar spectrum of possibilities, from self-seeking to self-denial; but the dominant schools that emerged, to influence Western ethical thought ever after, were the Epicurean and the Stoic.

Epicurus, founder of another academy in Athens, taught that by philosophy one could live "like a god among men." In making happiness the proper goal for man he did not, of course, spread the popular gospel of eat, drink, and be merry (this is a biblical phrase); happiness lay rather in a plain life of temperate pleasures, and especially in the uses of mind. Reason could deliver men from bondage to sensual pleasure, as from the need of worldly possessions, and make them superior to circumstance, liberate them from the control of necessity. Having within themselves all the resources they needed, men could always be free in mind and spirit. In particular Epicurus stressed freedom from fear: fear of death, fear of the gods, fear of a universe that leaves man alone. He was most original in his explicit rejection of religion, and of all ideas of man's dependence on the powers above.

Basing his ethics on the philosophical materialism of Democritus, which held that there were only atoms in a void, Epicurus denied the existence of an immaterial or immortal soul. Though not denying the existence of the gods too (perhaps out of prudence or temperance), he tucked them away in a corner of the universe, assured men that they had no concern with human affairs, and attacked the notion that good fortune was their gift, beyond man's own power. He was one of the very few Greek thinkers flatly to reject divination, as all magical means of predicting the future. And his Roman disciple Lucretius, who paid so reverent a tribute to his "holy father" Epicurus, had a saintlier zeal for emancipating men from slavery to superstition, especially the irrational hopes and anxieties of salvation cults. He insisted more passionately that in order to live "like a god among men" one had to banish all fear of the gods. "True piety is this," he wrote: "to look on all things with a master eye and a mind at peace." As a godless philosophy, Epicureanism was never very popular in the ancient world, and it has remained more or less disreputable to his day; but it has also remained among the permanent possibilities of intellectual liberty, periodically cropping out in new forms, as men stubbornly persist in the pursuit of happiness that gods and philosophers often frown on.

The Stoics won much more immediate prestige, and lasting influence, by resolutely opposing all desire for happiness as it is ordinarily conceived. As Epictetus later wrote, "There is but one way to freedom—to despise what is not in our power." Our earthly lot is not actually in our power; we can never hope to escape all pain, achieve all our desires, control our worldly circumstances or fate. Freedom therefore lies in being superior to pleasure or pain, indifferent to circumstances, able to endure any lot—ultimately in being free from all passion and desire. As Epictetus also said, once you give in to desire "you are a slave, you are a subject, you have become liable to hindrance and to compulsion." To fortify the will in choosing this hard way of life, the Stoics taught that it was a matter not of individual preference but of obedience to universal law. While they had different names for this law—Nature, Reason, Destiny, Providence, God, even Zeus—they all agreed that it was rational and right, and by their reverence for it made it essentially religious if not literally divine. In these terms, freedom lay in recognizing a principle of unconditional duty beyond individual desire, choosing to live in accordance with universal Reason or Nature.

In thus carrying through the universalism rather than the individualism of the Hellenistic age, the Stoics were led to their most influential principle—the concept of natural law. Zeno, the founder of the school, wrote a *Republic* (unfortunately lost) that was quite different from Plato's: his ideal state was not a *polis* but a *cosmopolis,* in effect rationalizing Alexander's dream of *homonoia.* His successors amplified the ideal of "one great City of gods and men," with its implications

of universal brotherhood. They deduced that the "natural law" governing this universal commonwealth, above all man-made law, embodied
a principle of equality; all men were equal by virtue of their common
possession of reason, common duty of obedience to the universal law.
Some Stoics explicitly concluded that slavery was unnatural, contrary
to reason. In the Roman Empire jurists would spell out these ideas in
legal terms.

We may postpone until then consideration of this lofty, cloudy,
ambiguous concept of natural law, since it had a negligible influence
on the laws and the politics of the Hellenistic states. Meanwhile we
may note that the Stoic philosophy afforded a Greek equivalent of the
Law of Israel and was free from the tribalism that the prophets repeatedly lapsed into, as well as from the ritualism of the priests. As
a sort of philosophical religion, without magic or miracle, it could
constitute a "free man's worship." Zeno said that temples were unnecessary because the human mind was God's temple, and his successors continued to affirm not only that men should choose to obey
God or Nature, but that they could do so by their own powers of
reason and will. The Stoics buttressed self-respect and self-reliance by
making no cheap concessions, offering no promises of earthly or
heavenly rewards. They maintained the loftiest tradition of pagan
ethics, insisting that men should do their duty and live right whether
or not it "paid." To the end of the ancient world, Stoicism nerved many
men to endure with fortitude an earthly lot that left a great deal to be
desired.

Yet this often painful lot brings up the apparent inconsistency of its
creed. The Stoics were forever insisting on the rationality and rightness
of the universal scheme—and insisting the more sententiously because
they never demonstrated it, never made intelligible the purposes of
Nature or God. Their resolute effort to suppress all passion and desire,
including wonder, was itself a confession that these purposes were
not at all clear or clearly good; otherwise acceptance of the universe
would not have required such arduous effort. And for ordinary human
purposes their wisdom was as sadly ambiguous. It may indeed be the
best kind of wisdom, especially for bad times; but in my lexicon freedom is not the word for it. The Stoics were renouncing all desire and
power to choose and carry out purposes—except the one purpose of
"choosing" whatever happened to be, the one desire to be imperturbable at any cost. In such calm or peace of mind they could and did
remark that a slave may be as "free" as any other man; and they could

ignore the fact that a slave is not actually a free man, and has good reason not to choose such a lot. Indeed, they made no resolute effort to abolish slavery, to write their natural law into legislation, or to realize their abstract ideal of universal brotherhood. Stoicism nerved many rulers and officials to keep doing their duty, but chiefly in maintaining the status quo, without too much concern over the lot of the many poor and ignorant, and without apparent love of God or man. Any deep, live concern would menace its ideal of imperturbable calm.

So we are brought to the social and political failures of the Hellenistic age, the losses in effective freedom. Stoicism was a symptom of these failures. With its rather pathetic worship of Freedom without choice, Purpose without purposefulness, Reason without reasonableness, Brotherhood without brotherliness, it amounted to a fatalistic acquiescence in the failures. And the philosophy of Epicurus, in theory radically different, came down to much the same impassivity. Stressing happiness rather than duty, he taught a more genial kind of wisdom, found more room for such values as friendliness and sweetness; yet he sought above all freedom from passion and concern. Typically he defined happiness in negative terms, as "the absence of pain in the body and of trouble in the soul." His design for living was a more explicit retreat from social problems, if in good order: "we must release ourselves from the prison of affairs and politics." In effect, the freedom he offered was freedom in a void. What filled the void in the Hellenistic world were ancient affairs—miracle, mystery, and authority.

2. *The Losses in Freedom*

The most conspicuous loss in freedom during the Hellenistic period was heralded by Alexander the Great. The self-proclaimed "liberator of Hellas" ruled as a king, deciding for himself what liberties to allow the Greeks to retain; and he became a self-proclaimed god too—the son of Zeus-Amon. In view of his dream of *homonoia* he may well have had statesmanlike motives in publicizing this seeming delusion of grandeur; his Asiatic subjects, unaccustomed to rule by mere mortals, might be more loyal to a god-king. In any case, his generals followed his cue. The victors in the wars over his empire all ruled as absolute monarchs, regarding the territories they conquered as their personal dominions. Their sons had them deified, and themselves began assuming such titles as Soter—"Savior"; in Egypt the Ptolemies became gods in their own lifetime. The Greek world had reverted to the ancient pattern of the sacred monarchy.

This was indeed more like Homeric kingship than Oriental despotism. The kings typically continued to allow considerable self-government in the old Greek cities in their realm, and to grant a measure of it to their new foundations. If their grace was chiefly a matter of prudence, since they needed help in their wars on one another, they were nevertheless respecting Greek tradition, "the autonomy of the Hellenes." Even in claiming divinity they might have been respecting the Greek demand for legitimate rule, for outside of Egypt few seem to have taken their divinity literally; it was the readiest way of sanctioning the power they actually wielded, and had to wield in order to rule effectively. In any case they could scarcely have established large-scale democracies. Their Asiatic subjects were wholly unprepared for self-government, their Greek subjects about as unprepared for federal or parliamentary government. The cities were not simply hostile to the kings, often conferring divine honors on them in gratitude for their protection or their generous patronage.

Yet monarchy had returned, and with it the idea of divine right. There were no constitutional checks on the royal power, no legal rights of citizenship in the royal dominions. The king was now the state, appointing and removing high officials at his own pleasure, making law by royal decree. Although there was often enough violent opposition to his person, there was little reasoned opposition to his institutional authority, and little effort to limit it by law. Plato's Academy, Aristotle's Lyceum, Zeno's Stoa—all the leading schools obligingly came out with defenses of kingship; characteristically the Stoics defined it as "noble servitude," but without proposing legal means of preventing ignoble tyranny. Traditionally devoted to the idea of rule by law, the Greeks grew used to rule by men. Athens itself had set the style by officially honoring the general Antigonus and his son as kings, even as "tutelar deities." Divinity became cheaper as cities competed for royal favors, and as only one of the Hellenistic kings is known to have scorned the fashion. (Antigonus Gonatas remarked of his godship, "The man who empties my chamberpot has not noticed it.") If most Greeks did not literally believe in the divinity of the kings, they grew used to this preposterous idea too.

In Egypt the Ptolemies approximated the "hydraulic society" of the pharaohs by reorganizing the traditional bureaucracy and regimenting the peasantry. They developed a planned, controlled economy that was highly efficient—for the purposes of enriching the rulers. Elsewhere the Hellenistic kings tended to become more despotic, but to less effect. Their dominions suffered more from deep confusions and divisions, the common failure of the savior-kings to unite their subjects or to inspire genuine loyalty to god, king, or country. The peasant masses remained much as they had been under Persian rule, probably no worse off, in any case passive or inert; if not brutally exploited, they were not Hellenized or in the least emancipated either. Many workers in the cities probably suffered more. Records of their condition are typically—and significantly—scarce, but the evidence indicates that the increased wealth of the age went increasingly to the wealthy, the poor became poorer; wages remained miserably low, while either hard times or prosperity might bring rising prices. The kings, busy with war or affairs of state, showed little if any concern over the lot of city workers. City officials might be as distracted or indifferent; the common people now had less political power, the rulers less urge to institute any fundamental reform. And all classes of Greeks suffered in more insidious ways from the subordination of the *polis*.

Civic spirit remained strong, to be sure. To the end the cities struggled to maintain what independence they could, and maintained their pride by splendor in building, adorning, and celebrating. The wealthier citizens paid their full share of the costs; they assumed public offices that generally were not opportunities for enriching themselves by graft (as in modern municipal government) but required them to spend of their own money in the upkeep of the city, and they sometimes made it outright donations in hard times. Still, this civic spirit was now more like modern pride in the home town, a local cause unlikely to inspire either daring enterprise or lofty idealism. Independent Rhodes accentuated the change in other cities. It nurtured a ruling aristocracy with a high sense of civic responsibility, even to requiring sons of the nobility to begin as common sailors; elsewhere the ruling class was more bourgeois than aristocratic, and had no such training for high command. That the cities had lost their freedom to make their own foreign policy was not simply a calamity, inasmuch as in practice this had meant chiefly a freedom to make war, but the royal wars went on anyway, for reasons less patriotic or in any sense ideal.[4] Citizens of the *polis* could no longer feel that they were in

---

[4] An exception that proved the generally shoddy rule was the campaign of King Attalus of Pergamum against the dreaded Gauls, who had long been ravaging Asia Minor. His

command of their destiny. So the one great historian of the age, Polybius, found his subject not in the feats of Alexander the Great or the expansion of the Greek world, but in the rise of Rome, which was putting an end to Greek independence.

In such a climate the freedoms enjoyed by the Greeks tended to become less meaningful, less fruitful. The more ambitious or more fortunate were freer from constraint as private individuals, they had a wider range of choice in means of self-realization, they could move about and practice their professions in a more variegated, open world; but they might suffer from the want of deep loyalties, steady responsibilities, high incentives, clear goals, and also from insecurity in a cloudy, windy world. On the one hand, the Hellenistic Greeks were given to ostentation, a complacence lacking either gusto or real composure. On the other, they were liable to anxiety, as pawns in a history not of their own willing. On both counts they began to lose the enterprise, the spirit of quest and adventure, that many had had in the dawn of the new era; and also to lose confidence in their own powers or in the prospects of their society. The ugliest sign was the growth of infanticide; inscriptions in Greece support the remark of a contemporary that "even a rich man always exposes a daughter," indicating that most upper-class families brought up only one son.[5] The upshot was a decline in creativity in all fields of culture—a decline that set in by the second century B.C., but that had been foreshadowed by the distinctive creations of the age.

Hellenistic art most clearly mirrored the superficial complacence, the underlying tensions, and the waning spontaneity of the age. Royal patronage encouraged the tendency to the theatrical and grandiose. The baroque possibilities of this art were best realized at Pergamum, especially in the great Altar of Zeus that commemorated the triumph of the Attalid kings over the barbarous Gauls by a powerful, if too muscular representation of the battle between the Olympians and the Titans. Such ideal significance, however, was lacking in most royal memorials. Unwittingly the kings of Pergamum also testified that Hellenistic king-

triumph made him widely admired as another liberator of Hellas, or champion of civilization against the forces of barbarism, and stimulated the effort of Pergamum to become the Athens of Asia. These Gauls, however, had been brought in and set loose by the rulers of Bithynia, another Hellenistic kingdom, in order to harry its neighbors; and the victorious kings of Pergamum went on to expand their dominions, exact tribute from other Greek cities, and become widely hated as tyrants.

[5] We may wonder how mothers felt about this practice, but we can only wonder. Women were not yet independent enough to voice their feelings in public records.

ship was not vital enough to inspire a grand imperial art: they started collecting older masterpieces, preparing for the routine industry that would keep sculptors busy turning out imitations or copies of the masterpieces. No more inspiring as patrons were the wealthy bourgeois, who enlarged the market for art. Their tastes ran to royal fashions, otherwise to realism, sentiment, fancy—to qualities of real interest and charm, but likely to become commonplace. A late fashion in pseudo-classicism gave a false air of composure to a society that was coming under Roman domination. Lacking deep roots in either the *polis* or the *oikoumene,* Hellenistic art was pretty much exhausted by the first century B.C.

Literature was mostly complacent all along, lacking depth in thought or feeling. About the highest endeavor was the work of the scholars, who reverently edited the classics but nevertheless were mostly pedants; they set up the classical standards of purity, propriety, and obedience to authority that made it easier to imitate the great poets, and almost impossible to emulate them. By establishing the Attic dialect as the standard literary language, they also assured the loss of almost all the works written in the living language of the Hellenistic world, but what is known of these works makes it doubtful that any masterpieces were lost. Writers embroidered the traditional myths and legends, bequeathing posterity a wealth of pretty fable and "poetic diction"; they created a world of fantasy in idyl, erotic tale, and romance, the latter in particular featuring puppet characters without force and episodic plots without logic; they plumbed the surface of their society in conventional satire, diatribe, and comedy of manners; as "educators" of Hellas they wrote a great deal of didactic poetry, versifying medical, geographical, and astronomical lore. In short, they freely exercised their wit, sentiment, fancy, and learning on almost every subject—except the basic social, political, philosophical, and religious issues of the age. The key to their superficiality was the pious performance of Athenian drama at the civic festivals. Except for the piety, these performances had little communal significance beyond another occasion for theatrical ostentation. They were "shows" in the modern sense: spectacles staged with ever more splendor, by professional troupes, to the greater glory of the producers and the star actors. No Hellenistic poet wrote any tragedy of note, as none wrote the epic of Alexander.

In another sense, show was the main object of Hellenistic education. This became a predominantly literary education, of a thoroughly academic kind. Students were taught to read, memorize, and recite the classics, especially Homer. In learning them by heart they might be taught to criticize, but only according to rule; there was little effort to train them to think for themselves, develop either independent critical sense or creative ability. Most symptomatic was the major subject—rhetoric. The teaching of rhetoric, begun by the Sophists, had been emphasized by Isocrates in fourth-century Athens for good civic reasons: its aim was to prepare men for public life by training them to debate public issues, address their fellow citizens on major public occasions. Now that great public issues were no longer being debated, in cities no longer independent, rhetoric became the rage. It taught men to orate about anything, or nothing; its aim was eloquence for its own elegant sake. It would remain a blight on literature and thought to the end of antiquity. Meanwhile it was in keeping with the Hellenistic curriculum: an education still humanistic, intended to cultivate the youth and make them good Greeks, but good for no particular purpose, vocational, political, or intellectual. It did not make them really good pupils of Homer either, for it began with a lesson in misunderstanding the great educator of Hellas. Among the first sentences the youngsters learned to copy down was: "Homer was not a man but a god."

For purposes of either social or intellectual enterprise, Hellenistic philosophy offered little better education. From the outset all its new schools had an escapist or defeatist cast. Hedonists turned their backs on all but private pleasures, with as doubtful good cheer as good will. The Cynics reverted to primitivism, praising "a dog's life" (in the words of Diogenes) above all the values of civilization, and managing to remain indifferent to the many poor who were less philosophical about the dog's life they were condemned to. The Skeptics, presumably impressed by the relativity of custom and belief in the *oikoumene,* denied outright the possibility of any certain knowledge, thus discrediting all serious inquiry, while failing to make clear just how they had come by this certainty of their own; generally they concluded that one might as well live by accepted custom. The Epicureans and Stoics taught more positive values, carrying the traditional faith in Mind to new heights as they asserted that man was equal to any Necessity, or in effect free from it; but they set sharp limits to purpose and choice, or to effective freedom. If reducing or suppressing desire is perhaps the best way to contentment, it is not a way to stimulate energy or enterprise, any active effort to make history rather than merely endure it. In general, all the schools were seeking some kind of freedom for the

Giguntomachia, from the Great Altar of Pergamum *Courtesy, Pergamon Museum, Berlin*

Gaul killing himself and his wife (Pergamum) *Courtesy, Terme Museum, Rome*

Laocoön
Courtesy, Vatican Mus

Representative coins
from early Lydian t
Hellenistic. At top,
second from left,
King Croesus type; a
far right, the Persi
imperial   *Courtesy*
Numismatic Society

ruscan Apollo
urtesy, Villa Guilia, Rome

Old Market Woman
Courtesy, The Metropolitan Museum of Art, Rogers Fund, 1909

Representative Roman patrician (Juni
Brutus) with busts of his ancestors
Courtesy, Palazzo Barberini

Roman Forum   *Courtesy of TWA*

Emperor Augustus   *Courtesy, Vatican Museum*

Marcus Aurelius
Piazza Campidoglio

Imperial family, from th
frieze of Ara Pacis
*Courtesy, Uffizi Gallery,
Florence*

Colossal head of Constantine the Great
Courtesy, The Metropolitan Museum of Art, Bequest of Mrs. F. F. Thompson, 1926

The Colosseum and the Arch of Constantine   *Courtesy, Italian State Tourist Office*

Early Christian art (fourth-fifth century): mosaic of Christ enthroned, Santa Pudenziana

Hagia Sophia, Turkey   *Photo by Fujihira, from Monkmeyer*

individual, apart from his political condition; but none proposed a kind that was calculated to encourage spontaneity and creativity, or a free, full development of individuality.

Meanwhile ordinary men were seeking a more familiar kind of "spiritual freedom." The want of a vital core in Hellenistic culture, the sense of a void beneath its splendors, might suggest another faithless, godless age; but actually it abounded in gods. More and more Greeks were living up to Whitehead's definition of religion: "what the individual does with his own solitariness." Enjoying virtually complete religious freedom, they now did a great deal with their solitariness. Only what they did revealed most plainly their want of confidence in their own powers.

Homer's blessed Olympians were fading out into thin air. As civic gods they were figureheads with only nominal functions and were accorded only formal respect, for old time's sake; they had nothing to offer the individual, especially the many unfortunates. The gods who were really worshiped were the mystery gods, come down from the ancient fertility rituals: gods with whom the individual could commune, in ecstasy or frenzy, and through whom he might hope for salvation, in this world or the next. Among the most popular were Cybele, the Phrygian Mother, and her dying, resurrected lover-son Attis. "Before her," wrote Apollonius in the *Argonautica*, "Zeus himself . . . doth somewhat yield, when from her mountains she ascendeth to the wide heaven." Zeus yielded as much to other Mothers, such as Isis and Astarte. He could not even compete with Serapis, a synthetic Greco-Egyptian deity invented by a Ptolemy for political purposes; although Serapis failed in his primary job of impressing the Egyptians, he traveled all over the Greek world and settled down in many a shrine. (The king had hired an Athenian sculptor to carve the god's likeness, an Athenian philosopher to celebrate his greatness.) Still more characteristic was the popularity of another upstart deity, Tyche—Fortune or Chance. Tyche was quite irrational and irresponsible, dispensing favors by whim, but she compensated for the uncertainty of her favors by the hope of deliverance from Necessity, or rational responsibility. And if all the attendant superstitions that swamped the late Hellenistic world were very old, not really strange to the Greeks, they look strange because of an increasingly morbid strain. Thus professional exorcists were now busy driving out demons—demons unheard of in Homer, or in Periclean Athens, but apparently too many even for the Great Mothers.

At its best, Hellenistic religion approached a loftier spirituality, with implications of universality, which helped to prepare the Greeks for Christianity. Commonly purified of their grosser rites, and tending to take on more ethical content, the mystery cults could induce a spiritual regeneration. Nevertheless, they remained essentially sacramental, miraculous means to a salvation that men could not achieve by their own virtue or wisdom, and that the individual sought by losing himself rather than by knowing himself. The continual gambling on new gods betrayed a feverish religiosity, a play for spiritual goods not really good for much in this world. By and large, the popular cults promoted neither sanctity nor sanity. They were symptoms of a decline in freedom of spirit, a failure of mind and nerve.

Now, the most apparent reason for this whole development was Oriental influence. The forms of the sacred monarchy, the new mystery cults, the flood of magic—all came out of the ancient East. Hence the paradoxical end result of Alexander's conquest and Hellenization of the East has become a historical commonplace. The conquered peoples clung to their own gods, never really took to the Greek way of life; the conquerors succumbed to the ways of their subjects. In other words, resurgent "Asia" won a spiritual victory over "Europe," long before the Arabs and the Turks sealed it by military victories. So the East would triumph over the conquering Romans too, setting the pattern of history to the end of antiquity, even to the end of the Byzantine Empire, the fall of Constantinople to the Ottoman Turks in 1453.

And so it bids us to pause again—and first to make some reservations about so neat a plot. "Asia" was no more villain than hero in the Hellenistic drama. For one thing, the Greeks had long had mystery gods in their own tradition, notably the most popular Dionysus. No strangers to magic either, they had perhaps known even the hordes of demons who apparently came in from Persia; the demons might have been there all along under different names, unknown to poets but familiar to peasants. In any case spiritual traffic with the East had been heavy since the dawn of the Greek world. Periclean Athens itself had welcomed foreign deities, including Cybele; Socrates had paid his respects to the snake-god Asclepius, whom Sophocles had put up in his own home. Though Oriental influence was unquestionably much more marked in the Hellenistic era, this only forces the obvious question: Why did the Greeks now succumb to it? Why the failure of mind and nerve? And though the obvious answers, already indicated, are perhaps sufficient, we again might consider more closely the underlying causes. The question is especially pertinent because the failure may appear to bear out the thesis of the Grand Inquisitor: the burden of freedom and open choice is too much for man.

As an aristocrat, however, the Grand Inquisitor was not speaking of his own needs—only the needs of the masses of ordinary men; and here is the immediate reason for closer inquiry. The Hellenistic masses were not clearly seeking escape from freedom. More clearly, they never enjoyed much effective freedom, had much real choice. The glimpses we catch of them give varied impressions, ranging from habitual industry and occasional gaiety to apathy, sullen alienation, and active discontent, but alike suggest no flight from responsibility. They cannot rightly be blamed either for the vulgarization of Hellenistic culture, especially religion, with which they have been charged. Mostly poor and uneducated, they were not so much fleeing from reason as banking on an ancient tradition of magic and miracle from which they had never been really emancipated; we might rather honor the democratic tendencies of the mystery cults, which were more hospitable than the Olympians to all races and classes of men, and to women too. Most clearly at fault were the Hellenistic rulers and the elite: the kings and their ministers, who displayed much energy in furthering their personal ambitions, somewhat less energy in efforts to promote the common welfare, much less in efforts to unite the Greek world; the wealthy bourgeois, who maintained the traditional modes of civic responsibility but displayed a characteristically limited capacity for enlightened self-interest, not to say vision; and the educators of Hellas—the writers and scholars, the teachers of rhetoric, the philosophers.

As we are dealing with a failure of mind, it is fair to concentrate on the Hellenistic thinkers. They were not the main cause of this failure, to be sure, if only because they were seldom leaders in the community. Nevertheless, they were deeply implicated in it, partly because they so often held themselves aloof from the community. In their typical indifference to the condition of the masses they subscribed, tacitly when not openly, to the Grand Inquisitor's thesis that the great majority of men are not fit for freedom or the life of reason. Only they proved incapable of his sophistication and cool detachment. They themselves mostly succumbed to the need of miracle, mystery, and authority, as if bent on proving that he was right for all mankind.

Before the first century B.C. Greek philosophy was on the decline that eventually carried it all the way back to the prehistoric myth and magic out of which it had arisen.

Although the Epicureans generally held out against the reigning superstition, their very loyalty to their master tended to make them ineffectual; his spirit gave them little incentive actively to combat the powers of darkness. The Skeptics were no less ineffectual, for in denying the possibility of any certain knowledge they had no way of declaring anything positively false. The Stoics, on the other hand, were not markedly disposed to further inquiry but were disposed to the kind of cosmic superstition represented by astrology—a new kind that came in from Babylon, and that with their aid became another typical Hellenistic rage. The fateful power of the stars was in keeping with the implicit determinism of thinkers who taught complete submission of man's purposes to a Nature or Destiny that had no demonstrable rational purpose. In the first century B.C. the authority of astrology was firmly established by the Stoic Posidonius, the last major philosopher of the age: a scholar so encyclopedic in his learning that he was admired as another Aristotle, and so basically uncritical that his learning was a hopeless muddle of fact and myth. And while ordinary Greeks now set about looking for miraculous means of escaping the fate inexorably decreed by the stars, all the leading schools except the Epicureans were embarking on comparable pursuits. They were becoming more like religious cults, giving up the disinterested pursuit of truth, seeking instead means of salvation or escape. Philosophers could no more endure a universe that left man free to choose and carry out his own purposes.

This intellectual failure might demonstrate again that "rationalism alone" is not enough. But in demonstrating as plainly that any old myth will not do either, it brought out the fundamental limitations or defects of Greek rationalism. The philosophers never developed the habit of regularly, systematically checking their thought against experience. Their characteristic passion for simplicity and order bred a positive repugnance to the world of diversity and change—the world in which history is made. Before Plato argued that true knowledge can be only of the changeless, Parmenides had achieved the ultimate by demonstrating that change was impossible: given the essential principle of Being, there could be no Becoming because this would require some admixture of Not-Being. It was only by as lofty a disregard for the facts of experience that the Stoics could assert the perfect rationality of

Nature, the entire rightness of things as they are. "Do your worst, pain, do your worst!" wrote Posidonius in a spell of misery: "You will never compel me to acknowledge that you are an evil." If the desperateness of his effort at logical consistency testified that he could not actually ignore the evidence of his senses, it also illustrated the fundamental incapacity of the Stoics to deal with the real evils of their time.

With the onset of astrology, philosophy became virtually divorced from science; but the divorce was unlamented, indeed unnoticed, for a similar reason. The Greeks never came to distinguish clearly between science and philosophy, or even to coin a word for "scientist." The brilliant Hellenistic scientists not only failed to formulate scientific method, or any systematic means to empirical certainty, but produced no Bacon or Galileo to champion empirical knowledge against traditional doctrine. Hence they had little influence on contemporary thought. They inspired no widespread faith in science, no further development of the scientific spirit. Thinkers did not go on to make empirical studies of man or society; the "Age of the Textbook" produced no texts on social or political science, beyond conventional defenses of monarchy. Much more conspicuous than the influence of any scientific thought was the power of classical tradition that led the Greeks almost unerringly to discard potentially the most revolutionary and fruitful theories, such as the evolutionary theory of Anaximander and the atomic theory of Democritus. Hipparchus and Ptolemy, the foremost astronomers of antiquity, succeeded in killing the Copernican theory of Aristarchus, which was awkward for religion and fatal to astrology; and though the observed data supported their preference for keeping the earth at the center of things, they proved their piety by endorsing astrology.

A particular reason why Hellenistic science failed to emancipate thought, or appreciably to influence society, was its aloofness from vulgar considerations of utility. The aristocratic tradition of contempt for the "base mechanic arts" grew stronger despite the growing materialism of the age. "Give me a fulcrum," boasted Archimedes, "and I shall move the world," but in fact nothing world-shaking came out of the science of mechanics he founded; although he won a legendary fame for his inventions, Plutarch recorded that he viewed engineering and all useful arts as "ignoble and sordid." Other Greeks explored the sources of power in water, steam, and air pressure, but made as little effort to apply their discoveries to industry or to substitute mechanical power for manual labor. Granted that improved technology alone could hardly have solved the social problems of the age, there was no necessary virtue either in a lofty indifference to utility that condemned the masses to drudgery and poverty. The indifference itself looks vulgar because technicians did apply their skills to such uses as new engines of war, and incidentally machinery for producing "miracles," or awesome illusions in temples. And theory too suffered from its divorce from practice. Applied science might have stimulated inquiry, suggesting new problems and possibilities; but as it was, science declined with philosophy and art. There were no important new theories or discoveries in the last century or so of the Hellenistic era.

In philosophy the aloofness from the common life was a more positive withdrawal, or retreat. The happiness sought by the Epicureans was not the happiness of the greatest number; they purchased their freedom by an indifference to political affairs that in Periclean Athens had branded a man as an "idiot." Stoics who maintained the principle of civic duty also suppressed on principle any live concern with poverty and pain, which they taught were not really evils. The age produced neither an Amos nor a Marx. None of the schools tackled its basic social and political problems, or sought to educate or uplift the common folk. And the thought of all of them suffered from their remoteness from the folk, or from the social realities of their time. The failure of the elite may be summed up by their blindness to the root evil of slavery.

By now, indeed, slavery was more widely condemned in principle, and it stirred some moral indignation because Greeks as well as barbarians were bought and sold. For the first time in history there were even some slave uprisings, both in Greece and in Asia Minor. Yet no serious effort was made to abolish the institution, which flourished on the continual wars of the period. With it flourished the holy island of Delos: this became an international market for the booming traffic in slaves, proud of its capacity to handle more than ten thousand a day. If some thinkers perceived the moral evil of slavery, none appeared to realize the economic and cultural evils. The abundance of cheap slave labor was a primary reason why wages of free workers remained wretchedly low, and why technicians neglected to develop mechanical power. It fortified the aristocratic prejudices of the elite; thinkers could afford their scorn of utility, and indifference to vulgar reality, because they lived comfortably off cheap manual labor. Hence free Greeks were themselves slaves to the institution, which fettered thought and narrowed enterprise in ways they could not perceive.

We may now get a better perspective on the Hellenistic world by reconsidering its superficial resemblances to our own. The expansion of commerce and industry, the advances in science, the rise of professionals and specialists, the more conscious individualism and mobility, the growing concern for private life and material well-being—all such developments, which made the Greeks more like modern bourgeois, still affected only a fraction of the populace, in a society fundamentally different from our industrial civilization based on the machine. The thesis of the Grand Inquisitor is much more pertinent for the modern democracies, in which the masses of men do enjoy freedom, and sometimes seem not really to enjoy it very much, or to want it as much as they want security, togetherness, adjusted personalities, and all the magic promised in ads. Yet the fact remains that ordinary men are much freer than they were in the Hellenistic kingdoms, have much more opportunity, and therefore have a quite different mentality. As workers they are not sullen or apathetic, in the countryside they are not illiterate peasants but farmers; everywhere they expect or demand much more of earthly life. The signs of a popular religious revival are still a far cry from the Hellenistic mystery cults.[6]

Above all, the modern world differs in its terrific dynamism, due immediately to the power of its machinery, more profoundly to its image of the future. While the modern faith in progress has been badly shaken, most men still have a live hope of a better future. Their very dismay is intensified by a feeling of immense potentialities—possibilities that may now seem all too dreadful, but that still include visions of new wonders (such as rocket flights to the planets) and that are still based on the possession of means undreamed of in past societies. After the initial expansion the Hellenistic Greeks had no such vivid feeling of potentiality, or driving faith in a better future. The Golden Age that they dreamed of, or that their scholars mulled over, was in the past. Their deeper thinkers saw history as an endless cycle, a perpetual recurrence of growth, decay, and death. Like the Stoics, they might declare the cycle rational, because ordained by Nature or Deity, but they might well feel it as meaningless; and at best it gave them little high incentive but to endure, or by miracle to escape.

---

[6] An incidental similarity is the vogue of astrologers, who run columns in scores of American newspapers, and perhaps outnumber as well as outprosper astronomers. This popular superstition is scarcely alarming, however, except perhaps as further evidence of the irresponsibility of a free, commercial press; it does not yet suggest a serious reversion to fatalism. The only stars that really sway the public are the Hollywood variety.

In this perspective we may finally add a reservation on the moral and intellectual failures of the Hellenistic Greeks. Real as these were, and perhaps sufficient to account for the decline in creativity, there were also untidy external reasons for the decline. One was malaria, which seems to have grown much more prevalent in this era: a disease the more blighting because it does not kill in large numbers, like the spectacular plagues, but debilitates its victims, leaves them prey to apathy or despondency. Another reason was the power of the Romans, who started building their great empire with no higher mission than to plunder and exploit. In the second century B.C. they flaunted their might by destroying Corinth, pillaging much of mainland Greece, and putting an end to the Achaean League, a belated Greek effort at federation. At the same time they set about weakening their loyal allies, Rhodes and Pergamum, the most energetic and promising of the Hellenistic states. In the following century Greek cities were more brutally exploited, especially in Asia Minor, to defray the costs of the senseless civil wars of Sulla, Pompey, Caesar, Brutus, and Mark Antony. Rome eventually made the Hellenistic Greeks look worse by unifying the *oikoumene,* establishing the law and order that they failed to achieve; but its depredations might also have been sufficient reason for the decline in creativity in the second half of the era.

At that, the Greek cities still had reserves of energy and enterprise. They flourished again after Augustus finally restored peace, producing some more great works. They retained enough vitality during another century or so of imperial misrule to contribute to the preservation of the Roman Empire in the East, while Rome itself fell to German barbarians. We can get no sum by casting up the failures of the Hellenistic Greeks against their achievement in preserving, extending, and transmitting their cultural heritage; but we must remember that as they failed they educated the Romans, and eventually the early Christians.

| # THE ROMAN EMPIRE

1. Myth and Reality

The Roman Empire has again come on bad times. Historians used to dwell on its grandeur, the tragedy of its decline and fall, the mystery of why so great an empire succumbed to barbarians—a mystery that was called "the most important problem of universal history." Haunted by its fate, they managed to find some fifty different reasons for its fall. Now universal historians in particular are more likely to dwell on it as the last stage in the degeneration of classical antiquity. They picture it as an essentially artificial state, which managed to organize the Hellenistic world but otherwise added nothing vital to classical culture, gave men no dynamic faith or high goal, and so preserved only a hollow, petrified culture. Meanwhile debunkers have pointed out that the tradition on which it was founded had little basis in fact: the patriotic image that the Romans had of themselves and their history, and that was accepted by Westerners down to the past century, amounted to a vulgar myth. In this view, the fall of the Roman Empire is no real problem. The only apparent mystery is why it held up so long.

Yet it did hold up for centuries, in spite of all the good reasons it had to fall—and fifty would seem quite a lot. Its famous decline took longer than the whole life span of many empires. Then the eastern half of the Empire did not fall, but went on for another thousand years, to become known as the Byzantine Empire—a fact ignored by some historians who have demonstrated that the fall of Rome was "inevitable." In Europe Roman tradition was vital enough to survive all through the Dark Ages, even to inspire the belief that the Empire had never really ended. It remained a major inspiration for the West as a grand symbol of commonwealth, ideals of universal law, order, and peace. The Founding Fathers of America were still studying Roman tradition when they devised a constitution for the land of freedom. Call it myth, and the fact remains that no other empire created so grand and enduring a one, as no other has been honored by so many explanations of its fall.

We may suspect that the ideas the Romans had of themselves were not *mere* fictions. They were neither dreamers nor fools, after all, else they could not have ruled so many for so long, and well enough to build so enduring a reputation. If they were deluded about their history, so might we be in our notions of what "really" happened (not to mention our notions about ourselves). And we will surely be deluded if we assume that ideas that seem mistaken or mythical to us could make no real difference in history. What men believe has happened may be just as important as what actually did happen; what they believe can happen or should happen may in the long run count for more than the fate that overtakes them. It is now easy to see that liberty, for example, became a catchword in the Roman Empire as men were in fact losing their liberty for good; yet they kept alive the tradition of antique liberty that would enflame the imagination of Renaissance Europe, thereby engendering more myths and gaining more historical force. Likewise the great Roman jurists were formulating the majesty of Roman law precisely when the Empire was in the throes of anarchy, and headed for outright despotism. They were preserving the cardinal principle of natural law: another idea that may look like a myth, that would become a powerful factor in Western political tradition, and that may not be a mere fiction—if the idea of our "common humanity" means anything.

The fact also remains that the Roman Empire began brutally and ended ignominiously, for reasons of major concern in a history of freedom. We cannot take the Romans at their own word. As we try to understand the collapse of their empire, and especially their loss of freedom, we must try to get at the actualities behind their beliefs. For among the reasons for their failure was the image they had of their ancestors: the image of a Republic that was all piety and patriotism. In glorifying the real virtues of their republican forefathers, the Romans failed to perceive the primitiveness of their religion, the poverty of their culture, and the narrowness of their idealism that helped to explain why their empire had begun so brutally, and why the Republic proved a dismal failure. Their national image exemplified the in-

veterate traditionalism that was the main strength of the Roman character, and the main weakness of the Roman mind.

In short, Roman history is considerably more ambiguous than
ordinary imperial history. We may take our cues from the work of Livy,
their first great historian and celebrant of their national ideals. His
History of Rome is incidentally full of auguries and prodigies, the
superstitions that always clouded the Romans' understanding of their
own achievements. Written during the reign of the Emperor Augustus,
at the dawn of the *Pax Romana* that made the Empire famous, it was
more profoundly characteristic of Roman piety in its nostalgia for the
good old days. Livy lamented the corruption of the Roman character,
a theme to become ever more notorious; but he failed to note that this
character had been corrupted by the time the Republic entered the
light of recorded history, before the Romans won the world. Now he
could see only that they had succumbed to luxury and avarice: "we can
endure neither our diseases nor their remedies"; whereas the Romans
would endure them for centuries. Although their diseases were indeed
plain enough, and never really remedied, they made almost all their
major contributions—to statecraft, law, architecture, literature, philosophy, and the Christian religion—after they had reputedly lost both
the wisdom and the virtue of their ancestors. There was evidently some
element of fiction in their corruption too.

Hence we must not only distinguish between Roman principle and
Roman practice, or between myth and reality, but keep an eye out for
deeper incongruities, of practice that might be more inspired than the
accepted principle, realities that might be more edifying than the
pious myths. We are dealing with a people who were much less brilliant, imaginative, versatile, and original than the Greeks, but whose
limited reach enabled them to grasp an empire and helped them to
achieve grandeur; a people who were among the greatest warriors in
history, and who became the greatest peacemakers, fulfilling the dream
of Alexander the Great by the most liberal imperial rule man had yet
known; an unspiritual people, brought up on a primitive tribal religion, who in political practice most nearly realized the universal ideals
implicit in the higher religions of the Axial period; an intensely conservative, Spartanlike people, lacking any passion for freedom, who
nevertheless wrote a major chapter in the history of freedom.

2. The Rise and Fall of the Republic

About their early history the Romans had suitable legends but so little certain knowledge that Greeks wanting their aid could sell them the idea that the founder of Rome was the Trojan hero Aeneas. We know that they were an Indo-European people akin to others in Italy, as obscure in their origin, with no more manifest destiny. If they entered Italy as war lords and worshipers of sky-gods, they emerged into history as a small tribe with a simple peasant culture, occupying a relatively unfavored region. Their rise in the world was obstructed but also greatly aided by more powerful neighbors with a much superior culture—the Etruscans. The history of civilization in Italy, as of Rome, begins with the non-Indo-European Etruscans.

This mysterious people probably came in from Asia Minor, but certainly owed much of their culture to Asia, and more directly to the Greeks.[1] Beginning about the eighth century B.C., they built up a number of city-states, apparently linked in some kind of federation, that dominated the region from modern Florence (Etruscan Fiesole) to Rome (itself an Etruscan name). Their essentially Grecian art reveals an often gracious, refined way of life shared by women, but it also reveals an obsessive anxiety—dread of demons and torments in the underworld, dread meanwhile of deities whose will the Etruscans sought to divine by a science of augury, especially a study of the livers of animals. Even the Romans were aware that they owed something to Etruscan religion. With the lore about omens they took over a medley of Etruscan ways, from the art of writing to the arch, the symbol of the fasces, gladiatorial combats, and perhaps the dignified status of women. Their extensive borrowings, however, emphasized one significant difference that may have been due to their Indo-European tradition. The Etruscans won among the ancients a reputation as a deeply religious people because they were hounded by the belief that man was nothing before the gods. The Romans, as scrupulous in their attention to ritual forms, were much more independent in spirit, confident of their own powers. If still quite unconscious of any mission, they were in this

---

[1] The recent decipherment of their language may throw light on their origins. Meanwhile the mystery of these origins has been deepened by the possibly needless assumption that they moved in as a nation and planted a fully developed culture. Where, one might ask, did the modern Italians come from?

THE RISE AND FALL OF THE REPUBLIC

respect prepared to take over the role of the Greeks in the drama of East and West.

As unconsciously they fitted themselves for such a role while throwing off the yoke of the Etruscan kings, the Tarquins. In the course of this struggle they got rid of their own kings too, and acquired their traditional hatred of kingship. The Roman city-state that emerged from the wars of independence was not a monarchy but a republic, resembling a Greek *polis*. While it no doubt owed something to the example of the Greek cities in southern Italy, it was developing its own distinctive forms, and exhibiting both political and military genius.

By the beginning of the fourth century B.C. the Romans had won their life-and-death struggle with the Etruscans. In the course of this century they succeeded in dominating most of Italy, and in the next century they won another life-and-death struggle, the Punic Wars with the greater power of Carthage. With the end of the Second Punic War (201 B.C.) they more consciously set about building an empire, though still with no declared sense of mission; they consolidated their dominions in Gaul and Spain, subdued Macedon and Greece, began dominating Asia Minor. One of their captives, Polybius, inaugurated the high tributes they would receive by writing the history of their conquests. Never before, he declared, had Fortune "accomplished such a work, achieved such a triumph" as this, which had brought "almost all the inhabited world under the single rule of the Romans in less than fifty-three years" (220-168 B.C.).

As a good Greek, Polybius knew that it was not really the work of "Fortune"—it was the Romans' own doing. He wrote his history in order to answer for posterity the obvious question: What had enabled them to achieve this unprecedented feat? The primary reason, he decided, was the excellence of the Roman constitution. This was a mixture of autocratic, aristocratic, and democratic elements so perfectly balanced that no one, "not even a native," could label it for certain by any of these terms. The seemingly absolute powers of the Consul were offset by exclusive fiscal and judicial powers of the Senate, which in turn were limited by legislative powers of the popular assembly, to which the Consul was also accountable. Polybius gave the first explicit, detailed account of the system of checks and balances that influenced the authors of the American Constitution, and that Americans have come to regard as the main political bulwark of their freedom.

Nevertheless, there is some question about the excellence of the Roman constitution. As in America, the checks and balances were also means to elaborate confusion, and might effectively prevent responsible rule; they included such provisions as two consuls, who could veto each other, and ten tribunes, any one of whom could veto the consuls and all the other tribunes.[2] It could be argued that the Romans proved their political genius chiefly by their ability to keep muddling through in spite of this fantastic system, were it not for another exception to the account of Polybius: there was in fact no such even balance of power. Power and initiative were mostly in the hands of the aristocratic Senate, whose authority was no less effective because it was derived more from custom than from legally constituted powers. At this stage the Senate made the Roman constitution look admirable because it had earned its authority, immediately by its steadiness during the worst crises of the Punic Wars, all along by its natural prestige as the one body of proved experience in rule (consuls and tribunes were elected annually), but in particular by the statesmanship it had demonstrated in the early Republic.

Rome had been torn by the class war of the Iron Age. Initially its patrician class had monopolized both political and religious offices; its plebeians had been not only completely barred from political life but prohibited from marrying patricians. When the plebs began to rebel, especially against enslavement for debt, the patricians had the wit to make some concessions, however grudgingly or bitterly. In the fifth century B.C. the famous code of the Twelve Tables, which inaugurated the tradition of Roman law and due process, was published largely in the popular interest. In the next century the Licinian Law decreed that one of the two consuls was to be a plebeian, and later the plebs were granted the right to elect their own magistrates, called "tribunes of the people," to protect their interests. They won the last say in government, as their assembly alone had the right to pass and repeal laws.

Such concessions never led to full equality even in theory. The principle of aristocracy was always deeply engrained in Roman tradition, accepted by common men too; they did not aspire to the *dignitas* of their superiors. Neither was there a declared ideal of freedom, such as Pericles proclaimed in the Funeral Oration; when Livy celebrated the

---

[2] The worst Roman disaster in the Punic Wars, the battle of Cannae, sprang immediately from an altercation between the two consuls, who alternated command; one was all for fighting in spite of a poor strategic position, the other wished to hold off. Come his turn to command, the former started the battle without consulting his colleague. "Fortune" was no more logical, for the rash consul was among the few survivors, taking to his heels, while the prudent one refused to desert his troops and died with them.

virtues of the ancestors he did not maintain that freedom was what had made Rome great. Yet all Romans did have a voice in their government. All were citizens with certain rights recognized by law, in a state conceived as a *res publica*—a public thing. It amounted to government chiefly by the Senate, but in theory it was of and for the people. If the Senate could and would abuse its power and privilege, the theory remained that it ruled by public consent, in the public interest. The Greeks early recognized that the Romans were not "barbarians."

The rulers of Rome displayed a more remarkable wisdom as they won dominion over most of Italy. They did not simply subjugate the other Italic peoples, or the Greeks in the south. While requiring them to acknowledge the supremacy of Rome and to provide soldiers for its armies, they permitted them considerable self-government and generally made a point of treating them to some extent as "friends and allies." Rome was on its way to a more genuine confederation than the classical Greeks ever achieved. And as it planted colonies to help control its dominions it overcame the inherent limitations of the classical *polis* by another major innovation: it began extending various grades of citizenship to other municipalities, up to the full rights of Romans. Already all roads were leading to Rome in a profounder sense, as for the first time in history a republic was developing into a large-scale nation. Hence its political experience would become much more important for the Western world than the political experience of the Greeks, since Periclean Athens could never serve as a model for nations.

These policies were dictated by expediency, not yet inspired by any conscious theory of confederation or ideal of *cosmopolis,* and they may now seem like elementary common sense. Nevertheless, this was a rare good sense, uncommon especially in the more brilliant Greeks. It brings us back to the celebrated Roman character. Character remains an old-fashioned concept, necessarily imprecise, not very satisfying for purposes of explanation since it has itself to be explained; yet it is not for such reasons any less real or important, especially in relation to the growth and maintenance of freedom. If Livy exaggerated the virtues of the old Romans, these virtues were as plain a reason as any for their extraordinary success.

They were to begin with the simple virtues of men of deeds—valor, loyalty, fortitude, steadfastness—which as in Sparta were fortified by an exceptional capacity for discipline and self-sacrifice. Unlike Sparta, however, Rome did not enslave its citizenry in the service of the state; the old Romans maintained their patriotic ideals with simply dignity, without any such rigorous, compulsory training. Their virtues were not necessarily products of the Republic, possibly antedating it, in any case contrasting sharply with the vivacious, volatile character that the Greeks developed in their *polis;* but at least they befitted a people that had rejected kingship. If the Romans were not a freedom-loving people, beyond the common desire for national independence, they became free and self-reliant enough to choose as well as do their duty, assume the responsibilities of their rights. The plebeians had won their rights by asserting an independent spirit, even to threatening secession from the state; their loyalty was no blind, passive, peasant obedience. Polybius observed that another reason for the rise of Rome was the superiority of its citizen armies over the technically better trained and equipped forces of Carthage, made up of foreign mercenaries. Thus the brilliant Hannibal won every major battle in the Second Punic War—except the last one.[3]

As old-fashioned a concept is the most apparent source of the Roman character—the family. It was a patriarchal family that instilled a reverence for the ancestors, the household gods, and the tradition of patriotism; the much-esteemed virtue of *pietas* signified devotion at once to the parent, the gods, and the state. As the father had absolute authority and all legal rights, the children only duties, the Roman family limited the freedom of the individual. The father himself was in practice typically bound by a deep sense of obligation, the need of respecting inviolable custom, or the traditionalism that limited the intellectual resourcefulness of the Romans. This traditionalism could also steady them, however, the more because they enjoyed in the ancestral home a wider margin of privacy than the classical Greeks had, and more security than the Hellenistic Greeks evidently had. The *lares* and *penates,* their household gods, long remained the most vital of their deities, giving the individual some measure of protection from his solitariness or something satisfying to do with it. Women in particular had a customary dignity as mothers that more than compensated for their lack of any legal power over their children, and in time they won a higher legal status too. The Roman matron was another celebrated

---

[3] Historians have puzzled over his failure to attack the city of Rome, after he had overrun Italy and marched triumphantly to its gates. Livy's explanation might be true, or ought to be. He writes that Hannibal was discouraged by reports that Roman troops had marched out of the city with colors flying, en route to Spain, and that the very ground on which his camp stood had just been sold, without any lowering of its price. There is no question that such faith in themselves enabled the Romans to survive terrible disasters and win the last battle.

type, virtually unheard of in classical Greece.

Much more anomalous was the role of Roman religion. This was a purely formal religion, a mass of primitive ritual untouched by either the loftier spirituality or the rationalism of the Axial period. It amounted to an essentially commercial transaction with hosts of vague deities hardly deserving the name: transactions conducted with the most painstaking thoroughness and punctuality, and with no spiritual pains to speak of. It was almost incredibly unimaginative, barren of myth, barren of possible inspiration for either art or speculation. When later Romans began to look into their ancestral religion they discovered that they had not the faintest idea of the motive or meaning of some rites they were performing, or the nature of some gods whose names were still inscribed in their calendar. Only the persistence of habit gave this religion any title to the holy name of "faith." To ordinary Romans it no doubt seemed completely intelligible because it was completely accessible and nonrational, providing deities and rites for every conceivable occasion, public and private, and raising no cosmic questions or painful mysteries. As F. E. Adcock remarked, had the Romans ridden bicycles they would probably have had a domestic goddess named *Punctura*.

We may therefore understand why Polybius (anticipating Marx) believed that the leaders of Rome deliberately used this religion as a tool, a means of keeping the multitude from getting unruly. They had not consciously designed it so, of course; yet the endless ritual did serve admirably the purposes of the state, instilling a deep sense of community and order. Primitive as this peasant religion was, it was at least free from the gross rites of the Oriental mysteries and from any inducement to frenzy or extravagance. Its merely prudential service of essentially nonmoral gods still engrained a moral sense of obligation, untroubled by any uncertainty about the nature of duty to god or state. Completely unexalted, it sanctified the native heath and hearth; idealizing nothing spiritual, it gave an ideal meaning to homely, daily concerns. By perpetual care to observe all the proper forms, it weakened the sense of care, giving ordinary Romans a "spiritual freedom" of a low sort but good for ordinary human purposes. (It took the Greeks to introduce a "care-destroyer.") And as the secret of its prosaic success remained that nothing was really secret or mysterious, there was nothing awe-inspiring either about the men who conducted the rites. The Roman priesthood never acquired the power of priesthoods in Oriental states.

Still, this religion was quite incapable of spiritual or intellectual development. Its low order of magic might not suffice as the Romans grew more worldly-wise, or acquainted with the powers of mystery gods. So the Great Mother Cybele came to Rome in 205 B.C., on a state invitation, when Hannibal was threatening the city; although Roman citizens were long forbidden to participate in her rather wanton festivals, she won immediate popularity by performing the miracles that the state gods were not up to. (She was credited with inducing Hannibal to quit Italy.) And the peasant religion of the Romans sufficed still less when they triumphed over Carthage, proceeded to build an empire, and so moved into a much greater world. For the governance of this world both the *pietas* and the constitution of the Republic proved utterly inadequate.

The Romans now illustrated the adage that nothing fails like success. With success that carried them far from the *lares* and *penates* they grew more militaristic, covetous, and shortsighted; they were much more interested in exploiting their subjects than in making "friends and allies" of them. But ordinary Romans at home were also impoverished by the spoils of victory. The spoils went largely to a wealthy few, who increased their wealth by acquiring land through loans and foreclosures and working their estates by increasingly abundant slave labor. The free farmer-soldiers who won an empire for Rome mostly lost their own land as a result. "The wild beasts that roam Italy have their dens and lairs to shelter them," cried Tiberius Gracchus, "but the men who fight and die for Italy have nothing but air and light. . . . They are called masters of the world, they have no clod of earth to call their own." In 133 B.C. Tiberius, an aristocrat, got himself elected tribune and started a program to help the landless, only to be murdered by an aristocratic mob. Ten years later his brother Gaius took up his program, to meet a similar fate. The wild beasts continued to have the better of it.

Gaius tried as unsuccessfully to extend the rights of Roman citizenship to the Italian allies, or "Socii," who had likewise borne the brunt of victory, serving in the Roman armies. In 90 B.C. the allies revolted. As a result of this "Social War" all free Italians won the franchise, signaling another major phase in the development of the Roman state; but immediately their victory meant little because the struggle merged into a war between the generals Marius and Sulla, inaugurating the civil wars that convulsed the Republic to the end. Generals were now the real powers in Rome. The needs of maintaining the far-flung empire had brought about the replacement of the citizen militia by a professional standing army, and these paid troops gave their primary loyalty to their generals, who secured their pay; the generals might march on Rome to enforce their demands for benefits. They fought among themselves until Augustus finally restored order by ruling as an emperor. For practical purposes the Republic ceased to exist long before its official end, usually dated 27 B.C.

Now, the most apparent reason why the Republic failed was the notorious corruption of the Roman character. Polybius predicted that success would lead to degeneration, through a scramble for wealth and power. The patricians grabbed everything within sight to feed their new taste for luxury; the Senate became so addicted to the giving and taking of bribes that the cry went up that everything was for sale in Rome. A rising "equestrian" class, made up of businessmen, was as avaricious, and co-operated in transforming the state into a virtual oligarchy. The ruling class now lacked both the good sense and the good will to do anything on behalf of the common people, in particular the landless who kept drifting into Rome, where there was little industry to sustain them. While worrying over the threat of this embittered proletariat, the rulers fought every effort to improve its condition or to curb their own power and greed; after the Gracchi their common policy was violence or murder. Although they had to worry too about the generals, who might support the popular cause, they found a champion in Sulla. In the course of a bloody dictatorship over some years, Sulla transferred his practically unlimited power to the Senate, thereby assuring the rule of personal ambition, greed, and hatred in political life. The civil wars that destroyed the Republic were the more senseless because they were fought over no clear principles or programs.

But the Romans suffered as well from the defects of their virtues. These were grounded on an unreasoned piety that was not conducive to sensitivity or enlightenment, was more liable to coarseness and callousness. Thus the brutal gladiatorial combats were introduced during the First Punic War, long before the corruption set in, and they rapidly became popular, growing into immense shows as captives provided an abundance of gladiators; but no Roman leader spoke out against the degrading effects of these spectacles. Certainly not Cato the Elder, known to his fellows as the very model of an "old Roman." (His celebrated maxims incidentally included advice on how to get the most out of slaves: when not sleeping they should always be working, and when old should be sold off.) What worried Cato was the growing addiction to Greek culture as well as to luxury, or in particular to Greek philosophy—such "meddlesome" fellows as Socrates. There was some good reason for this worry, and for the policy that temporarily banned all philosophers from Rome: the inquiring, critical spirit of the Greeks unquestionably tended to undermine the traditional pieties, as did the substitution of Greek sculpture for the old earthen images of the gods. Nevertheless, the Republic suffered as obviously from the lack of enlightenment, or of thought free enough to be critical of tradition.

Imperial success accentuated the basic defects of the constitution praised by Polybius. It had taken a Greek to narrate this success and analyze this constitution; the Romans had built up their empire almost absent-mindedly, as one war led to another, and they had little political theory beyond a reverence for traditional forms. Given large provinces to govern, the Republic developed no civil service or trained administrators; the offices of proconsul and tax collector were plums for the wealthy. The Senate grew more powerful because it remained the only experienced body, with a bigger job on its hands and more plums at its disposal. And all political authority was centered in Rome. In extending the rights of citizenship the Romans failed to develop a practicable system of representative government; they had only the clumsy fiction of "tribes"—some thirty-five for all Italy—in which voters were enrolled, and which had a single vote each in spite of vastly increased, uneven numbers. The right of franchise meant little because in order to vote all men had to come to Rome. For wealthy landowners such inconveniences were offset by obvious advantages, especially because no quorum was necessary for voting, and no voting was allowed on market days. The Senate found it easier to bribe, browbeat, or trick the common people, of whom the many thousands in Rome were enrolled in only four tribes, and the thousands outside Rome might be represented by a few strays. Among the senatorial tricks that modern politicians might envy was putting off voting by finding the omens unfavorable.

Similarly the Republic failed to develop any system of public education. By the second century B.C. upper-class Romans were harping on the perennial theme of the ignorance, stupidity, and irresponsibility of the common people; but they did nothing whatever to educate or enlighten the people, fit them for responsible voting, just as after the Gracchi they made no effort to deal with the basic causes of popular unrest. Romans of the old school were mostly incurious about the world they were ruling, except as a source of plunder. The Roman masses knew nothing about it, except that they were not sharing the plunder.

Hence it was not democracy that failed in republican Rome. Democracy might not have saved the Republic either, but in any case it was given no chance. True, the common people always retained some potential power because of their numbers and their voting privileges. They had to be cajoled, bribed, or intimidated; they could be of use to demagogues and ambitious generals; they might be given some bread, or cheap corn, along with the circuses that kept them amused; and they were generally demoralized enough to look like the "mob" that has always frightened aristocratic thinkers. Nevertheless, they had no effective say in their government, or means of informed, intelligent say. They had no organized party or trained leaders to represent their interests. The senatorial machine that ran the government sought only to keep the popular assembly ineffectual, and in this it succeeded. The assembly ceased to be a real arm of the government, remaining at most something of a nuisance to the rulers.

The Roman Republic accordingly ended as a clear example of the Marxist description of modern democracy—class government masked by democratic forms. Its fall was not due, however, to class war. Bitter as class feeling might be, the common people of Rome were too poor, ignorant, weak, and dispirited to carry on a concerted class struggle, or to start anything like a revolutionary movement. The one significant revolt after the "Social War" was an uprising of slaves, led by gladiators, who proved their desperation, and the sorry state of affairs in Rome, by holding out for two years in southern Italy, defeating two armies, before they were put down and crucified by the thousands. Otherwise the civil wars were due immediately to the ambitions of generals, ultimately to the failures of the Roman aristocracy. The Senate proved too selfish, irresponsible, and witless to maintain its authority against the generals.

Yet the end of the Republic was not the end of Rome. Although the reasons for its collapse seem plain, they recall us to the underlying ambiguities of Roman history. These would become more pronounced in the remarkable achievement of the Emperor Augustus, who "restored" the Republic by establishing absolute monarchy. In the last years of the Republic they were epitomized in the works of its two most famous sons—Cicero and Julius Caesar. Utterly different types, these men alike signaled the grandeur to come, and also the basic weaknesses of imperial Rome.

Although devoted to the traditional ideals, Cicero was not literally an old Roman but a "new man"—a provincial and a member of the equestrian class. He was decent, moderate, and reasonable, more liberal than most of the aristocrats. As governor of a province in Asia Minor he was conscientious and honest, anticipating the benevolent rule that Rome was to provide. As a senator at home he urged methods of persuasion instead of force, and hoped to restore order by uniting the aristocratic and the middle classes, the Romans and the Italians. Although by no means an unswerving idealist or a heroic type, he played a relatively dignified part in the sordid drama of his day, and finally died for his republican ideals. More important, he was also a "new man" as an urbane, cultivated one, steeped in Greek thought. Under Greek tutelage he became a rationalist and humanist, a major figure in the transmission of classical culture. Never highly imaginative, original, or profound, Cicero was to have an everlasting influence on Western history by his exposition of the ideal theory of natural law, and of the state as a "partnership in Justice."

Still, Cicero failed the Republic, as it failed him. Apart from his considerable vanity, there was always something stagey about his principles: a rhetorical quality that heightened his immediate effectiveness as an orator, but at some expense of statesmanship, and more of clarity, consistency, and honesty in thought. "Liberty has no dwelling place in any state," he wrote grandly, "except that in which the people's power is the greatest, and surely nothing can be sweeter than liberty; but if it is not the same for all, it does not deserve the name of liberty." Actually, Cicero was not at all devoted to an ideal of democracy or equal rights. He made no serious effort to restore the people's power or to secure sweet liberty for all; he spoke contemptuously of the common people when he mentioned them at all. As a bourgeois he forgot his Stoic conception of the state as a "partnership in Justice," declaring that its main object was "the security of private property," and denouncing a "radical" orator who complained because not two thousand men in Rome owned any property; like some modern bourgeois, Cicero regarded the mention of disagreeable truths as an incitement to class war. Such attitudes limited his political intelligence too, making him incapable of adapting his ideal theory to Roman actualities. Like almost all the old Romans, he kept lamenting the loss of the old civic virtues instead of trying to get at the basic causes of corruption, or to institute any basic reforms. His traditionalism was neither practical enough nor idealistic enough. Essentially it was sentimental.

Julius Caesar, unlike Cicero a great gambler, was much more realistic and effective, even if he too got himself murdered. Historians are still debating his motives, his plans, and his ideals—if any. The uncertainties involve no question of his great abilities, however, and what is definitely known about him is significant enough. Whether his ambitions were selfish or patriotic, Caesar plainly used demagogic means as he rose to power, lavishing great sums of money on spectacles for the Roman masses. As plainly, he did not offer them a revolutionary program or promise them a full-fledged democracy; if he had their interests at heart, he felt no need of any popular slogans of liberty and equality. His army had been enough to make him master of the Roman world. In 49 B.C. he opened his decisive struggle with his great rival Pompey by crossing the Rubicon and marching on Rome, he finished off Pompey the next year, and two years later he made his mastery official by getting himself appointed dictator for ten years, then having the term extended for life.

Although little more than a year of life was left to Caesar before his assassination, in this time he amply proved his claims to statesmanship. From the moment of his triumph over Pompey he had astounded his political enemies by his clemency, pardoning instead of proscribing or slaughtering them. He then put to shame the rhetoric of Cicero by pushing through a remarkably ambitious program of economic and political reforms. At home his measures included a public works program, a reorganization of the fiscal system, a reduction of debts, and agrarian reforms. Abroad he extended the rights of citizenship, granted self-government to new cities, made freedmen eligible for high office, and provided for responsible administration by abolishing the system of tax farming, in which Roman businessmen had collected taxes at huge profit to themselves. For posterity he introduced a reformed calendar (prepared at Alexandria) accurate enough to serve more than fifteen hundred years.

The trouble remained that Caesar literally dictated his whole program. Controlling the army and the treasury, he showed scant respect for republican institutions. While he swelled the ranks of the Senate with provincials, he reduced it to a rubber stamp for approving his edicts, and he reduced popular elections to as nominal forms for approving the officials he appointed. Although he refused the offer of a crown, he incurred suspicion by accepting such trappings of royalty as the purple robe. As significantly, he was the first Roman to have his own portrait engraved on coins—a custom that had been introduced in the Greek world by the Hellenistic kings. And he proposed no new constitution for Rome, made no provision for his succession. What Caesar was up to remains uncertain; but his legacy to Rome was "Caesarism"—autocracy.

At any rate, he got an extraordinary lot done in his short time. The best of him lived after him too: his adopted son Octavian, the Augustus to be, built on the foundations he laid. The boldness and imaginativeness of Caesar emphasized that Rome was far from moribund in spite of all the flagrant corruption. Its empire had continued to expand throughout the civil wars; Pompey had extended and secured its dominions in the East, Caesar had secured the province of Gaul and invaded Britain. The Romans looked worse than they were because the spotlight was always on Rome, the main seat of brawl and corruption. We may assume that the rest of Italy housed many decent, honest, responsible citizens, and that the industrious towns had no such degraded masses as the capital. Provincials, represented by Cicero, were already providing Rome with fresh sources of energy and ability. Both Cicero and Caesar were rising above the narrow tribal ideals and the primitive pieties of the old Romans, anticipating the universalism of the Empire.

3. The Grandeur of the Empire

As Julius Caesar had some apparent hankering for royalty, Marcus Brutus, Caius Cassius, and their fellow conspirators murdered him in the name of republican liberties. Brutus may well have been as sincere as tradition had it. He was a patrician, however, and showed little concern over the liberties of common people. (Shakespeare probably did not know that like other patricians, his noble Brutus practiced usury, charging 48 per cent interest on loans.) His class had raised no republican banner against the dictatorship of Sulla, imposed in its own interest, and it still had no program to offer the Republic. Within a few weeks after the murder of Caesar, Cicero lamented that the lofty deed was in vain; a new civil war was under way. A triumvirate of Mark Antony, young Octavian, and Lepidus, formed to carry on the cause of

Caesar, took over the state, condemned to death many of his enemies (including Cicero), and defeated the forces of Brutus and Cassius, which had been armed by extortions from the unhappy Greeks in Asia Minor. Antony and Octavian then eliminated Lepidus, only to begin conspiring against each other. They squared off at the battle of Actium, in 31 B.C., in which Antony was finished by a crushing defeat. As he had married Cleopatra of Egypt and taken on the airs of an Oriental monarch, Octavian had been able to pose as the champion of old Roman tradition, or of the West against the East. His victory at Actium stirred wild enthusiasm in Italy.

In the course of succeeding to the mastery of the Roman world, Octavian had been as unscrupulous as Julius Caesar, but much more ruthless and vindictive. On his record, only Romans taken in by his propaganda could have believed that he was a devoted patriot, just as they were deluded into believing that Antony intended to bequeath their empire to his Oriental queen (who was actually a full-blooded Macedonian). Nevertheless, they were right: the victor of Actium was indeed the savior of Rome. Following his victory, Octavian was as generous as Caesar, refusing to punish those who had borne arms against him, and he proved to be a wiser statesman, or at least a more successful one. Beyond all question he became a dedicated patriot.

Immediately Octavian not only restored peace but inaugurated the long era of the *Pax Romana,* and with it an unprecedented prosperity. He gave up wars of aggression to concentrate on the task of consolidating the Empire, really unifying it for the first time. Like Caesar, he was liberal to provincials, giving them the right to appeal directly to him, and depending on their services to help build an honest, efficient civil service lacking under the Republic; he enforced responsible rule by the provincial governors. At home he exercised as much power as Caesar had but showed much more respect for traditional forms. In 27 B.C. he officially surrendered his powers as dictator, restoring the state to the Senate and the Roman people, thereby winning his reputation as a "champion of liberty." The Senate and people reciprocated by delegating supreme authority to him for a ten-year term, and kept renewing the delegation to the end of his life. They also formally gave him his name of Augustus, which connoted sacred and superhuman, and later the title "Father of his Country." The Greek cities in Asia Minor were more extravagant in their gratitude, officially conferring on him such titles as "Savior of all mankind" and "Founder of the whole Universe." He was at least the founder of a new political order, which his long reign of more than forty years firmly established.

This order, the celebrated "Principate," was an absolute monarchy under the guise of republican forms. In deference to the traditional hatred of the name of king, Augustus was called *imperator,* or commander in chief, and himself chose the title of *princeps,* or "first citizen" of the state; as such, he took pains to have the Senate approve all his decrees. Most historians assume that he retained republican forms only to disguise the monarchy he deliberately established. Others (like Ferrero) believe that he was genuinely devoted to the republican ideal, and that he consented to rule as a monarch all his life only because the people forced him to, sharing their fear that his retirement would bring on civil war again.[4] Whatever his motives, there is no question about his autocratic powers. He reinforced his authority by legally constituted powers, taking on such offices as consul, censor, and tribune; he retained full control of the army and the treasury, together with direct control of the stronger provinces; and he made war and peace, as he made the laws that the Senate approved. By the end of his long reign, only some oldsters had personal memories of the Republic that Cicero had died for; "Caesarism" had permanently replaced republican government. It has also been called Fascism.

The Principate may therefore be regarded as a grand hoax, or a myth. We need to keep in mind its obvious shortcomings by republican standards, in particular the failure of Augustus to build in safeguards against abuses of the power he wielded. But first we need to realize that his principate was by no means a mere myth. Augustus had himself set a high example of responsible rule, proving that power does not always corrupt (else there is no hope for the human race), proving it more strikingly because he had virtually absolute power. More important for the long run, he had not claimed the rights of an absolute monarch, or asserted the duty of unquestioning obedience. As *princeps* he had committed himself to Cicero's ideal theory of the state.

In this theory the state was a commonwealth, the property of the people, who were the source of all authority. The emperor was a servant of the people, ruling by common consent, exercising only the authority they had delegated to him; his office was the highest form of

---

[4] Toward the end of his life Augustus prepared an account of his stewardship, which was inscribed on the walls of various temples. In this he emphasized that he had "restored liberty to the state" and remained obedient to the will of the Senate and the people. The fullest copy that has survived is in Ankara, ancient Ancyra. The ghost of Augustus might rejoice in the knowledge that Ankara was made the capital of Turkey by Kemal Atatürk, another dedicated dictator and Father of his Country.

civic duty, not a personal privilege. Hence the deification of the emperor, a custom that began when Augustus conferred divine honors on Julius Caesar, was not the source of his power but a symbolic blessing, or posthumous reward for high service. The best of the Roman emperors were perhaps as worthy of worship as many of the saints to come. They kept restating the ideal theory: "the idea of a kingly government," in the words of Marcus Aurelius, "that most of all respects the freedom of the governed." Some other emperors made such a farce of it that unsympathetic historians have described it as a vulgar fraud; yet the ideal was vital enough to survive all corruption and abuse, outlive the Empire itself. It enshrined the basic principle of constitutional government, kingly power limited by law. It became a cornerstone in Western political tradition, providing a basis for opposition to tyranny long before the separation of powers was worked out in constitutions.

By his liberality to the provinces Augustus also stimulated loftier ideas of Rome's imperial mission. His policy was a blend of tribalism and universalism that fell short of Cicero's ideal of "a single commonwealth of gods and men," but that still impressed men as the dawn of a new era in history. It inspired Virgil's *Aeneid,* the grandest statement of the Roman mission. Aeneas was no Homeric hero, seeking personal glory and fame, but the dedicated founder of the Roman nation; his travails were epical because this nation represented "a new hope for the human race, a hope of peace, of order, of civilization." As the Principate maintained peace and order for two centuries, the ideal of *cosmopolis* grew more pervasive and explicit. "For me as Antoninus," wrote Marcus Aurelius, "my city and fatherland is Rome, but as man, the world"; and he took for granted that his highest obligation was to the world. The less exalted emperors before him had generally shown enough sense of obligation to the provinces to win more popularity abroad than at home. Greeks declared not merely loyalty but a fervent gratitude. "You Romans," cried the orator Aristides, "are the only rulers known to History who have reigned over free men. . . . The lustre of your rule is unsullied by any breath of ungenerous hostility; and the reason is that you yourselves set the example of generosity by sharing all your power and privileges with your subjects . . . so that in your day a combination has been achieved which previously appeared quite impossible—the combination of consummate power with consummate benevolence. . . . Rome is a citadel that has all the peoples of the Earth for its villagers."

This was rhetoric, of course: Roman imperial rule was never so unsullied or consummate. Nevertheless, the Romans were indeed the only rulers known to history to win from subjects such praise as guardians of universal freedom. In A.D. 212 their conception of empire as a commonwealth culminated in a measure quite unprecedented: an edict of the Emperor Caracalla conferred Roman citizenship upon virtually all the free men of the Empire. Admittedly his motive was not idealistic —it was primarily to swell the number of taxpayers; and by this time Roman citizenship conferred no political rights of participation in the government. Yet it did mean equality before the law. What had been a jealously guarded privilege in Athens, comparable to membership in an exclusive club, became the right of all free members of the community. The Romans gave the West the concept of "the people," unknown in classical Greece. By law the citizen was a *persona:* a man with private rights to life, liberty, and property—rights declared and protected by the state. For the Romans had developed a law appropriate to a universal commonwealth.

The development was typically anomalous. Roman law began like all other law as tribal custom, "sacred" only because it was merely tribal and more ritualistic than reasoned. As the Romans built up their empire, with no ideal purpose in mind, they had to administer law to diverse peoples with alien customs; and though they found the task distasteful, they gradually evolved a *jus gentium,* a "law of nations" different from their own civil law, or "law of the citizens." The *jus gentium* became a law of contract, applying to all men alike regardless of their tribal status, and it therefore implied a principle of equity or "natural" justice above mere convention. With the help of Greek philosophy, to which old Romans had been hostile, this principle became explicit.

Under the Principate the Romans also began to develop a unique class of jurists to rationalize and systematize their law, make it a science, as the much more intellectual Greeks had never done. (Plato's *Laws* remained an academic performance.) Generations of magistrates and jurists, mostly anonymous, mostly very practical men and no doubt conservative, worked quietly to build up a system of law that was one of the most impressive intellectual achievements of antiquity, and in effect a social revolution. In general it was by all odds the most equitable, reasonable, and enlightened law that man had yet formulated, far transcending the hodgepodge of "God-given" laws in the Old Testament. It was an essentially rational law, governed by the logic of equity, based on the premise that men were responsible beings who of their own volition entered into contractual relations, reciprocal rights and duties. In particular the jurists most clearly transcended tribal and class prejudice, by the concepts of *cosmopolis* and natural law. Roman law thereby became one of the major emancipations in history.

Cicero, again, had summed up the premises of natural law: "Since there is nothing better than reason, and since it exists both in man and God, the first common possession of man and God is reason. But those who have reason in common must also have right reason in common. And since right reason is Law, we must believe that men have Law also in common with the gods. Further, those who share Law must also share Justice; and those who share these are to be regarded as members of the same commonwealth." The actual laws of nations fell short of such justice, reflecting "bad habits and false beliefs," but "true law" remained universal, unchanging, and everlasting because it was founded "not upon men's opinions, but upon Nature." And true law incorporated a basic principle of equality, underlying all differences of class, race, and culture, because of men's common possession of reason. Accordingly, the jurist Ulpian asserted that slavery was strictly unnatural even though it was written into the laws of all nations: "So far as *jus civile* is concerned, slaves are not counted as being persons; but this is not so under *jus naturale*, because so far as it is concerned all men are equal." His contemporary Tryphonimus likewise asserted that "liberty is included in natural law." As Cicero had put it, "We are servants of the law in order that we may be free."

That the Romans continued to count slaves as not persons reminds us again how far their practice fell short of their ideal theory. But again the theory made a real difference, and in the long run counted for much more. It is hard to realize how much more because we now take for granted a great deal of Roman law, beginning with its stress on due process and the simple idea (in Ulpian's words) of "giving every man his own." And of the close to a billion people who now live under codes indebted to the Romans, those in the Western democracies are indebted above all to the concept of natural law. Passing into Christian thought, this became so deeply embedded in Western tradition that it entered silent assumptions as well as conscious theory. Men were disposed to resist arbitrary law or exercise of power long before they invoked natural law to support the doctrine of "natural rights." Americans were speaking out of ancient tradition when they appealed to "the laws of nature and nature's God" in the preamble to their Declaration of Independence.

So we might now pause to consider this "myth." Hellenistic thinkers, such as the skeptic Carneades, had pointed out the plain objections to the Stoic doctrine: law is on the face of it a matter of convention, reflecting radically diverse customs and beliefs, emphasizing that men do not in fact agree on a universal, everlasting law. Cicero himself gave this away when he ventured to cite an example of natural law: "No one shall have gods to himself, either new gods or alien gods, unless recognized by the state." His "right reason"—always something different from the other fellow's reason—likewise failed to dispel the ambiguities of his key term "Nature." So capitalized, it means or connotes something divine, but all religious history testifies that men cannot agree on the nature or will of God, if any. In the sense of the physical universe, "nature" scarcely authorizes any law of justice; the most apparent law of life is the law of tooth and claw. "Natural" too may mean many different things, from customary or appropriate to essential or ideal. For such reasons the doctrine of an eternal, immutable law may always be used to sanctify the status quo. Conservatives have not needed Cicero's cue to sanctify property rights in particular, though these obviously temporal, mutable arrangements always deprive many men of property and involve apparent injustice. (The Roman jurists did not agree on whether property was natural or conventional.) Nor is it ever clear whether natural law requires men to obey or to resist actual laws that seem unjust.

Yet the concept is not so meaningless as current fashions in realism would have it. Another common meaning of "nature" is human nature: the nature, one may say on wholly realistic grounds, of a social animal who does in fact possess a power of reason, who has common basic needs, and who can live only by living with his fellows. Hence men everywhere recognize the necessity of law and for the most part obey it, at considerable sacrifice of their immediate selfish interests. Granted that law is primarily a matter of custom and convention, it everywhere involves some element of rationality and some idea of impartiality; no known code declares in so many words that the strong have a right to do whatever they please to the weak. Historically law has involved some virtually universal principles of justice, resting on the permanent needs of social life. All codes, for example, normally prohibit murder and theft within the community, and require men to keep their plighted word. And especially important in a history of freedom has been a different meaning of "natural" law—natural as designating not what is but what ought to be. Generally the Stoics proposed it as a fact, an everlasting law somehow written into the constitution of the universe; they were most vulnerable when they asserted, as Cicero did, that "law is not a product of human thought." Yet they always distinguished it from actual law, and proposed it as a norm. It is reasonable at least as an ideal of equity, a necessary means of declaring some actual laws unjust, or of opposing such institutions as slavery. It puts the basic law where it must be in any free society, beyond the whim of the rulers or the interests of any one class.

At any rate, roughly universal principles of justice are indispensable when men try to set up international law, as they are now doing in the United Nations, and as the Romans did in the course of administering their heterogeneous empire. What gave the Roman Empire its grandeur, and its abiding influence, was not its wealth and power but these ideas of a universal commonwealth and a universal law. The "stupendous majesty of the Roman peace" that awed Pliny was no mere myth.

Immediately the *Pax Romana* meant two centuries of relative peace and order such as the Mediterranean world had never known before, and would never know again. But unparalleled as it was in the history of empire, it meant much more than the mere absence of war. It gave birth to a positive hope that men could live together in harmony and security, in an ordered civilization, under the reign of justice. A century after Augustus the hope became a positive faith under a series of exceptionally devoted, high-minded emperors—Nerva, Trajan, Hadrian, Antoninus Pius, and Marcus Aurelius. Coins of this period bore legends of the Times of Happiness, and of everlasting promise. This was a sad illusion, we now know; but it spread the dream of Alexander the Great, a dream of world order that would haunt the imagination of the West ever after, and eventually would be embodied in a United Nations. It led to glimmerings of a faith in progress. Early Christians themselves were sometimes dazzled, in spite of their disposition to be horrified by the wickedness of pagan Rome, and to welcome the prospect of the end of this corrupt world. Tertullian wrote: "The world is every day better known, better cultivated, and more civilized than before."

The civility was largely confined to the cities, of course, but there were many hundreds of these, still distinctive for the splendor of their public works. The Romans had carried on the Hellenistic tradition, founding many new cities and granting considerable municipal self-government. The spirit of the *polis* was still alive, in an empire that

had something of the feel if not the forms of a confederation. Freedom of movement was supplemented by more social mobility than there had been in the Republic, more opportunity for the energetic and enterprising; a rising class of freedmen took over much of the business of administering the Empire. The upper classes maintained the tradition of civic responsibility, serving as public officials without pay, and spending lavishly for civic purposes. The Roman were in some respects not only more practical but more imaginative than the Greeks in promoting the amenities of civic life. As architects they went beyond the simple post and lintel, exploring the possibilities of arch and vault in monumental public buildings; as engineers they contributed to both health and comfort by introducing sewers, baths, and central heating, while also building their superb roads and their massive aqueducts to bring in the life-giving waters—for want of which the sites of scores of splendid cities in the Near East now support only a poor village.[5] In the midst of all this munificence most people remained very poor, and their condition must concern us shortly; but in the cities a fairly large proportion were able to enjoy a high standard of comfortable, civilized living.

They recall the most obvious contribution of Rome—the preservation and transmission of Greek culture. Although Romans of the old school typically professed some contempt for the Greeks as corrupt and effete, their high culture was essentially Greek by the time of Augustus; in the well-known words of Horace, Greece had "taken captive her rude conquerors." The captives produced important works in their own right, developing such new forms as the satire of Horace, using Greek forms to express their own distinctive ideals, as in Virgil's *Aeneid*, and creating a few masterpieces that survived the loss of the Greek originals that had inspired them, as the great poem of Lucretius *On the Nature of Things* did more for the philosophy of Epicurus than the extant fragments of his own work. Their

---

[5] Asia Minor, now Turkey, gives perhaps the most haunting impression of the vanished splendors. Although the most progressive country in the Moslem Near East today, Turkey is only beginning to approach the level of wealth and culture in Asia Minor under Roman rule, when there were several hundred cities important enough to issue their own coins. Almost all its major towns occupy the sites of ancient cities, and only a few of them have any public monuments worthy of a moment's comparison with the countless temples, theaters, colonnades, baths, and gymnasia the ruins of which still litter the land. Many once-famous sites—Ephesus, Miletus, Nicaea, Laodicea, Sardis, Xanthus, and Troy, to name only a few—are now either deserted or occupied by a few peasants. Elsewhere chunks of Corinthian columns embedded in the walls of peasant huts or stables may remind a traveler that a city once flourished in the vicinity.

basic contribution, however, is represented by the work of Cicero. Unoriginal, unspontaneous, and unsparkling, but sensible and tactful, he transmitted Greek thought in a somewhat diluted form that might be better suited to the needs of ordinary men and daily life, especially in the still-backward region of western Europe. He also heralded an important type bequeathed by the Romans—the type of cultivated gentleman, at once man of letters and man of the world, who need not be a man of noble birth. Cicero could make an admirable educator for humanistic purposes, even for democratic purposes unlike his own. Not very attractive as a person, or ever really distinguished as a mind, he in this view merited the reverence accorded him by Westerners to this century, and may symbolize the achievement of the Empire ordered by the man who had him killed.

Altogether, this achievement was impressive enough to justify the exceptional attention the Roman Empire has got from historians, from Polybius on. As we approach its end we might consider the testimony of another Greek historian, Ammianus. Writing in the fourth century A.D., when Rome had long since fallen on bad times, he could no longer dwell on its excellent constitution. He had instead many harsh things to say, about not only the proverbial vices of the capital but the brutal oppression of common men—symptoms of a degeneration worse than Polybius had predicted. Nevertheless, Ammianus was much more devoted to Rome, now become venerable, even writing in Latin instead of his native Greek. Himself still a pagan in an empire also become officially Christian, he was a lover of classical culture; and Rome was to him the bulwark of this culture against the rising barbarism. Although in the next century it was to succumb to the barbarians, it impressed him as virtually immortal. He anticipated the myth of the "Eternal City," as Rome was christened by Rutilius, the last of the pagan poets, after it had been sacked by Alaric in the year 410. By his fidelity Ammianus lent dignity to the myth, exemplifying why the fall of Rome seems more tragic than that of any other empire.

Yet it no longer seems at all mysterious, or simply tragic. We can make out plenty of signs of inner rot long before the barbarians took over Rome, as they could not have done in a healthy empire—barbarians had been on its borders all along. At that their invasions were not dramatic conquests, only periodic raids, followed by a gradual infiltration of the Roman army and government; so when Rome officially "fell," in the year 476, contemporaries were unaware of any epoch-making event. The barbarians had long been controlling the government; now they merely dispensed with the fiction of Roman rule. It is easy enough for us to see the beginning of the end in the Principate that won Augustus universal acclaim as the "Savior of all mankind."

4. *The Decline and Fall*

It appears that Augustus suffered from a feeling of failure in his old age, saddened by the vice in his capital, even within his own family; but the irony went deeper than he knew. While he had set his heart on reviving the old-time religion and morality, the peace and prosperity he restored were more likely to give men a false sense of security than a high sense of dedication—false because he had not built really strong foundations, political, economic, or spiritual. In particular, the pious fiction of his principate that veiled the end of the old republican order also veiled the basic defect of the new order. Everything had depended upon him. The emperor was indeed "the soul of the Empire," as Seneca was to say; only he was a fallible mortal, and the Empire had no sound constitutional body. Although Augustus arranged for his stepson Tiberius to inherit his powers, he made no constitutional provision for the regular election of emperors, as none for the protection of their subjects against abuses of their powers. The fate of the dynasty he founded foreshadowed the political fate of the Empire.

Some fifty years after his death, this dynasty ran out in Nero (d. A.D. 68). The successors of Augustus had included the ferocious Caligula, who expressed the wish that the Roman people had but a single neck for him to wring, and who for want of any better method was removed by assassination; the infamous Nero averted a similar fate by committing suicide. By this time armies were making emperors, outside of Rome. Vespasian, a sturdy commoner who took the name of Caesar as he restored order, demonstrated that the Roman character had survived its celebrated corruption, as did the remarkable series of emperors from Trajan to Marcus Aurelius, who fulfilled the promise of the Augustan Principate; but Marcus, the noblest of them all (d. A.D. 180), himself inaugurated another century of convulsion by naming as his successor his preposterously worthless son Commodus. Before he was throttled, Commodus distinguished himself by superlative folly and crime.[6] Shortly thereafter the Praetorian Guard in Rome put up the imperial office for sale, briefly bestowing it on the highest bidder. A strong emperor, Septimius Severus, again restored order for a time by making the army his chief concern, advising his sons first of all to "enrich the soldiers and scorn all other men." The army proceeded to make and unmake emperors at will—in one period of fifty years as many as twenty-six, only one of whom died in bed. Assassination had at first been the fate chiefly of the monsters, such as Caligula and Commodus; now it was more likely to overtake the most patriotic emperors. Other than patriotism, however, the emperors had no political principle or program until the reign of Diocletian (284-305). A truly great statesman, he ended the anarchy and prolonged both his own life and that of the Empire by dropping all pretense of republican government, setting up an Oriental court, shutting himself off from his subjects, and ruling as an out-and-out absolute monarch.

As might be expected, the material prosperity of the Empire declined sharply during all this disorder, which was aggravated by the ravages of Gothic raiders and wars with the rising Sassanian Empire in Persia. Diocletian accordingly sought to restore economic order too by arbitrary methods. He bound peasants to the soil, bound artisans and city officials to their jobs, fixed wages and prices, and in general tried to freeze the economy. As in Ptolemaic Egypt, this "socialism" was designed primarily for the benefit of the rulers, not of the toiling masses; rigid order was the only kind of order that now seemed feasible, more especially because the economy had long lacked resilience. Diocletian's program was a belated acknowledgment of another basic weakness of the Roman Empire.

The prosperity of the Augustan era had not led to a steady growth of commerce and industry. After the first century A.D. the Romans made no important advances in technology, no marked economic progress of any kind. When the Empire ceased to expand and to bring in captured wealth, it developed no new resources, but in effect began to live off its capital. There were signs of serious trouble as early as the "Times of Happiness" from Trajan to Marcus Aurelius: the em-

---

[6] Probably he was mad. The historian Dio Cassius records that his messages to the Senate took this form: "The Emperor Caesar Lucius Aelius Aurelius Commodus Augustus Pius Felix Sarmaticus Germanicus Maximus Britannicus, Pacifier of the Universe, Invincible, the Roman Hercules, Pontifex Maximus, Holder of the Tribunician Authority for the eighteenth, Imperator for the eighth, Consul for the seventh time, Father of his Country, to consuls, praetors, tribunes, and the fortunate Commodian senate; Greetings." A possible excuse for his madness was the absurdity of his power.

perors were finding it harder to make both ends meet. Then they
could think of nothing better to do than debase the imperial coinage,
which they proceeded to do steadily. But their troubles had not resulted from anything like state socialism. Although historians disagree
on the extent to which the Romans approached "capitalism," business
at least remained in the hands of private businessmen. If the emperors
might embarrass businessmen, like everybody else, by extraordinary
levies or compulsory services in emergencies, they otherwise followed
a policy of *laissez faire*—as Augustus had. More strictly, they had no
real economic policy. The economic stagnation was due not to any
restrictions on free private enterprise, but to a lack of enterprise in
both businessmen and the emperors.

Imperial Rome had preserved the traditional aristocratic disdain of
economic activity and the mechanic arts. The senatorial class had been
debarred from trade and industry, or any business except usury and
farming; high interest rates, landed estates, and abundant slave labor
enabled them handsomely to afford their disdain of business. The successful bourgeois were inclined to ape their patrician betters. They
produced few real entrepreneurs or captains of industry, generally
investing their wealth in land or gold rather than business enterprise;
Cicero set the genteel fashion when he argued that merchants could
not be honest but might become respectable by buying landed estates
with their ill-gotten gains. The emperors typically remained indifferent
to economics except for some concern over the growth of *latifundia,*
the large estates that were ruining agriculture in Italy. Aside from
unsuccessful efforts to deal with this problem at home, they made as
little effort to strengthen or stimulate the economy as to regulate it.
Their necessary concern over their own income never led them to
adopt such measures as annual budgets, national loans, or any long-
range fiscal policies. No Roman thinker produced a treatise on economics.

Meanwhile there were always the many poor, who naturally suffered when business was bad, and gained little if anything when it
was good. In the palmy days of the Empire wages were kept low by
the many millions of slaves, as well as by the want of industrial enterprise. Although some emperors made efforts of sorts to relieve or
protect the poor, none was ever farsighted enough to attempt either
long-range economic programs or basic social reform. At its best their
attitude was typified by a story Suetonius told, about a man who
showed the Emperor Vespasian a model of a machine that would enable

him to build great public works with fewer laborers and at great savings. Vespasian praised and rewarded the inventor, then had his model destroyed. Suetonius cites the story as proof of the emperor's wisdom, since the machine would have put men out of work; and under the circumstances his policy was doubtless humane. For the long run it guaranteed that laborers would remain poor and relatively unproductive. Similarly the munificence of the emperors at home only guaranteed that Rome would remain a parasitic city, growing ever larger and showier, and producing very little in return for the wealth it lived off; here the common people came to be provided with free corn, free shows on 175 days of the year, and almost a thousand public baths. Elsewhere they were busier but not much better off. Emperors, businessmen, and intellectuals alike remained unaware that their poverty was another basic cause of economic stagnation, in that they provided no market to stimulate enterprise.

Such indifference to economics might have been more seemly had the Romans not been so practical, even materialistic a people, or especially had they been devoted to cultural enterprise. As it was, cultural stagnation was more pronounced, and set in earlier. In litera-ture the golden age was the Augustan, of Virgil, Livy, and Horace. A "silver age" that followed in the first century A.D. got some luster from such names as Seneca, Tacitus, Pliny, and Juvenal, but gave signs of decadence in increasing affectation and strain; and it petered out early in the second century. The glorious age of the Empire, from Trajan to Marcus Aurelius, was about the least creative in Western history. The Stoic philosophy then found classic expression in the *Meditations* of Marcus, but the high-minded emperor added nothing new, as no other Roman had to any school of philosophy; and his melancholy intimated the inadequacy of his philosophy for both intellectual and political needs. In the three centuries that followed until the fall of Rome, the Romans wrote no masterpieces of any kind. As for art, they had always left sculpture and painting to the Greeks, pleased to buy the products but to disdain the profession; and it too deteriorated. By the fourth century most sculptors were unable to carve the human form correctly, in the realistic manner that the Romans had always preferred.

The one art that flourished to the end was rhetoric. Taken over from the Hellenistic Greeks, this became the main subject of higher education and gave increasing prestige to teaching, which the Romans had at first treated as the lowest of the professions. In the words of

Henri Marrou, Roman education represented an "ideal of humanism that was unconcerned with, unconstrained by, any sordid technical or utilitarian considerations." In other words, it was divorced both from political realities and from any pursuit of new knowledge or truth. Education has seldom been more revered than it was in the last days of the Empire, and has seldom had less content.

One apparent exception to the decline of classical culture, the growth of Christianity, calls for a separate chapter. In the present context it was among the obvious symptoms of decline, and pointed to the underlying reasons for it. In trying to buttress his Principate by the traditional religion of Rome, Augustus had displayed more piety than wisdom. This religion could still foster the traditional virtues of the Romans, and did so to the end; yet the motives of the dignified men of the old school who continued to revere the gods of Rome were more patriotic than truly religious. Few educated men could really believe in the primitive religion of the forefathers, or in the imperial cult wedded to it. Neither could the state religion inspire the common people, still less console them in times of stress; if they might pray for the great and good emperors, they could hardly pray to them. Like the Hellenistic Greeks, the Romans took to savior gods. Their invitation to the Great Mother Cybele in the days of Hannibal was prophetic; her cult became immensely popular all over the Empire, rivaled only by other Oriental mystery cults, as of Isis and Mithra. At their best these cults were means of regeneration, but as in the Hellenistic era their popularity was generally not a sign of renewed faith. It indicated rather a loss of vital faith, a spiritual malaise—a dependence again on miracle and mystery.

Augustus had inspired more complacence than fervor or zeal. Seeking primarily to order and consolidate, he had not given the Empire a dynamic faith or a spirit of adventure. Even in his day Romans were prone to nostalgia; like Livy, they looked backward instead of forward. As time went on, orators vied in celebrating the deathless glory and felicity of the Empire, or an adventure that was over, but the most serious thinkers were generally the least hopeful. Stoics, always the dominant school, still saw history as an endless cycle, and typically felt that their age was on the downswing, not the upswing; the Necessity they worshiped looked pretty much like a necessary evil, no less when Marcus Aurelius noted that "the rational soul comprehends that those who come after us will see nothing new." Marcus set the grandest and most melancholy example as he gave his all to the service of the commonwealth, without stint or complaint, and without faith, without hope, without love. On a lower plane the common symptom of a want of fervor or faith was self-indulgence. Augustus had warned the Romans that sterility would deliver their city to the barbarians, and issued laws penalizing celibacy and childlessness, but to little avail; many upper-class Romans were disinclined to go to the trouble of rearing families. Ordinary Romans were given to the simple callousness expressed by one of them in a fond letter to his pregnant wife: "If it is a boy, let him live; if it is a girl, put it out."

All this one might write off again as the old story of moral decay, except that morality did not clearly degenerate after the Augustan age, and corruption was never so flagrant as in the Republic. Apart from a few monsters, the emperors maintained an exceptionally high average in responsible, patriotic rule, as did most provincial governors. The state of morals looks worse than it was because most literary accounts of it come down from the parasitic capital; provincials generally had more virtue and sense than the idle rich and the idle poor of Rome. They belie, too, the popular racial theory that the decline of the Roman Empire was due to the deterioration of the old Roman stock; after Augustus almost all the greater Romans were of provincial stock, "tainted" by foreign blood. They suggest rather that we look again to the basic limitations of the Roman mentality, the basic defects of the Roman character.

The most curious thing about these empire builders is how essentially incurious and unadventurous they were, how little interest they showed in the world they were masters of. In taking over Greek culture, they could not by an effort of will have acquired the spontaneity, versatility, and creativity of the Greeks, but they might have picked up something of their eager curiosity and gone on to inquire and explore for themselves. As it was, they made no contributions worth mentioning to natural science, mathematics, medicine, geography, or any major branch of inquiry, and made no explorations at all. Having gone on the defensive with Augustus, they began living off their cultural as well as economic capital, resting on authority instead of risking experiment or innovation. They reduced literature to a source of models and rules, the proprieties spelled out in Horace's *Art of Poetry*. Except for law, their one great intellectual achievement, they only mulled over the philosophy they had learned from the Greeks, venturing no new ideas out of their own experience. Having made an extraordinary history, in a world greater than the Hellenistic *oikou-*

mene, they made no advance whatever in historical understanding, failing even to match the effort of Polybius. Their imperial historians, indeed, most clearly demonstrated their inability to comprehend either their achievements or their failures.

Tacitus, the greatest of these historians, was unconsciously the most revealing. His greatness lies wholly in his powers of narration and delineation of character, not his powers of insight or analysis. Thus in trying to explain happenings he sometimes invokes natural causes, sometimes Fortune, sometimes Inexorable Fate. Understandably, his *Annals* of the early Empire is purely military and political history, with only casual reference if any to social conditions, the economy, law, education, art, and other such matters commonly neglected by ancient historians; but he shows surprisingly little interest in the provinces, the Roman Empire at large. He indicates not the least understanding of the achievement of Augustus, which alone gave greatness to his subject. He offers a positively misleading account of the succeeding emperors, in particular Tiberius and Claudius. If what he says about their personal vices is true, he ignores their proved capacities as administrators and statesmen, who earned the gratitude of the provinces by maintaining the just, responsible rule inaugurated by Julius Caesar and Augustus.

No more did Tacitus understand himself—if we take him at his own word. "Unmoved, as I have no reason to be moved, by either hatred or partiality," he begins his *Annals;* and he proceeds at once to display his animus against Augustus. The key to both his partiality and his narrowness is his bias as a patrician. Because the Republic was no more, "there was not a vestige left of the old sound morality"; but what he meant was that the Senate had been stripped of its power. He mourned the loss of freedom, meaning only the freedom of the patrician class; mourned the fate of the "Roman people," though expressing only an aristocratic contempt of the common people. He was indifferent to the blessings of good government in the provinces, as the senators of old had been; for the real evils of his time he had no solution but a return to power of the senatorial class, which had failed miserably in the Republic. While the emperors continued to make the only real effort at promoting the common welfare, he could only yearn for a restoration of the civic virtue that his class had not in fact upheld. In short, he had learned nothing from either the failure of the Republic or the feats of Augustus. Despite his austere manner, he was essentially a sentimentalist, like Cicero; and like him he spoke for the Roman elite.

Tacitus accordingly exemplified the severe moral as well as intellectual limitations of the Romans. Unquestionably sincere, if somewhat theatrical in his gravity, he may sound hollow because his devotion to "Rome" involved no apparent concern over the welfare of the great bulk of the Roman people. His moral insensitivity helped to blind him to the political realities, past and present. Because of such insensitivity Romans in general failed to see through their political myths: they were untroubled by the glaring discordancy between their ideal theory of commonwealth and the actualities of poverty and oppression. There was always a purely formal quality in their idealism, as in their religion and their classicism, or in the rhetorical republicanism of Tacitus. So Cicero could write eloquently about virtue as its own reward, and he could also write, "What is the use of being kind to a poor man?" Seneca could preach stoical indifference to external circumstances and sing the praises of poverty while managing to become one of the richest men in the Empire, in particular by exploiting the aristocratic tradition of usury.

At their worst the Romans were simply callous. The notorious example is their passion for gladiatorial games, which throughout their history almost none of them—not even the noble Marcus Aurelius—ever spoke out against. Short of this brutality, a streak of coarseness ran through their whole society. It came out in the vulgar materialism of their upper classes, a love of money and ostentatious luxury the more conspicuous because they paraded their piety, their gravity, their disdain of business. It appeared in the common grossness of their art—an official, complacent, monotonous art that at best expressed power rather than freedom, voiced matter more than spirit, and never voiced the wonder that it may evoke by its massiveness and splendor. In this aspect the Roman Empire may be symbolized by its architecture: ornate marbled surfaces, concealing a core of brick, mortar, and rubble, and adorned with columns serving no functional purpose. And even at its best the Roman character was wanting in both humanity and spirituality. Virgil, one of the very few Romans who seemed deeply stirred by the spiritual ferment of the Axial period, offered Aeneas as their best: a hero who was the paragon of Roman virtue, all *pietas* and *dignitas*, ever dutiful, ever prepared to sacrifice his happiness to his grand mission of founding Rome, "a new hope for the human race";

M*

yet a pretty boring hero, unimaginative and humorless, lacking spontaneity and zest, lacking any passion for goodness apart from duty, ever prepared to sacrifice the happiness of others too (as he sacrificed Queen Dido) to an official mission that was more political than truly religious or humane.

In philosophy, a more pertinent, influential example was set by Seneca, who was to become the most popular exponent of Stoicism in the Western world. As the tutor and later the chief minister of Nero, he gave the emperor lofty precepts about his duty to the commonwealth, in keeping with the ideal theory of Augustus. He soared higher than other Stoics, conceiving a God who was father of all mankind; so Christians would make him out to be a disciple of St. Paul, even forging letters between him and Paul. Yet there was very little spirit of brotherhood in Seneca, as little faith, hope, and charity. He represented most explicitly the inhuman logic of the Stoic ideal. "To feel pain at the misfortune of others," he wrote, "is a weakness unworthy of the wise man." And while he himself seems to have been pained somewhat by his feeling that the Roman world was decaying, he provided the most depressing evidence of the actual decay of classical culture by writing tragedies. Supposedly modeled upon Greek tragedy, but as lacking in Greek as in Christian spirit, his plays are distinguished by their bombast, their crude horrors, and their incredibly abominable taste.[7] Accentuating his incapacity for both pity and awe, they give another slant on the tragic fall of the Roman Empire: the Romans lacked a tragic sense of life.

Immediately Seneca leads us to a fundamental issue. In the course of making his fortune under Nero, he sometimes departed from his Stoic principles by gross flattery of his royal pupil; he could then argue that the emperor was above the law, not bound by it. Even his most serious thought led him to such conclusions. Although he expressed the conventional admiration of the Roman Republic, he was more profoundly pessimistic than Tacitus, hardly dreaming of its restoration; he dreamed rather of a "Golden Age" before civilization, in a state

---

[7] An example of his taste is the scene in *Hippolytus* following the death of the hero, who has been torn to pieces: the hero's father sets about collecting the pieces, trying to fit them together, and speculates on one he is unable to identify or place. A student of literature may be still more depressed by the thought that the plays of Seneca were long much admired, especially by Elizabethan poets; generations of Western critics ranked them with the masterpieces of antiquity. A measure of compensation is the humility this thought might induce, in an awareness that current fashions in literary taste may not be the last word either.

of nature (a myth that Rousseau would revive). He departed from the whole classical tradition, which had represented the *polis* or the state as the necessary means to virtue and civility, by representing government as a necessary evil, made necessary by human wickedness. Such views disposed him to authoritarianism, the more because he had an especially low opinion of common men. Despotism was "natural" enough, given the viciousness of the masses, and certainly preferable to any rule by them. It is accordingly ironical that Seneca himself fell victim to the despotism of Nero, who turned on him and ordered him to commit suicide. Like a good Roman Stoic, he obeyed and went to his death with calm fortitude, if also with a characteristic suggestion of staginess. (Tacitus reports that he invited friends in for the occasion, and when he was not allowed to draw up a will, told the friends he would leave them "his only, but fairest possession, the pattern of his life.") But his fate was dramatically appropriate even aside from the opportunity to prove or parade his dignity; for his thought was profoundly symptomatic of the actual loss of freedom in the Roman Empire.

Now, in view of the fifty reasons historians have found for the fall of the Empire, one can hardly maintain that this loss was the "real" cause. Nevertheless, there unquestionably was a distinct loss in political and intellectual freedom, and on the face of the record it was an important factor. Its importance becomes plainer if we look beyond the Romans themselves. Their empire embraced millions of Greeks and Oriental peoples, it civilized other peoples in western Europe, it finally extended citizenship to all of them; yet neither the Greek tradition nor the fresh blood availed against the growing paralysis and sterility. In a history of freedom, at any rate, we must dwell on the actual loss in freedom, and consider its possible consequences.

5. *The Relation to Freedom*

"As to peace," wrote Plutarch about A.D. 100, "there is no need to occupy ourselves, for all war has ceased. As to liberty, we have that which the government leaves us; and perhaps it would not be good if we had any more." *Perhaps:* Plutarch was still a good enough Greek to have some doubts, possibly some inkling of the thesis of John Stuart Mill. A benevolent despotism, Mill argued, was in the long run likely to be more fatal than a brutal one. Harsh rule may stir a struggle for liberty, whereas under a benevolent despotism men naturally tend to become passive, submissive, dependent; content to be ruled by others, without active participation in their government, they lose the habit of initiative, enterprise, and self-reliance in public life; and eventually they lose all capacity for self-rule. History offers no better evidence for this thesis than the Principate established by Augustus. For two centuries the Roman Empire basked in the peace he restored, men grew complacent under as generally mild, benevolent rule as monarchy has ever provided; and when the political honeymoon ended with Commodus, the people proved utterly helpless.

From the outset the emperor had decided how much liberty to leave them. He made the laws that in theory proceeded from the community, he made all the crucial decisions of war and peace. His authority was strengthened by the fiction of his deification, even if most Romans did not take it literally; as Pliny told the Emperor Trajan, "The gods have given thee supreme power and control over all things, even over thyself." Hence Roman jurists were understandably of two minds, sometimes asserting that the emperor was under the law, sometimes acknowledging that he was its author. Ulpian himself decided that the pleasure of the *princeps* had the force of law, since "the people confers on him and into his hands all its own sovereign power and authority." And if, Pliny notwithstanding, the gods sometimes neglected to give the emperor control over himself, he might suffer as much as the people from the absence of any other legal control.

The Romans never developed institutions, legislative or judicial, to make good their theory of constitutional, limited government. The formality of the popular assembly was dropped as early as the reign of Tiberius. This left the Senate as the only constitutional body, and it had no legal power to veto the emperor, as no control over the treasury and the army. Although most emperors were careful to show respect to so venerable an institution, it was a purely formal respect. Senators were often inclined to feel as bitter as Tacitus did over their impotence, or as jealous of favors shown to the provinces; but then they might be worse than futile, as they found devious ways to vent their injured dignity or their spleen. The early emperors were habitually fearful of conspiracy; the best of the later ones might suffer from senatorial backbiting and scandalmongering, as Hadrian in particular did. On the other hand, when the army began making and breaking them, the emperors could not count on effective support from the Senate. They had to reckon with the fact that they got their power from the army, not the gods, and were always liable to assassination. From first to last emperors needed exceptional gifts of self-control as they exercised a supreme power on which there were no legal checks, in the face of a republican tradition that was just strong enough to make them vulnerable to the charge of tyranny, never strong enough effectively to curb a disposition to actual tyranny.

Such dispositions had freer rein because of the ancient confusion between society and the state, or failure to delimit clearly and consistently the domain of the state. Although the Romans built up a law that protected a domain of personal rights, they did not consciously seek to extend this private domain or to hedge the traditional primacy of the state. Augustus felt free to invade private life, penalizing celibacy and childlessness in the interest of the state, and like Cicero he took for granted that religion was a department of the state—a view that would trouble the most conscientious emperors when the "atheistical" Christians spurned the state gods. They were the more troubled because of their consistent opposition to any private associations except those for the most harmless recreational purposes, or burial societies for the dead. There were no political parties in the Roman Empire, no labor unions, farm bureaus, or chambers of commerce, no societies for the promotion or prevention of anything in the public interest. The emperors banned all associations that might have the least political purpose or power, thereby betraying a distrust of the people, and in any case denying them means to political education. As for a Roman Civil Liberties Union, it was simply unthinkable. If some emperors affirmed the principle of freedom of thought and speech, there was never a constitutional right to such freedom; and in practice the right was arbitrarily restricted or denied.

Augustus had instituted censorship in the interest of morality and religion, for instance exiling the poet Ovid. His successors, fearful of their personal safety, had more despotic ideas about public enemies. Tiberius broadened the law against treason to include any show of disrespect to the emperor and his family. Under it a new precedent was set when a writer was formally condemned for publishing a history in which he praised Brutus and Cassius; a supine Senate then voted to burn his books. Caligula proposed to remove from public libraries such subversive books as the works of Homer, Virgil, and Livy. Philosophers were especially suspect to the Flavian dynasty that succeeded the Augustan; the Emperor Domitian banished them all from Rome (among

them the Stoic Epictetus) and put to death many Romans who had
been corrupted by their teaching. Even the more admirable emperors
testified to the precariousness of civil liberties, as Nerva acquired a
reputation for liberality by exempting senators from imperial inquisition. Later emperors were less inclined to such liberality, or less able to
afford it. Caracalla, who extended the rights of citizenship to all free
men, also decreed death for any of them who so much as wrote or spoke
the name of his brother Geta, a rival to his throne whom he had
murdered. Among his victims was the famous jurist Papinian.

An incidental consequence of these repressive tendencies was the
rise of a class of professional informers, who flourished by reporting
to the emperors all blasphemies, or signs of disrespect. A more pervasive consequence was the growth of a servile spirit. The many "clients"
who hung around wealthy households, willing to fawn on their patrons
for the sake of crumbs from their table, were no more of a disgrace
to the Roman tradition of sturdy character than were the many senators who played sycophant to the emperor; Seneca's rank flattery of
Nero was typical. But the loss of intellectual freedom had profounder
effects on culture. Tacitus complained bitterly of the book-burnings,
the expulsion of the philosophers, the exile of "every liberal art";
and though the emperor reigning in his day permitted such complaints,
Tacitus believed that the spirit essential to a great literature had been
killed. "Genius," he concluded, "died by the same blow that ended
public liberty." Longinus, who probably wrote his essay *On the Sublime* at about the same time, pronounced much the same verdict. The
sublime was no more: "We never drink from the fairest and most
fertile source of literature, which is freedom, and therefore we show a
genius for nothing but flattery."

Given the historical record, freedom is not in fact clearly essential
to literature: poets in many societies got along without drinking from
this fair source, or ever mentioning it. Yet the Romans had learned
about literature from the Greeks, had known freedom; and the record
also suggests that the loss of it had much to do with the cultural sterility
of the Empire. It helped to kill whatever chance the Romans might
have had to develop a spirit of eager inquiry and searching criticism.
It strengthened their disposition to an unreasoned conservatism that
impeded independent, adventurous, creative thought and effort. It
confirmed the tendencies to official monotony in art, to superficiality
and irrelevance in literature, to an exclusive concern with style rather
than substance in rhetoric, to fatalistic acquiescence or passivity in

philosophy. It helped to smother any live sense of new possibilities, any enthusiasm; so when the Romans dreamed it was of a mythical Golden Age—in the past. They grew less bitter than Tacitus as they grew less aware of their lost freedom, but they gave more meaning to the comment on the *Pax Romana* that he attributed to a barbarian: "They make a desert and call it peace." They made a cultural desert too. Among other things, the Empire died of boredom.

Although the Romans themselves suffered most directly and conspicuously, the Greeks and other provincials exhibited much the same symptoms. The Greeks continued to produce some notable works, as of Plutarch in literature, Strabo in geography, Epictetus in philosophy, Ptolemy and Galen in science. Chiefly, however, they produced orators and historians: the one practicing rhetoric and delivering panegyrics to their rulers, the other writing academic studies of the past with little feeling for either the actual future in store or a possibly better future. Plutarch, whose *Lives* contributed so much to the cult of liberty in later Europe, helps to explain why the Greeks contributed very little to it under the Roman Empire. Deeply devoted to the antique republican tradition, he was primarily an antiquarian, and his work an anachronism. In his piety he chose to serve as priest in the shrine of Apollo in Delphi and tried to revive the worship of the Olympian gods, who were long since dead for religious purposes. He also served as local magistrate, carrying on the tradition of the *polis*. The *polis* was still alive; but it too was dying, losing the spirit of liberty.

As the Greek cities prospered under the *Pax Romana*, they vied in lavishing divine honors on the emperors, even the monsters. Assus in Asia Minor, for example, hailed the reign of Caligula as the inauguration of a blessed new era "when the Universe found unmeasured joy, and every city and every nation has striven to behold the God." They were more complacent because they still enjoyed considerable self-government, and could boast of being "free and autonomous from the beginning by grace of the Augusti." Still, this freedom was by "grace" —it was never within their own power. They had no voice whatever in the selection of the God they beheld, or in the determination of imperial policy. They vied in making up grandiose titles for their benefactors, and as grandiose legends about their own dignity, because they had no major public issues to debate, no political affairs of serious consequence to handle on their own. Their range of interest and responsible choice, already narrowing, was further restricted by imperial fears of private associations. (Thus Trajan refused to allow an organization of 150 firemen in one city, declaring that such organizations were dangerous.) And the most conscientious emperors might intrude on municipal affairs, or take control of municipal finances, for the sake of efficiency. In competing for empty honors the cities tended to reckless extravagance, sometimes to scandalous mismanagement of their affairs; the emperors had to send officials (as Trajan sent Pliny) to straighten them out. Hadrian, the most fervent admirer of the Greeks, did most to restrict the effective autonomy of the cities as he reorganized the imperial government, centralizing power in an imperial bureaucracy.

By his time popular government within the cities was dead. The Greeks clung to their popular assemblies longer than the Romans did, but as the assemblies had little power or serious business to transact, the cities eventually followed the example of Rome and dropped them. The wealthy class took over the whole business of government. Although still typically public-spirited, they were not simply enthusiastic over unpaid honorary offices that could be a heavy burden, especially when they had to meet extraordinary capital levies; so far from resenting infringements on local sovereignty, they were likely to be pleased to dump their problems on the emperors. Then, with the breakdown of the *Pax Romana,* they were denied this pleasure. The Emperor Severus imposed rigid controls in order to collect the heavy taxes now required by his military establishment. Local magistrates were made responsible for the full burden, which they could escape only by flight; benefactions by the wealthy that had been matters of custom were made obligatory. Local self-government became a sham, maintained only in so far as it served the purposes of the imperial bureaucracy. Except for the growing power of the army and the bureaucracy, the Roman Empire was beginning to realize an actual kind of equality—equality in bondage to the state.

The common people might have taken some comfort in the thought that the wealthy were now suffering too, only they themselves generally suffered more, and by this time they were mostly too apathetic for any serious thought. The felicity of the *Pax Romana* had never gone wide or deep; peasants and city workers—the great majority of the nominally free population—had not enjoyed their share of the prosperity brought by Augustus. The prosperity tended rather to widen the gap between the cities and the peasantry, and within the cities between the proletariat and the upper class. The tradition of popular government remained strong enough to cause more active discontent than in Oriental societies, as we hear of occasional strikes and riots, and possibly, too, peasants in the armies took out their resentment of the city bourgeois during the civil wars; but in general the poor were either too helpless or too listless to indulge in the excitement of class war. There was never any widespread uprising, anything like a popular revolution. In the greater cities the masses demanded only bread and circuses.

From some historians the common people have accordingly received harsher treatment: they have been held up as the prime exhibits of the degeneration of the Roman Empire. Even Rostovtzeff, who dwelt on the poverty and oppression from which they suffered, summarized the whole drama as "the gradual absorption of the educated classes by the masses and the consequent simplification of all the functions of political, social, economic, and intellectual life, which we call the barbarization of the ancient world." Certainly there was little conspicuous virtue in the masses. While most of them may well have been decent and hard-working, at least outside the capital, what appears in the record is chiefly their passion for vulgar, brutal spectacles. Yet as certainly whatever effect they had on the educated classes was due to no active effort of their own. They had no political power or direct voice in their government, no means of becoming responsible citizens. Mostly very poor and unschooled, they had little or no opportunity of realizing their best selves, and never enough effective freedom to be justly charged with irresponsibility. As in the Hellenistic world, the fault was most obviously in the privileged ruling class, who did little to satisfy either the material or the spiritual needs of the common people.

It recalls us to the abstract, rhetorical, academic quality of Roman idealism: the failure not only to realize the ideal fictions but to make a steady, serious, intelligent effort to do so. A government that in theory respected most of all "the freedom of the governed" was rarely concerned about the want of actual freedom for the many. "There is an abundant and beautiful equality," Aristides orated, "of the humble with the great and of the obscure with the illustrious, and above all, of the poor man with the rich and of the commoner with the noble." There was in fact nothing like such equality, least of all of the poor man and the commoner with the rich and the noble. There was at most an equality in citizenship, before the law, which would become an influential ideal in the Western world, but which had a sharply limited meaning in the Roman world, and a steadily diminishing value. The ideal of justice, the most majestic achievement of the

Roman Empire, is also the measure of its failure. "Justice is the fixed and constant purpose that gives to every man his due," reads the ideal theory, preserved in the preamble of Justinian's *Institutes*. As the theory was being formulated, apparent social injustice was becoming more fixed, the due of a great many men was bondage, and it is fair to say that purpose had never been controlled by the simple sentiment that every man ought to be given a fair chance. Men will forever disagree on what constitutes social justice; but at least there is no question that without assured rights and opportunities the many cannot enjoy freedom to choose and carry out their own purposes.

We can never be certain, either, that a really free citizenry would have saved the Roman Empire. We can say positively that the Empire was weakened by a dispirited populace, lacking the energy, resolution, and self-reliance that freedom might have maintained. In spite of all the panegyrics, its rulers failed to inspire a deep sense of community among the masses, or a patriotism to match their own. Hence the common people did not put up a valorous, determined resistance to the invading barbarians; we rarely hear of a heroic stand or fight to the death. All along they had had little chance or incentive to realize whatever special abilities they might have had. The economic and the cultural stagnation were both cause and effect of the waste of human resources. "The invention of a valve in the bellows used in iron furnaces to create a continuous blast," Tenney Frank observed, "an improvement that any intelligent and interested workman might have conceived, would have revolutionized the iron industry by making smelting and casting possible on a large scale." Slaves and underpaid workmen lacked the interest and the ability to make this simple invention, or any invention that revolutionized any industry. No Whitmans came out of the folk either, no great writers or artists of any kind.

In justice we may then add some excuses for the Romans. The Principate of Augustus was perhaps the only feasible solution for a people who, in the words of Tacitus, were "capable of neither complete servitude nor of complete freedom," but more especially for an empire too heterogeneous and far-flung to become a republic. It is hard to conceive how Augustus or his successors could have transformed this empire into a democratic state, or anything comparable to the United Nations. Even had their subjects clamored for representation in a federated government—as they never did—communications were too slow and uncertain to make such a government practicable. And as usual we need to supplement the good moral or philosophical reasons for the decline of the Roman Empire. The decline was due as well to external causes, including accidents. The devoted Marcus Aurelius in particular had good excuse for his melancholy. His reign was heralded by scattered calamities of flood, earthquake, and famine; presently all Europe was devastated by one of the worst plagues on record; and with his treasury almost empty, he was obliged from then on to wage constant campaigns against new tribes of Germans pouring in from the north. Thereafter the Empire was under constant pressure from barbarians on its borders. In the fourth century, after Diocletian had by desperate measures managed a partial recovery, it had to contend with the worst of the invasions: the Huns flooded in, not only ravaging Europe but driving Gothic tribes into the Empire. Visigoths annihilated a great Roman army in a battle at Adrianople—an "irreparable disaster" with which Ammianus concluded his history, regarding it as a turning point. Even so, we must be wary of the popular conclusion that the fall of Rome was inevitable; for in the East the Empire again recovered.

Finally, we need to be still more wary of the popular analogies (drawn by Spengler and Toynbee, for example) between the declining Greco-Roman world and modern civilization, and in particular between the Romans and the as practical, materialistic Americans. The analogies are indeed closer than those with the Hellenistic world, and are especially pertinent for Americans devoted to cake and TV instead of mere bread and circuses. But we cannot hope to understand either the ancient or the modern world unless we attend first and last to the fundamental differences between them in every major respect—economic, political, cultural, spiritual. The Romans had nothing like modern science and technology, the material means to world order, or to world destruction; nothing like modern democracy, with free public education for all, and wide opportunity for self-realization, or for irresponsibility; and nothing, once more, like the terrific dynamism, the immense potentialities for better or worse—for almost anything except stagnation. At the end, the most conspicuous thing the Roman Empire had in common with the modern West was the Christian religion; but this gives further reason to discount the popular analogies, aside from the unpopular fact that Christianity failed to save the Empire in Europe. It was as profoundly different from Christianity in America today as Rome was from New York.

Chapter Ten

THE TRIUMPH OF CHRISTIANITY

1. The Basic Ambiguities

By all odds the most important historical occurrence in the last centuries of Rome was the slow, obscure, unspectacular growth and spread of Christianity, and its eventual triumph as the imperial religion. In the third and fourth centuries A.D. it emerged as the only really dynamic movement of the age, the principal source of creativity in thought and culture. It helped the eastern half of the Empire to endure, becoming the heart and soul of the Byzantine Empire. In Europe it survived the fall of Rome, preserved the remnants of classical culture through the Dark Ages that followed, and provided the foundation of a new civilization. It then became a major factor in the history of Western freedom. Lord Acton, who first proposed to write this history, believed that the realization of human freedom was the very mission of Christianity, or God's plan for man.

Even so, Christianity calls for no more than a chapter at this stage, for a simple reason: its early leaders had a quite different idea of their mission. It had little effect on freedom in the ancient world, beyond an adverse effect when it became the imperial religion. To its converts—long a very small minority—it indeed brought "spiritual freedom," or peace of mind through hopes of the Savior; it began to realize the possibilities of ordinary freedom implicit in its message of brotherhood, by its charitable endeavors on behalf of its own poor and needy; and it raised the new issue of freedom of conscience, as Christians refused to make the ceremonial obeisance to the imperial cult, submitting to martyrdom rather than violate their conscience. When they triumphed, however, Christians soon made it clear that they did not

believe in religious freedom—they wanted it only for themselves. They
began oppressing pagans and Jews, and then turned violently on
heretical fellow Christians; they repudiated freedom of religious
thought and conscience with an explicitness and thoroughness never
before known in history. Meanwhile Christianity was supporting an
imperial regime that was doing away with the remnants of political
freedom, and still oppressing the poor. In the nascent Byzantine Empire
the Christian God was pressed into the service of another Oriental
sacred monarchy. In the West the Church grew stronger than the
increasingly feeble emperors, but it did not exert its authority on behalf of either political freedom or basic social reform.

Our present concern is primarily the relations of Christianity to the
ancient world, the final perspective it affords on both the achievements
and the failures of the Greeks and Romans. This requires consideration of its potentialities for the life of freedom, but also requires a constant awareness that these potentialities were not generally realized
until much later in Western civilization. It at once forces attention to
the basic ambiguities of Christianity. Eminent thinkers are still prone
to easy pronouncements about *the* Christian or biblical view of man
and history, slighting the radically different views that have made
Christian history, and that are upheld by other eminent thinkers. Sin,
Reinhold Niebuhr has said, is "the refusal to admit finiteness." If so,
a historian of freedom may hope to be freer from sin than most
theologians; and immediately he may find in ambiguity the key to
comprehensive understanding, or to finite justice.

Thus Christianity was the profoundest revulsion against the ancient
world, a break sharp enough to warrant the dating of a new era from
the birth of Christ (though the exact year of his birth is unknown);
and it was also a culmination, the last great creation of the ancient
world. It was for good reason a scandal to the Jews, a foolishness to the
Greeks, an "atheistical" superstition to the Romans; and it was profoundly indebted to all of them, incorporating much of their loftiest
aspiration. On both counts it triumphed over all the rival mystery
religions, to which it was likewise much indebted. As a synthesis of
elements from such diverse sources it embraced beliefs logically incompatible, attitudes diametrically opposed—contradictions that grew
more pronounced as it preached a message of regeneration to a society
that kept on dying. It embarked on its career as the most catholic, flexible of the higher religions, and the most exclusive and inflexible in its
insistence on the absolute, inalterable truth of its doctrines. It soon

gave promise of becoming as well the most dynamic of the world's religions, directly because of its missionary zeal, but also because of the high tension generated by its paradoxes or contradictions.

In the light of later history, the obvious paradoxes begin with the simple teaching of Jesus himself, which came to be regarded as a unique revelation. He spoke as a Jew, of course, directly out of the tradition of the great prophets. Although his teaching may be considered purer or loftier than theirs, it was essentially the same call to repentance and righteousness, in the service of the same God; he was less original than they, or than the other religious pioneers of the Axial period. According to the Synoptic Gospels, he made no open claim to divinity, and had no plain intention of founding a new religion. (His "church" is mentioned in but a single text, in Matthew.) Some of his recorded sayings indicate a belief that the world was soon to end, the Kingdom of God was at hand—even in the lifetime of "some of them that stand here." Other extreme teachings, notably the sublime, impossible ethic of the Sermon on the Mount, become more understandable in the light of this belief. His early followers unquestionably expected the imminent coming of the Kingdom; so in time Christians had to readjust their faith to a world that bid fair to go on indefinitely. Yet they were still affected by the symptoms of decay, and then more deeply affected by the breakdown of the Roman Empire in the West. Essentially Christianity in antiquity remained what it began as, an end-of-the-world religion, only less literal in its immediate hopes, more intense in its anxieties.

St. Paul, the greatest of the Apostles, did most to found the Christian Church, though with no idea of building it for the long run (he hoped and prayed for the Second Coming of the Lord in his own lifetime), and with some ideas rather different from those of Jesus, whose followers he had at first persecuted. Not having known the historic Jesus, he seldom referred to his humanity or his life on earth. What he knew and preached was the resurrected Christ, who had called to him from the heavens when he was on the road to Damascus. Because of this blinding, overwhelming mystical experience, he knew a Savior-God, similar to those worshiped in the mystery religions, but superior. Paul bequeathed Christianity its most original doctrine, that of the Redeemer: unlike other savior-gods, Christ had deliberately sacrificed himself in order to atone for the sins of mankind, to free man from "the law of sin and death." At the same time Paul burdened mankind with an absolute need of redemption: he bequeathed as well the novel

doctrine of original sin, the Fall of Man unmentioned by either Jesus
or the prophets of Israel. And he insisted that salvation was possible
only through Christ. In his mystical exaltation, and his sense of
desperate urgency, he sought to become "all things to all men"—an
aspiration that would have seemed strange to the prophets, or to
Buddha and Confucius; only he separated all men into believers and
unbelievers, a division more inhuman than that between Greek and
"barbarian" because he denied all things to unbelievers.

First, however, Paul had made his crucial decision to preach Christ
to the Gentiles. He was led to exempt them from the ceremonial
requirements of the Jewish Law despite the opposition of St. Peter
and James, "the brother of the Lord," who would have kept Christianity a Jewish sect.[1] After Paul, the Gentiles had ever more say. The
Gospel According to St. John identified Christ with the Greek *Logos*,
reinterpreting his mission in the light of Greek thought; it featured
symbols of "light," "freedom," and "truth." Nevertheless, it deepened
the ambiguities of Christianity, immediately by illustrating how "revealed" truth may shut out light, freedom, and truth by ordinary
human standards; it was the most authoritarian of the Gospels, the
most insistent on the absolute necessity of belief in Christ, and the
most hostile to the Jewry from whom both Jesus and Paul had sprung.
Proper belief about the nature of Christ then became the major concern of his followers, at some expense to his gospel of brotherhood and
love. The early disagreement between Paul and the conservatives, and
the continuing disagreements indicated in his Epistles, deepened into
schism; by the second century A.D. there were some twenty varieties of
Christianity, by the fourth century at least eighty. Efforts to preserve
unity in the scattered congregations led to the growth of an authoritarian church. The Church would succeed in maintaining sufficient
unity among most Christians, but at the cost of violent, permanent
disunity, and for the sake of doctrines, as about the Trinity, preached
by neither Jesus nor Paul.

Meanwhile the growth and spread of Christianity had been aided

---

[1] Although orthodox Christians deny that James was actually the brother of Jesus,
inasmuch as the Virgin Mary could not have had other children, in the Bible he is literally
called so. Most of the authors of the New Testament presumably did not know of the
virgin birth of Jesus, which is mentioned only by Luke and Matthew, or if they had heard
of it, they might have dismissed it as a pagan superstition. Some Greeks had grown fond
of such legends, which conferred virgin mothers on various of their great men (among
others Plato and Alexander the Great); but the idea of a Mother of God was naturally
alien to the pure monotheism of Judaism.

as well as impeded by conflict with the Roman authorities. If the martyrs of persecution were many fewer than later legends made out, they did set an example of integrity and fortitude that could inspire their fellow Christians, and might impress Romans too. The emperors had further reasons to distrust these "atheists," it is true, since many Christians agreed with Tertullian that "no thing is more alien than the public thing"; yet they were hardly more lacking in active civic virtues than were the Roman masses, and generally they were less demoralized, more sober and responsible. Diocletian, the greatest states-man among the later emperors, paid them tribute by instituting the most thorough persecution of them; although his motives are uncertain, his edicts having disappeared, he evidently considered them a force to be reckoned with. They were strong enough to stand up under this persecution, and so to profit from his achievement as a savior of the Roman Empire. To help him defend and rule the harassed Empire, Diocletian had appointed three other Caesars, among them the father of Constantine the Great. When Constantine succeeded his father he set about disposing of the other Caesars; and in the year 312, in the course of his wars with them, he became a convert to Christianity. Upon winning complete control of the Empire, he subsidized Christian-ity and set it on the way to becoming the imperial religion.

Even so, Constantine's motives were not clearly inspired. His con-version was due to a vision of the Cross he had had upon entering a battle—a kind of vision that the pagan gods often vouchsafed their worshipers, but that might obscure the nature of the Christian God of love. It was hardly comparable to the mystical experience of St. Paul; Constantine became at best a sincere Christian, far from a saintly one. Neither was he clearly farsighted enough as a statesman to recog-nize in a still small minority sect the one vital force that might pre-serve the decadent Empire, for he seemed unaware that his empire was decadent. There is no question, however, that his conversion was timely. While consolidating the work of Diocletian, he established Christianity firmly enough to withstand the pagan revival later at-tempted by Julian the Apostate, and to carry on as the state religion of the Eastern Roman Empire. Although he further weakened Rome by building himself a new capital at the ancient Greek city of Byzan-tium, henceforth to be known as Constantinople, the Church in the West would at least have more than a century in which to strengthen its position, and to begin converting the barbarians who were taking over the Empire. If Constantine was no saint by nature, and could never have foreseen the long-range consequences of his handiwork, the Church still had good reason to canonize him, as it soon did, and to hail him as the "Thirteenth Apostle" even before he was baptized on his deathbed.[2]

Historians have as good reason for describing the contribution of the embattled emperor as a "fatal gift." Christianity to Constantine was a worldly success religion, proved by the victory he had won after his vision of the Cross. In setting up his new state cult, he conceived himself as the imperial deputy of a God of power, the "Mighty One," who sanctioned his supreme authority; and grateful churchmen agreed that the Equal of the Apostles had been divinely appointed. Hence he inaugurated the lasting confusion in Christendom between the things that are Caesar's and the things that are God's. Though eventually the distinction made by Jesus would become a bulwark against tyranny, Constantine saw no real difference between these things, and Caesar would long have all the better of it. At the same time he gave the Christian Church great power as the ministry of his state cult. It was now able to begin enforcing uniformity of belief, permanently alienating large bodies of Christians. With its worldly power the Church acquired a material wealth that tended to corrupt churchmen, or at least distracted many from concerns with a spiritual kingdom "not of this world." In protest against such worldliness many other Christians took to asceticism, fleeing to cell or desert. "Wonderful irony of history!" Theodore Zahn commented. "So long as the world was honestly heathen the earnest Christian could live in it. The practice of otherworldliness was then all-too-possible in the world. But in Constantine's New Jerusalem, this kingdom of God so happily realized upon earth, the real Christian was not at home."

Only the question remains: Who is this "real" Christian? Must he believe that God's creation is essentially evil, a devil's snare, at best a vale of tears? Could he be really holy only by turning his back on society, seeking a private salvation? Or might not his Christian duty of loving his fellows signify that life on earth was potentially good, not vain? Might not there be good even in the vile flesh, which Christ had assumed? For that matter, might not Constantine be right in his belief—shared by the prophets of Israel—that God rewards proper worship and punishes sin on earth, in history? Christianity was already

---

[2] His belated baptism is no reason for doubting the sincerity of his conversion. Early Christians commonly put off the rite, in the belief that any sins committed after this cleansing might be fatal to their chances of salvation.

answering Yes and No to these and many other questions.

Yet for such reasons too its triumph over all the rival mystery religions was not fortuitous. It was more ambiguous than any other cult because it was at once the most inclusive in its affirmations and the most positive in its negations. It had absorbed more of the best in the classical world, while it had broken more radically with much that was evil, false, or futile. It could appear as an ideal synthesis of Greek rationalism and Roman discipline with the religious fervor of Judaism, and so an ideal means to the universal community that the ancient world had dreamed of ever since Alexander the Great. What Christianity actually became was rather different; but first we need to consider more closely the reasons why it triumphed, in particular why it was actually too a means of regeneration.

2. *The Break with the Classical World*

To repeat that the essential teachings of Jesus were drawn from the great prophets of Israel is to emphasize now that they were literally revolutionary, and will always remain so if they are taken seriously. His gospel was purer chiefly in its greater stress on their subversive doctrines. He condemned more insistently the formalism and legalism in which the respectable might find refuge; he more clearly transcended the narrow loyalties to family, tribe, and nation; he was more eloquent in preaching brotherhood and love, even to sinners and heathen Samaritans; he was more consistently hostile to wealth and privilege, the sources of division and oppression. If there is some question whether the disciples of Jesus realized how subversive his teachings were, there is little question that the high priests and the Roman authorities realized it. His crucifixion was due to no mere difference in theological opinion.

Although his revolutionary gospel was soon obscured by hopes of the resurrected Christ, and later by controversy over his exact relation to the Godhead, the spirit of Jesus was never quenched. It was much more potent than one would gather from most Christian documents of the early centuries, which reflected chiefly the doctrinal controversies. It could work on his lowly followers the better because they overlooked an ambiguous aspect of his gospel, as a gospel of brotherhood so radical that he could say he came to bring "not peace but a sword";

too lowly to take to the sword or employ the vocabulary of rebellion that later generations would find in it, they read a gospel of peace and good will. Above all, Christianity retained the concern of Jesus for the lowly and needy. While the other mystery religions were democratic enough to welcome men of all races and ranks, their initiation rites were typically costly, and their greatest gift was "secret knowledge," which the initiates were sworn never to divulge. (Thus Apuleius, who was blessed with such knowledge by Queen Isis, wrote proudly of how he had spared no expense to get it—expenses carefully detailed beforehand by the priests of his adorable queen; and later he had to sell the clothes off his back to learn the secrets of Osiris.) Christianity alone sought out the poor, offered a gospel free and open to all. No other religion preached so active a love; none engaged in such extensive charitable enterprises on behalf of the poor, the widowed and orphaned, the sick and the aged.

Julian the Apostate testified to the power of the Christian gospel of love when he tried to revive his religion of Hellenism. "Atheism owes its success above all to its philanthropy," he warned the pagans, rebuking them for "a slackness and indifference that are not merely a disgrace to our religion but a downright betrayal of it." One reason why he failed to arouse them is that strictly their indifference was not a betrayal of their religion. A spirit of brotherly love had rarely informed the humanistic ideal of Hellenism, the abstract Stoic concept of equality, the abstract Roman idea of *humanitas;* many cultivated pagans disdained the masses on aristocratic principle, just as they scorned the manual labor of the poor. For all its divisions, the Christian community most nearly realized the ideal of community that the classical world proclaimed but fell short of in both theory and practice. *The Shepherd of Hermas,* one of the first Christian writings, stresses the qualities not only of humility, gentleness, and love but of gladness—a cheerful service of both God and man. "For every man that is glad doeth the things that are good, and thinketh good thoughts, despising melancholy; whereas the melancholy man is always committing sin." The paintings in the catacombs of Rome—so often childlike in their expression of peace, hope, love, and joy—support the testimony of the good Shepherd that the ethic of Jesus was a living inspiration to simple worshipers.

For such reasons Christianity gave new meaning to the *persona* recognized in Roman law. In view of the millions of slaves, the ancients still had little idea of the dignity and worth of the individual, much less of the sanctity of the person; there was no word yet for "personality" in classical philosophy. There was none in early Christian writings either, nor any developed theory of the rights of the individual; Christians too accepted the institution of slavery, which Jesus had not attacked. Nevertheless, he had implicitly asserted the dignity of the person, within whom was the Kingdom of God. Immediately the person was the neighbor one should love as oneself; ultimately he was one who had been created in the image of God. He had an immortal soul, which Christians believed was a personal soul—a belief denied by Neo-Platonists, as by the holy men of India. In establishing their own communities apart from the state, moreover, Christians naturally grew more concerned with a realm within the privacy of their souls. They had to maintain the sanctity of this personal realm against the pressures of the state, as few pagans had had to do since Socrates. (Such comparable renegades as the Cynics were merely ridiculed, not persecuted.) Lacking a legal right to their "atheism," they moralized the rights of the individual against the state. They started something their own Church could not stop when it came into power; for heretics ever after would maintain their own ways in defiance of both church and state.

By this time the Christian Church had developed other profoundly illiberal tendencies, mostly deriving from the somber teachings of St. Paul about man's utter dependence on God. Nevertheless, it was above all the Apostle of the Gentiles who made Christianity a gospel of regeneration. In all history there is no more striking demonstration than Paul's of the power of the perennial religious cry: "Ye must be born again!" Such religious conversions as his were very rare in antiquity. We hear of many men who felt healed, purified, inspired by initiation into the pagan mysteries, but we know of none who became so wholly transformed and wholly dedicated to the service of the god; like Apuleius in *The Golden Ass,* who adored Queen Isis, the initiates commonly continued to shop around in other mysteries. Paul was indeed, as he said, a "new creature": a man reborn through Christ, who ever after his mystical experience lived only for Christ, laboring without rest, daring all perils and pains, suffering martyrdom—sacrificing everything to make his Lord known to other men. One may add that he began by unwittingly sacrificing the historic Jesus, the man he knew only by hearsay; yet the life "in Christ" as he preached it offered a fulfillment in hope, faith, and charity beyond anything known to the pagans.

To begin with, he remained true to the great prophetic tradition behind Jesus. Paul relieved the Gentiles only of the purely ritual requirements of the Jewish Law (such as the embarrassment of circumcision); he held them to the moral law, not merely promising but demanding a thorough regeneration. While he transformed Jesus into the Christ, a savior-god, he made Christianity more ethical than all the other mystery religions, discouraging any merely sacramental or magical means of salvation. As the Apostle of the Gentiles, moreover, he most explicitly made it a universal gospel. In the life "in Christ" all men were one: "There is neither Jew nor Greek, there is neither bond nor free, there is neither male nor female." But most compelling remained the new hope he held out to both Jew and Gentile, the highest hope that religion had yet held out to man: the stupendous idea that God himself had appeared on earth and suffered in order to save man. As Paul preached it, in the fervor born of his mystical experience, it was no mere hope but a wholehearted faith, a flaming certainty that could survive the disappointment of his immediate hopes of the Second Coming. By his missionary fervor he likewise generated a moral strenuousness or willfulness that could survive his teaching of man's complete dependence on the grace of God, and his dark notions of predestination; he never for a moment desisted from his own work, which was nothing less than an effort to Christianize the whole Roman Empire. He was the first of a long line of typical Christian saints: men not really meek or poor in spirit, sometimes fierce, often tormented, rarely so serene as the holy men of the East, but by the same token as rarely quiescent.

In Paul's own day, early in the *Pax Romana,* few cultivated pagans felt an acute need of a new hope and faith; Christianity long appealed chiefly to the many poor who did not share in the felicity of the age. As the Roman Empire decayed, however, it became clearer that Christianity was no mere negation or solace but a new start, a positive inspiration. "Amid the ruins of a falling age," wrote Bishop Cyprian, "our spirit remains erect." In fact Christians were never given to the apathy of the Roman masses, or to the fatalistic resignation of the philosophers; and in the worse days that lay ahead they would not take to quietism. They clung to their cardinal virtue of hope, and like Paul kept backing it up by works. No doubt they were buoyed up primarily by their hope of personal immortality, even to the wildly improbable hope of bodily resurrection; but they were also buoyed up as no pagan could be by the belief that the coming of Christ was the climax of history, the key to the whole meaning and purpose of man's history on earth.

The long uncertainty over the precise nature of Christ never obscured the essential idea, that he had lived and died on this earth: "The Word became flesh and dwelt among us." Although in the Synoptic Gospels Jesus is represented as rather strangely secretive about his identity, even to forbidding his disciples to announce that he was the Messiah, he at least carried on the messianic tradition that took history seriously. When he departed from this tradition by talking of a kingdom "not of this world," he never suggested that this world was illusory, or this life simply vain; his parables always implied the reality of the natural, temporal world, and often implied its value. His followers were indeed prone to strong otherworldly tendencies, to which we must keep returning, but officially they never succumbed to them. The test came with the rise of the Gnostics, an influential school of thought with deep roots in Platonism and Greco-Oriental religion. Seeking a mystical salvation through union with Christ, the Gnostics insisted on the irremediable evil of the material world, and so denied the humanity of Christ—putting on the flesh was an unthinkable degradation; while as logically they divorced this world from God, arguing that a good God could never be responsible for so evil a creation. (Some made it the handiwork of the primitive, blundering Yahweh of the Old Testament.) Just as logically, the Church condemned Gnosticism as heresy. Christianity would never formally renounce the world in which its Lord had appeared, never consistently preach the ideal of non-attachment maintained by Hindus and Buddhists, as by many of its own saints.

For the Gentiles in particular, Christ gave a new meaning to history. He was a Person, not an impersonal Necessity. Unlike the gods of all the other mystery religions, he was clearly a historic founder. Unlike them, too, he did not die annually, cyclically; he might appear to do so in the ritual of the Mass, or later in Passion plays, but Christians always knew that his crucifixion was a unique historic event. Potentially it held a unique promise of a new and better life, not merely more of the same. If early Christians still had little hope of earthly progress, none adopted the classical view of history as endless cycle: a view that might offer the solace of resignation to the uniform, inevitable fate, as Marcus Aurelius insisted, but that was more likely to make history seem meaningless, pointless, as the melancholy of Marcus testified. After the sack of Rome by Alaric, St. Augustine emphasized the futility of the cyclical theory, arguing that only Christianity made history meaningful.

In his own theory of endless struggle between the Earthly City and the City of God, Augustine indicated less consciously the dynamic possibilities of Christianity. These possibilities had little scope in his crumbling society; churchmen were busy administering or holding their own, and their surplus energy went chiefly into the furious theological controversies that were splitting Christendom. Yet the very violence of the controversies was a sign of vitality, making plain that the leaders of Christendom were not at all impassive or resigned. It was due in part to a passion for truth that by this time was rare in the pagan world.

Still, this passion was a legacy of the Greek spirit: the Apostles had not been truth seekers, much less theologians. The unclassical violence was more anomalous because the controversies were centered on doctrines that had been evolved by the rationalism of classical tradition. It might have been much better for humanity, and for the cause of freedom, had the simple gospel of brotherly love won the ancient world. As it was, the Sermon on the Mount was hardly a primary reason for the triumph of Christianity, any more than it converted the warring Constantine. Christianity had to overcome the best as well as the worst in the ancient world, and it got its most effective weapons from its enemies. For better or worse, it won out over the rival mystery religions with the help of the Greeks and the Romans, in particular of two major aids—a developed theology and an organized church.

3. The Indebtedness to Classical Culture

"What in common have Athens and Jerusalem? the Academy and the Church? heretics and Christians?" exclaimed Tertullian. "Let them see to it who teach a 'Stoic,' a 'Platonic,' or a 'dialectic' Christianity! We find no need of curiosity reaching beyond Christ Jesus, nor of inquiry beyond the gospel. When we believe, we need nothing further than to believe. Search that you may believe; then stop." The first of the Latin Church Fathers, Tertullian expressed the common hostility of early Christians to classical culture, shot through as it was with pagan religion. In the sixth century A.D. the hostility culminated in the edict of the Emperor Justinian closing down the philosophical schools of Athens, sealing the end of the ancient world.

Yet Christianity never did reject pagan culture, if only because it could not possibly do so. Tertullian himself had received a classical education, the only education available. He was addicted to sermons, a practice grown out of the classical rage for rhetoric. He thought and wrote in Latin, not the Aramaic spoken by Christ Jesus, and the gospel that to him made all inquiry unnecessary was written in Greek, which had given Jesus the name of "the Christ." Himself a theologian of sorts, he had had to make some inquiry in order to ascertain and defend the beliefs he proclaimed necessary; and unhappily, the beliefs he stopped at included some that his Church would declare heretical. He remained important only as the forerunner in the Latin West of a theological tradition that had grown up in the Greek East, an inquirer who gave this tradition a typically Roman cast by his very practical interests and his legal bent. He was grateful for the law and order provided by the godless "public thing," the Roman Empire—in his belief a "respite" from the "terrible woes" threatening the whole earth, and in fact a respite long enough for his Church to build up an organization that would enable it to survive the woes. "In the Emperor," he wrote, "we reverence the judgment of God, who has set him over the nations."

For such reasons Christianity did in fact become Stoic, Platonic, and dialectic, among other things, while developing a Roman Church. Its deep, everlasting indebtedness to the classical world was initiated by the Apostle of the Gentiles. "Verily a man which am a Jew," St. Paul was yet no man of Judaea. He began life as Saul of Tarsus: Roman citizen of a Greco-Oriental city in Asia Minor, which he noted with some pride was "no mean city." Having been reared in such an atmosphere, he could more readily recognize his Savior in a dying, resurrected God—a pagan, not a Jewish idea. Above all, he could believe that Christ had died for all mankind: in Tarsus, then the main seat of the Stoic school, he had breathed the air of *cosmopolis*. There was little spirit of universalism in the Jerusalem of his day, where he had been opposed by James, the brother of the Lord, and everywhere he met the fiercest hostility from the chosen people. According to Acts, it was this hostility that led to his epoch-making decision: at Antioch-in-Pisidia in Asia Minor he turned from the "blasphemous" men of Israel to the Gentiles, announcing that the Lord had commanded him to be a light to them and bring salvation "unto the ends of the earth." And as a light-bringer, Paul proceeded to reason with the Gentiles in their own terms, "pray with the understanding also." He wrote his

Epistles not merely to exhort but to educate, expounding a gospel much more sophisticated than the simple gospel of repentance and salvation attributed to the other Apostles by Acts.

Asia Minor, where Paul did most of his preaching, remained the spiritual center of Christianity for the first century or so. Early tradition placed St. John in Ephesus, then its greatest city. While identifying Christ with the Greek *Logos,* or Word, John lent Greek clarity to his mission; according to his Gospel, Jesus was not at all secretive about his identity, but announced unequivocally from beginning to end that he was the Son of God, come to earth so that men might have "eternal life." John was still unaware of the Trinity, since Jesus could say both that "the Father and I are one" and that "the Father is greater than I," but such uncertainties about the Godhead would call for more Greek thought. As meanwhile the Apologists began to explain their faith, and to defend it against the suspicion or the scorn of cultivated pagans, they drew more directly on Greek philosophy. Others took to the allegorical method of interpreting Scripture, which the Greeks had developed in order to explain away the seemingly unholy fables of their beloved Homer. In this way they could gloss over many embarrassing texts in the Old Testament, and some difficulties presented by the human life of Jesus; and though Tertullian denounced the method as blasphemous, it continued to inspire much Christian literature, eventually culminating in the Divine Comedy of Dante.

Most important was the development of systematic theology, beginning with Clement of Alexandria—a philosopher who had been converted to Christianity. How profoundly this transformed Christianity may be realized simply by turning from the Synoptic Gospels, in particular the Sermon on the Mount, to the Nicene Creed, formulated in A.D. 325 by the first Ecumenical Council. The Gospels are concerned primarily with righteous conduct and are almost wholly innocent of metaphysics, of which there is no trace whatever in the Sermon. The Nicene Creed is concerned wholly with correct belief; it is all metaphysics, with no ethical content whatever. Its key terms would have been virtually unintelligible to the early disciples of Jesus. For that matter, few Christians today can understand the theological uproar at Nicaea before the Council settled on the formula that Christ was "of one essence with the Father" and "begotten, not made." Or more precisely, failed to settle the whole problem. Many churchmen were still unhappy because the phrase "of one essence with" nowhere appears in Scripture, while many more worried over the nature of

Christ—whether as both man and God he had one nature or two separate natures, and one or two wills; so fierce battles continued to rage all over Christendom. Centuries later the Western and Eastern churches would split permanently over the *filioque,* another nice question about the internal relations of the Trinity: whether the Holy Ghost proceeded from the Father, or from both the Father and the Son.

We must therefore note at once that the heritage of Greek philosophy was not a pure boon to Christianity. Immediately it inspired an impossible effort to define precisely the nature of God, an effort the more hopeless because Christian theologians could not be content with the simple monotheism of Judaism. Confusion was deepened as they introduced the philosophical Absolute of Aristotle and others—an Unmoved Mover, impersonal, ineffable, utterly self-sufficient—and then tried to identify it with the intensely personal Yahweh, a Father and a Lord incessantly concerned with the goings-on in his temporal creation. All such insuperable difficulties were aggravated by the common assumption of Greek philosophers that there were simple, certain answers to metaphysical questions, and in particular by the early agreement of the theologians that a jealous God demanded certainty and uniformity in metaphysics. The endless disagreement failed to shake their belief that any basic disagreement was blasphemous, or simply unthinkable; so they went on with their dreary word game, making the Godhead ever more incomprehensible, more remote from the concerns of Jesus, but always insisting that they were laying out the word of God, not speaking their own word. The Council of Nicaea called out a long series of councils, which kept anathematizing large bodies of Christians in decisions that, as Archbishop Benson noted, were almost uniformly "uncharitable, unscriptural, uncatholic, and unanimous," and were as uniformly unintelligible to most simple Christians then and now.[3] Altogether the development of Christian theology may

---

[3] The many losers in these battles—Arians, Nestorians, Monophysites, etc.—are now unknown to most Christians, and like all the losers in history are likely to be judged harshly; so in justice to them it should be remarked that they not only were as sincere Christians as the victors, but generally were trying to make the faith more intelligible. The common-sense Arian view, for example, that the Son was lesser than God—a view usually implied when not explicitly stated by Jesus in the Gospels—has remained pretty much the thought or feeling of ordinary Christians. Among other casualties of the warfare were such genial ideas as Adoptionism, implicit in the Gospel According to Mark. As Mark says nothing about a virgin birth, but has it that the Spirit descended upon Jesus after his baptism by John, it could be that Jesus was an inspired man, like Buddha, who earned divinity by his works—works that might be even more inspiring if regarded as a human effort rather than a set plan. Otherwise his agony on the cross, lasting only a few hours as it did, can seem a trifling sacrifice for a God who sentenced men to an eternity of torture in hell.

appear to bear out the warning of Tertullian against such profane
curiosity. It satisfied the pride of many theologians, but otherwise
satisfied no emotional, imaginative, aesthetic, or moral needs to speak
of.

Yet it was a quite natural development, beginning with the Epistles
of the Apostle of the Gentiles, and for the long run an indispensable
one. If it was not clearly inevitable, inasmuch as there was no comparable development in the rival mystery religions, by the same token it
gave Christianity a clear advantage over its rivals. Mithraism, for example, offered almost everything else that Christianity did: a god who
had saved the human race, a brotherhood that admitted the lowly, the
sacraments of baptism and communion, a promise of resurrection,
and an inspiring ethic, especially popular among the soldiers who were
defending the Roman Empire because of its emphasis on the stoical
virtues. Nevertheless, it failed to take hold in the Greek world: it was
only another mystery cult, with little claim to intellectual respect.
Christianity alone appealed to the mind as well as the heart of the ancients, and put mind to work. While the theologians set the Godhead
beyond the ken of simple believers, they also kept Christianity above
the vulgar superstition that simple believers are always prone to. They
gave it a philosophical basis solid enough to survive the barbarism of
the Dark Ages, and to become the basis of a new culture.

Say the worst about it, theology represented an effort at understanding. It was an absolutely necessary effort if the claims of reason were
to be recognized. From Tertullian to this day, these claims would be
repeatedly attacked, and reason denied any rights in matters of faith;
yet the very attacks indicated that the theologians had won it some
rights. And since its claims are essential to the realization of human
freedom, we may pardon their departures from the recorded teachings
of Jesus. These teachings are not, after all, very clear or consistent
about his identity and his mission. In any case they had to be interpreted and adapted to the needs of a society more sophisticated than
his own, less able to "receive the kingdom of God as a little child,"
and as a still going concern forced to consider the interests of "the
wise and prudent" from whom God had "hid these things."

Immediately there was some excuse for the remarkable passion engendered by the supersubtle theological distinctions, apart from the
impossibility of drawing a clear line between self-respect and self-
righteousness, or earnestness and arrogance. The churchmen of course
had to preserve the divinity of Christ if he were to be the Savior, but

the acute Greeks among them could see the necessity of preserving as well his full humanity, the Incarnation called for by the logic of the Atonement. Hence they fought the more Hebraic or Oriental thinkers who wanted to minimize his manhood, or keep his divine personality pure and single. At the same time they had to insist on the unity of the Godhead, to avoid the appearances of polytheism. Over the admission of the Holy Ghost into the Trinity there was little controversy, but again Greek thinkers could appreciate its logical convenience, as a means of constant spiritual relations with an utterly transcendent God. So they finally worked out the unique doctrine of the Trinity, in which Christ retained his two natures "without confusion, without change, without division, without separation"—a concept that is not very lucid, but that made the most of Christ, perhaps the best of an extraordinary logical problem. At least it maintained the ground of a free man's worship, the belief that the ways of God did not pass all understanding.

For the long run the embattled theologians builded both better and worse than they knew. Their excesses were in the tradition of Greek philosophy—an emancipation of mind that led to new forms of tyranny over thought, but nevertheless kept thought active. They set about reducing the faith to rigid dogma, imprisoning the religious mind they had emancipated, but they continued to undermine their claims to finality or fixity. Every new dogma was proclaimed as immutable truth, divinely revealed, beyond all question; the business of proclaiming, revealing, and questioning went on. Hence the theologians assured the permanent possibility of heresy, a means of keeping Christian thought alive and to some extent free. And among the Greek ideas they introduced into the Christian scheme was the basic idea of a lawful, orderly world, befitting a rational God: a metaphysical assumption that would become a premise of the most revolutionary and fruitful of heresies—modern science. With it entered the principle of natural law in human affairs, the premise of natural rights.

The whole theological enterprise was in turn abetted and hampered by an official church. The ecumenical organization of the Christian Church was another quite natural development, in keeping with a world-wide empire, but again it was not clearly inevitable: none of the other mystery religions had such an organization, or official leaders. It gave Christianity perhaps its greatest advantage over its rivals, as it certainly enabled the Church to assume the responsibilities of an imperial religion.

This too may be traced to the unwitting handiwork of St. Paul, who by his Epistles tried to hold together his scattered congregations, serving as a kind of bishop without portfolio. Each of the Christian communities then came to elect its own pastor, or bishop. By the third century many of these communities were large enough to require numerous aides for the bishop, from presbyters and deacons to readers and doorkeepers. Gradually the priesthood settled into an ordered hierarchy, whose members usually worked their way up the scale. Meanwhile some organization between the scattered communities developed as gradually, out of a desire to maintain uniform ritual and doctrine. Neighboring bishops met to talk over their problems; the meetings grew larger and more formal, at length resembling embryonic synods or councils. By the time Constantine the Great adopted Christianity, its organization was thorough enough to enable him to summon an Ecumenical Council, and authoritative enough to enable the Council to issue official decrees supposedly binding on all churches.

As an unplanned growth, this organization was hardly a conscious imitation of the Roman imperial government. It lacked most conspicuously any central authority comparable to the emperor, since there was as yet no pope; and ordinary Christians would no doubt have been indignant if told that they were aping their pagan rulers. Yet there is no doubt either that their leaders were influenced by the administrative system of the Romans. St. Paul, a Roman citizen, had set the tradition that came down through Tertullian by expressing nothing but respect for the Roman state. The imperial bureaucracy was a model for the hierarchical priesthood, as the imperial theory of commonwealth was a spur to ecumenical organization. At any rate, Christian leaders displayed a Roman genius for order, generally lacking in the Oriental mysteries. With the triumph of Christianity the correspondences became closer, as bishops began aspiring to imperial authority. In the fourth century Bishop Damasus of Rome proclaimed the supremacy of the Roman See; the doctrinal basis for his claim was the tradition that St. Peter had founded the Roman Church, but his prestige owed most obviously to the political authority of Rome. (He had won his appointment by a political struggle, ending in a battle that according to Ammianus cost 137 lives.) The principal rival of the Bishop of Rome was the Bishop of Constantinople, who eventually became the Patriarch of the Holy Orthodox Church. Although Constantinople dug up an apostle, St. Stephen, as the founder of its church, this legend transparently counted for much less than the political prestige of the New Rome.

As necessarily a kingdom of this world, the organized Church was bound to make concessions to worldly interests that would dismay high-minded Christians. First, however, we must remark the spiritual as well as the practical value of the Roman order and discipline it introduced. With the help of begging priests and wandering prophets, other mystery cults flourished like weeds, but remained weedy. Christian bishops soon began exercising authority over their flock, more especially when they had to deal with some men who felt filled with "the Spirit," as St. Paul had been—men always fervent, seldom reasonable, possibly exalted or possibly deluded. If the churchmen's criterion for distinguishing between true and false prophets was somewhat arbitrary or unclear, they generally tended to curb extravagance. Similarly the later Church curbed the Christian tendencies to excess in otherworldliness and asceticism by channelizing the fervor into the institution of monasticism, putting it under rule; the rule of St. Benedict in particular was a classical example of disciplined piety, setting the unworldly spirit to work in the maintenance of an ordered, self-sufficient community that was something like a Christian *polis*. There was a degree of classical measure even in the apparent concessions that the Church made to vulgar needs, as like all established churches it returned to the formalism denounced by its founder, for its sacraments discouraged the frenzy as well as the ecstasy of pagan rites.

Above all, in view of later history, the Church became a school for statesmanship. It produced such types as St. Ambrose, Bishop of Milan: an administrator in the Roman tradition, tireless in duty, calm and unfaltering in the exercise of authority, who forced the mighty Emperor Theodosius to do public penance for defying the spiritual authority of the Church. Ambrose wrote an influential manual of ethics that owed more to Stoicism than to the Sermon on the Mount, and he was well versed too in Roman law, which the Church Fathers adopted; the basic law of Christendom remained Roman, not Christian. Hence the Roman Church was able to take over the responsibilities of the state when the Empire crumbled in the West. In the darkest days of Western Christendom, at the end of the sixth century, it produced another savior, Pope Gregory the Great. Except for his work the then wretched, defenseless city of Rome might well have gone down in a sea of barbarism; and his greatness derived not only from his saintliness but from his genius and resolution as administrator, organizer, and statesman. Gregory fulfilled the tradition inaugurated by the Apostle of the Gentiles in that he expected and prayed for the speedy end of the world—of the Earthly City, which because of his extraordinary effort was able to carry on under Christian auspices.

Yet his Church was indeed an earthly kingdom, on the Roman imperial model. It had become a wholly authoritarian church. Gregory called for unquestioning obedience to both God and earthly rulers; his Christian subjects were long since unaware that the Greeks had not considered obedience a primary virtue. He himself had no ideal whatever of freedom, political, intellectual, or religious. In his barbarous age an authoritarian church was doubtless the only kind that could maintain any semblance of law and order; but a student of freedom must now note that its organization had entailed a positive loss in freedom.

Having at first elected their own bishops, parishioners long continued to have a voice in their election, sometimes overriding the wishes of their shepherds. As a hierarchy developed, however, the clergy had an increasing advantage, and in the century following the installation of Christianity as the imperial religion they largely won the exclusive right to election. The Church remained democratic in that it recruited its priesthood from the common people, on the basis of ability rather than birth or rank, but its government became a self-perpetuating aristocracy; it taught the people that they must obey their betters, and had no right to decide who their betters were. Similarly a hierarchy developed among the bishops, in spite of a theoretical equality. Those who presided in the great cities naturally had more prestige, and as naturally tried to acquire more power, through jurisdiction over churches in neighboring provinces. At the Council of Ephesus the lesser bishops warned them against the "pride of worldly power," lest Christians lose "that freedom which our Lord Jesus Christ, the Liberator of all men, purchased for us with his blood." Nevertheless, Christians lost that freedom: authority became more highly centralized, until even the greater bishops had to acknowledge the supremacy of the bishops of Rome and Constantinople—the emperors of the Church. The formal requirement of unanimity only disguised the failure of the Church to develop genuinely representative government. Like the Roman state, the Christian Church became government in ideal theory for the people, but of and by a priestly bureaucracy, under a Holy Father.

As early as the second century, Bishop Irenaeus staked out the essential claims of the Church. In a legalistic spirit suggestive of the Pharisees but more especially of the Romans, he formulated the whole scheme of salvation, making its primary requisites right conduct, right faith, and the sacraments of baptism and the eucharist. Right conduct was sufficiently defined by the Ten Commandments, but right faith had to be defined by the Church. Irenaeus was the first known bishop to assert the absolute, infallible authority of the bishops, as heirs of the Apostles, and to insist on their right to outlaw heretics. As for the sacraments, they were founded on the simple rites practiced by Jesus, but the idea of their magical efficacy derived rather from Greco-Oriental sources; and Irenaeus went further in insisting on their absolute necessity. The Church would go still further, adding more sacraments until it reached the magic number of seven, becoming the most thoroughly sacramental of the mystery religions. Meanwhile it had complete control of the essential means of salvation. As Bishop Cyprian summed it up in the next century, "Outside the Church there is no salvation."

Given secular power, the Christian Church triumphant was able to enforce these claims. The consequences are now familiar, but at the time seemed strange to Greeks and Romans. While they had always taken for granted the necessity of formal respect of the state gods, they had never set up authorities to determine and enforce correct opinions about the gods; their characteristic ideal of stability and order had not induced the Christian passion for uniformity of belief, or horror of diversity. Constantine the Great was still half pagan when he issued his celebrated, if possibly legendary Edict of Milan (A.D. 313), decreeing that "Christians and all others" should enjoy freedom of worship—the first explicit declaration of religious freedom in the ancient world. As a Christian emperor, he soon learned that his new God prohibited such freedom to those who held erroneous opinions. If heresy were tolerated, he announced, "God may be moved not only against the human race but against me myself." Later the pagan Symmachus tried to persuade Bishop Ambrose that reverence itself called for diversity of belief, since "the heart of so great a mystery can never be reached by following one road only"; but Ambrose knew better. Theodosius, the emperor he humbled, issued an unprecedented decree depriving heretics of civil rights. For the first time in history, religious orthodoxy became a requisite for citizenship. By the fifth century Pope Leo the Great endorsed the death penalty for erroneous belief; and the Spaniard Priscillian, with six followers, made history as the first heretics to be tortured and burned to death.

Short of such barbarities, the principle of compulsion was not an ideal way to regenerate the ancient world. Rather it emphasized that Christianity had pretty thoroughly succumbed to the more ancient tradition of "miracle, mystery, and authority." We are brought back to the reasons why its triumph led to no real improvement in earthly history at the time, by either Christian or classical standards, least of all by the standard of freedom.

4. The Costs of Success

"The service of Jesus is perfect freedom," wrote St. Gregory of Nazianzus. In the first centuries many Christians must have felt so. Memories of Jesus were still green, in Gospels that were living literature; the "good news" of his sacrifice for men was really news, still thrilling. The service of Jesus was performed in communities that could be havens of peace, brotherhood, and mutual aid. Voluntary, cheerful service, of the kind celebrated by the Shepherd of Hermas, is indeed a lofty mode of freedom. Early Christians might give lessons in self-realization to some of their go-getting descendants.

Nevertheless, their feeling of perfect freedom was a subjective affair, somewhat at variance with the objective conditions of their lives. It came down to a hope of such freedom in a life to come. Early Christians had no dream of political freedom, of course; the ideals of Pericles were simply irrelevant to the gospel alike of Jesus and St. Paul. No more were Christians dedicated to any social program for improving the lot of common men, beyond the brotherhood within their little communities. If the appearance of Christ gave vital meaning to earthly life, they still had no faith in progress nor any real philosophy of history, for the simple reason that the Gospels know nothing of such philosophy. And in all such respects the triumph of Christianity brought no real change. By this time the Roman Empire in the West may well have been too far gone to be saved by it; but in any case it stirred no new hopes of a better life on earth in either East or West. At most, as the worldly success religion it seemed to Constantine, Christianity took over the functions of the old state gods.

Immediately, it blessed the state that Diocletian and Constantine had made over into an outright Oriental despotism. "The powers that be are ordained of God," St. Paul had written. "Whosoever therefore resisteth the power, resisteth the ordinance of God; and they that resist shall receive to themselves damnation." In view of his hopes of the imminent Second Coming, he was perhaps expressing chiefly his indifference to politics, but as the world went on, all the Church Fathers agreed with him in counseling obedience to the powers that be. It occurred to none of them that more democratic or constitutional powers, or any powers that succeeded in displacing the autocratic emperor, would then be ordained by God—just as he was obliged to ordain some emperors who murdered their rivals or predecessors (as the sainted Constantine had). If their oversight was understandable, given age-old tradition, it nevertheless meant that Christianity succumbed to this tradition. As patriots devoted to the preservation of the Roman Empire, Diocletian and Constantine had not clearly betrayed any principle when they dropped the pretenses of republican government. The Church can hardly be blamed for welcoming the power it got from Constantine, but in the exercise of this power it can be charged with betraying its Christian faith.

Neither the Christian emperors nor the Church made any serious effort to Christianize the social structure of the Empire. At most the emperors passed a few new laws in keeping with their new faith, such as Constantine's repeal of the penalties on celibacy, and the Church continued its philanthropic work on behalf of the needy. A few of its leaders kept alive the Hebraic tradition of indignation at social injustice, John Chrysostom in the East and Bishop Ambrose in the West preaching some eloquent sermons contrasting the luxury of the rich and the wretchedness of the poor. Yet they did not urge either the emperors or the poor to do anything about such injustice. Now powerful and wealthy, the established Church formed the invariable historical alliance with the ruling class. Its leaders began openly justifying the subjection of the many, even to defending slavery. The early Church Fathers had followed St. Paul, who recommended a humane treatment of slaves while also exhorting slaves to be content with their lot; the later Fathers argued more explicitly for the propriety of the institution, as a consequence of original sin. Like Bishop Ambrose, they might add that slaves were blessed by a superior opportunity to practice the Christian virtues of humility and patience.[4]

---

[4] One Isidore of Pelusium set an early high for casuistry by pointing out that slaves might be better off than freemen at the Last Judgment: they could perhaps pass off on their masters responsibility for the sins they committed.

On the whole, the triumph of Christianity resulted in a distinct lowering of its ethical standards. If no established church in a great society could be expected to maintain the revolutionary ideals of Jesus, the misfortune remains that its leaders specifically repudiated much in the social gospel that most clearly distinguished Christians from pagans, and that might have given ordinary men more real freedom. Thus many early Christians, believing their Lord's teachings about nonviolence, had refused all military service, but in obedience to the powers that be churchmen began to hedge: they accepted "just" wars, while leaving forever uncertain how to tell them from unjust wars. In the fourth century pacifists were declared heretical. Thereafter the Christian Church would give more open support to war than any other of the higher religions, save only Mohammedanism; and while many ordinary Christians would perish by the sword, many more would be oppressed in states organized primarily for military purposes. Similarly the Church grew more tolerant of the possibilities of worshiping both God and mammon: by the fifth century a council condemned the old-fashioned idea that the rich could be saved only by renouncing their wealth. Christian camels could now pass through the eye of a needle.

The grosser concessions to wealth, luxury, and ease were no doubt exaggerated by the holy men who took to cell and desert. St. Jerome, for example, was shocked by the degeneracy in Rome, but he sounds much like the old Roman moralists—Christians were only rehearsing the old story. Certainly the corruption within the Church was by no means so flagrant as it became in medieval and Renaissance Europe. Yet the moral tone in the leading Christian centers, from Rome to Antioch, was no better than it had been in the old pagan days, and was plainly worse than the tone of early Christian communities. The saints themselves did not help to regenerate society when they simply fled it, to seek their own salvation. As they became objects of worship, they contributed instead to the one unfailing service performed by the Church on behalf of the poor: it offered them spiritual solace. Only this was a familiar kind of solace, not very spiritual. It betrayed an imperfect freedom, menaced by pathetic needs, harking back to a much older story; for all along Christianity had been taking on a cargo of prehistoric magic.

According to the Gospels, Jesus himself accepted some of the superstitions that had grown popular in Judaea. Unlike the great prophets of Israel, but like other wandering prophets of his time, he repeatedly performed miracles, in particular by driving out demons—the dread cause of disease. His followers played up the miraculous much more if only because the whole Christian faith rested on the supreme miracle of his resurrection. Thus the Eucharist, which as described in the Gospels seems like a simple memorial, became "the drug of immortality" celebrated by St. Ignatius; churchmen daily transformed the bread and wine literally into the flesh and blood of Christ. Likewise the familiar initiation rite of baptism was transformed into a magical cleansing of original sin. Christians were somewhat embarrassed, indeed, because other mystery religions practiced similar rites—a coincidence they could explain only as the work of the devil. They might have been as embarrassed by their mythology of saints and martyrs, which was more banal than that of the pagan gods and heroes; but presently this yielded new miraculous possibilities. Helena, the mother of Constantine the Great, inaugurated an immensely popular fashion by digging up in Jerusalem the True Cross. Many other relics of Jesus turned up, and soon were supplemented by prodigious quantities of bones and relics of saints and martyrs. Some saints did double duty by replacing pagan gods in shrines famous for their cures. (In the East they became so good at working cures that a number of them survived the coming of the Arabs and Turks, and continued to serve Moslems.) Angels too—especially the Archangel Michael—rode the floodtide into orthodox piety, though St. Paul had warned against the worship of them.

Now, the growth of such vulgar idolatry—the most universal element in the world's religions—was by no means surprising, nor simply humiliating. From the outset Christianity appealed chiefly to the lowly, or in the charitable words of Paul, to congregations including "not many wise, not many mighty, not many noble"; the magic and miracle solaced men who had little other recourse. About them as about the masses of men throughout history, the most depressing thought is their helpless need, not their spiritual shortcomings. None the less the spreading superstition was both cause and consequence of the failure of Christianity spiritually to regenerate the ancient world. It pointed to another reason why the service of Jesus represented considerably less than perfect freedom. For this was a compulsory service, bound by drastic penalties; it was coupled with not only promises of eternal rewards but threats of eternal torment. Men had more dire need of supernatural aid as Satan—a migrant to Judaea long before the time of Jesus—now came into his own.

All the Gospels agree that Jesus accepted the new ideas of heaven and hell that had also grown popular in Judaea (although they never became official dogma in Judaism). Even in the Sermon on the Mount he conjoined all the beatitudes with promises, ending his preamble "for great is your reward in heaven"; and as he went on he kept remarking that the alternative was punishment in hell. Usually he spoke of hell-fire as a bald matter of fact, not dwelling on it as his later ministers would, but by the same token he seemed not greatly concerned that only a few men are chosen, most are doomed to burning.[5] St. Paul likewise took heaven and hell literally, as did all the authors of the New Testament. Black-and-white ideas of the here-after, with angels and demons to match, became bedrock dogma in Christianity. Although Origen of Alexandria maintained that hell was really only a purgatory, and that God would finally save all men, even the demons—an idea that would seem becoming to an all-powerful God of love—the Church Fathers would have none of it. Satan was given eternal sovereignty over hell. A common argument for the resurrection of the body was that the damned souls needed flesh in order to burn and suffer to the full.

It is too much to say that Christians were hounded by fear. Early Christian art gives little evidence of fear, and later Christian behavior foretold the futility of the millions of sermons to come: the endless threats of damnation would never scare Christendom into godly behavior. For most men the conceit of personal immortality was presumably assurance that hell was where the other fellow went—first of all the unbeliever. Yet the fate of this unbeliever intimated why Christians would suffer as much from religious terrorism. It is not surprising that they made little apparent effort to love their enemies, or their heretical neighbors, inasmuch as God himself treated his enemies to everlasting torture. A more natural consequence was the spirit of hatred—the hatred that inflamed the lurid fantasies of the Book of Revelation, and gave early Christians the reputation of "enemies of the human race." When backed by worldly power, it became more virulent. Experience, observed Ammianus, had taught the Emperor Julian the Apostate that "most Christians behave more savagely to one another than wild beasts do to mankind." They anticipated the atrocities of the Inquisition, the savage wars between Protestants and

---

[5] Suzuki illustrates the rather different ideal spirit of Buddhism. If he believed in heaven and hell, he has said, he would certainly insist on going to hell to share the sufferings of the damned.

Catholics—the hell on earth that Christianity made on principle, as it directly inspired more hatred than has any other religion.

At best, the insistence on heaven and hell precluded the freedom of disinterested service, disinterested love. It lessened the chances of a moral regeneration of the ancient world, since conduct inspired by hope of reward or fear of punishment is not strictly moral at all—it is merely prudent. In this respect Christian ethic was plainly inferior to the loftiest pagan ethic, which from Socrates down through the Stoics had consistently taught virtue for its own sake. Even the Sermon on the Mount fell short of a prayer left by an obscure pagan named Eusebius: "May I be no man's enemy, and may I be the friend of that which is eternal and abides. May I never quarrel with those nearest to me; and if I do, may I be reconciled quickly. May I never devise evil against any man; if any devise evil against me, may I escape uninjured and without the need of hurting him. May I love, seek, and attain only that which is good. May I wish for all men's happiness and envy none. May I never rejoice in the ill-fortune of one who has wronged me. . . ." So his prayer went on; and it was addressed to no God of power, accompanied by no petition for either material or heavenly reward. Eusebius was saying simply, Let me be good.

Knowing that ordinary pagans did not live in the spirit of Eusebius, one may add that no doubt most ordinary Christians did good without thought of eternal reward, simply because it made them feel good. Yet his prayer brings up another major consideration. While Christianity broke with much that was sterile in classical tradition, it also rejected much that was admirable. The wisdom of the Greeks that seemed "foolishness" to St. Paul still looks like wisdom to most of us. If such judgments are obviously debatable, they involve some unquestionable matters of fact that are as obviously significant in a history of freedom. Early Christianity bred no live concern for earthly freedom, beyond the mixed by-products of the service of Jesus. In making this service the end-all and be-all for man, it undermined some essential conditions of freedom as we know it.

The most apparent break was with the ideal of human self-sufficiency that had ruled classical thought ever since Homer. Whatever their concept of excellence, all thinkers had agreed that man could achieve it by his own natural powers of reason and will, without supernatural aid. To Christians this faith was the deadly sin of pride. Jesus himself might not have thought so: while he took for granted the necessity of belief in the God of Israel, his recorded teachings implied that men could freely repent, enter the Kingdom of God by their own efforts, and he sufficiently stressed an apparent freedom of choice to warrant his indictment by Dostoyevsky's Grand Inquisitor. But St. Paul knew otherwise. Having been miraculously saved by Christ, he taught that man could know nothing and achieve nothing except by the grace of God. When so many of God's chosen people perversely refused to recognize the Christ, he also concluded that God denied grace to many men, for reasons unclear: "Therefore hath he mercy on whom he will, and whom he will he hardeneth." At any rate, those who had been blessed by grace should never attribute it to their own merits. "By grace are ye saved through faith; and not of yourselves: it is the gift of God; not of works, lest any man should boast." Call this attitude humble or call it abject, it plainly followed that no man was entitled to a mind, a faith, and a life of his own. Christians could still seem proud enough in their faith, even arrogantly self-righteous; but the orthodox belief remained that they were utterly dependent on the grace of God, and that the Greek faith was deadly sin.

As revolutionary was the related Christian shift from a way of life theoretically based on reason to a way emphatically based on faith, without which there could be no salvation. If the faith of ordinary Christians came down to simple credulity, like that of ordinary pagans, St. Paul had been too fervent to worry over such possibilities; he never bothered to demonstrate the crucial truth of the resurrection of Christ, simply saying, "He was seen." This may be called a truth transcending reason, as it certainly passeth ordinary understanding; or it may be called a defiance of reason, as Tertullian proudly maintained when he said, "I believe *because* it is absurd"; but anyway reason was never allowed to question faith in the resurrected Christ, or to deny its primacy. Although in spite of Tertullian theologians continued to appeal to reason, as they were bound to do in their professional capacity, their whole intellectual enterprise was severely confined by the requirements of faith. As they were led to metaphysical doctrines that free speculation would scarcely have arrived at, so they were debarred from speculating on other religious possibilities, and denied the freedom of doubt. Soon Christian thinkers were no longer able to separate philosophy from religion. By the end of the ancient world there was virtually no more disinterested inquiry, no pursuit of truth for its own sake.

As naturally Christians lost sight of the Greek ideal of all-around excellence. Jesus himself had preached nothing like this, showing no interest in art, literature, philosophy, or in general the values of civilization. St. Paul, better acquainted with Greek culture, was more positively hostile to its stress on natural possibilities of truth, goodness, beauty, and joy. For he had considerably darker ideas about the nature of man. By judicious selection, liberal Christians have been able to find an essential humanism in the gospel of Jesus, describing it as a religion of joy that strengthened the spirit of man; but there is no making a humanist of St. Paul. He suffered from a deep sense of man's unworthiness, if only because he himself had been a persecutor of the disciples of Jesus. Hence he was led to his novel idea of original sin—an idea that might induce humility, but would hardly encourage aspirations to freedom or to fullness of life.

While bitter experience had made Greeks and Romans sufficiently aware of man's propensities to evil, they had no such idea of ineradicable evil at the very heart of man; their ethical thought typically implied that goodness was natural for man, and that he was more or less perfectible. Judging by the *Shepherd of Hermas,* many early Christians were happy enough in the service of Jesus to think likewise. Yet the official view became that man was a fallen creature, born to sin. The Church Fathers used this doctrine to justify their acceptance of despotism and slavery, as conservatives would always use it to oppose social reform; any apparent social evils were natural for a naturally depraved creature. At the same time, a sense of sin became a hallmark of Christian spirituality. Simple sinners might be absolved by penance, but earnest spirits were prey to much deeper anxieties than were pagans, or for that matter Hindus, Buddhists, and Confucianists. More than any other religion, Christianity fostered a sense of guilt—again a possible means to humility, but not conducive to freedom of mind or spirit.

Similarly Paul deepened the ambiguities of Christian idealism by his dark views of earthly life, and his yearning for the life to come. "If in this life only we have hope in Christ," he wrote, "we are of all men most miserable." The otherworldly tendencies of Christianity grew more pronounced as the Roman Empire decayed. Officially it would never declare flatly that God's creation is as evil as Buddha said it was; if many saints and hermit-monks said as much by fleeing the world, their judgment did not become dogma. Nevertheless, their say was influential, for they were considered the holiest of Christians; and many ordinary Christians had plain reasons to agree with the view that made "this world" a synonym for sorrow and evil. In partic-

ular the holy men accentuated a radical dualism of body and soul
that was foreign alike to Judaism and to the recorded teachings of
Jesus. This was a heritage of Platonic idealism, or immediately of
Neo-Platonism, but in Christianity it led to much more fear or hatred
of the flesh than the ancients had ever shown.

Though early Christians seem generally to have mortified the flesh
no more than Jesus did, St. Paul foreshadowed this development too
when he wrote that those who live in the Spirit "have crucified the
flesh." By the fourth century we hear increasingly of the sinful, vile
flesh. Men were forgetting that Jesus had assumed it without apparent
shame, and that it was due to be resurrected.[6] Characteristically, Christians proceeded to carry their aversion to unclassical extremes. "Do
not suppose," Plotinus had written, "that a man becomes good by
despising the world and all the beauties that are in it"; but many a
Christian supposed just this. Their faith produced the ideal type of
the solitary ascetic monk—a type the very opposite of the antique
ideal, Greek or Roman. "How absurd is their choice!" exclaimed the
poet Rutilius, "how perverse their understanding!—to dread the evils,
without being able to support the blessings, of the human condition."

As mortification of the flesh became another hallmark of Christian
spirituality, and physical filth acquired its odor of sanctity, Christian
literature began to reek with a still more distinctive theme—the fear
of hatred of God's plan for the procreation of mankind. Not money
but sex was the root of all evil. All sexual desire was branded as lust,
all sexual intercourse as a shameful thing. It was through this shameful act, St. Ambrose pointed out, that Adam had transmitted his sin to
mankind. All men were fit for hell because all had been born out of
lust.

The immediate victims of this pathological obsession, needless to
say, were women. Although they had fared well with Jesus, appearing
as central figures in many of the gentlest parables and episodes of the
Gospels, their degradation began with St. Paul. He took very literally
the myth of Eve. While he remarked in passing that male and female

---

[6] Some contemporary Christian thinkers, notably Christopher Dawson and Reinhold
Niebuhr, make much of the extraordinary doctrine of the resurrection of the body, as a
symbol of an ideal unity of body and soul, a means to a complete fulfillment of life in the
hereafter. In proposing such unity as "the" Christian view of man, however, they
minimize the quite different tradition stemming from early Christianity, and forget that
the classical Greeks much more clearly stated and nearly realized the ideal of harmony
and wholeness. Incidentally, they also neglect to demonstrate the plausibility of the
doctrine, which to men of other creeds seems as preposterous as it did to the philosophers
of Athens who listened to St. Paul.

were one in Christ Jesus, he taught more emphatically that on earth woman should be subject to her husband "in every thing," as one who had been created for the sake of man. Even so, Paul did not really approve of her creation: he said it was better for men to remain bachelors, like himself, and accepted marriage only grudgingly, as a lesser evil than fornication. Later Christian writers almost all agreed that celibacy was holier than marriage, St. Jerome and St. Augustine even worrying at some length before they decided that married people could get into heaven. And churchmen worried most, naturally, over the dangers to men. They saw in women only the cause, not the victim of man's lust. Tertullian summed up their outrage: "Woman! You are the gateway of the devil. . . . Because of you the Son of God had to die. You should always go dressed in mourning and in rags." As all this implied, woman still had sufficient natural power over men, and she too could attain the holiness of celibacy; yet she was not allowed to forget that she was the daughter of Eve, the cause of original sin. At her lowliest she had never before been so insistently degraded, nor so violently denounced as a positive menace to man.

Men suffered as well from this kind of spirituality, however—and not merely the many monks tormented by carnal desire. As the natural love between man and woman was excluded from the ideal Christian life, so the love of all things natural and human was clouded by the morbid fear that identified the world with the flesh and the devil. It discouraged any rational pursuit of happiness, or the simple idea that happiness was a reasonable end for man. An incidental symptom was the disappearance of the smile from art, as of humor and vivacity from literature. (It is hard to imagine the Church Fathers laughing or joking.) The pall cast on all civilized interests except religion perhaps made little difference, considering the barrenness of classical culture in the last centuries of Rome; but by old Greek standards man had indeed fallen from natural grace.

For all such reasons early Christianity failed to realize its great potential gift to mankind—the person. Ideally, once more, the new faith gave the individual more dignity as one created in the image of God, assured a realm of privacy apart from the things that were Caesar's; it encouraged him in somewhat more dubious ways by promising him personal immortality—even in heaven he would be himself; and at worst it could make him feel more self-righteous than he could on principle as a pagan. Yet on all counts Christianity deprived him of much of the actual freedom he had enjoyed in classical Greece, and gave him less encouragement to develop and express his personality. It specifically denied him rights of conscience, or personal belief; there was nothing sacred in the person of a heretic or unbeliever. As specifically it denied him rights in the Kingdom of God based on personal merit alone. It declared no ideal of self-realization except through the prescribed service of Jesus; it never proclaimed the value of individuality, or of the "happy versatility" that Pericles boasted of in his fellow Athenians, for it saw no good in diversity of interest. The person it prized most was not the real self, body and mind, but a spiritual type that sought holiness by sacrificing wholeness. Thus it encouraged ascetics to assert themselves strenuously by self-denial instead of mere self-control (though we may assume that some of these virtuosos were not wholly unconscious of the worldly fame they might win—especially by living on the tops of pillars). Ordinary Christians it relieved of the possible burden of self-assertion, promising heaven to the meek and the poor in spirit, but by the same token it did not promote self-reliance. Among the lowly, the person was ideally anonymous.

On every count there remain the ambiguities of Christianity, the contrary tendencies to rationalism, humanism, naturalism, individualism. When a new civilization arose in Europe, fired by a remarkable energy and enterprise, Christianity would begin to realize its potentialities for more than "spiritual" freedom, if by less than perfect service of Jesus. At this stage, as we take leave of the classical world, the appropriate theme is "Hail and Farewell!" And to make it momentous, to keep it suitably ambiguous, there came at the end St. Augustine. His *City of God*, inspired immediately by the fall of Rome to Alaric, was the first comprehensive, ordered statement of the Christian faith. It was an extraordinary synthesis, embracing all that was most vital and distinctive in Christianity, all that it owed to classical culture, all that it suffered from the decay of a world it was failing to save; and his work was to have an immense influence, providing the intellectual foundations of the Catholic Middle Ages, as later of the Protestant Reformation. It was a Janus monument, facing both a past that Augustine largely repudiated and a future that he little relished. It marks a major turning point in the history of Western man.

5. *Epitome:* City of God

In piety to the ancients, let us heed the great classical scholar Wilamowitz. "The tradition is dead," he wrote; "our task is to revivify life that has passed away. We know that ghosts cannot speak until they have drunk blood; and the spirits that we evoke demand the blood of our hearts. We give it to them gladly; but if they then abide our question, something from us has entered into them." The tradition of St. Augustine is far from dead, nor is he a speechless, bloodless ghost; he spoke most eloquently in his own *Confessions,* through which we know him more intimately than we know any other man in antiquity. Nevertheless, we must be prepared to give him something of our blood, and even so to remain uncertain whether he will abide our questions. If he could have dreamed of the likes of most of us, he would have been simply appalled, confirmed in his worst fears about man. His spirit is considerably more remote from ours than is the spirit of Socrates or Cicero, Pericles or Augustus. Men are still evoking it, more especially since the state of our world has appeared to confirm his fears; only they evoke different Augustines, to suit as different purposes.

Thereby, however, they give the obvious cue for our immediate purposes. St. Augustine, Bishop of Hippo, was a many-sided man: mystic, theologian, rhetorician, psychologist, churchman, administrator. He may abide many a question, or not abide by his answer to it, because he tried to reconcile all the major conflicting tendencies of Christianity. As rigorous as fervent in his devotion at once to the spirit, the logic, and the letter of the Christian faith, he strained spirit, logic, and letter to the utmost in order to glorify an irresistible divine grace that man was always resisting, to educate an essentially depraved creature who was totally obliged to serve his self-sufficient Creator, to support a wretched life made tolerable only by the hope of another life, which only a few Elect would enjoy—to embrace beliefs that to many of us look like hopeless contradictions, or that may be described more piously as paradoxes, but that in any case summed up both the ambiguous achievement and the ambiguous promise of Christianity.

Born in North Africa in A.D. 354, at a time when Christianity was still combating strong pagan opposition, Augustine was prepared for his historic role from the day he was conceived by his Christian mother and his pagan father. He was given the best classical education available, during which he enjoyed the simple pagan pleasures normal to youth that later gave him a terrible sense of guilt; the "hideous" sins detailed in his *Confessions* were mostly forms of love of play. (Perhaps the most serious of them was his indulgence in a mistress, who bore him an illegitimate child; but he was faithful to her for years, giving her up only when his pious mother begged him to look for a rich wife instead.) He began studying all the philosophical and religious movements of his time, but not in a spirit of eager curiosity; enough of a Christian to know that doubt or error meant eternal damnation, he was engaged in a compulsive quest for certainty. For a while he took to Manicheism, since it provided the most logical explanation of the evil in God's world by making Satan an independent power, not a creature of God's. He was more inspired by Neo-Platonism, which explained away evil as a mere absence of good, and acquainted him with a purely spiritual Absolute free from the apparently naïve anthropomorphism of God as often described in the Bible. Bishop Ambrose then eased his difficulties with the Bible by teaching him the classical method of interpreting it allegorically. Finally the reward for his travails was a mystical experience. This experience, which in the year 386 made him a wholehearted convert to the Lord Jesus Christ, may be said to mark the watershed between the classical and the medieval-Christian world.

The Lord prepared him for conversion by bringing him face to face with himself: "I beheld and loathed myself," seeing "how foul I was, and how crooked and sordid, bespotted and ulcerous." Thereafter Augustine was a "new creature" much like St. Paul. His compulsive quest ended in as ardent a compulsion to resolve all the doubts of his fellow Christians, give them the certainty and peace of mind he had come to know.

The *Confessions* that recorded his conversion was itself a unique work. In writing his autobiography, as no pagan thinker had, he displayed not only a candor but a psychological subtlety and acuteness beyond anything in classical literature. If his awareness of the "abysmal depths" of personality sprang from his sense of guilt, it nevertheless meant a deeper kind of self-consciousness, a deeper concern with personality, which eventually would distinguish a Hamlet from both King Oedipus and Socrates. Immediately it led

Augustine to differ from classical philosophers in stressing the primacy of will, not reason. He then had to wrestle with the problem of free will, which had never seriously troubled them; for men could not logically gainsay the will of an all-powerful God. He was more troubled because he knew man's will as primarily a will to evil, both from his own youth and from his hard work as Bishop of Hippo. But he also knew a will to impossible perfection. "Be ye perfect, even as your Father which is in heaven," Christ had commanded. In his exalted moods Augustine would have nothing of the classical principles of limit, measure, proportion; his spiritual reach was infinitely beyond his grasp. He set the style for the distinctive "Faustian" spirit of Western civilization.

As a theologian who had had mystical visions, he accordingly tried to utter the absolute, unutterable perfection of God. This he declared was so far beyond all rational conception that any assertion about God —even the assertion that he was ineffable—was impermissible. Nevertheless, he knew by intense personal experience a personal, providential God, quite unlike a mere philosophical Absolute. His Lord therefore retained some of the anthropomorphic traits of the old Yahweh, and involved him in more theological difficulties; but first and last he insisted on a divine purposefulness that gave man a high purpose on earth. When Christians and pagans alike were appalled by Alaric's sack of Rome, he responded by writing the *City of God,* projecting a theory of history that was to be universally accepted in Western Christendom until recent centuries. He attacked point-blank the common notions of the rule of Fortune or of Fate, especially as implied by the classical theory of cycles: under the divine providence history must have point and direction. The direction was for him the City of God in the hereafter, nothing like progress on earth; yet it left the future open and put its issues squarely up to man. And Augustine broadened as well as deepened the meaning of human history. For the greater historians of antiquity the most momentous events had naturally been political events in their own time and place—the Persian Wars, the Peloponnesian War, the Roman conquest of an empire. For Augustine history was a universal drama. True, he knew very little about world history, and his ignorance of it was embalmed in Christian tradition down to the age of the Enlightenment; but his idea of universal history also came through.

This idea, however, owed more clearly to Stoic thought than it did to Christian Scriptures. So too the whole effort of Augustine to systematize the Christian faith was an essentially classical enterprise, far beyond the ken of the early Apostles. In carrying it out he was deeply indebted to classical philosophy, especially Platonism, in which he remarked that he found every Christian doctrine except the Incarnation. At a time of increasing anarchy, when God seemed unconcerned about the fate of the Christian Roman Empire, he sought to maintain not only faith in the divine providence but classical ideals of order. The Christian faith might well have survived anyway, as it did in the East with little or no help from St. Augustine. He built into the faith principles of spiritual, intellectual, and political order that could and did serve as a foundation for Western Christendom when it eventually emerged from the anarchy.

An incidental but striking example was his definition of virtue as "the order of love." Whereas for Jesus love had no order or bounds, for Augustine a boundless love of God called for discrimination among the lesser objects of love on earth, a scale of values that ideally meant right order and harmony. Much more influential was the authority he lent to the Greek idea of an ordered universe. While as a devout believer in Scripture he perforce believed in miracles, he was impressed by the most wondrous miracle, the regularity of nature: "Nature is all order and all miracle, but the miracle is the order." In a similar spirit he transmitted the Stoic ideal of *cosmopolis*, now backed by the authority of God: "There is one commonwealth of all Christian men." With this he passed on to the Middle Ages the idea that an unjust law was really no law. He was much more concerned with law and order in the commonwealth than were either the authors of Scripture or his philosophical mentors, the Neo-Platonists. Whereas Plotinus had simply ignored the community or the state, the Bishop of Hippo remained in the line of older classical tradition.

Hence he qualified his theory of the two radically opposed cities: the City of God, "built by the love of God," made up of those destined to be saved; and the Earthly City, "built by the love of self," represented by the state—the Rome that was falling. Augustine's primary concern was naturally the City of God, and he saw all history as a constant conflict between it and the Earthly City, which was effectively ruled by Satan. Nevertheless, he did not conceive the state as simply of Satan: it too had been willed by God, as "the life of the wise man must be social." He had much to say on peace and justice, to which the state ideally was a means. He could even resist his strong impulse to despise the flesh that had got him into so much trouble; he fitted the flesh into his order of good, granting it value "in its own kind and degree." In general, he equipped the Christian life with a degree of classical reasonableness. Christopher Dawson, one of his many contemporary admirers, asserts that he "first made possible the ideal of a social order resting upon the free personality and a common effort towards moral ends."

But this tribute brings us up sharply. St. Augustine himself hardly declared an ideal of the "free personality," and certainly his influence promoted no such ideal in the long centuries ahead. The weight of his immense authority was decidedly against all ideals of freedom in the Greek or the modern sense. Given a system that remains one of the marvels of human thought for its wealth of apparent contradiction, later Christians could extract much from it to support their different purposes; but immediately it marked a historic turning point by its flat repudiation of the humanistic ideals of the ancient world.

His miraculous conversion gave Augustine a vivid sense of utter helplessness, utter dependence on the grace of God. He was led logically to the belief that men must make it their whole effort to love and serve God, but he also concluded that they could not even love God unless granted grace—as on the face of it the great majority had not been. Similarly he was a "new creature" in a depressing sense, as one afflicted with an appalling sense of guilt. He stressed much more vehemently than St. Paul that the whole human race was cursed by original sin. He drew the blackest picture of the unutterable misery of its condition, in which all the natural calamities of storm, flood, earthquake, poison, pestilence, and famine were intensified by the depravity of man.[7] In keeping with this view of the human condition, which was to remain the orthodox Christian view for a thousand years, he confirmed the morbid Christian fear of natural pleasures. While admitting some good in the flesh, he wrote much more eloquently about its evils; it was safer for men to be always on guard against its dangerous delights. He had a particular horror of sexual intercourse, calling attention to the shameful commingling of the

---

[7] A typical catalogue of woes begins with "gnawing cares, disquiet, griefs, fears, wild joys, quarrels, lawsuits, wars, treasons, angers, hatreds, deceit, flattery, fraud, theft, robbery, perfidy, pride, ambition, envy, murders, parricides, cruelty, ferocity, wickedness, luxury, insolence, impudence, shamelessness, fornications, adulteries, incests, and the numberless uncleannesses and unnatural acts of both sexes, which it is shameful so much as to mention: sacrileges, heresies, blasphemies, perjuries, oppression of the innocent, calumnies, plots, falsehoods, false witnessings, unrighteous judgments, violent deeds, plunderings," etc. St. Augustine did not take classical pains in drawing up an order of vice.

excretory and sexual organs through which original sin was transmitted; he permitted intercourse only for the purpose of procreation —though even then men must be careful not to enjoy it. He was not inclined to cherish the "free personality" of women.

This spirit helps to explain why, in spite of his sophistication and his spirituality, St. Augustine lent his authority to vulgar belief that inspired fear. As he took literally the myth of Adam and Eve, so he took seriously the hosts of demons who preyed on their accursed descendants, and insisted on the material reality of the "eternal fire" that awaited most of them. The torment was properly everlasting; Augustine said it was "very absurd" to hope or pray for an end to the agonies of the damned. His logic only made the divine providence more appalling. To the doctrine of predestination it added a nice rational calculation: so as to maintain the order of heaven, the number of those predestined to be saved must equal the number of fallen angels. His main concession to justice in the divine scheme was the possibility of different degrees of pain in hell.

The absolute certitude that blessed St. Augustine with a feeling of spiritual freedom did not dispose him to be sweetly reasonable, or to permit freedom of thought in others. Reason had not led him to Christ—it had led him only into doubt, when not astray into such heresies as Manicheism. Although his system represented a remarkable effort at understanding, he put his seal on another tradition that was to last for over a thousand years: belief came first, only belief made understanding possible. And as even then reason could not prove the truth of Christ, but kept suggesting possible objections to it, he naturally described its claims as "intellectual arrogance," or more roundly as "the sacrilegious and impious darings of reason." In denying the claims of doubt he was the more dogmatic because his own belief seemed arrogant to pagans. In the sympathetic words of Christopher Dawson, "The idea, so shocking to the Hellenic mind or to that of the modern rationalist, that God intervenes in history and that a small and uncultured Semitic people had been made the vehicle of an absolute divine purpose, was to him the very center and basis of his faith."

Augustine was most emphatic about another idea as shocking to the Greek or the modern mind—the idea of St. Paul that men could claim no merit for their own good works, which were simply the gift of God. In his celebrated controversy with Pelagius he again marked a turning point in history. A British monk known for his sanctity, Pelagius denied the curse of original sin, arguing reasonably that all men, like Adam himself, were free to choose and could earn salvation by their own efforts: "Everything good and everything evil is *done by us,* not *born with us.*" Although he hoped thereby to give Christians a keener sense of personal responsibility, to Augustine such responsibility looked like deadly pride. As he saw it, the sacrifice of the Redeemer would be unnecessary if men had it within their own power to save themselves, and anyhow his own experience taught him that they had no such power. He succeeded in getting the Pelagian teaching officially condemned as heresy; and heresy it remained. Man was free to choose evil and earn hell, but not to earn heaven on his own.

All such ideas, and the dangerous pride that induced men to oppose them, naturally induced Augustine to confirm the authoritarianism of the Church, even to justifying the use of force in dealings with unbelievers and heretics. He wrenched a text from a parable of Jesus, "Compel them to come in," but his main concern was to keep out heretics. As Bishop of Hippo he had had immediately to put down the Donatists, who maintained that the sacraments were valid only if administered by pure priests—a seemingly reasonable position, but fatal to the authority of the Church and the necessary efficacy of the sacraments.[8] In particular, Augustine laid the foundations of the medieval papacy. He did not yet recognize the primacy of the Bishop of Rome, to be sure, much less any claims to papal infallibility, nor did he identify the Church with his City of God; this was an "invisible" society, whereas the Church on earth was a visible society that obviously included some sinners and might err. Yet for all practical purposes he maintained the infallibility of the Church. Though admitting the theoretical possibility that even councils might err, he banked on their authority in defining the true faith (as when he managed to get Pelagius condemned). He provided no clear means of distinguishing the Visible from the Invisible Church, and in his exalted moods plainly did tend to identify them. "Therefore even now," he could write, "the Church is the Kingdom of Christ and the Kingdom of the Heavens." As plainly he set church above state. He had little influence in the East, on the nascent Byzantine Empire, but the Roman Church would

---

[8] This heresy was an incidental by-product of the persecution by the Emperor Diocletian, during which some churchmen had prudently renounced the Christian faith rather than suffer martyrdom. When these backsliders were pardoned and restored to their ministry, the Donatists would have none of them, holding that spiritual shepherds ought to be better than their flock.

lean heavily on his work when it laid claim to papal supremacy. His *City of God,* written to justify the fall of Rome, did more than Scripture or any other work to maintain the importance of Rome through the Dark and Middle Ages.

By the same token it did much less for the Earthly City, in which ordinary freedom must be realized. For the long run Augustine made a potential contribution by depriving the state of sanctity, as well as by his concern for justice, but he also degraded the state by treating it chiefly as a necessary evil, made necessary by original sin. Classical Athens was for him only a city of Satan, no better than Babylon. He talked of Rome too as "the second Babylon," but because of its materialism, not its political oppression. He went further than the Church Fathers before him in endorsing the powers of the emperors, counseling obedience even to wicked rulers, since God had ordained them as a punishment for our sins: God "gives kingly power on earth both to the pious and the impious, as it may please Him, whose good pleasure is always just." Similarly he called on slaves to serve their masters "heartily and with good will" even if the masters were wicked, because slavery was a "result of sin." He neglected to demonstrate that slaves were in general more sinful than their masters, or even to consider the question.

It may be said that St. Augustine kept his eyes on a higher purpose, the most important concern for man—the relation of man to God, not the mere reorganization of society. Or that, like the great prophets of Israel, he sought to make over the hearts of men rather than their social institutions, perhaps in a more conscious belief that no new laws or institutions would avail unless the hearts of men were improved. Thus he described as a "vice" of the classical *polis* its concern with merely political justice. But then this is to say that Augustine broke more radically with a tradition unknown to the prophets. Whatever his effect on the heart, he gave more positive support than they had to seemingly unchristian institutions that kept the many in subjection or bondage.

Likewise classical culture suffered more directly from his teaching. Augustine had no use for science, natural philosophy, or any independent inquiry. The only knowledge that mattered was knowledge of God, which was to be found in Scripture; so the curiosity of the Greeks was a foolish distraction when not a positive menace. "Wretched that man who knows all philosophies, and knows not Thee; blessed is he who knows Thee, though ignorant of all those matters." The subject of history as passed on by Augustine was vitiated by the same incuriosity. He gloried in a divine order of history that was fully known to God, though "hidden from us"—enough that God knew it; his remarks on the actual order of past history were mostly trivial or routine, betraying not only considerable ignorance but little idea of natural causation. As for the great poets and artists of antiquity, there was no room for them in the City of God. The love of God was not only the supreme good—it was the source of all good; and the love of any earthly goods for their own sake was damnably sinful. The immediate effect of Augustine's teaching was as destructive of culture as were the depredations of the Vandals who were besieging Hippo when he died. Thereafter high churchmen did little to resist the increasing barbarization of Europe. By the time of Gregory the Great, Western Christendom was sunk in an ignorance that looked more barbarous than blessed.

Farewell indeed! And yet hail too: for Gregory vindicated the faith of St. Augustine. The Vandals who were besieging Hippo soon overran North Africa, and later the Arabs swept out almost every trace of Christianity in the region where Augustine had worked so hard to save souls (even though God had predestined their fate); but his Church did not go down. Gregory the Great, who maintained both its spiritual and its worldly authority during the darkest age of Rome, had studied the City of God. This was indeed the great educational work that Augustine intended, even as he scorned the profane educational ideals of the ancients. Still, it suggests a final verdict rather different from his own as we say farewell to the classical world. Without its culture he could not possibly have written his City of God. He transmitted much of its thought, something of its spirit. In justice —in a spirit of Christian charity too—the last word about it is properly a word of gratitude for its enduring contributions to the life of freedom.

| # *EPILOGUE: THE BYZANTINE EMPIRE*

In the spirit of St. Augustine, C. N. Cochrane has explained the fall of Rome by a fatal error that began with Constantine the Great: the rulers of the Empire identified the City of God with the Earthly City. They tried to enlist Christianity in the service of a state that was decadent, but it was impossible anyway to reconcile Classicism and Christianity, as Augustine knew; so it was "inevitable that *Romanitas,* despite her pretension to eternity, should perish from the earth." This explanation might seem plausible as well as wholesome were it not for an odd oversight. The Eastern Roman Empire persisted in this fatal error, rejecting the wisdom of Augustine; and it went on for more than a thousand years, defying the inevitable until the fall of Constantinople to the Turks in 1453. It lasted much longer than all the previous empires in the region—Hittite, Assyrian, Persian, Hellenistic—while outliving too the contemporary empires of the Sassanian Persians and the Arabs. Only Egypt and China surpassed it for longevity.

Cochrane's oversight is characteristic of Western prejudice against this remarkable Byzantine Empire. Originating in jealousy between the bishops of Constantinople and Rome, the prejudice grew stronger with the revival of civilization in the West, under a "Holy Roman Empire"; the idea grew up that this was the true heir of Rome, Byzantium only a bastard offspring. The final break between the Roman Church and the Holy Orthodox Church, in the eleventh century, then made heretics of the Byzantines—a viler species than infidels. But they fared no better when historians began rising above this religious bias, in the age of the Enlightenment. To rationalists and freethinkers their holy empire looked like only a benighted despotism. Gibbon pronounced the verdict that was generally accepted until recent times: "In the revolution of ten centuries, not a single discovery was made to exalt the dignity or promote the happiness of mankind. Not a single idea has been added to the speculative systems of antiquity. Not a single composition of history, philosophy, or literature has been saved from oblivion by the intrinsic beauties of style or sentiment, of original fancy, or even of successful imitation."

One may therefore feel proud that in our godless century the Byzantine Empire has at last received sympathetic attention. Spengler and Toynbee fitted it into the regular cycles they found or imposed on the history of civilization—a somewhat dubious honor, but at least implying that it had as much intrinsic dignity as other civilizations. Appreciation was also stimulated by the belated discovery of the glories of Byzantine art, especially the mosaic; the revolt against realism made it easier to do justice to the formalism that Renaissance art had broken away from. At the same time, historians studying the roots of our civilization began to realize how deeply Europe was indebted to Byzantium, directly for its civilizing influences, indirectly for the bulwark it had provided against the surge of Islam. Russian historians took a particular interest in it, since Russia owed far more to it than to Rome; and their studies inspired Jack Lindsay to reverse Gibbon's verdict. He goes so far as to argue that in the course of creating a magnificent culture of its own, Byzantium "laid the foundations which made Europe possible," and held "the main road of human advance."[1]

As usual, however, the pendulum has swung too far. Granted its impressive achievements, the Byzantine Empire certainly made no significant advance toward freedom of any kind. Most obviously it laid the foundations of czarist Russia, which was hardly on the main road of human advance. Otherwise it survived chiefly in its Holy Orthodox Church, which prided itself on not having moved from where it stood in the early centuries of Christianity, in fact remained more strictly orthodox than the Roman Church, and set the tone of the whole society. Despite its important contributions to Europe, Byzantium did not lay the foundations of Europe; Western civilization was essentially an independent development, which from the outset took a quite different course. The Byzantine Empire rightly looks to us like an ancient affair, another Oriental sacred monarchy. It still has intrinsic dignity and historical importance; but these too are most

---

[1] His work is entitled *Byzantium into Europe* (London, 1952). The work by Cochrane that I quoted from is *Christianity and Classical Culture* (Oxford, 1940). Any similarity between these works is strictly coincidental.

apparent when it is viewed as an epilogue to ancient history, not a prelude to Western history.

Its tenacity alone suggests that it was an honorable epilogue. Byzantium demonstrated the vitality of classical culture, which was not so hopelessly decadent as one might gather from studying Rome or Europe alone. In the sixth century it built its superb cathedral of Hagia Sophia, a masterpiece in a new style, as Greek architects solved the problem of setting an immense dome on a square interior. This was a monument to its Christian faith, but the faith was indeed bent to the service of an imperial Roman state, and in time to the conscious preservation of its Greek legacy. Greco-Roman tradition survived the new influences from the East that helped to make Byzantine culture distinctive, earning it its new name.[2] The Empire retained its early consciousness of a high mission, which was the main source of both its dignity and its importance to the West. It was dedicated to the defense not only of Christianity against the infidels but of civilization against barbarism.

In this view its survival of the fall of Rome is less mysterious than may at first appear (or than it seemed to me when I wrote *The Uses of the Past*). Byzantium could draw on the greater wealth, the more highly developed economy, and the more deeply rooted culture of the East. In Constantinople, the "New Rome," it had the advantage of a capital exceptionally well situated for purposes of both commerce and defense. The Greek East was not given to the Roman disdain of trade and business; by the fifth century Constantinople was a metropolis of a million people, far more industrious than Rome had ever been, which for some centuries remained the greatest city in the world. Behind its strong walls, with the wealth drawn from commerce, its rulers carried on the administrative and military traditions of Rome. A generally efficient, if often oppressive bureaucracy maintained a stability that in fiscal affairs was unprecedented, and is still unparalleled; backed by a government that never defaulted, Byzantine coinage was accepted as standard all over the commercial world for eight

---

[2] Historians differ about when the Eastern Roman Empire became Byzantine, dating the change anywhere from the fourth to the eighth century, but their disagreement emphasizes the fact that it was a gradual change, not at all revolutionary. None deny the continuance of Greco-Roman tradition. Arnold Toynbee, who has tried hardest to define Byzantium as a new civilization, in order to keep his cycles neat, declares that it made the fatal error of trying to revive the "ghost" of the Roman Empire and admits that it achieved a "recognizable reproduction." Let us add that it was an uncommonly robust, lively ghost.

hundred years. The Byzantine army was as proficient on organization, which made warfare a science, while some inventor gave its fleet a terrible secret weapon, "Greek fire."

Such explanations are not wholly satisfying to the moralist or the philosopher of history, still less to a lover of freedom. They involved a flagrant disregard of both Christian and classical idealism—the unscrupulousness, deceit, treachery, and cruelty for which Byzantine history is notorious. Neither do they wholly explain the survival of the Empire, which more than once was on the verge of apparent doom, and immediately was saved by the unpredictable emergence of a great emperor or general. But these recurrent crises recall us to the most honorable aspect of its history. The high mission of Byzantium was never an easy one, nor was it supported by a belief that the New Rome was an Eternal City. The Byzantines did not have to study Augustine to learn that no earthly city is eternal—they knew this from their Greek ancestors, and from long experience in living dangerously. They were generally ambitious and often aggressive, dreaming imperial dreams; but as often they were on the defensive, fighting against odds. They most nearly anticipated Western history by the turbulence of their history, in which crisis might almost be called the normal state. There was never a *Pax Byzantina*.

Byzantium enjoyed its first brilliant age in the first half of the sixth century under Justinian the Great, the most Roman-minded of its emperors and one of the greatest builders in history. It paid heavily in taxes, however, for his imperial splendors, and it was further exhausted by one of the most devastating plagues on record. By the end of the century it was tottering under the blows of the Sassanians, whose armies overran most of the Empire, three times reaching the capital itself. Its savior at this desperate juncture was the Emperor Heraclius. But even as he concluded a successful counterattack the Arabs were pouring out of their desert under the banner of Mohammed; before his death they had permanently won the provinces of Egypt, Palestine, and Syria. Their drive continued until 717, when they laid siege to Constantinople by land and sea. Here, in one of the most momentous struggles in history, the all-conquering Arabs were finally repelled by the Emperor Leo III. Otherwise they might well have overrun all Christendom, and Charles Martel had no chance to win his reputation as the savior of Europe by defeating a relatively small plundering expedition in far-off France. "Under the shelter of that defense of the Eastern gateway western Europe could refashion its own life," Norman

Baynes concluded: "it is hardly an exaggeration to say that the civilization of western Europe is a by-product of the Byzantine Empire's will to survive."

The tenacity of the Byzantines was accentuated by the failure of the Sassanian Empire, which had quickly succumbed to the Arabs. Early in the third century A.D. beginning to revive the power and the glory of the former Persian Empire, this had become an impressive empire by Oriental standards. The Sassanians developed a brilliant art that contributed much to Islamic art. They fell in with the universalism of the age by producing the prophet Mani, an avowed follower of Zoroaster, Buddha, and Jesus, who combined their teaching in a religion designed for all races and classes of men, and who died a martyr (c. 275). The Magian priesthood that persecuted the Manichees, with a zeal anticipating Christianity, at least gave the state religion of Zoroastrianism its scriptures, the Zend-Avesta. Most novel was another religious movement, the Mazdakite, so revolutionary that it has been described as Iranian Communism: it not only preached but tried to realize an ideal of social equality, instigating uprisings against the nobility. And a few of the Sassanian monarchs won some fame for their enlightenment as well as their military prowess. Chosroes I, a contemporary of Justinian the Great, welcomed at his court the Greek philosophers from the schools of Athens that Justinian closed down; and when they found Zoroastrian orthodoxy no more congenial, he magnanimously arranged with Justinian for their return home without penalty.

It is significant, however, that they left. The Sassanian Empire failed to fulfill any of its unusual promise, settling down into the ancient ways of the Oriental monarchy. It was periodically disrupted by conflicts between the King of Kings and a feudal aristocracy, or sometimes the priesthood, but these generated no new conception of government. The class structure remained more rigid than most; the Mazdakite movement, like the Manichee, was properly crushed. The popularity of these movements testified chiefly to the oppression of the masses, which grew harsher; the peasantry was reduced to serfdom. No idea of personal liberty seeped in from the Greco-Roman world. Justice was still a royal favor bestowed on subjects, not a legal right of citizens. The Sassanian monarchs accumulated a vast wealth, which might or might not be used to advance the public welfare, and eventually enriched the rude Arabs. The Empire ended ignominiously, as its aristocracy fought among themselves, virtually exterminating the royal family, and no leader and no class put up a determined resistance to the Arabs.

Following the successful defense of Constantinople, the Byzantine Empire demonstrated more staying power than did these Arabs too. Through the ups and downs of the next few centuries it reached the peak of its power and wealth, while the Empire won by the followers of Mohammed soon began to break up because of internal failures —not external pressure. It was such pressure that marked the beginning of the end for Byzantium: in 1071 Seljuk invaders won a decisive victory at Manzikert and proceeded to overrun most of Asia Minor, the heartland of the Empire. Its decline thereafter was painfully slow because it kept struggling to the end, stubbornly refusing to die, or to accept barbarian rule as Rome had. Western Christendom, now coming up in the world, was too bigoted and ignorant to appreciate its debt to the defenders of Constantinople, instead killing whatever chance the Empire might have had to survive. In 1204 Constantinople fell to the barbarians of the Fourth Crusade—the first time it had fallen since its foundation almost nine hundred years before; and after pillaging and massacring to their heart's content, the Crusaders sat down to enjoy their loot in preference to marching on to the Holy Land. (As one of them wrote, "Since the world was created, never had so much booty been won in any city!") Some fifty years later the Byzantines recovered their capital, but then they had to cope with the Ottoman Turks, who were taking over the short-lived Seljuk Empire. They were no longer wealthy, Venetians and Genoese having drained off most of their commerce. Even so they struggled for two more centuries, until their dwindling empire was little more than a huddle about their once mighty capital, now a city of fewer than a hundred thousand people. At the end, in 1453, the Emperor Constantine Palaeologus died fighting on its walls.

So the victorious Moslem Turks completed the spiritual resurgence of the East, which began even as Alexander the Great conquered it. The conclusion is too pat; yet there is both rhyme and reason in it. The Byzantine Empire had been centered in the *oikoumene* of the Hellenistic Greeks. A contemporary historian of its fall, Kritovoulos, rounded out the drama by harking back to Homer: he reported that Sultan Mohammed, the conqueror of Constantinople, paid a visit to Troy and there remarked that he had at last avenged the Trojans, punishing the Greeks "for their injustice to us Asiatics." The last of the Constantines had displayed as appropriate historical sense in dying like an old Roman, after trying to hearten his people by reminding them of the feats of their Roman ancestors. For though Greek had long since become the official language of the Byzantine Empire, to the end it called itself the "Empire of the Romans"—and to the Turks too it was always *Rum*. The fall of Constantinople, which forever ended Greco-Roman rule in the East, brings us back to the enduring power of the classical tradition.

From the outset this empire had in a real sense been an "Empire of the Romans." Although there is some question of the depth of Constantine the Great's devotion to the Christian God, there is no question about his devotion to the cause of the Empire. However autocratic in fact, he still subscribed to the ideal theory of a universal commonwealth and even preserved something of the forms of the Augustan Principate. In founding his capital, he provided it with a splendid Senate House and brought in enough old Roman families to form an undistinguished, shadowy, but still visible Senate. In Byzantine theory, the Senate had a voice in electing the emperor, as did the army and the people of Constantinople. If in practice the electors almost always approved whomever the emperor designated (usually his son), or whoever managed to dethrone him, the forms helped to keep alive the idea that the sovereign was a servant of the people; more than once popular clamor set a popular favorite on a contested throne. Like the Roman emperors, the sovereigns of Byzantium maintained a fairly high average in responsible rule, and were more disposed to consider the public weal or will than were the Sassanian kings or the contemporary caliphs of Baghdad. Their civil service always remained open to able plebeians, giving Byzantine society something of a democratic air.

In particular Byzantium retained the traditional reverence for law. The most influential work of Justinian, his complete codification of Roman law, included a *Digest* opening with a quotation from Ulpian that defined the "true philosophy" of law as justice, "the art of the good and the fair," and the lawyer as a "priest" of justice. This spirit lent an aura of sanctity to a law that was thoroughly secular, with only incidental Christian trimmings (chiefly about sexual behavior). Moreover, the tradition was strong enough to inhibit outright despotism. Though Justinian pronounced officially that as emperor he was above the law, because its source, his code preserved elements of the older constitutional principles. It was felt that somehow the emperor was beneath the law too; Byzantine sovereigns typically proclaimed their devotion to the law, not their right to make it to suit themselves.

As essentially a department of the state, the Holy Orthodox Church helped to inspire devotion to it but otherwise played a generally uninspiring political role; it had no zeal for upholding constitutional principles of government or any notions of political freedom. Still, its patriarchs were not wholly subservient to the emperor, sometimes criticizing or even defying him. In their own realm they were never so arrogant as to claim infallibility or establish an Inquisition; rejecting on principle the demand of Rome for absolute submission, the Orthodox Church required no such submission of the Slavonic and Caucasian churches established by its missionaries. In spite of its conservatism it was Greek enough to tolerate some dangerous speculation over ideas come down from its pre-Christian heritage, so long as intellectuals subscribed to its basic dogmas. And indirectly it contributed to the revival of the Greek heritage.

This was an ironic outcome of the furious controversy over Iconoclasm that began with Leo III, the savior of Byzantium from the Arabs, and raged for more than a century. In trying to suppress the popular worship of images, the iconoclastic emperors had something of a Semitic spirit but also a Roman spirit: they were combating the monasteries, which had grown immensely wealthy on the superstitious reverence of their ikons and were a heavy drain on both the manpower and the material resources of the beleaguered Empire. The churchmen who defied the emperors, on the other hand, had somewhat impure motives. They might defend ikons by Platonic arguments, saying that the visible image only symbolized the invisible reality, but there was little question that the popular worship of images was as idolatrous as lucrative; the most impassioned defenders were neither humanists nor saints. The Council that finally settled the controversy by anathematizing all who refused to worship images still had an unspiritual air, for it had been summoned by the Empress Irene, a headstrong partisan who ascended the throne by deposing and blinding her son, and it had to reverse a previous council that had as unanimously proclaimed images to be inventions of the devil. Nevertheless, this was a victory for Christian art, which had grown out of classical art. By implication it lent dignity to the natural world in which Jesus had appeared, the human form that he had assumed. At any rate, it was followed by a revival of Greek humanism in art and thought.

In his aspirations to imperial grandeur, Constantine the Great had prepared the way for this too. He had adorned his New Rome with hundreds of statues looted from the cities of Greece and Asia Minor, and had stocked libraries with Greek manuscripts in order to make it a center of learning too. Pagan literature survived the bigotry of Justinian the Great, who had decreed that anyone "infected with the madness of the unholy Hellenes" should be prohibited from teaching any subject. His own reign was both commemorated and excoriated by Procopius, the last of the greater historians of antiquity. In his century Latin ceased to be the official language of the Empire, leaving Greek as the language in which all subjects had to be taught. More Greek literature and learning were incorporated in education, which was always highly prized as a token of Byzantine superiority over the barbarians. The centuries following the defeat of the Iconoclasts were marked by an outspoken reverence for the Greek classics, especially Homer, whom writers quoted more often than they did the Bible itself. "Hellenism," a horrid word to Justinian, became not only a good word but almost a holy word. The Byzantines were never so proud of their classical heritage, or so busy studying and elaborating upon it, as in the last centuries of their doomed empire. They even produced a freethinker, Plethon, so bold as to declare Christianity a menace to thought.

By this time their scholars were helping to educate western Europe, which knew no Greek, as long before they had helped much more to educate the Arabs. The direct contributions of Byzantium to the new civilization, such as Justinian's Code and Platonism, belong to another story. Here we need remark only that all along, through diplomatic relations with Rome and through trade, it helped to keep Europe literate and semicivilized. Italy profited most from intercourse with it, especially Venice—the one European city to flourish during the Dark Ages; but its influence was felt even on the distant borders. Thus in the seventh century it gave England Theodore of Tarsus (St. Paul's city), who brought along some precious books, became Archbishop of Canterbury, and organized the English Church. Almost everything that Europe got from it was to the good, simply because it was a civilizing influence. The growing hostility to Byzantium as Western Christendom began to flourish was not due to any passion for liberty, any high political, civil, or religious principle. It was due to doctrinal differences, which were intensified as Europe grew strong enough to indulge its political jealousy and its rapacity.

Yet the new civilization was already displaying much more enterprise and creativity than Byzantium had since the age of Justinian.

In its early centuries it produced such men as Peter Abelard, Thomas Aquinas, Roger Bacon, Dante, Chaucer—names not to be matched in the whole of Byzantine history. Islam too had gone on to much more impressive achievements in philosophy and science. Gibbon's verdict remains substantially true: Byzantium made no major discoveries, added no new ideas to ancient systems of thought, produced no masterpieces in history, philosophy, or literature. Except for its art and architecture, it created nothing of enduring importance, nothing that has entered the stream of world culture; no one except scholars reads any of its books. As an epilogue, its history sets off the much greater radiance of Greece and the greater majesty of Rome.

The consciousness of a high mission that dignified Byzantium was in another aspect a blight. From first to last it was intensely conservative, in a basically incurious, uncritical fashion. It conserved some of the best in classical tradition, but typically in the spirit of Justinian's Code: a pure digest of Roman law, supplemented by no effort at innovation or even reinterpretation. Lacking the free Greek spirit that had created its classics, and that might have inspired new adventures in thought, it did little but annotate its heritage. Its ideal was the academic classicism of the Hellenistic age, epitomized by its revival of the "pure" Attic dialect: a dead language, which had to be used by all writers of any pretensions to culture, and which thus discouraged any possibility of a vital native literature, especially of a poetry worthy of its achievements. And in this slavish piety Byzantium conserved some of the worst in classical tradition too—above all the accretions from the Orient.

In heart and soul the Byzantine Empire was always an Oriental sacred monarchy. Its Roman forms were much less conspicuous than the much older forms suited to an emperor who (like Justinian) signed himself a "divine and pious despot," always wore a halo in his portraits, held court in a "Sacred Palace," called his edicts "celestial commands," even assessed taxes under the name of "the Divine Delegation." The imperial pageantry—maintained in full splendor to the end of the impoverished Empire—included the characteristic Oriental custom of prostration before the throne. The Apostolic Emperor was no more immune than other Oriental monarchs to palace intrigue and assassination (fewer than half of the Byzantine emperors died a natural death), but whoever deposed him acquired his halo.[3] If the Church

---

[3] One royal protective device was the employment of eunuchs in high positions, since their ambitions could not extend to dreams for sons or dynasties of their own. Boys

might now and then quarrel with a vicious emperor, or more especially a "heretical" one such as the Iconoclasts, it never seriously challenged the office of the "Autokrator." Neither did any important political leader or thinker. Sympathetic historians explain that the Byzantines had no reason to question an order that had been willed by God; but the significant fact remains that unlike the Greeks and the Romans, they produced no political theory.

By the same token, their sacred monarchy was as unplanned a growth as it had been in the ancient East. The result of no plot by cynical power seekers, neither was it a conscious effort to unite the divine oneness with political authority. Constantine the Great simply took for granted his autocratic powers, the complete control he inherited of the army, treasury, civil service, and all legislative functions. As a Christian emperor, soon to be hailed by grateful churchmen as "Peer of the Apostles," he acquired more than a nominal sanctity, and was naturally led to assert the principle of "caesaropapism," the supremacy of state over church. Churchmen themselves taught him that it was his imperial duty to enforce correct belief and depose heretical bishops; so it was in a dedicated, not a presumptuous spirit that he told the bishops they were within the Church, he was "divinely appointed Bishop-General outside the Church." Some churchmen were uneasy about this appointment, and some later emperors may well have been cynical about their divine status, as they were certainly often unscrupulous in the exercise of their divine power; but generally the Byzantines accepted without question a marriage between state and church in which the emperor represented the superior male principle. They accordingly simplified the Christian life by relieving it of a dual obligation, making little more distinction between the things that are Caesar's and the things that are God's than had the sacred monarchies before them. For the same reason they established no firm basis for resistance to tyranny, or claims to rights against the state, such as Europe would build.

Given the recurrent crises of Byzantine history, the sacred monarchy was not in fact so static as its conservative ideal would have made it, or as God may have willed. It underwent not only some efforts at administrative or fiscal reform but the rise of a feudal aristocracy,

---

deliberately castrated for this purpose in fact provided the empire with many capable administrators, as well as patriarchs. I have remarked elsewhere that castration is possibly as good a qualification for responsible statesmanship as success in manufacturing automobiles or selling soap; but it is not a mode of political freedom.

which from the tenth century on often resisted the emperor or provided his assassins. This, however, was no herald of Western feudalism (as Jack Lindsay tries to make out in order to make Byzantium conform to the Marxist dialectic). Essentially it was a repetition of the struggles that Oriental monarchs, from Pharaoh to the Sassanian King of Kings, had periodically had with their nobility. It led to no contractual system of rights, no Magna Carta, no specified limits on the power of the emperor. The basic structure and theory of the Byzantine state remained unchanged to the end. Excepting the conspirers and the assassins, nobles rose to power and privilege chiefly as generals or officials in the imperial bureaucracy, and as in the ancient East, this bureaucracy was appointed by the emperor, responsible only to him, dependent upon his favor.

Over business the state exercised much more control than the Roman state ever did until the time of Diocletian. It monopolized large-scale industry and trade, controlled workers and wages through guilds, and closely regulated commerce. Worried conservatives today may accordingly see in the Byzantine state the seeds of modern socialism (as Lindsay does for his Marxist purposes), but again this was nothing new—it was as old as Pharaoh. Likewise businessmen had yet to awaken to the historic mission assigned them in both conservative and Marxist theory. If more private enterprise conceivably might have led to more political freedom, the business class displayed little passion for either such enterprise or such freedom. It never became strong enough to offset the centralized power of the state, or to carry on an energetic class struggle against the landed aristocracy. Outside the shop or the counting room it was largely passive, if not conservative on principle. It generated no fresh developments.

The common people were no more given to active class struggle. Although they still got some protection from Roman law, citizenship had pretty well lost its original meaning, and only something of the turbulent Greek spirit remained. In Constantinople they were more insubordinate and irreverent as well as more industrious than the Roman masses had been; on occasion they felt free to revile the Apostolic Emperor. But some uprisings that looked like popular revolutions amounted only to riots, never leading to any concerted movement for popular rights or an assured voice in the government. Fabled Constantinople had no aura like that of republican Rome, not to mention democratic Athens; it was fabled only for its imperial splendor and monumental religiosity. In the countryside the Sassanian and

Arab inroads had an ironic by-product, liberating many peasants as landlords fled to the walled capital; an independent, sturdy peasantry, which carried on a guerrilla warfare against the invaders, apparently contributed to the resurgence of the Empire. With its resurgence, however, they were mostly reduced to tenants or virtual serfs on the estates of monasteries and the feudal nobility. The army that the Byzantine Empire depended on was a professional, not a citizen army, typified by its armored horsemen. Few "citizens" were fighting on the walls of Constantinople when it fell to the Turks.

Outside the capital municipal liberties had disappeared many centuries before. Whatever tradition of self-government had survived Constantine the Great was virtually ended by Justinian. While he repaired and adorned many of the ancient cities, he brought them all under the complete control of the imperial bureaucracy, enforcing service on the city council simply to carry out the orders from Constantinople. Even freedom of movement was denied in a world once full of wanderers; escape to the capital legally required an official permit. Although the old Greek cities in Asia Minor evidently kept busy in commerce and industry, abetted by their wonder-working shrines and the flourishing traffic in holy relics, one hears very little of them in Byzantine annals, except for their fall to Arabs and Turks. The most famous of them—Miletus, Ephesus, Pergamum, Sardis, Tarsus—dwindled and crumbled, as Athens had earlier. Their physical decay was poetically appropriate, for the Byzantine Empire had ended the history of the classical *polis,* and of the Greek as a political animal. The incubus of its sacred monarchy was plainer because during its last centuries the free town was emerging in Europe, to become the main center and the spur of progressive development.

Its natural tendency to arrest was no less apparent in art, the most original creation of Byzantium. No longer autonomous, this was a profoundly conservative force because it was an ultraimperial art, directed from Constantinople, for fixed purposes of royal and religious propaganda. Once having achieved their masterwork in Hagia Sophia, Byzantine architects clung ever after to its basic design of dome over square, but never again attempted to build on so mighty a scale; only the imperial capital was worthy of such a cathedral. Mosaics were as conventionalized as the ritual of the Mass they were designed to illustrate. Within the set conventions artists achieved considerable variety, and in time moved toward a more naturalistic style, but from first to last the basic forms and aims of their art remained unchanged. Any bold innovation would have seemed subversive or blasphemous.

We are accordingly led back to the Christian legacy that the Byzantines also conserved so zealously. In their way, they were always intensely religious. Aside from war and business, Christianity governed all their major cultural interests, premising and crowning their most serious thought. It was the deepest source of unity in a racially heterogeneous empire, consecrating the emperor in Hagia Sophia, serving as the primary inspiration of the masses, who did not share in the classical culture and often groaned under "the Divine Delegation." But the Holy Orthodox Church thereby emphasized that Christian spirituality does not necessarily foster earthly freedom. Critics of the classical tradition have observed that both the Greek *polis* and the Roman *cosmopolis* failed to reconcile the need of moral, spiritual unity in society with the need of individual freedom. The Orthodox Church never attempted such a reconciliation, or even conceived such a problem.

It was most distinctively Christian in its exclusive, doctrinaire piety. In the early centuries this inspired considerable persecution, which seriously weakened the Empire. One reason why Egypt, Palestine, and Syria were permanently lost to Christendom was that their populace had been alienated by persecution, due to their Nestorian or Monophysite inclinations; they offered little resistance to the Arabs, many even welcoming the more tolerant rule of the Moslems. After the defeat of the Iconoclasts there was little more persecution, but chiefly because there were no more major controversies. The Church now settled for the orthodoxy that ended its religious growth: what has been called a splendid loyalty to the faith of the Fathers, or what may be called a bigoted conceit. Either way, it meant that no new ideas or ideals came out of Byzantium. It had a provincial aspect, as contemporary chroniclers quite ignored the final break with the Roman Church; and in the last centuries it again exacted a considerable price. When emperors sought a reconciliation with the Roman Church, for the sake of European aid against the Ottoman Turks, their efforts at compromise were fiercely resented by the bulk of the clergy and the indoctrinated masses. Shortly before the fall of Constantinople, a dignitary immortalized the spirit of Eastern Christendom: "It is better to see in the city the power of the Turkish turban than that of the Latin tiara!"

In helping to complete the triumphant resurgence of the East, the Holy Orthodox Church was perhaps fulfilling its historic destiny, if not

God's plan.[4] To a Western eye it looks more Oriental than Greek because of its primary devotion to miracle and mystery. At its best it inspired a pure devotion to the "Mystery of mysteries, the Sacrifice above all other sacrifices" that it celebrated so gloriously by its art and its liturgy; its ideal was a mystical otherworldliness, or the lofty aloofness of Mount Athos. At its worst it encouraged much vulgar superstition, especially the worship of saints and relics; the booty in Constantinople that so dazzled the Crusaders included a stupendous quantity of holy relics. In any case its preoccupation with the supernatural led it to degrade the natural world. The reverence of Byzantium for its Greek legacy fell short of any declared ideal of all-around excellence or fullness of life, and never approached the popular reverence for the monk, the stylite, the ascetic saint. The avowed scorn of the flesh helps to explain the routine cruelty in Byzantine life. Countless men, including apostolic emperors, had their noses cut off and their eyes put out on the assumption that this was an eminently Christian mode of punishment, which might help the victim tc renounce the world and save his immortal soul; and many a scoundrel spent his last days in a monastery.

Such otherworldliness also had something to do with the notorious worldliness of· Byzantium, and the routine corruption. While supporting autocracy and war, the Holy Orthodox Church did little to Christianize life in the temporal social world. No influential saint echoed the indignation of John Chrysostom over the misery of the poor; no high churchman led any popular movement for social or political reform. As a privileged institution, the Church not only acquiesced in the status quo but took advantage of its opportunities for exploitation. Monasteries—havens from the evil world—accumulated vast wealth by expropriating peasants as well as cashing in on the magical virtues of their ikons and their relics. Monks generally offered the most determined and successful resistance to the emperors, but principally to those emperors who tried to curb their power or limit their worldly possessions.

Altogether, the Orthodox Church was a bulwark against new aspiration as well as barbarism. It did an incalculable service to Christendom by converting the rude Slavic peoples and inspiring resistance to the Arabs; but it had little to offer peoples already civilized, and nothing

---

[4] It should be noted that the Church indeed made out better under the power of the Turkish turban. The sultan not only granted it religious freedom but gave it civil jurisdiction over all Greek Christians—a freedom and power it could hardly have expected to enjoy under the domination of Rome.

more to the Byzantines when they had to contend with the rising power of the Turks and the Europeans. Still devoted to its mysteries and its miracles, it could only conserve, stand fast to the end. In Constantinople the end was inglorious: the great bulk of its people spent the day of its fall in their churches, praying to their saints instead of fighting on their walls. The miracle they prayed for would only have deepened the mystery of the divine will, for in the order ostensibly ordained by God there had been little spirit of a Christian commonwealth. Outside the churches, a visitor from another society might never have guessed that this was a Christian commonwealth.

Still, the inconsistencies between the belief and the behavior of the Byzantines were no more glaring than the inconsistencies of medieval Europe, above all of its Crusaders. They may be detected even in modern America (more especially since it has passed a law putting itself "under God"—as if a Christian country could be anywhere else). In natural piety, the last word about Byzantium too might well be a word of gratitude and respect.

The dying Empire did more than maintain the dignity of its ancient mission. While its Church displayed both intellectual energy and integrity as it fought political concessions to the Roman Church, a movement toward mystical quietism, approaching heresy, inspired some of its best religious writings. In Greece popular reformers known as the Zealots led a struggle against the wealthy and fought valiantly, if vainly, to establish free cities, like those in Italy that were reviving memories of the antique *polis*. Perhaps most valiant was a cultural renaissance that lent a glow to the last centuries of Byzantium. The fall of Constantinople to the Fourth Crusade was followed by the most brilliant period in philosophy and learning; Nicaea became celebrated as a second Athens. When the capital was recovered, cultural activity grew more intense and more humanistic as the city grew poorer and shabbier. The Church of the Chora (or Karieh Cami) was adorned with the lightest, brightest, warmest of Byzantine mosaics. Frescoes uncovered in the same church are so suggestive of the Italian Renaissance that scholars at first thought they must have been painted by some pupil of Giotto, but in fact their style antedated Giotto, and they may make his art seem naïve. As the "decadent" ancient world had had enough vitality to create the magnificent art of Byzantium and to make Constantinople the greatest city in the world of its time, so the spirit that had defended its legacy for a thousand years conceivably might have awakened to a new life. Westerners who now enjoy a freer life at least owe it to Byzantium to honor this spirit.

BIBLIOGRAPHY

Given so large a subject, the following bibliography is of course selective, and only in the roughest sense comprehensive. Except for a few specialized studies to which I am directly indebted, it is designed for the general reader, not for historical scholars.

GENERAL

Albright, William Foxwell: *From the Stone Age to Christianity*, Baltimore, 1940.
Becker, Carl: *Progress and Power*, New York, 1949.
Berdyaev, Nicolas: *The Meaning of History*, London, 1936.
Burckhardt, Jacob: *Force and Freedom*, New York, 1943.
Cambridge Ancient History, 12 vols., 1923-39.
Childe, V. Gordon: *Man Makes Himself*, New York (Mentor Books), 1951.
———: *New Light on the Most Ancient East*, New York, 1953.
Cohen, Morris: *The Meaning of Human History*, La Salle, 1947.
Coon, Carleton S.: *The Story of Man*, New York, 1954.
Dawson, Christopher: *The Age of the Gods*, New York, 1938.
———: *Progress and Religion*, New York, 1938.
De Burgh, W. D.: *The Legacy of the Ancient World*, 2 vols., London, 1947.
Dewey, John: *Freedom and Culture*, New York, 1939.
Hauser, Arnold: *The Social History of Art*, Vol. 1, New York (Vintage Books), 1957.
Heichelheim, Fritz M.: *An Ancient Economic History*, Vol. 1, Leiden, 1958.
Huntington, Ellsworth: *Civilization and Climate*, New Haven, 1922.
Jaspers, Karl: *The Origin and Goal of History*, London, 1953.
Kroeber, A. L.: *Configurations of Cultural Growth*, Berkeley, 1944.
———: *The Nature of Culture*, Chicago, 1952.
Langdon-Davies, John: *A Short History of Women*, New York, 1927.
Linton, Ralph: *The Tree of Culture*, New York, 1955.
Lovejoy, A. O., and Boas, George: *Primitivism and Related Ideas in Antiquity*, Baltimore, 1935.
MacIver, R. M.: *Community*, London, 1924.
McIlwain, Charles H.: *Constitutionalism Ancient and Modern*, Ithaca, 1940.

Maine, H. S.: *Ancient Law,* London, 1908.

Marrou, Henri: *A History of Education in Antiquity,* London, 1956.

Moore, George F.: *History of Religions,* 2 vols., New York, 1913-19.

Parkes, Henry Bamford: *Gods and Men, The Origins of Western Culture,* New York, 1959.

Roelofs, H. Mark: *The Tension of Citizenship,* New York, 1957.

Sabine, George: *A History of Political Theory,* New York, 1955.

Sarton, George: *A History of Science, Ancient Science Through the Golden Age of Greece,* Cambridge, 1959.

Seltman, Charles: *Women in Antiquity,* London, 1956.

Shotwell, James T.: *The Long Road to Freedom,* New York, 1960.

Singer, Charles (ed.) and others: *A History of Technology,* Vols. I and II, Oxford, 1954-56.

Toynbee, Arnold J.: *A Study of History,* 11 vols., London, 1935-59.

Whitehead, Alfred North: *Adventures of Ideas,* New York, 1933.

EARLY CIVILIZATIONS   (Chapters 1, 2, 3, and 4)

Braidwood, Robert J.: *The Near East and the Foundations for Civilization,* Eugene, 1952.

Chadwick, H. Munro: *The Heroic Age,* Cambridge, 1912.

Cottrell, Leonard: *The Bull of Minos,* London, 1953.

Coulborn, Rushton: *The Origin of Civilized Societies,* Princeton, 1959.

Frankfort, Henri: *The Birth of Civilization in the Near East,* Bloomington, 1951.

———: *Kingship and the Gods,* Chicago, 1948.

——— and others: *Before Philosophy,* Harmondsworth (Penguin Books), 1951.

Ghirshman, R.: *Iran,* London, 1954.

Glotz, Gustave: *The Aegean Civilization,* New York, 1925.

Gurney, O. R.: *The Hittites,* London, 1952.

Huizinga, Johan: *Homo Ludens,* Boston (Beacon Books), 1955.

James, E. O.: *Myth and Ritual in the Ancient Near East,* London, 1958.

Kramer, Samuel Noah: *From the Tablets of Sumer,* Indian Hills, 1956.

Levy, Gertrude R.: *The Gate of Horn,* London, 1948.

Olmstead, Albert T.: *History of the Persian Empire, Achaemenian Period,* Chicago, 1948.

Pallottino, M.: *The Etruscans,* London, 1955.

Raglan, Lord: *The Hero,* New York, 1937.

Redfield, Robert: *The Primitive World and Its Transformation,* Ithaca, 1953.

Rostovtzeff, M. I.: *A History of the Ancient World,* Vol. 1, Oxford, 1926.

Weisinger, Herbert: *Tragedy and the Paradox of the Fortunate Fall,* London, 1953.

Wilson, John A.: *The Burden of Egypt*, Chicago, 1951.
Wittfogel, Karl A.: *Oriental Despotism*, New Haven, 1957.
Woolley, Charles L.: *Digging Up the Past*, Harmondsworth, 1954.
————: *Excavations at Ur*, London, 1954.

JUDAISM   (Chapter 5)

Albright, William Foxwell: *The Archaeology of Palestine*, Harmondsworth, 1949.
Bevan, Edwyn R., and Singer, Charles (eds.): *The Legacy of Israel*, Oxford, 1927.
Finkelstein, Louis (ed.): *The Jews*, New York, 1949.
Gordon, Cyrus H.: *The World of the Old Testament*, Garden City, 1958.
Orlinsky, Harry M.: *Ancient Israel*, Ithaca, 1954.
Parkes, James: *Judaism and Christianity*, Chicago, 1948.
Wright, G. Ernest: *The Challenge of Israel's Faith*, Chicago, 1944.
(See also the relevant chapters in the works of Dawson, De Burgh, Moore, Parkes, and Roelofs listed under *General*.)

GREECE   (Chapters 6, 7, and 8)

Barker, Ernest: *Greek Political Theory, Plato and His Predecessors*, London, 1947.
Bevan, Edwyn R.: *Stoics and Sceptics*, Oxford, 1913.
Bowra, Cecil Maurice: *The Greek Experience*, New York, 1958.
Burnet, John: *Early Greek Philosophy*, London, 1920.
Bury, J. B.: *A History of Greece to the Death of Alexander the Great*, New York (Modern Library), 1937.
Claggett, Marshall: *Greek Science in Antiquity*, New York, 1955.
Cornford, Francis M.: *From Religion to Philosophy*, London, 1912.
Dodds, E. R.: *The Greeks and the Irrational*, Berkeley 1951.
Farrington, Benjamin: *Greek Science*, 2 vols., London, 1944.
Guthrie, W. K. C.: *The Greeks and Their Gods*, London, 1950.
Hadas, Moses: *Humanism, The Greek Ideal and Its Survival*, New York, 1960.
Hamilton, Edith: *The Greek Way to Western Civilization*, New York, (Mentor Books), 1948.
Harrison, Jane Ellen: *Themis, A Study of the Social Origins of Greek Religion*, Cambridge, 1912.
Havelock, Eric A.: *The Liberal Temper in Greek Politics*, New Haven, 1957.
Herodotus: *The Persian Wars*, New York (Modern Library), 1947.
Hogarth, David G.: *Ionia and the East*, Oxford, 1909.
Jaeger, Werner: *Paideia: The Ideals of Greek Culture*, 3 vols., New York, 1943-45.

Jones, A. H. M.: *Athenian Democracy*, Oxford, 1957.

Kitto, H. D. F.: *The Greeks*, London, 1951.

Livingstone, Richard W. (ed.): *The Legacy of Greece*, Oxford, 1928.

Murray, Gilbert: *Five Stages of Greek Religion*, New York, 1925.

———: *The Rise of the Greek Epic*, Oxford, 1924.

Nillson, Martin P.: *Greek Piety*, Oxford, 1948.

Oates, Whitney J.: *The Stoic and Epicurean Philosophers*, New York, 1940.

Popper, K. R.: *The Open Society and Its Enemies*, Vol. 1, London, 1945.

Rostovtzeff, M. I.: *The Social and Economic History of the Hellenistic World*, 3 vols., Oxford, 1941.

Routh, H. V.: *God, Man, and Epic Poetry*, Cambridge, 1927.

Snell, Bruno: *The Discovery of the Mind*, Cambridge, 1953.

Tarn, W. W.: *Hellenistic Civilisation*, London, 1947.

Thucydides: *The Peloponnesian War*, New York (Modern Library), 1934.

Zimmern, Alfred: *The Greek Commonwealth*, London, 1931.

ROME AND EARLY CHRISTIANITY   (Chapters 9 and 10)

Adcock, F. E.: *Roman Political Ideas and Practice*, Ann Arbor, 1959.

Bailey, C. (ed.): *The Legacy of Rome*, Oxford, 1923.

Barker, Ernest: *From Alexander to Constantine*, Oxford, 1956.

Cochrane, C. N.: *Christianity and Classical Culture*, Oxford, 1940.

Cowell, F. R.: *Cicero and the Roman Republic*, New York, 1948.

Eyre, Edward (ed.): *European Civilization, Its Origin and Development*, Vol. 2: *Rome and Christendom*, London, 1935.

Ferrero, G., and Barbagallo, C.: *A Short History of Rome*, 2 vols., New York, 1919.

Frank, Tenney: *An Economic History of Rome*, Baltimore, 1927.

Gibbon, Edward: *The Decline and Fall of the Roman Empire*, 2 vols., New York (Modern Library), 1932.

Guignebert, C. A. H.: *Jesus*, London, 1935.

Hadas, Moses: *A History of Rome*, New York (Anchor Books), 1956.

Hatch, Edwin: *The Influence of Greek Ideas on Christianity*, New York (Harper Torchbooks), 1957.

Laistner, M. L. W.: *The Greater Roman Historians*, Berkeley, 1947.

Lake, Kirsopp: *Landmarks in the History of Early Christianity*, London, 1920.

Lot, Ferdinand: *The End of the Ancient World*, New York, 1931.

McGiffert, A. C.: *A History of Christian Thought*, 2 vols., New York, 1932.

Magie, David: *Roman Rule in Asia Minor*, 2 vols., Princeton, 1950.

Marrou, Henri: *St. Augustine, and His Influence Through the Ages*, London, 1957.

Newman, John Henry: *An Essay on the Development of Christian Doctrine*, New York, 1949.

Nock, A. D.: *Conversion, The Old and the New in Religion from Alexander the Great to Augustine of Hippo,* London, 1933.

Polybius: *The Histories,* 6 vols., New York (Loeb Classical Library), 1922-27.

Ramsay, William M.: *The Cities of St. Paul,* London, 1908.

Rostovtzeff, M. I.: *The Social and Economic History of the Roman Empire,* Oxford, 1926.

Schweitzer, Albert: *Paul and His Interpreters,* London, 1948.

Tacitus: *Complete Works,* New York (Modern Library), 1942.

THE BYZANTINE EMPIRE   *(Chapter 11)*

Baynes, Norman H.: *The Byzantine Empire,* London, 1925.

——— and Moss, H. St. L. B., (eds.): *Byzantium,* Oxford, 1948.

Burckhardt, Jacob: *The Age of Constantine the Great,* New York (Vintage Books), 1956.

Bury, J. B.: *History of the Later Roman Empire,* 2 vols., London, 1923.

Diehl, Charles: *History of the Byzantine Empire,* Princeton, 1925.

Lindsay, Jack: *Byzantium into Europe,* London, 1952.

Runciman, Steven: *Byzantine Civilisation,* London, 1933.

Vasiliev, A. A.: *History of the Byzantine Empire,* 2 vols., Madison, 1928-29.

INDEX